Voluminous States

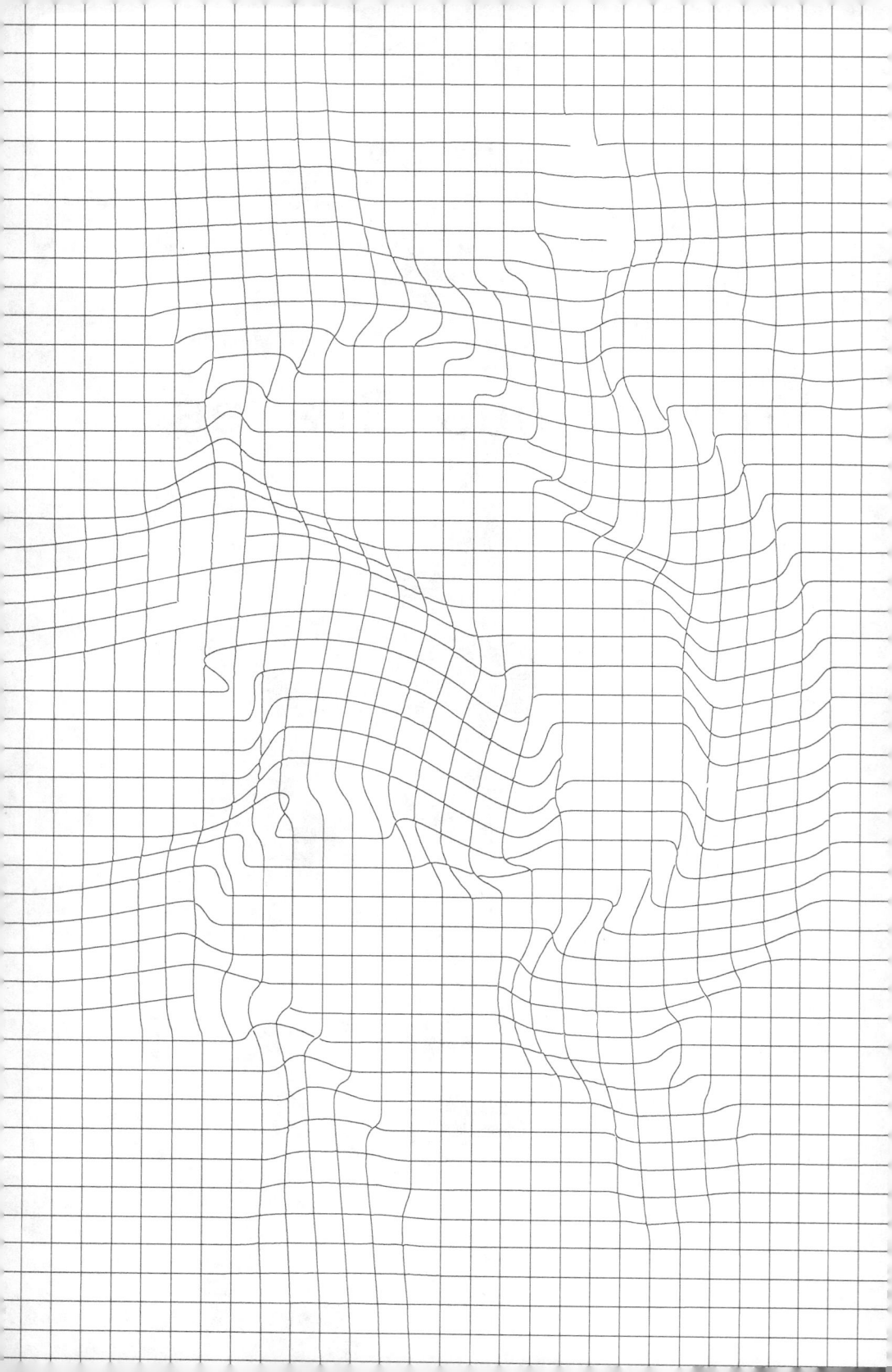

Voluminous States

Sovereignty,
Materiality,
and the
Territorial
Imagination

Edited by
Franck Billé

Duke University Press
Durham and London
2020

Designed by Drew Sisk
Typeset in Portrait Text and IBM Plex Mono by Westchester
Publishing Services

Library of Congress Cataloging-in-Publication Data Names:
Billé, Franck, editor.
Title: Voluminous states : sovereignty, materiality, and the
        territorial imagination / edited by Franck Billé.
   Description: Durham : Duke University Press, 2020. |
   Includes bibliographical references and index. Identifiers:
LCCN 2019054631 (print)
LCCN 2019054632 (ebook)
ISBN 9781478007913 (hardcover)
ISBN 9781478008422 (paperback)
ISBN 9781478012061 (ebook)
Subjects: LCSH: Sovereignty. | Boundaries. | National
   security.
Classification: LCC JC327 .V67 2020 (print)
LCC JC327 (ebook)
DDC 320.15—dc23
LC record available at https://lccn.loc.gov/2019054631
LC ebook record available at https://lccn.loc.gov/2019054632

Cover art: Brian Tomlinson, Liquid 12, 2017. Courtesy of the
artist. www.bt-photography.co.uk.

For Valerio, Milo, and Max

CONTENTS

Materiality

Territorial Imagination

ACKNOWLEDGMENTS

I am incredibly grateful to the fifty-five scholars who thought along with me on the topic of volume over the last four years, and who agreed to write contributions to this book or to one of the two companion collections in *Cultural Anthropology* and *Society and Space*. It is a rare privilege to have so many wonderful scholars engage with one's work and give so generously of their time. It is through conversations with them that the book grew into its present form. Thank you Ross Exo Adams, Peter Adey, Andrea Ballestero, Debbora Battaglia, Lauren Bonilla, Dylan Brady, Ashley Carse, Wayne Chambliss, Shiuh-Shen Chien, Jason Cons, Nancy Couling, Jeremy Crampton, Hilary Cunningham, Elizabeth DeLoughrey, Klaus Dodds, Elizabeth Dunn, Stuart Elden, Adam Fish, Bradley Garrett, Gastón Gordillo, Sarah Green, Gökçe Günel, Tina Harris, Carola Hein, Stefan Helmreich, Caroline Humphrey, Tim Ingold, Anna Jackman, Rikke Bjerg Jensen, Agnieszka Joniak-Lüthi, Eleana J. Kim, Marcel LaFlamme, Austin Lord, Nayanika Mathur, Evangeline McGlynn, Marilu Melo Zurita, Ekaterina Mikhailova, Lisa Sang-Mi Min, Alex Nading, Yael Navaro, Aihwa Ong, Madeleine Reeves, Paul Richardson, Douglas Rogers, Aditi Saraf, Rachael Squire, Nicole Starosielski, Phil Steinberg, Malini Sur, Helga Tawil-Souri, Jennifer Telesca, Michael Vine, Clancy Wilmott, Max Woodworth, and Jerry Zee.

Thanks also to Arjun Appadurai, Marilyn Strathern, Jason Dittmer, Tim Choy, James Ferguson, Hyun-Gwi Park, Umut Yıldırım, China Miéville, Tung-Hui Hu, Philippe Descola, Yu-Kai Liao, Natalia Ryzhova, Richard Fraser, Adam Levy, Alexander Murphy, Lisa Parks, Steven Connor, William Stafford, Limor Darash, James Sidaway, Rosanna Carver, and Mel Ford who have offered comments, encouragements, and feedback at different stages of the project, as well as Dominic Boyer and Cymene Howe, my interlocutors at *Cultural Anthropology*, and Lauren Martin and Charmaine Chua at *Society and Space*.

I thank my editor Elizabeth Ault at Duke University Press for her enthusiasm, support, and vision for this project, as well as her assistant Kate Herman.

This project began at the University of Cambridge and was finalized at the University of California, Berkeley. I was lucky to be surrounded by wonderful colleagues and friends at both institutions—in particular Caroline Humphrey, Paula Haas, Nayanika Mathur, Chris Kaplonski, and Libby Peachey at Cambridge; and Kiela Diehl, Alexei Yurchak, Aihwa Ong, Angel Ryono, Sanjyot Mehendale, Karen Clancy, and Martin Backstrom at Berkeley.

As ever, I am grateful to my parents Jean-Pierre and Vita, my sister Lori and brother-in-law Peter, as well as my Italian family Emanuela, Antonio, Fabrizio, and Silvana.

Lastly, and most importantly, I wish to thank three very special individuals: my husband Valerio and our two little ones, Milo and Max. Valerio, to whom I first pitched the idea of the book, believed in the project from the start and remained an unwavering source of support. The arrival of baby Milo in our lives in August 2018 has been an endless source of joy and wonder. His sunny disposition, infectious laughs, and appetite for life remind us every day about what really matters. Max, furry brother extraordinaire, keeps me in shape by taking me on daily "smell walk" adventures around the neighborhood. It is to them I dedicate this book.

Voluminous

An Introduction

FRANCK BILLÉ

Early 2018, Singapore's Urban Redevelopment Authority announced a proposal for an underground masterplan, with pilot areas to be unveiled in 2019. Extending dozens to possibly hundreds of meters below the city-state, the masterplan will free up surface land by stacking up a wide range of human activities and urban infrastructure, from rail and road networks to bus interchange stations, and from substations to reservoirs and sewage systems.[1] While usage of subterranean space is not novel[2] and is indeed the privileged space for the cable and pipe infrastructure that makes urban life possible, the scale and depth of Singapore's plans are particularly ambitious. Unlike subterranean extensions that tend to be spaces where the entangled messiness of urban life support can be tidied away, Singapore's plans represent nothing less than an unequivocal embrace of the subterranean as urban realm and domain amenable to colonization and control. Singapore's aspiration to make the most of its subsoil and submarine environments echoes statist territorial ambitions elsewhere.[3]

From the Arctic to the South China Sea, states are vying to secure sovereign rights over vast maritime stretches, undersea continental plates, shifting ice floes, and aerial volumes. These vertical inroads are comparatively new, but the three-dimensional nature of property law has a long genealogy. Well before technology made it possible, ownership of a plot of land was legally understood to represent the intersection of the Earth's surface with a conical property extending upward and downward from that surface. *Cuius est solum, eius est usque ad coelum et ad inferos,* or "Whoever's is the soil, it is theirs all the way to Heaven and all the way to Hell," as the Latin maxim goes.[4] But if the three-dimensional nature of land was common knowledge among lawyers, it remained largely a theoretical issue until the advent of air travel and the development of effective ground-excavating methods. Of course, subsurface mineral deposits have long been the subject of territorial disputes, while "aerial arts of war," in the form of painting, land surveys, and later photography, predate modern technologies such as digital imaging.[5] However the first genuine attempts to territorialize aerial, maritime, and subterranean spaces only emerged through transformative technologies that made it possible to control, colonize, and populate beyond-the-human worlds previously considered asocial.[6] Until recently many of these three-dimensional spaces were seen as beyond effective political control: the United Nations Convention on the Law of the Sea (UNCLOS) for instance only came into force in 1994, and there is still no international legal agreement on the vertical extent of sovereign airspace.

The definition and contours of volumetric sovereignty are in constant evolution,[7] partly through the possibilities afforded by new technologies, but partly also in response to economic opportunities and geopolitical imperatives. The notion of airspace sovereignty was recognized for instance just after World War I as a reaction to aerial reconnaissance and bombings, while the concept of "territorial waters," in existence since the late eighteenth century and generally limited to three nautical miles (the typical range of cannon fire from shore), began to be challenged in the 1940s. The United States sought to expand it in its pursuit of oil and gas, while for smaller countries like Chile and Iceland, the rationale was greater control over fishing resources.[8] More recently, the notion of continental shelf—defined as the shallow seabed that extends from the part of the shore permanently submerged down to the continental slope, typically at a depth of one hundred to two hundred meters— has provided coastal states with further possibilities to extend their sovereign rights beyond their exclusive economic zone (EEZ) (see figure I.1).[9]

Such extensions of sovereign rights do not necessarily index an extension of sovereign territory, nor indeed the ambition to acquire any,[10] but they have made the political map more complex, in that territory and sovereignty are now rarely coextensive. As geographer Ian Shaw notes, now more than ever, the planet's "mosaic of distinct states has melted into a more distorted painting: a scattershot of statelets, militarized cities, and transnational flows."[11] The entanglement of the governmental and the corporate, deeply embedded within the infrastructural stratum of our political and economic environment—what

INTERIOR WATERS ART. 8

TERRITORIAL WATERS ART. 2 AND 3

CONTIGUOUS ZONE

EEZ PART V. ART. 57
200 NAUTICAL MILES

EXTENSION OF EEZ ART. 76
MAX +150 NAUTICAL MILES

HIGH SEAS / INTERNATIONAL WATERS
ART. 1.1.1 AND PARTS VII, XI

OR MAX −2500 m   +100 NAUTICAL MILES

12   12

0
−200 m   NORMAL BASELINE (LOW WATER LINE)

END OF (GEOLOGICAL) CONTINENTAL SHELF

FLOOR OF SLOPE

OR d

60 NAUTICAL MILES

−2500 m   SEDIMENTARY ROCK

CONTINENTAL CRUST

sediment thickness min. d/100

OCEAN CRUST

ZONE OF CONTINENTAL MARGIN

CONTINENTAL SLOPE

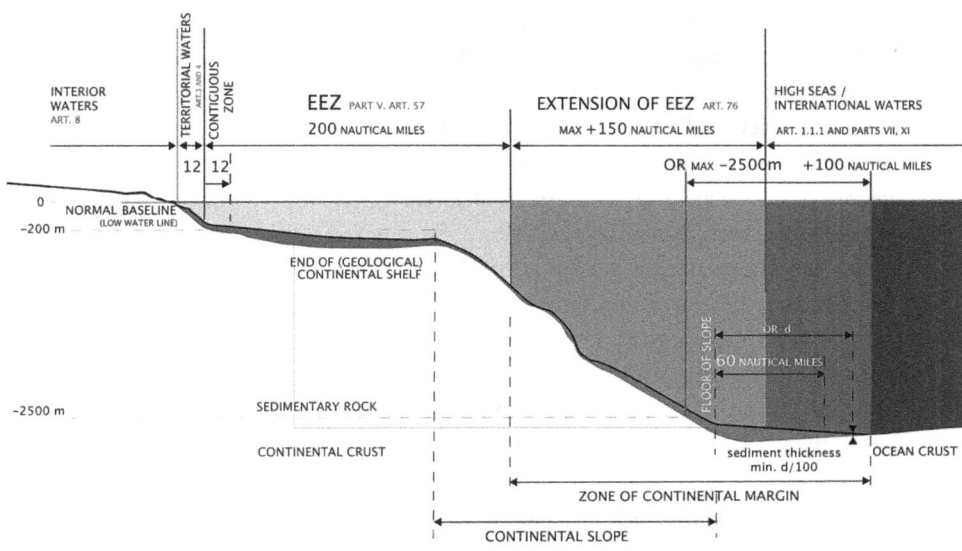

Figure I.1. The exclusive economic zone offshore, UNCLOS. © Nancy Couling.

Keller Easterling has termed *extrastatecraft*—further complicates the practice of territory.[12]

This complexity, somewhat naively imagined as a borderless world in the early 1990s following the collapse of the Soviet Union, has more recently given rise to a propensity to equate the multiplicity, complexity, and increasingly staggered and dispersive nature of border control as a harbinger of deterritorialization.[13] Yet, as Étienne Balibar notes, the multiple, heterogeneous, hypothetical, and fictive nature of political borders—and by extension the territorial sovereignty they index—does not make them any less real.[14] The discreteness of the nation-state as container may be a potent fiction but it is one to which we are all committed and in which we remain deeply invested. David Ludden's assertion that we are unable to imagine political space beyond a cookie-cutter world of national geography, and that scholars work within that everyday experience, holds true fifteen years later.[15] Almost in spite of ourselves, the state continues to hold our collective political imagination.[16]

More than two decades ago, John Agnew warned us about the "territorial trap" that shapes the ways in which international relations are studied.[17] Yet the recent proliferation of border walls is testimony to the continued belief of governments and their citizens in the seductive fiction of the territorial nation-state.[18] In the last few years, this trend appears to have increased even further with the election of Donald Trump, the United Kingdom's Brexit vote, as well as the rise and consolidation of autocratic regimes in Europe, China, Russia, Turkey, India, and elsewhere. This despite the fact that, as Michael Dear has pointed out, not only is partition the crudest tool in the armory of geopolitics, it is an overt confession of failed diplomacy.[19] Walls are potent symbols of "territory's continued allure,"[20] standing tall to "patch" gaps in political borders, aiming to keep at bay feared cultural ingress and economic leakage. But they are also a symptom of weakness, of waning sovereignty as Wendy Brown has argued. For Brown, "rather than resurgent expressions of nation-state sovereignty, the new walls are icons of its erosion."[21]

Walls also project a vision of the world that is resolutely horizontal. As such, they tend to be largely ineffective as barriers to movement: people go around them, above them, below them. More than two hundred tunnels linking Mexico to the United States have been discovered since 1990, the majority of them used for drug trafficking. Walls are also woefully inadequate to stem illegal migration, let alone address larger phenomena requiring containment such as the effects of climate change.[22] If walls are a symptom of waning sovereignty, then, they also reveal a recalcitrant tendency to apprehend the world in two dimensions. Recent geopolitical forays into vertical spaces such as the atmosphere or the subterranean have in fact proven extremely challenging to represent, either cartographically or mentally. From the God's-eye perspective to which we are accustomed, the vertical axis collapses on itself and, reduced to a single point, becomes invisible. Such challenges are typically encountered in vertical urban environments such as Hong Kong where the multilevel urban fabric makes it complex to map. Two points may share the same coordinates but be located on a different surface altogether.[23]

With scholars in a vast array of disciplines becoming increasingly alert to the necessity of a three-dimensional perspective, the last few years have witnessed a veritable efflorescence of publications on the topic of volume. A seminal intervention that appears to have given the impetus for much of this "volumetric turn" was Stuart Elden's 2013 paper, "Secure the Volume," in which he argued for the necessity to rethink geography in terms of volumes rather than areas.[24] While Elden was not the first scholar to draw attention to volumes—indeed his article cites an extensive literature engaging with spaces beyond the surface—he was instrumental in identifying commonalities shared by scholars interested in aerial spaces such as Peter Adey, Derek Gregory, or Alison Williams, and subterranean realms like Eyal Weizman or Bradley Garrett, and to call for an integration of these various strands into a more comprehensive and coherent volumetric framework.[25] Heeding Elden's agenda-setting call, a number of geographers began engaging more actively with the volumetric.[26] In parallel with this incipient development, anthropologists and cultural theorists are also becoming increasingly concerned with three-dimensional realms such as air, oceans, riparian environments, and outer space as well as with their social, political, and cultural reverberations.[27]

Voluminous States brings into crossdisciplinary dialogue these converging interests in volumetric sovereignty and more-than-human geographies. The contributors suggest that this theoretical confluence can be especially illuminating for border processes and phenomena that deploy beyond the two dimensional. As the authors in *Voluminous States* show, the fact that political battles are increasingly being waged in more complex volumetric geographies does not suggest a weakening or dilution of the logics of territorial control. The political and cultural colonization of sea, air, and ice—framed primarily through a land-based imagination, whether through the creation of islands as toeholds in the South China Sea or the planting of flags on ocean floors or ice sheets—is in fact subject to similar cartographic anxieties.[28]

Conceiving sovereign space as volume is crucial insofar as it reflects the three-dimensional nature of modern territorial control. Airspace surveillance, maritime patrol, and subterranean monitoring are all integral to maintaining territorial sovereignty, yet these dimensions of bordering are rarely if ever addressed by border studies scholars. *Voluminous States* argues that a three-dimensional approach to studying borders and territoriality is imperative to understand how the Westphalian logic of bordering has evolved since the seventeenth century to frame contemporary territorial incursions, especially into places where human interventions are recent and technologically mediated. A two-dimensional analysis feels clearly obsolete when battles are increasingly waged in volumetric space in the form of drone strikes or the amorphous threats of biological warfare and cyberattacks.[29]

Speaking Volumes

The theoretical ambition of the book is threefold, as reflected in the book's subtitle. *Voluminous States* is concerned on the one hand with the extension of sovereignty into spaces previously beyond the realm of human intervention. Polar regions, high-altitude mountains, the air, the sea, and the subterranean are some of the locations discussed by the authors. These spaces are more than simply a backdrop to the discussion; their materiality is key to the discussion. If the growing literature on volumetric sovereignty is making significant forays into previously unexplored realms, comparatively few scholars have been as attentive to the entanglement of axes and layers, and to the "stuffness" of this resultant volumetric space. The term *voluminous* in the title—rather than a more abstract *volumetric*—alludes here to the significance and physical presence of the state. Several chapters in the book, such as Jerry Zee's on dust, Jason Cons's on floods, or Clancy Wilmott's on fluctuating sea levels, foreground the material entanglements, constraints, and elusiveness of this three-dimensional space.[30] This very complexity, as geographer Jason Dittmer has argued, speaks to an apprehension of systems as "always dynamic and interacting in ways that defy attempts to model them."[31]

While all chapters are concerned with an evolving imaginary of territorial sovereignty, a number of chapters address it more specifically. Wayne Chambliss's contribution on military incursions into the subterranean realm evokes for instance an incipient downward extension of territorial sovereignty through subsurface mapping.[32] Aihwa Ong's analysis of land reclamation in Singapore also suggests a steady expansion of the state to encompass both watery and subterranean spaces—an ambition China has also pursued, albeit differently, through the notion of "blue territorialization." Emerging three-dimensional views of national territory make a stark contrast with the wall-building exercises being deployed around the world, yet these views are not mutually exclusive. Calls for an old-school US-Mexico border wall thus cohabit, uneasily, with an imaginary of warfighting that is increasingly nonplanar, noncontiguous, and deterritorialized.[33]

The three keywords—*sovereignty*, *materiality*, and *imaginary*—that contour the narrative arc of the book run in some form through all the chapters. As such, the chapters' distribution and order in the book denotes emphasis of content rather than exclusive focus. Because of the way the project has grown over the last three years, organically and in dialogue between the authors and editor, there is much entanglement between the chapters. The book should be seen primarily as a jigsaw puzzle, each piece bringing further clarity to the topic of volumetric sovereignty. The puzzle made up by this edited collection also extends beyond the book, with two online collections of fifty short essays, published across two journals in the two core disciplines: *Cultural Anthropology* (2017–18) and *Society and Space* (2019).[34]

Sovereignty

Over the last decade, the field of border studies has grown exponentially, largely in reaction to ever more complex and sophisticated forms of border control and to the considerable human suffering they engender. The recognition that borders impact individuals very differently depending on their ethnicity, economic status, and national origin, and the realization that the early 1990s notion that borders were becoming obsolete came from a place of privilege, contributed to the deconstruction of the concept of *border* and to numerous studies of processes, such as document procurement, offshore detention facilities, data monitoring, and immigration raids, that take place far from the geographical border.[35]

The increasingly staggered nature of the border and border controls, combined with constraints placed on sovereignty with regards to exchange rates, monetary policy, arms control, chemical weapons, landmines, warfare, environmental control, minority rights, etc., can convey the impression that the omnipotent nature of sovereignty is in recession.[36] It is worth reiterating here, as political theorist Joan Cocks has argued, that sovereignty is an illusion insofar as the "power to command and control everything inside a physical space" is unattainable, and never more so than today. And yet, the longing for that sovereign power clearly continues to haunt contemporary politics, thereby reifying this illusion.[37] Counterinstinctively perhaps, the very interconnectedness of sovereignties, rather than weakening the concept, may actually be strengthening it.[38] Thus the presence of US border controls at European airports for instance, thousands of miles away from US territory, does not signify a waning or blurring of territorial sovereignty. To the extent that these practices are mutually agreed upon and potentially replicated by European partners, they help bolster border controls as well as reinforce the very idea of territorial sovereignty that is indexed by borders. It is also worth keeping in mind that "attack" and "defense" rely on very different assumptions: if powerful states routinely encroach upon the territorial sovereignty of weaker states, the reverse is not true. Borders are lines only the powerful may trespass.[39]

The persistent currency of the notion of territorial sovereignty is evident from the spatial extensions of sovereign power currently taking place across maritime, aerial, and subterranean spaces. By using rocks and shoals as footholds to solidify (in the sense of treating as solid) the fluid geographies of the South China Sea, China has been actively engaged in expanding its territorial foothold.[40] Islands allow states to claim additional territorial waters to a radius of twelve nautical miles but since 1982 they have also granted them authority to exploit resources within an EEZ extending to two hundred nautical miles. As a result, terraforming has proven a very effective way to claim sovereign rights to vast expanses of what were previously classified as "high seas."[41] Expanding further on the EEZ jurisdiction, the Straddling Stocks Fish Agreement (entered into force in 2001) grants each coastal state the authority to regulate exploitation of highly migratory species and straddling stocks in areas of the high seas adjacent to its EEZ so as to conserve the abundance of these species within its EEZ.[42] The United Nations Convention on the Law of the Sea (UNCLOS) grants coastal states additional sovereign rights over extended continental shelves, up to 350 nautical miles from the coastal baseline, provided certain geological and bathymetric conditions are met. These sovereign rights do not imply full territorial sovereignty: relating to the subsurface only, they have no incidence on the legal status of the superjacent waters as high seas or that of the airspace above those waters. But they speak to a gradual arrogation of spaces previously found beyond the realm of human existence and colonizing possibilities.

Increasingly the reach of the state has also been directed downward, penetrating ever deeper into the subterranean realm. With so much of its power relying explicitly on visuality, the opacity of the Earth's surface has long marked a hard ontological boundary for the state. The triumph of the surface, in Ryan Bishop's phrasing, has thus been echoed by a subterranean impotence.[43] Unsurprisingly, as Caroline Humphrey, Elizabeth Dunn, and Wayne Chambliss all discuss in their respective chapters, the underground has frequently been a space associated with resistance, a place of escape from the state's sight and control. In the context of the city of Odessa, Ukraine, as Humphrey discusses, if the maze of tunnels beneath the city has been used for most of its history as a nexus of resistance and evasion, the position of the subterranean vis-à-vis the state is more complex and not necessarily always adversarial. The evolving and adaptable use of Odessa's catacombs is, for Humphrey, a symptom of the very nature of this kind of space. As cellular social places that have developed incrementally, warrens obey their own infrastructural regimes, ultimately escaping the grasp of their original architects.[44]

If the subterranean realm is one often occupied and taken advantage of by nonstate actors,[45] Eyal Weizman's work on the Israel-Palestine border has shown this facile dichotomy does not necessarily hold true everywhere.[46] Faced with threats both within and under urban environments, the Israeli army has been exploring new strategies to destroy underground tunnels but also to short-circuit and recompose the architectural and urban syntax.[47] Avoiding the streets, roads, alleys, and courtyards that define the logic of movement through the city, Israeli soldiers are punching holes through walls, ceilings, and floors, moving across a three-dimensional volume of dense urban fabric.[48]

Similar spatial processes are explored in Elizabeth Dunn's chapter on the Roki Tunnel linking Russia and Georgia. The aim of the tunnel, initially envisioned in the 1960s and completed in 1984, was to cut across the Greater

Caucasus mountain range that had proven a near impassable wall on Russia's southern border. In bypassing the six mountain passes that allowed movement but also acted as chokepoints,[49] the tunnel would literally flatten volumetric space, ignoring its vertical dimension and turning it into what Deleuze and Guattari have called a "smooth space" where the mountainous topography on which locals relied could be obliterated.[50] But in doing so, the tunnel also created a "striated space"—a conduit able to channel, and therefore control, movement. What ultimately makes tunnels (potentially) successful political technologies for state actors, Dunn argues, is their capacity to *collapse* the volume, to make the terrain legible and controllable, and to force conflict back onto terrain where the state has considerable technological advantage.

Pushing back ever further on the ground's intrinsic opacity, state actors have been relying on new technologies—such as magnetometers and other metal detectors, electromagnetic induction, electrical resistivity, gravity measurement technology, and seismic and acoustic sensors—to map the subsurface and combat "striated space."[51] Of all these techniques, Wayne Chambliss argues, gravity measurement technology is especially promising in that it relies on differences in materials' density and, unlike LIDAR, multispectral cameras, or ground-penetrating radars that can be thwarted by various countersurveillance tactics, gravimetry recruits the Earth itself as informant. Because the Earth's composition is not homogenous, the force of gravity varies at every point of the Earth's surface by a tiny amount. As Chambliss explains, the US military is currently mapping the subterranean to create a baseline. Subsequent changes in the gravitational fields, such as the creation of underground bunkers or a military facility, will alter the structure's gravitational signature, making the structure visible. If it is feasible in theory to spoof these mapping technologies (by adding heavy material to counterbalance the missing soil), it will prove increasingly difficult to do so as the technology becomes more sophisticated.

With the Earth plumbed at increasing depths and resolutions, well beyond what was previously imagined possible, new resource exploitation opportunities have opened up, extending the remit of state sovereignty and complicating the relationship between the surface and the subsoil. Fracking and horizontal drilling have caused the emergence of the issue of extralateral rights, i.e., the right to chase resources beyond the surface boundaries of an initial land grant—essentially allowing serpentine underground claims to supersede the surface grid.[52] Counterintuitively, technological advances have reduced rather than extended the state's lower and upper limits. The assumption that sovereignty extended upward and downward ad infinitum was only challenged when the technological means to colonize these upper and lower reaches became available. It was only then that limits had to be determined—though paradoxically it is anticipated that they will be extended and revised further as technology develops.

Just as exploitable depth will eventually reach a point where pressure and temperature render the issue of property moot, the upper bound to sovereignty is generally agreed to be the Kármán line, sixty-two miles above sea level, where the atmosphere is no longer sufficiently dense to provide any appreciable aerodynamic lift. An upper limit is in any event necessary given that the Earth is in motion; without one, nations would be sovereign over a constantly changing sliver of space.[53] As multimedia artist Dario Solman stated, "verticality pushed to its extreme becomes orbital." At such point, "the difference between vertical and horizontal ceases to exist."[54] This is not to say that sovereignty cannot be extended to outer space—there are in fact over four hundred communication satellites in geosynchronous orbit—only that it can no longer operate along the same spatial logic of terrestrial sovereignty, as a mere vertical extrapolation of terrestrial borders. The politics of tethering here are of a different nature. The geosynchronous orbit, located at 22,236 miles above the equator and with an orbital period matching that of the Earth, has become incredibly valuable real estate as it is ideally positioned to monitor weather, communications, and surveillance. This is especially true of the geostationary orbit, a segment of the geosynchronous orbit located right above the equator in which an orbiting satellite will appear stationary with respect to Earth. So valuable is the geostationary orbit that it is increasingly clogged up by satellites belonging to a handful of states.[55] As Gbenga Oduntan suggests, the very fact that an object hangs permanently over a state suggests it has a special relationship to it, which cannot be easily overlooked.[56]

The terrestrial referent, speaking to a land-based imagination, has in fact been regularly noted in state incursions into more-than-human spaces.[57] In her discussion of the International Space Station in the afterword to this collection, Debbora Battaglia notes that at the end of a working day or in the event of an emergency, astronauts return to their slice of national territory as it is constructed onboard. In my own chapter on the enclave complex of Baarle-Hertog and Baarle-Nassau, we witness a strong will to twist and bend the material and social fabric of the two towns in ways consonant with a Westphalian imaginary—in spite of the highly fractured nature of the enclaves, which ultimately makes it impossible. The development of oceanic space is similarly framed by a land-based imagination, "mobilizing territorial metaphors similar to the terrestrial equivalent of land grabbing," even though the established and fixed grid coordinate system of terrestrial boundaries is poorly suited to accommodate the unique aquatic materiality of ocean space.[58] In the

context of the South China Sea, the People's Republic of China has been rep-
licating narratives of development in Xinjiang and other remote borderlands.
Its new official map, unveiled in 2014, makes assertive claims toward enlarge-
ment of its territorial footprint by claiming sovereignty over vast expanses of
oceanic space, but it also does much more than that. Unlike the previous map
which depicted noncontiguous territories in cutaway boxes—as is the case
for instance with the United States' customary representation of Alaska and
Hawaii—the so-called vertical map is singular and continuous and includes
the vast body of water south of Hainan Island.[59] In the new map, the mainland,
islands, and claimed waters in the South China Sea are all featured on the same
scale in one complete map, thereby placing the islands, but also the entirety of
the maritime space, in direct visual equivalence with the mainland.[60]

In spite of its shortcomings vis-à-vis territories beyond land and beyond
the horizontal, cartography continues to hold a crucial place in the way territorial sovereignty is imagined and borders are managed.[61] In her chapter on
the Sino-Indian border across the Himalayan range, Tina Harris explores the
challenges of bordering at sixteen thousand feet. As she shows, the siting of
border posts remains constrained by limitations imposed by the environment:
the India-China boundary line is actually too high to be physically occupied
by humans, and military bases are therefore placed in more habitable zones,
far away from the "actual" border zone. Natural seasonal and environmental
changes such as the freezing of mountain passes or monsoon-related landslides
in the Himalayas may also shift the border to new locations or may mean that
humans can only access it at specific times of the year. There is a sense however that the Indian and Chinese sides are creeping toward full appropriation
of the border with the aid of new technologies such as laser fences, motion
sensors, CCTV cameras, and a network of radars, and that the gap—or *lag* in
Tina Harris's phrasing[62]—will eventually disappear.

This gap between confidently mapped borders and actual realities on the
ground is especially vivid at the India-China border but even the most established borders are never as stable as they claim. Italy's northern border with
Austria and Switzerland follows the watershed that separates the drainage ba-
sins of Northern and Southern Europe. Running at high altitudes, the border
crosses snowfields and perennial glaciers—all of which are now melting as a
result of anthropogenic climate change. "As the watershed shifts so does the
border, contradicting its representations on official maps. Italy, Austria, and
Switzerland have consequently introduced the novel legal concept of a 'moving border,' one that acknowledges the volatility of geographical features once
thought to be stable."[63] A grid of twenty-five solar-powered sensors has been

fitted on the surface of the glacier at the foot of Mount Similaun; every two hours these sensors record data, allowing for an automated mapping of the shifts in the border. In these two very different border contexts, technology aims to close the gap between physical reality and representation, between map and territory. The promissory role of sensors tracking borders in real time, or of drones surveilling spaces beyond human reach, assuages cartographic anxieties and maintains the totalizing fiction of the nation-state in suspended belief. The more precise and sophisticated these technologies, the more ontologically secure the borders.

The process of terrestrial globalization, Peter Sloterdijk writes, reached its completion "with the installation of an electronic atmosphere and a satellite environment in the earth's orbit."[64] The provision of television, radio, and internet signals serve as confirmation of sovereign power insofar as states are invested in providing access to the entire territory over which they have sovereignty, and as gaps in coverage tend to be perceived as symptomatic of state weakness.[65] As early as 2011, China Mobile announced for instance that residents of the Spratly Islands (which until recently were uninhabited) would be enjoying full cellphone coverage. Elsewhere, telephone signals have been known to mold more overtly patterns of human settlement. In occupied Palestine, the erection of a cellphone tower by the Israel Electric Corporation allowed a settler outpost to emerge and grow steadily, highlighting the capacity of technology to act as a prosthetic device for territorial sovereignty.[66]

Often, these technologies originate with the military and later enter the civilian domain. As Caren Kaplan writes, military ways of seeing and doing have been foundational to whole areas of culture that compose the ground of everyday life—including those that might seem unrelated to the project of state security or waging war, such as modes of making and reproducing art, or industrial design and technologies.[67] In his chapter based on research carried out in North Dakota, Marcel LaFlamme looks at how the maturation and proliferation of unmanned aircraft or drones, greatly aided by smartphone applications, is posing significant challenges to existing regimes of traffic management and is giving rise to new modes of volumetric sovereignty. Unlike many countries that have already transferred system management to various corporate structures, LaFlamme explains, the United States continues to retain direct responsibility over its air traffic control. However, various emerging forms of marketization are gradually transforming the way in which sovereignty is governed across borders as well as within them.

LaFlamme's chapter brings into sharp relief the fractured and nonhomogeneous nature of political space, a point other scholars have made with respect to digital enclosure, territorial airspace, or the management of oil pipelines.[68] This complexity highlights the importance of apprehending the state as a volumetric entity, rather than the mere intersection of the horizontal and the vertical. As Jason Cons and Michael Eilenberg have recently noted, we need to attend to the assemblages "constituted of intertwined materialities, actors, cultural logics, spatial dynamics, ecologies, and political economic processes."[69] As the next section discusses in more depth, these state assemblages—these "acephalous ad hoc groupings of diverse elements"[70]—are more than a set of discrete layers: they interact and provoke cross-scale entanglements that can remain beyond the threshold of conscious detectability yet have deleterious or even lethal consequences on the body.[71] It is both timely and imperative that we attend to their material presence, to the vibrant matter that composes them— the swirling of the air, the roiling of the water, the churning of the soil, the melting of the ice.

Materiality

Voluminous States challenges an imaginary of space that is disembodied and abstract, taking issue with the notion propounded by some cartographers that the move from map to GPS has caused an uncoupling of territory and sovereignty and has led to a predominance of coordinates beyond any geographic commitment.[72] As our bodies grate against the textured materiality of that purportedly empty space, as we choke on its dust, as our lungs struggle to fill with oxygen, and as our social lives become enmeshed in and demarcated by invisible electromagnetic fields, we are continually confronted with the textured and voluminous presence of this space.[73]

Remaining attuned to the sensory (even *sensuous*) and synesthetic texture of this three-dimensional space is an important thread linking all contributions and in particular the five chapters found in the "Materiality" section. That "volume" and "materiality" cannot be dissociated from each other is especially evident in Klaus Dodds's chapter focusing on the Arctic.[74] Drawing on the notion of fissure to foreground the elemental and more-than-human qualities of territory, Dodds reflects on what is at stake when ice, land, air, and water crack up and scramble established imaginative legacies of place framing. In the two Cold War–era vignettes he presents, on secret subterranean operation Camp Century/Project Ice Worm and the USS *Skate* submarine, the Greenlandic ice sheet ultimately proved to be a noncompliant and undomesticated partner. Geopolitical forays into the Arctic—an increasingly attractive site of resource extraction and global navigation given the compounding effects of climate change—have underscored the complex and materially recalcitrant nature of the region, neither solid nor liquid. The symbolic planting of a flag, if attempted at the surface of the North Pole, would not take place on "solid, spatially fixed land but on a mathematically determined spot marked on a maze of mobile and shifting ice floes."[75] Russia's planting of a titanium flag on the bottom of the Central Arctic Ocean in August 2007 circumvented this icy conundrum by choosing earthly attachment instead.[76]

As geographer Philip Steinberg has argued, sea ice holds particular interest precisely because of its liminality: while it is juridically and cartographically of the sea, its tactile, functional, and visual properties more closely resemble land.[77] This very material liminality became in fact a point of contention in a murder case that took place in 1970 on T-3, an ice island that from 1952 through 1978 served as a US Navy research station as it floated around the Arctic Ocean. At the time of the murder, T-3 was situated in international waters, though it had originally calved off Canada's Ellesmere Island. Should T-3 be considered a vessel, under the jurisdiction of the United States, or a piece of sovereign territory, and therefore Canadian?[78] As a prosthetic technology of territory, Johanne Bruun and Philip Steinberg write, T-3 operated as an elemental nodal point, pulling together a complex territorial assemblage of matter and meaning in an environment whose physical properties crack apart commonplace understandings of terrain.[79]

Voluminous space is an entanglement of materialities but also of scales, from the planetary to the granular. "Seemingly insignificant 'specks' accumulate, taking shape from barely noticeable singularities to unavoidably complex entities. As discrete units that aggregate to immense numbers, they exhibit a continuous fluid medium of their own—viscous, gravitational, flowing, blowing—constantly composing, and recomposing itself, instigating morphological variation."[80] A pertinent example of this transscalar multimateriality is the so-called Great Pacific garbage patch—a plastic vortex of flotsam and jetsam whose contents and boundaries defy both spatial definition and visibility. Larger than Texas—and possibly twice the size of America[81]—evaluations of its size speak to the ambition, and ultimate impossibility, of comparing it to a landmass since the nature of the patch invalidates attempts at territorial referentiality.[82] As the gyre churns vast quantities of discarded plastics, the material is broken down into ever smaller components. Most of the contents of the garbage patch are in fact so small that they are invisible to the naked eye, yet the impact of its overall mass—amounting to as much as a six-to-one ratio of plastic to zooplankton—is all too real. In suspension below the ocean's surface, these particles alter the usual transparency of the water, blocking sunlight in part or completely.[83]

Frequently imagined as a vast floating collection of refuse, the garbage patch is a ghostly presence reaching across scales, both immense and minuscule.[84]

The complex planetary assemblage of the Great Pacific garbage patch is also palpable through its environmental impact. The harmful effect of microplastic on fish, birds, and other animals is well known but other classes of organisms actually benefit from the plastic debris. Water skater insects that live on hard surfaces in the water, for instance, have been laying their eggs on pieces of plastic in much greater numbers than ever before, extending their range considerably as a result.[85] Examples such as these speak to the complexity of entanglements between human and nonhuman animals, the organic and nonorganic, the animate and the inert. They also shed light on the planetary scale of environments and (mega)events such as climate change—as the work of Tim Morton on hyperobjects has shown.[86]

Similar processes inform atmospheric entanglements. In his chapter on the movement of airborne particulate matter across the Pacific, Jerry Zee notes that the impact that dust storms originating in China have on California's air quality is often so significant that they can push air quality over regulatory thresholds. In measuring the quality of the air before it is impacted by domestic pollution, analyses carried out by the Lawrence Berkeley National Labs on the summit of Mount Tamalpais, north of San Francisco, are able to provide a "fingerprinting of the inbound airmass" and estimate how much of China drifts into American air. As Zee notes, these floating dusts blast apart a distinction between land and air, solid and gas, dramatizing their continuity as a choreography of materials.

As dust plumes move across and between continents, heavier dust particles are among the first elements to descend, while finer dusts that carry highly carcinogenic toxic material (far more likely to be inhaled deeply) travel to more geographically distant locations.[87] Importantly, these dust plumes are an assemblage of both organic and inorganic material. Suspended in the estimated two billion metric tons of dust lifted in the atmosphere every year are soil pollutants such as herbicides and pesticides, as well as microorganisms (bacteria, viruses, and fungi) in such quantities that sediment-borne bacteria could form a microbial bridge between Earth and Jupiter.[88] The astonishing magnitude by which desert soils are aerosolized into the giant clouds of dust discussed by Zee means that the sediments and their tiny inhabitants, once airborne, can settle thousands of miles from their site of origin, impacting the health of human and nonhuman animals where they make landfall.[89]

These "bacterial passengers" do more of course than merely hitch a ride on dust particles. They are an intrinsic part of both human and nonhuman animal bodies insofar as microorganisms outnumber human cells in the body by a ratio of ten to one.[90] The increasing recognition of widespread bacterial and cross-species entanglements means that symbiogenesis—the horizontal transfer of genetic traits—is gradually replacing the cruder model of neo-Darwinian evolutionary theory. From biotic entities organized into clusters of genomes with unstable group boundaries (in the case of some influenza strains) to organisms such as certain fungi where the concept of species is largely irrelevant, scholars are increasingly attuned to the coevolution of organisms.[91]

This dramatic shift in conceptual models has had important repercussions on the way state borders are conceptualized and approached.[92] In a chapter deploying the concept of ecotone—the interface between two different ecological habitats—Hilary Cunningham embraces a volumetric sensibility in order to remain attuned to the different kinds of space, bodywork, and somatic edges that are created by borders, especially as they impact the nonhuman. Ecotones, she writes, exhibit a rich variety and abundance of life. The potential erection of a US-Mexico border wall, in addition to its intended effect on human movement, will turn this particular ecotone into what she terms a *necrotone*—a death-dealing place. Not only will a continuous border wall interrupt the migratory patterns and ranges of animals living at the surface, but its subterranean extension will impact the burrows and movements of subterrestrial animals, while artificial light and the creation of twenty-four-hour daylight conditions will create maladaptive behaviors and disrupt bird flights and migrations.[93] A volumetric approach, Cunningham argues, situates human and nonhuman wellbeing at the same crossroads, recognizing that the planet's most vulnerable human and nonhuman populations are on the frontiers of social marginalization and ecological destruction.

The planned border wall is an especially egregious disruption of the thickness and mobility inherent to transitional zones, but of course all borders, including "natural" ones, are political and cartographic fictions imposed on the world.[94] Sarah Green's evocative metaphor of the tidemark to refer to the temporal oscillation of lines of sovereignty over space is particularly useful here in that it is alert to more-than-human forces, but it may be productive to extend it along a vertical axis as well to give it volume.[95] Thus in her chapter on Hong Kong, Clancy Wilmott traces how surfaces are imagined, produced, and lived in the context of voluminous urban spaces. Measuring height, she writes, is both situated and relative, since landscapes rise and sink, the tide washes up and down, and the oceans are not consistently level across the world. In a city like Hong Kong where building space is limited, upward construction has been accompanied with extensive land reclamation,[96] but the baseline for this urban expansion—the "surface" of the city—lacked stability and definition. In 1866 a copper bolt was driven into the naval dockyard's pier to determine a consistent sea level for the measurement of the hills, but when the dockyard had to be rebuilt, this led to a new, unfixed zero point, somewhat lower than when it was last checked. When the dockyard was moved a second time, the bolt was repositioned again, and a few more feet were lost.[97]

Doreen Massey wrote that the Euclidean notion of space as a stable surface provides "unwelcome constraints that separate spaces from the matter and meanings that occur within." Because the foundational space that remains after substance has been stripped away is empty, abstracted, and atemporal, this makes for a poor foundation for theorizing relational geographies of immanence.[98] Mining the gap between *volumetric* and *voluminous*—between measured abstract space and lived space—and tracking Hong Kong's urban evolution through its verticality, materiality, and temporality, Wilmott is also attentive to the "chaotic underpinnings and experience of place."[99]

Philip Steinberg and Kimberley Peters have argued that the ocean is an ideal spatial foundation to challenge approaches that portray space as dematerialized, static, and periodized. As a voluminous and material environment undergoing continual reformation, the persistent and underlying churn of the ocean is ideally suited, they write, to "reinvigorate, redirect, and reshape debates that are all too often restricted by terrestrial limits."[100] Their oceanic "wet ontology" is theoretically productive, especially as chaos and turbulence are not the exclusive property of liquids. Solids can also become turbulent under extreme conditions, or relative to geologic time.[101] As Nigel Clark reminds us, "strata-forming processes are incessantly active, and the uppermost layers of the Earth's crust are in constant interaction with the swirling mobility of air, water, and life at the planet's surface."[102]

The notion of turbulence brings in an important elemental dimension which has thus far remained unexplored in the emerging literature on volume, that of gravity. As Gastón Gordillo writes in his contribution, gravity affects everything that exists, lives, and happens on Earth. If this statement appears self-evident, it does not diminish its force in any way. In fact, this very assumed and invisible omnipresence tends to obfuscate the implications of thinking gravity materially, territorially, and philosophically.[103] Like Wayne Chambliss discusses in his chapter on gravimetry, attentiveness to gravity reveals the irreducible materiality of the planet's terrain. In his essay, Gordillo foregrounds the body as the main recipient of what Derek McCormack terms *elemental envelopment*.[104] The microphysics of warfare in Afghanistan which Gordillo describes reveal the ways in which the power of gravity over human action has contingent yet consequential impacts on the deployment of state sovereignty. In an echo of the battles waged between Russian and Caucasians that are discussed in Dunn's chapter, warfare in Afghanistan brings to light the stark differences in the way terrain is apprehended by invading armies and local fighters. These distributive differentials, in turn, demand renewed attention to the ways in which the world that envelops us is experienced, embodied, and imagined.

Territorial Imagination

Just as space is never empty, time is never even, Karen Barad writes. Time is "drawn out like taffy, twisted like hot metal, cooled, hardened, and splintered."[105] Temporality is an important aspect of the concept of tidemarks deployed earlier as well as a significant dimension of border control, as is nicely illustrated in Harris's ethnographic case. While temporality in the Himalayas is uniquely shaped by altitude, temperature, plate tectonics, and climate change, time is a universal (though unequal) factor of border crossings—if only in terms of the time it takes to physically go through customs and passport controls, and/or scramble over mountainous terrain, trek across desert, and cross rivers in an attempt to avoid official border crossings.[106]

Time is also experienced differently depending on the scale that is privileged.[107] In her chapter on the Greek-Albanian border region of Epirus, Sarah Green fuses human and geological perspectives—a two-speed ethnography—to highlight the productive intersections that inform the relations of local people with their politically and tectonically unstable region. Being attuned to these different temporalities brings into view certain spaces that were assumed to be static and immobile,[108] and is also key to understanding different logics of spatiality—in this case the Westphalian logic of the nation-state; the remaining traces of the Ottoman Empire's logic of statecraft; and the social logic of the people of the Greek-Albanian border.

The complex entanglements of time, space, and materiality—what Karen Barad terms *spacetimemattering*[109]—do not always take place in spaces or timeframes accessible or even perceptible to prosthetic-free human experience.[110] As scholars in the humanities and social sciences gradually take these different temporalities into their stride,[111] the importance of taking volume into consideration is gaining recognition in analyses of social and political life. In urban contexts in particular, Stephen Graham has argued, horizontal imaginations are woefully inadequate to understand the urban labyrinths which seamlessly weave together the surface, the overground, and the subterranean. If they fail to apprehend cities as volumes, he continues, urban planners and researchers "will struggle to contest their designs and exclusions and address their palpable problems."[112]

A volumetric imaginary is also eminently suited to exploring amorphous and seemingly immaterial realms such as radio and sonic waves or the invisible topographies of electromagnetic space, none of which overlay precisely onto a geopolitical organization of space but instead have the capacity to crisscross, bleed through, and undermine political boundaries.[113] Again, their nonlinear and leaky qualities are not foreshadowing deterritorialization necessarily. As Keller Easterling reminds us, despite being atomized and airborne, mobile telephony must nonetheless "tap into that physical broadband network, and at these or any other switching points, a bottleneck or monopoly can develop."[114] A similar argument was developed by Nicole Starosielski in her work on undersea cables. Signal traffic, she writes, is "wired rather than wireless; semicentralized rather than distributed; territorially entrenched rather than deterritorialized; precarious rather than resilient; and rural and aquatic rather than urban."[115] Contrary to popular representations, only a very small proportion of this traffic is actually airborne.[116] It is also highly concentrated, due in part to the considerable costs of each system and the presence of existing networks, originally designed for older technologies such as the telegraph and the telephone.[117] Not only are communications networks "grounded" in particular topographies but their design and placement take into account the local geography, climate, and existing infrastructure. Mindful of the high temperatures generated by search engines, Google has for instance chosen to locate some of its European servers in Hamina, Finland, where the seawater cooling system can be more energy efficient.[118] While the coldness of the Arctic is proving a useful accomplice for global infrastructures, the physical geography of the seabed has proven an essential partner for transoceanic cabling, providing a resting space that is far removed from the hulls of passing ships.[119]

The two case studies in Aihwa Ong's chapter show particularly well the tension and play between an imaginary of the nation-state as fixed and bound by its borders, and sovereign practices that are increasingly complex and deterritorialized—a phenomenon she termed *graduated sovereignty* in an earlier text.[120] In Singapore, the seaward extension of territory, in the form of land reclamation and novel usages of oceanic surface, is seeing the island nation's geobody technologically sustained in a fluid material environment. Reimagined as a hydroterritorial entity,[121] Singapore has literally become buoyant. China has also, in very different forms, sought to extend its territorial footprint to spaces beyond terra, embarking on a process of technological and ecological manipulation of land/sea/sky interfaces. The imaginary here is one of flows and connections, reliant on the Maritime Silk Road project to weave an extensive economic and political web well beyond China's mainland. If Singapore's volumetric expansion is sustained by a terrestrial referent, in that buoyancy implies an upward force resistant to gravity, the infrastructural assemblage behind the extension of China's volumetric sovereignty is less reliant on geographical constraints. Borrowing deterritorializing moves from America's hyperpower playbook, Ong writes, China has been able to leverage its political and economic clout to reinterpret and bend territorial sovereignty rules. Still, even here, the metaphoric references remain terrestrial and horizontal: "Great Firewall," "Great Wall of Sand," "Great Wall in the Sky."

The flows and forces discussed by Ong depart in important ways from the abstract and immaterial models that some imagined would be replacing the bipolar world order that had defined global relations until the collapse of the Soviet Union in 1991. The material nature of these flows is foregrounded even further in Jason Cons's chapter on Bangladesh's delta region. Noting how anticipatory fears of inundation dominate imagined geographies, Cons urges us to pivot away from catastrophic events as the primary logic of the future and focus instead on alternative visions of environmental transformation. Equally pressing—less dramatically apparent but with important implications for a better understanding of borders and volume—the notion of seepage, Cons argues, is a more useful tracker of anthropogenic change. A significant dimension of material and volumetric instability in the delta comes from river siltation, a consequence of the shrimp industry as well as upstream dams and barrages on major rivers in India that subsequently flow into Bangladesh. These processes are also more-than-human: plate tectonics are causing the Sundarbans region itself to seep out of India and into Bangladesh, a gradual eastward flow that has led to speculative plans to rethink the delta space. The fugitive nature of matter brings different planes into relation in "ways that are constitutive of new, multidimensional spatial forms," blurring "borderlines not only between spatial planes, but also in terms of experiences of territory."[122]

Such spatial entanglements substantiate Steinberg and Peters's assertion that a wet ontology can be productively extended to spaces beyond the oceanic. Territorial management indeed appears to be increasingly predicated on mobility across planes and scales. Layered representations of the state—to say nothing of flat cartographic models—are poorly suited to reflect the complexities of territorial control. Such is this complexity that organizational models are gradually skewing human/nonhuman assemblages in favor of nonhuman models.[123] Technological-entomological amalgams such as the swarm give precedence to autonomy, emergence, and distributed functioning, and operate at speeds and altitudes beyond human capabilities. As the breach widens between human experience and the new realities of territorial management, a volumetric imaginary attuned to these evolving paradigms has become critical.[124]

Counterintuitively perhaps, a sensorial, synesthetic approach grounded in human experience might be the best way to achieve this. A "confusion of the sensorium," Ryan Bishop has argued, is key to the status of the subject with regard to agency and control,[125] working here against the privileged position that sight has long occupied in geopolitics.[126] More proxemic senses such as sound, smell, or touch can open up different perspectives insofar as they are tied to bodily presence.[127] Thus, as architectural theorist Juhani Pallasmaa reminds us, in a large or dark environment, it is through the echoes of our own footsteps or the sound of dripping water that the ear can carve a volume and make sense of the surrounding space.[128]

In her chapter about the demilitarized zone (DMZ) separating North from South Korea, Lisa Sang-Mi Min deploys the notion of echolocation to come to terms with the paradox of an experience that is heavily reliant on the optical yet leaves the observer strangely disoriented. Optical techniques to locate the DMZ, such as large panoramic windows, binoculars, or guard posts, invoke a sense of frozen staticity. Sound, by contrast, relates to the border in ways that elude the burden of these optics. "Sound cannot be contained in the same way that optics seek maintenance upon territory," she writes. While vision renders the landscape flat, the sonic environment is voluminous, embracing, expanding, contracting. Min describes how the rolling sounds of propaganda, world news, K-pop, military marches, and songs of love, longing, and loss are reflected and deflected by topography and weather. Echolocation is more than wayfinding. It is, first and foremost, a way of being in the world.

Perhaps even more than hearing—which Pallasmaa considers, along with vision, one of the two privileged sociable senses—smell and touch can be productive contributors to a synesthetic and *voluminous* spatial imaginary. These senses tap into an apprehension of space that is generally relegated to the private realm, "archaic sensory remnants . . . usually suppressed by the code of culture."[129] Smellscapes, immersive and volatile, can help map elusive olfactory traces that index tangible social inequalities,[130] while alertness to tactile and haptic dimensions brings to the fore an intersensoriality in politics that is rarely made explicit yet molds international relations and policy.[131] Vibration, implicating both sound and touch, similarly opens up volumetric dimensions that are difficult to map or visualize. In the context of horizontal drilling and fracking, the anthropogenic nature of induced vibration engages subterranean spatial logics that contrast dramatically with territorial encounters as well as challenge the cohesion implicit in Steinberg and Peters's notion of wet ontology.[132] Effects of vibrations on the body itself can be harmful, if not lethal, even if they are not consciously registered. Frequencies of seven hertz, coinciding with theta rhythms, can induce moods of fear and anger, while infrasonic resonance can produce intense friction between internal organs. The weaponization of vibratory space, with infrasonic acoustic guns or through the panic-inducing violence of high-volume frequencies, is another example of the mobilization of voluminous space for political aims.[133]

Untethered Spaces?

On September 5, 1962, a fragment of the Soviet spacecraft Sputnik IV crashed in Manitowoc, Wisconsin. This more-than-Earth encounter remained a local news story until 2007, when the town launched the now yearly Sputnikfest, with contests such as the Ms. Space Debris Pageant, open to "all human life forms."[134] In Kazakhstan and in the Russian Altai Republic, both on the rocket flightpath of the Baikonur Cosmodrome, Russian space debris are a far more common occurrence.[135] This has caused a niche scrap metal economy to develop in Kazakhstan, with groups of specialized collectors combing the steppe after each launch in search of salable metals. Through established norms and principles, as well as per the 1974 Convention on Registration of Objects Launched into Outer Space, while outer space is considered neutral territory, human-made objects remain the property of the launching state—constituting in effect orbital ambulatory exclaves of sovereign territory.[136] For Kazakhstan, both Baikonur and the space objects taking off from it remain intimately entangled in debates about the meaning of national sovereignty, as well as about Russia's protracted presence in post-Soviet Central Asia.[137]

Like the economic zones discussed in Ong's chapter, these territorial fragments constitute spaces of exception within the recognized world state system but belong to a specific subset insofar as their sovereign status is predicated on movement. Like a ship or aircraft registered under a particular flag but crossing other sovereign spaces, their jurisdiction is dependent on location. These mobile pieces of sovereign territory also share characteristics with the cross-border movement of water and sewerage discussed in the context of Baarle-Nassau and Baarle-Hertog which pass from a sovereign space to another and require mutual agreement to sustain the illusion. Unlike economic zones that are carved out for specific (usually economic) aims, ambulatory spaces and temporal exceptions function as devices designed to work within the agreed system without having to challenge its core tenets. An extreme example is Suite 212 at Claridge's Hotel in London—a temporary Yugoslavian enclave that was created for a single day in 1945 to ensure the heir of the throne would be born on Yugoslavian soil.[138]

These spaces of volumetric exception illustrate the difficulty of creating imaginaries of political order beyond the nation-state or forms of sovereignty that are truly deterritorialized.[139] Even utopian projects like the sixty or so micronations that have been declared worldwide have a territorial referent: a sliver of no-man's land (Liberland), a city's neighborhood (Christiania), an off-shore platform in the North Sea (Sealand), a section of ocean space (Republica Glaciar), a satellite in outer space (Asgardia). As geographer Alastair Bonnett notes, "the notion that sovereignty can be based within a network of people and not defined by borders isn't easy to get one's head around."[140] Surprising contenders may be supranational organizations or networks such as the internet or the International Organization for Standardization (ISO). Writing of the latter, Keller Easterling notes that some observers regard it as the beginnings of a "world state" in that it "formats the performance and calibration of many components of infrastructure space at every scale, from the microscopic to the gigantic."[141] The internet has also been described as a sovereign territory even if such statements belong in the domain of the metaphorical since, in practice, the United States exercises superjurisdiction over it.[142] Yet it is these novel and volumetric geographies—specifically the planetary-scale computation which Benjamin Bratton terms *the Stack*—that are set to have the most dramatic impact on our geopolitical realities: "Planetary-scale computation takes different forms at different scales—energy and mineral sourcing and grids; subterranean cloud infrastructure; urban software and public service privatization; massive universal addressing systems; interfaces drawn by the augmentation of the hand, of the eye, or dissolved into objects; users both over-outlined by self-quantification and also exploded by the arrival of legions of sensors, algorithms, and robots."[143] Together, these computations distort and deform modern political geographies, producing new territories in their own image and ushering in a new model of geopolitical architecture. The gap between human imaginaries and the new realities of territorial management and sovereignty appears however to be widening and deepening, as cartographic two-dimensional representations continue to hold sway and elicit much affective force in spite of their inadequacies.[144]

NOTES

1   Jun Sen Ng, "Masterplan of Singapore's Underground Spaces Ready by 2019," *Straits Time*, February 5, 2018, https://www.straitstimes.com/politics/masterplan -of-spores-underground-spaces-ready-by-next-year.
2   See discussion in Humphrey, this volume.
3   See also Jerome Whitington, "Modernist Infrastructure and the Vital Systems Security of Water: Singapore's Pluripotent Climate Futures," *Public Culture* 28, no. 2 (2016): 415–41.
4   Stuart Banner, *Who Owns the Sky? The Struggle to Control Airspace from the Wright Brothers On* (Cambridge, MA: Harvard University Press, 2008).
5   Caren Kaplan, *Aerial Aftermaths: Wartime from Above* (Durham, NC: Duke University Press, 2018).
6   Carl Schmitt, *Nomos of the Earth in the International Law of Jus Publicum Europaeum* (New York: Telos, [1950] 2003).
7   See, for instance, Irus Braverman, Nicholas Blomley, David Delaney, and Alexandre (Sandy) Kedar, *The Expanding Spaces of Law: A Timely Legal Geography* (Stanford, CA: Stanford University Press, 2014).
8   William Rankin, *After the Map: Cartography, Navigation, and the Transformation of Territory in the Twentieth Century* (Chicago: University of Chicago Press, 2016).
9   As defined by the International Seabed Authority (ISA). The ISA was established under UNCLOS to control activities within areas of the seabed located outside national jurisdiction (see International Seabed Authority, "Continental Shelf," official website of International Seabed Authority, accessed January 17, 2019, https://www .isa.org.jm/continental-shelf). As Klaus Dodds writes, registering for extended continental shelf (ECS) status is an expensive and technical business (Klaus Dodds, "Our Seabed? Argentina, the Falklands and the Wider South Atlantic," *Polar Record* 52, no. 266 [2016]: 536). Claims are based on geological and geographical criteria including distance, thickness of sedimentary rock, and water depth. The various zones found between territorial waters and the high seas in figure I.1 represent different ways of calculating the maximum extension of the EEZ. The maximum limit is generally set at 350 nautical miles, or 100 miles from the 2,500-meter isobath, whichever is greatest. But coastal states can also claim an extension of their 200-mile EEZ to include the continental shelf. The claimable area is 60 nautical miles from the foot of the continental shelf, or the distance from the foot of the shelf to the part of the seafloor that has 1 percent sediment (*d*).
10 Coastal states are seeking primarily to define areas in which they have sovereign rights, with the view to exploit natural resources. As Philip Steinberg, Jeremy Tasch, and Hannes Gerhardt point out, the common portrayal of seabed-mapping missions as a "competitive mad dash to gain sovereign territory" is misleading. They are marking "limits," not "boundaries" (Philip E. Steinberg, Jeremy Tasch, and Hannes Gerhardt, *Contesting the Arctic: Politics and Imaginaries in the Circumpolar North* [London: IB Tauris, 2015], 32).

11 Ian Shaw, *Predator Empire: Drone Warfare and Full Spectrum Dominance* (Minneapolis: University of Minnesota Press, 2016), 15.

12 Keller Easterling, *Extrastatecraft: The Power of Infrastructure Space* (London: Verso, 2014).

13 See, for instance, Sandro Mezzadra and Brett Neilson, *Border as Method, Or, the Multiplication of Labor* (Durham, NC: Duke University Press, 2013); or Nira Yuval-Davis, Georgie Wemyss, and Kathryn Cassidy, *Bordering* (Cambridge: Polity, 2019).

14 Étienne Balibar, *Politics and the Other Scene* (London: Verso, 2002), 76.

15 David Ludden, "Maps in the Mind and the Mobility of Asia," *Journal of Asian Studies* 62, no. 4 (November 2003): 1058.

16 Stefanie R. Fishel, *The Microbial State: Global Thriving and the Body Politic* (Minneapolis: University of Minnesota Press, 2017).

17 John Agnew, "The Territorial Trap: The Geographical Assumptions of International Relations Theory," *Review of International Political Economy* 1, no. 1 (Spring 1994): 53–80.

18 Reece Jones, *Violent Borders: Refugees and the Right to Move* (London: Verso, 2016).

19 Michael Dear, *Why Walls Won't Work: Repairing the US-Mexico Divide* (Oxford: Oxford University Press, 2013), 177.

20 Alexander B. Murphy, "Territory's Continuing Allure," *Annals of the Association of American Geographers* 103, no. 5 (2013): 1212–26, https://doi.org/10.1080/00045608 .2012.696232.

21 Wendy Brown, *Walled States, Waning Sovereignty* (New York: Zone Books, 2010), 24.

22 Close to half of all undocumented immigrants come to the United States legally but then overstay their visas. Many of them travel by air, making walls doubly ineffective.

23 Clancy Wilmott, "Surface," Theorizing the Contemporary, *Cultural Anthropology*, October 24, 2017, https://culanth.org/fieldsights/surface?token=540.

24 Stuart Elden, "Secure the Volume: Vertical Geopolitics and the Depth of Power," *Political Geography* 34 (2013): 35–51.

25 Peter Adey, *Aerial Life: Spaces, Mobilities, Affects* (Malden, MA: Wiley-Blackwell, 2010); Derek Gregory, "From a View to a Kill: Drones and Late Modern War," *Theory, Culture and Society* 28, nos. 7–8 (2011): 188–215; Alison J. Williams, "A Crisis in Aerial Sovereignty? Considering the Implications of Recent Military Violations of National Airspace," *Area* 42, no. 1 (2010): 51–59; Eyal Weizman, *Hollow Land: Israel's Architecture of Occupation* (London: Verso, 2007); Bradley L. Garrett, *Explore Everything: Place-Hacking the City* (London: Verso, 2013).

26 Elaine Campbell, "Three-Dimensional Security: Layers, Spheres, Volumes, Milieus," *Political Geography* 69 (2019): 10–21; Ian Klinke, *Cryptic Concrete: A Subterranean Journey into Cold War Germany* (Chichester: Wiley-Blackwell, 2018); Marilu Melo Zurita, "Sinkhole," Volumetric Sovereignty forum, *Society and Space*, March 17, 2019, http://societyandspace.org/2019/03/17/sinkhole; María Alejandra Pérez, "Exploring the Vertical: Science and Sociality in the Field Among Cavers in Venezuela," *Social and Cultural Geography* 16, no. 2 (2015): 226–47.

27 Andrea Ballestero, *A Future History of Water* (Durham, NC: Duke University Press, 2019); Dominic Boyer and Cymene Howe, *Wind and Power in the Anthropo-*

cene (Durham, NC: Duke University Press, 2019); Timothy Choy and Jerry Zee, "Condition—Suspension," *Cultural Anthropology* 30, no. 2 (2015): 210–23; John Hannigan. *The Geopolitics of Deep Oceans* (Cambridge: Polity, 2016); Stefan Helmreich, *Alien Ocean: Anthropological Voyages in Microbial Seas* (Berkeley: University of California Press, 2009); Lisa Messeri, *Placing Outer Space: An Earthly Ethnography of Other Worlds* (Durham, NC: Duke University Press, 2016); Laura A. Ogden, *Swamplife: People, Gators, and Mangroves Entangled in the Everglades* (Minneapolis: Minnesota University Press, 2011); Eric Paul Roorda. *The Ocean Reader: History, Culture, Politics* (Durham, NC: Duke University Press, 2020); Jennifer E. Telesca, *Red Gold: The Managed Extinction of the Giant Bluefin Tuna* (Minneapolis: University of Minnesota Press, 2020).

28   On cartographic anxieties, see Franck Billé, "Introduction to 'Cartographic Anxieties,'" *Cross-Currents* 21 (2016): 1–18, http://cross-currents.berkeley.edu/e-journal /issue-21.

29   Grégoire Chamayou, *Théorie du drone* (Paris: La Fabrique, 2013); Gregory, "From a View to a Kill"; Shahar Hameiri and Lee Jones, *Governing Borderless Threats: Non-Traditional Security and the Politics of State Transformation* (Cambridge: Cambridge University Press, 2015); Lisa Parks and Caren Kaplan, *Life in the Age of Drone Warfare* (Durham, NC: Duke University Press, 2017).

30   A very powerful description of such entanglements in three-dimensional space is provided by Eyal Weizman in his book *Hollow Land*. The "Tunnel Road," linking Jewish Jerusalem and the West Bank settlement of Gush Etzion, crosses a volumetric space. "Although the road is under Israeli control, both the valley it spans and the city it runs beneath are areas under Palestinian control. As the road threads itself through this folded, topographical arrangement of different jurisdictions, Israeli territory finds itself alternatively above and below the Palestinian. . . . When the bridge's columns rest on Palestinian ground, the 'border' runs, presumably, through the thermodynamic joint between the column and the beams" (Weizman, *Hollow Land*, 180).

31   Jason Dittmer, "Geopolitical Assemblages and Complexity," *Progress in Human Geography* 38, no. 3 (2014): 390.

32   If the technologies Chambliss discusses are currently used exclusively by the US military, the "fluid movement between military and civilian populations and machinery," as Caren Kaplan has written, suggests that the popular imagination of the underground as static and inhibitive of movement, and thus less amenable to geopolitical mobilizations, will increasingly give way to a more dynamic view (Caren Kaplan, "Drone-O-Rama: Troubling the Temporal and Spatial Logics of Distance Warfare," in *Life in the Age of Drone Warfare*, ed. Lisa Parks and Caren Kaplan [Durham, NC: Duke University Press, 2017], 171). See also section XI, "Militarism and Technology," in Roberto J. González, Hugh Gusterson, and Gustaaf Houtman, *Militarization: A Reader* (Durham, NC: Duke University Press, 2019).

33   Martin Coward argues that this new military imaginary is blind to contiguity and perceives only a constellation of noncontiguous entities without any territorial reference (Martin Coward, "Networks, Nodes and De-Territorialised Battlespace: The Scopic Regime of Rapid Dominance," in *From Above: War, Violence and Vertical-*

26   Franck Billé

ity, ed. Peter Adey, Mark Whitehead, and Alison J. Williams [Oxford: Oxford University Press, 2013], 112). However, his privileging of connections in the form of nodes and networks leaves unexamined the material texture of space.

34 The two collections are available online in Open Access: "Speaking Volumes," Theorizing the Contemporary, *Cultural Anthropology*, 2017–18, http://culanth.org /fieldsights/1247-speaking-volumes; Volumetric Sovereignty forum, *Society and Space*, 2019, http://societyandspace.org/2019/04/10/volumetricsovereigntyforum.

35 Corey Johnson, Reece Jones, Anssi Paasi, Louise Amoore, Alison Mountz, Mark Salter, and Chris Rumford, "Interventions on Rethinking 'the Border' in Border Studies," *Political Geography* 30 (2011): 61–69.

36 Gbenga Oduntan, *Sovereignty and Jurisdiction in the Airspace and Outer Space: Legal Criteria for Spatial Delimitation* (London: Routledge, 2012), 23.

37 Joan Cocks, *On Sovereignty and Other Political Delusions* (London: Bloomsbury, 2014), 2–3.

38 Oduntan, *Sovereignty and Jurisdiction*, 24.

39 See, for instance, Daniel Immerwahr, *How to Hide an Empire: A History of the Greater United States* (New York: Farrar, Straus and Giroux, 2019).

40 Even if China is not the only nation involved in terraforming—Vietnam has also carried out land reclamation on Sand Cay Island—the extent of its activities remains unmatched.

41 Fiery Cross Reef (*Yongshu jiao* 永暑礁) has, for instance, grown in stunning fashion "from a single coral head that peaked a mere meter out of the waves" into an island "attaining a size of over 200 hectares of reclaimed land—roughly equivalent to about 280 football pitches" (Howard W. French, "What's behind Beijing's Drive to Control the South China Sea?," *Guardian*, July 28, 2015).

42 United Nations, *Agreement for the Implementation of the Provisions of the 1982 United Nations Convention on the Law of the Sea Relating to the Conservation and Management of Straddling Fish Stocks and Highly Migratory Fish Stocks*, A/CONF.164/ 22/Rev. 1 (New York: United Nations, 1995). See discussion in Philip E. Steinberg, *The Social Construction of the Ocean* (Cambridge: Cambridge University Press, 2001), 172.

43 Ryan Bishop, "Project 'Transparent Earth' and the Autoscopy of Aerial Targeting: The Visual Geopolitics of the Underground," *Theory, Culture and Society* 28, nos. 7–8 (2011): 270–86, https://doi.org/10.1177/0263276411424918.

44 The Odessa Catacombs, like their Paris counterpart, have now become important tourist attractions. Elsewhere, other subterranean formations have also led to profit-making enterprises. As Marilu Melo writes, if sinkholes have caused substantial damage and even deaths when the surface suddenly collapses in urban environments, they have, in places like Mexico's Yucatan Peninsula, transformed into tourist commodities. Taking advantage of the emergence of a sinkhole market, some "land" owners have opted to dynamite the surface to accelerate the creation of sinkholes—thereby manufacturing recreational volume for tourist consumption (Melo Zurita, "Sinkhole").

45 Daphné Richemond-Barak, *Underground Warfare* (Oxford: Oxford University Press), 2018.

46 Weizman, *Hollow Land*.

47 With space theorists such as Gilles Deleuze, Félix Guattari, and Guy Debord on the reading lists of some of the contemporary military institutions, Israeli military tactics have been relying on postcolonial and poststructuralist theory (Weizman, *Hollow Land*, 187).

48 Weizman, *Hollow Land*, 185–86.

49 For more on chokepoints, see the recent collection curated by Ashley Carse, Jason Cons, and Townsend Middleton (*Limn* 10 [2019]).

50 Guy Deleuze and Félix Guattari, *A Thousand Plateaus: Capitalism and Schizophrenia*, trans. Brian Massumi (Minneapolis: University of Minnesota Press, 1987).

51 Richemond-Barak, *Underground Warfare*, 93–104.

52 Evangeline McGlynn, "Quake," Volumetric Sovereignty forum, *Society and Space*, March 12, 2019, http://societyandspace.org/2019/03/12/quake.

53 Banner, *Who Owns the Sky?*, 266.

54 Cited in Stephen Graham, *Vertical: The City from Satellites to Bunkers* (London: Verso, 2016), 25.

55 In 1976, eight equatorial nations proclaimed sovereignty over segments of the geosynchronous orbit. Brazil, Colombia, Congo, Ecuador, Indonesia, Kenya, Uganda, and Zaire were primarily motivated by the fear, not entirely ungrounded as it turned out, that the first countries capable of launching satellites would fill up the orbit before poorer nations could acquire satellites of their own (Banner, *Who Owns the Sky?*, 286–87).

56 Oduntan, *Sovereignty and Jurisdiction*, 301.

57 Thus regulations about the subsoil are being implemented through UNCLOS, while the management of outer space is taking the high seas commons as its primary narrative.

58 Jon Phillips, "WATER | Order and the Offshore: The Territories of Deep-Water Oil Production," in *Territory beyond Terra*, ed. Kimberly Peters, Philip Steinberg, and Elaine Stratford (London: Rowman and Littlefield International, 2018), 67; Katherine Genevieve Sammler, "The Deep Pacific: Island Governance and Seabed Mineral Development," in *Island Geographies: Essays and Conversations*, ed. Elaine Stratford (London: Routledge, 2016), 14. See also Irus Braverman and Elizabeth R. Johnson, *Blue Legalities: The Life and Laws of the Sea* (Durham, NC: Duke University Press, 2020).

59 See Alessandro Uras, "The South China Sea and the Building of a National Maritime Culture: A New Chinese Province in the Making," *Asian Survey* 57, no. 6 (2017): 1008–31.

60 This equivalence, Ross Exo Adams argues, is in fact multidirectional. In his recent study of urbanization, he argues that the oceanic imagination has also imparted specific ways of conceptualizing the urban, a "maritimization" of urban space in effect. See Ross Exo Adams, *Circulation and Urbanization* (London: Sage, 2019).

61 A British company has recently divided the world into a grid of three-by-three-meter squares and assigned each one a unique three-word address. What3words

can pinpoint an exact location and direct a user to it—a very useful advantage for countries like Mongolia with little infrastructure and no street addresses. The system is however poorly suited to identify elevation.

62   The idea of lag presupposes isomorphism in that it implies that the space that is absent will be the same as the one that already exists (Marilyn Strathern, personal communication). On the political fiction of homogeneous space, see Franck Billé, "Territorial Phantom Pains (and Other Cartographic Anxieties)," *Environment and Planning D: Society and Space* 32, no. 1 (2014): 163–78.

63   Marco Ferrari, Elisa Pasqual, and Andrea Bagnato, *A Moving Border: Alpine Cartographies of Climate Change* (New York: Columbia University Press, 2018). See also the project on which the book is based, at the Italian Limes website, accessed October 3, 2019, http://italianlimes.net.

64   Peter Sloterdijk, *In the World Interior of Capital: Towards a Philosophical Theory of Globalization*, trans. Wieland Hoban (Cambridge: Polity Press, 2013), 12.

65   Ekaterina Mikhailova, "Broadcast," Volumetric Sovereignty forum, *Society and Space*, March 3, 2019, http://societyandspace.org/2019/03/03/broadcast.

66   The outpost of Migron is now one of the largest of the 103 outposts scattered throughout the West Bank (Weizman, *Hollow Land*, 2). As of 2011 it had a population of 260.

67   Caren Kaplan, "The Balloon Prospect: Aerostatic Observation and the Emergence of Militarised Aeromobility," in *From Above: War, Violence and Verticality*, ed. Peter Adey, Mark Whitehead, and Alison J. Williams (Oxford: Oxford University Press, 2013), 21–22.

68   See, respectively: Helga Tawil-Souri, "Digital Occupation: Gaza's High-Tech Enclosure," *Journal of Palestine Studies* 41, no. 2 (Winter 2012): 27–43; Weiqiang Lin, "AIR | Spacing the Atmosphere: The Politics of Territorializing Air," in *Territory beyond Terra*, ed. Kimberly Peters, Philip Steinberg, and Elaine Stratford (London: Rowman and Littlefield International, 2018), 35–49; Andrew Barry, *Material Politics: Disputes along the Pipeline* (Oxford: Wiley-Blackwell, 2013).

69   Jason Cons and Michael Eilenberg, "Introduction: On the New Politics of Margins in Asia Mapping Frontier Assemblages," in *Frontier Assemblages: The Emergent Politics of Resource Frontiers in Asia*, ed. Jason Cons and Michael Eilenberg (London: Wiley, 2019), 3.

70   Jane Bennett, *Vibrant Matter: A Political Ecology of Things* (Durham, NC: Duke University Press, 2010), 23–24.

71   The 2010 eruption of the Eyjafjallajökull Volcano in Iceland caused major disruptions in global air traffic yet the fine particles of volcanic ash were largely invisible to the naked eye (Peter Adey, *Air: Nature and Culture* [London: Reaktion Books, 2014], 172–73).

72   Rankin, *After the Map*, 4.

73   Timothy Choy, *Ecologies of Comparison: An Ethnography of Endangerment in Hong Kong* (Durham, NC: Duke University Press, 2009); Lisa Parks and Nicole Starosielski, *Signal Traffic: Critical Studies of Media Infrastructures* (Urbana: University of Illinois Press, 2015).

74 See also Klaus Dodds, *Ice: Nature and Culture* (Chicago: University of Chicago Press, 2018).

75 Steinberg, Tasch, and Gerhardt, *Contesting the Arctic*, 40.

76 See Klaus Dodds, "Flag Planting and Finger Pointing: The Law of the Sea, the Arctic and the Political Geographies of the Outer Continental Shelf," *Political Geography* 29, no. 2 (2010): 63–73.

77 Philip E. Steinberg, "Of Other Seas: Metaphors and Materialities in Maritime Regions," *Atlantic Studies: Global Currents* 10, no. 2 (2013): 163.

78 For a discussion of this fascinating legal case, see Steinberg, Tasch, and Gerhardt, *Contesting the Arctic*, 45–47.

79 Johanne Bruun and Philip Steinberg, "ICE | Placing Territory on Ice: Militarisation, Measurement and Murder in the High Arctic," in *Territory beyond Terra*, ed. Kimberly Peters, Philip Steinberg, and Elaine Stratford (London: Rowman and Littlefield International, 2018), 149–56.

80 Katrin Klingan, Ashkan Sepahvand, Christoph Rosol, and Bernd M. Scherer, *Textures of the Anthropocene: Grain, Vapor, Ray* (Cambridge, MA: MIT Press, 2015), 7. On viscosity, also see Nancy Couling and Carola Hein, "Viscosity," Volumetric Sovereignty forum, *Society and Space*, March 17, 2019, http://societyandspace.org/2019/03/17/viscosity.

81 Comparisons to "America" likely have the United States as referent, but the very looseness of the term (potentially indexing the entire continent) speaks to the amorphousness of the Great Pacific garbage patch and to the impossibility of circumscribing it mentally or territorially.

82 Jennifer Gabrys notes that "the relative invisibility and inaccessibility of the patches render them as looming imaginative figures of environmental decline and yet relatively amorphous and unlocatable and so seemingly resistant to environmental action" (Jennifer Gabrys, *Program Earth: Environmental Sensing Technology and the Making of a Computational Planet* [Minneapolis: University of Minnesota Press, 2016]).

83 Te Punga Somerville, Alice, "The Great Pacific Garbage Patch as Metaphor: The (American) Pacific You Can't See," in *Archipelagic American Studies*, ed. Brian Russell Roberts and Michelle Ann Stephens (Durham, NC: Duke University Press, 2017), 323.

84 Te Punga Somerville, "Great Pacific Garbage Patch as Metaphor," 331.

85 Miriam C. Goldstein, Marci Rosenberg, and Lanna Cheng, "Increased Oceanic Microplastic Debris Enhances Oviposition in an Endemic Pelagic Insect," *Biology Letters* 8, no. 5 (2012): 817–20.

86 Timothy Morton, *Hyperobjects: Philosophy and Ecology after the End of the World* (Minneapolis: University of Minnesota Press, 2013).

87 Hilary Cunningham, "Permeabilities, Ecology and Geopolitical Boundaries," in *A Companion to Border Studies*, ed. Thomas M. Wilson and Hastings Donnan (Chichester: Wiley-Blackwell, 2012), 379. As Cunningham further notes, "what may be regarded as the 'local' or 'regional' impacts of the dust storms may in fact be quite differentially global, both in scope and in effects" (379).

88   Dale W. Griffin, Christina A. Kellogg, Virginia H. Garrison, and Eugene A. Shinn, "The Global Transport of Dust: An Intercontinental River of Dust, Microorganisms and Toxic Chemicals Flows through the Earth's Atmosphere," *American Scientist* 90, no. 3 (May–June 2002): 228.

89   A seventeenfold increase has been reported for instance in the incidence of asthma on the island of Barbados since 1973, which corresponds to the period when the quantities of African dust in the region started to increase (Griffin et al., "Global Transport of Dust," 233).

90   As per a Human Microbiome Project analysis published in 2010, cited in Fishel, *Microbial State*, 59.

91   See, respectively, Celia Lowe, "Viral Clouds: Becoming H5N1 in Indonesia," *Cultural Anthropology* 25, no. 4 (2010): 625–49; and Anna Lowenhaupt Tsing, *The Mushroom at the End of the World: On the Possibility of Life in Capitalist Ruins* (Princeton, NJ: Princeton University Press, 2015), 231. A more classic example perhaps is that of the lichen. Neither green alga nor a fungus as was initially presumed, the lichen is the coevolution of at least three distinct species (Fishel, *Microbial State*, 65).

92   Donna Haraway's book, *When Species Meet* (Minneapolis: University of Minnesota Press, 2008), was an especially important milestone in reframing human-nonhuman relationships. More recently, Jane Bennett's notion of vibrant matter has also been helpful in highlighting the complex entanglements of nonhuman material with the human, showing how "human agency is always an assemblage of microbes, animals, plants, metals, chemicals, word-sounds" (Bennett, *Vibrant Matter*, 120).

93   See also Eleana J. Kim, "Flyways," Theorizing the Contemporary, *Cultural Anthropology*, June 27, 2018, https://culanth.org/fieldsights/flyways.

94   Of all borders aligned on natural features, river borders are perhaps the most recalcitrant, creating misalignments as they alter their course. The border dispute between Croatia and Serbia arose during the twentieth century as natural meanderings and hydraulic engineering works contributed to altering the course of the Danube. Such changes frequently lead to overlapping territorial claims, but in the case of the Croatian-Serbian border it also opened up cartographic breaches, creating patches of land unclaimed by either side. One of these gaps was seized by activist Vít Jedlička who proclaimed the micronation of Liberland in April 2015.

95   Sarah Green, "A Sense of Border," in *A Companion to Border Studies*, ed. Thomas M. Wilson and Hastings Donnan, 573–92 (Chichester: Wiley-Blackwell, 2012).

96   So extensive was this reclamation that the naval dockyard had to be moved twice as it was no longer on the shore.

97   This shifting baseline is a good illustration of the argument recently made by Kate Sammler that the level of the sea constitutes a political surface. In demarcating territory, she writes persuasively, rising sea levels impact legal baselines and shift national terrestrial and maritime borders inland. Katherine Genevieve Sammler. "The Rising Politics of Sea Level: Demarcating Territory in a Vertically Relative World," *Territory, Politics, Governance* (2019) https://doi.org/10.1080/21622671.2019.1632219.

98   Doreen Massey, *For Space* (London: Sage, 2005), qtd. in Philip Steinberg and
      Kimberley Peters, "Wet Ontologies, Fluid Spaces: Giving Depth to Volume
      through Oceanic Thinking," *Environment and Planning D: Society and Space* 33, no. 2
      (2015): 248.
99   Steinberg and Peters, *Wet Ontologies, Fluid Spaces*, 247.
100   Steinberg and Peters, *Wet Ontologies, Fluid Spaces*, 247–48. In a later piece, Peters
      and Steinberg add a caveat to their original argument, noting that "the ocean
      is not simply liquid. It is solid (ice) and air (mist). It generates winds, which
      transport smells, and these may emote the oceanic miles inland." Kimberley
      Peters and Philip Steinberg, "The Ocean in Excess: Towards a More-than-Wet
      Ontology," *Dialogues in Human Geography* 9 (2019): 293.
101   Austin Lord, "Turbulence," Volumetric Sovereignty forum, *Society and Space*,
      March 17, 2019, http://societyandspace.org/2019/03/17/turbulence.
102   Nigel Clark, "FIRE | Pyropolitics for a Planet of Fire," in *Territory beyond Terra*, ed.
      Kimberly Peters, Philip Steinberg, and Elaine Stratford, 69–85 (London: Row-
      man and Littlefield International, 2018).
103   Gravity, as Marx once declared, is all around us: "The atmosphere in which we
      live weighs upon everyone with a 20,000 pound force. But do you feel it?" (cited
      in Choy, *Ecologies of Comparison*, 145).
104   Derek P. McCormack, *Atmospheric Things: On the Allure of Elemental Envelopment*
      (Durham, NC: Duke University Press, 2018). On thinking with the elements
      that literally fill and underpin space, see also Rachael Squire, "Rock, Water, Air
      and Fire: Foregrounding the Elements in the Gibraltar-Spain Dispute," *Environ-
      ment and Planning D: Society and Space* 34, no. 3 (2016): 545–63.
105   Karen Barad, "No Small Matter: Mushroom Clouds, Ecologies of Nothingness,
      and Strange Topologies of Spacetimemattering," in *Arts of Living on a Damaged
      Planet*, ed. Anna Tsing, Heather Swanson, Elaine Gan, and Nils Bubandt (Min-
      neapolis: University of Minnesota Press, 2017), G106.
106   In the fraught environment of Israel and Palestine, border controls also involve
      a number of techniques such as curfews, and work and travel permits that
      temporally delineate border crossings. The fact that daylight saving times are
      not synchronous on both sides brings in an additional layer of complexity by
      separating the fractured geography of the region into two different time zones
      for part of the year. See Helga Tawil-Souri, "Checkpoint Time," *Qui Parle* 26,
      no. 2 (2017): 383–422.
107   Marcia Bjornerud uses the term *timefulness* to draw attention to the need for
      a polytemporal worldview that registers overlapping rates of change (Marcia
      Bjornerud, *Timefulness: How Thinking Like a Geologist Can Help Save the World*
      [Princeton, NJ: Princeton University Press, 2018]).
108   The underground for instance has recently been discovered to be teeming with
      life, at depths, temperatures, and pressures far beyond what were previously as-
      sumed to be absolute limits. The bacteria, archaea, and other microbes that exist
      in such extreme environments grow at extremely slow rates, but their carbon
      mass is 245 to 385 times greater than that of all humans on the surface (Terry

Collins and Katie Pratt, "Life in Deep Earth Totals 15 to 23 Billion Tonnes of Carbon—Hundreds of Times More than Humans," official website of the Deep Carbon Conservatory, December 10, 2018, https://deepcarbon.net/life-deep -earth-totals-15-23-billion-tonnes-carbon).

109   *Spacetimemattering* for Barad marks the inseparability of space, time, and matter, while the gerund indexes the dynamic reconfiguration of a field of relationalities among "moments," "places," and "things" (Barad, "No Small Matter," GIII).

110   See Helmreich, *Alien Ocean*, 16.

111   See, for instance, Adam Bobbette and Amy Donovan, *Political Geology: Active Stratigraphies and the Making of Life* (London: Palgrave Macmillan, 2019); Nigel Clark, *Inhuman Nature: Sociable Life on a Dynamic Planet* (London: Sage, 2010); Jeffrey Jerome Cohen, *Stone: An Ecology of the Inhuman* (Minneapolis: University of Minnesota Press, 2015); and Douglas Rogers, *The Depths of Russia: Oil, Power, and Culture after Socialism* (Ithaca, NY: Cornell University Press, 2015).

112   Graham, *Vertical*, 237. See also Jeremy Crampton, "Vortex," Volumetric Sovereignty forum, *Society and Space*, March 3, 2019, http://societyandspace.org/2019 /03/03/vortex.

113   See Louise Amoore, "Cloud Geographies: Computing, Data, Sovereignty," *Progress in Human Geography* 42, no. 1 (2018): 4–24; Steve Goodman, *Sonic Warfare: Sound, Affect, and the Ecology of Fear* (Cambridge, MA: MIT Press, 2010); Tung-Hui Hu, *A Prehistory of the Cloud* (Cambridge, MA: MIT Press, 2015); Nicole Starosielski, *The Undersea Network* (Durham, NC: Duke University Press, 2015).

114   Easterling, *Extrastatecraft*, 17–18.

115   Starosielski, *Undersea Network*, 10.

116   Representations of communications infrastructures direct our gaze upward: handheld devices, laptop computers, wireless routers, cell phone towers, "cloud" computing, and satellites. As a cable engineer told Starosielski, "satellites are simply just 'sexier' than cables" (Starosielski, *Undersea Network*, 5).

117   Almost all of Australia's internet traffic goes out through a single thirty-mile stretch. These concentrations have vast repercussions for resiliency, as became evident in 2011 when a woman in Georgia shut down much of the internet in Armenia when she dug up two fiber-optic lines while looking for scrap metal (Starosielski, *Undersea Network*, 11).

118   Lisa Parks and Nicole Starosielski, "Introduction," in *Signal Traffic: Critical Studies of Media Infrastructures*, edited by Lisa Parks and Nicole Starosielski (Urbana: University of Illinois Press), 2015, 1-2.

119   Klaus Dodds, personal communication. See also Starosielski, *Undersea Network*, 2015.

120   Aihwa Ong, *Neoliberalism as Exception: Mutations in Citizenship and Sovereignty* (Durham, NC: Duke University Press, 2006).

121   See also Franck Billé, "Murmuration," Volumetric Sovereignty forum, *Society and Space*, April 10, 2019, http://societyandspace.org/2019/04/09/murmuration.

122   Lauren Bonilla, writing about the Mongolian desert in "Voluminous," Theorizing the Contemporary, *Cultural Anthropology*, October 24, 2017, https://culanth .org/fieldsights/voluminous.

123 Jeremy Packer and Joshua Reeves, "Taking People Out: Drones, Media/Weapons, and the Coming Humanectomy," in *Life in the Age of Drone Warfare*, ed. Lisa Parks and Caren Kaplan (Durham, NC: Duke University Press, 2017), 261–81.

124 Billé, "Murmuration."

125 Bishop, "Project 'Transparent Earth,'" 277.

126 See for instance Kaplan, *Aerial Aftermath*.

127 Rachael Squire, "'Do You Dive?': Methodological Considerations for Engaging with 'Volume,'" *Geography Compass* 11, no. 7 (2017): 1–11.

128 Juhani Pallasmaa, *The Eyes of the Skin: Architecture and the Senses* (Chichester: Wiley Academy, 2005), 50. See also Mack Hagood, *Hush: Media and Sonic Self-Control* (Durham, NC: Duke University Press, 2019).

129 Pallasmaa, *Eyes of the Skin*, 16.

130 Think for instance about how London's industries have traditionally been located in the east, downwind, whereas well-to-do residential areas were west of the city. On mapping smellscapes, see Sybille Lammes, Kate McLean, and Chris Perkins, "Mapping the Quixotic Volatility of Smellscapes: A Trialogue," in *Time for Mapping: Cartographic Temporalities*, ed. Sybille Lammes, Chris Perkins, Alex Gekker, Sam Hind, Clancy Wilmott, and Daniel Evans (Manchester: Manchester University Press, 2018), 50–90.

131 Franck Billé, "Skinworlds: Borders, Haptics, Topologies," *Environment and Planning D: Society and Space* 36, no. 1 (2018): 60–77. See also John Protevi, *Political Affect: Connecting the Social and the Somatic* (Minneapolis: University of Minnesota Press, 2009).

132 McGlynn, "Quake."

133 Goodman, *Sonic Warfare*, 18–19.

134 Agnieszka Joniak-Lüthi, "Orbital," Volumetric Sovereignty forum, *Society and Space*, April 10, 2019, http://societyandspace.org/2019/04/09/orbital.

135 The Russian spaceport Baikonur is located in an area of southern Kazakhstan leased to Russia. After the disintegration of the Soviet Union, the Russian base became an extraterritorial space in the newly independent state of Kazakhstan.

136 Jill Stuart, "Unbundling Sovereignty, Territory and the State in Outer Space," in *Securing Outer Space*, ed. Natalie Bormann and Michael Sheehan, 8–23 (London: Routledge, 2009). See also G. E. Hall, "Space Debris—An Insurance Perspective," *Proceedings of the Institution of Mechanical Engineers* 221, part G:J, Aerospace Engineering (2007): 915–24.

137 Joniak-Lüthi, "Orbital."

138 Evgeny Vinokurov, *A Theory of Enclaves* (Lanham, MD: Lexington Books, 2007), 41.

139 An exception is the Order of Malta, a legal oddity which claims to be a sovereign state and a sovereign subject of international law, but has no territory at all.

140 Alastair Bonnett, *Beyond the Map: Unruly Enclaves, Ghostly Places, Emerging Lands and Our Search for New Utopias* (Chicago: University of Chicago Press, 2018), 88.

141 Easterling, *Extrastatecraft*, 171–72.
142 Hu, *Prehistory of the Cloud*, 92.
143 Benjamin H. Bratton, *The Stack: On Software and Sovereignty* (Cambridge, MA: MIT Press, 2015), 4–5.
144 Billé, "Murmuration."

Sovereignty

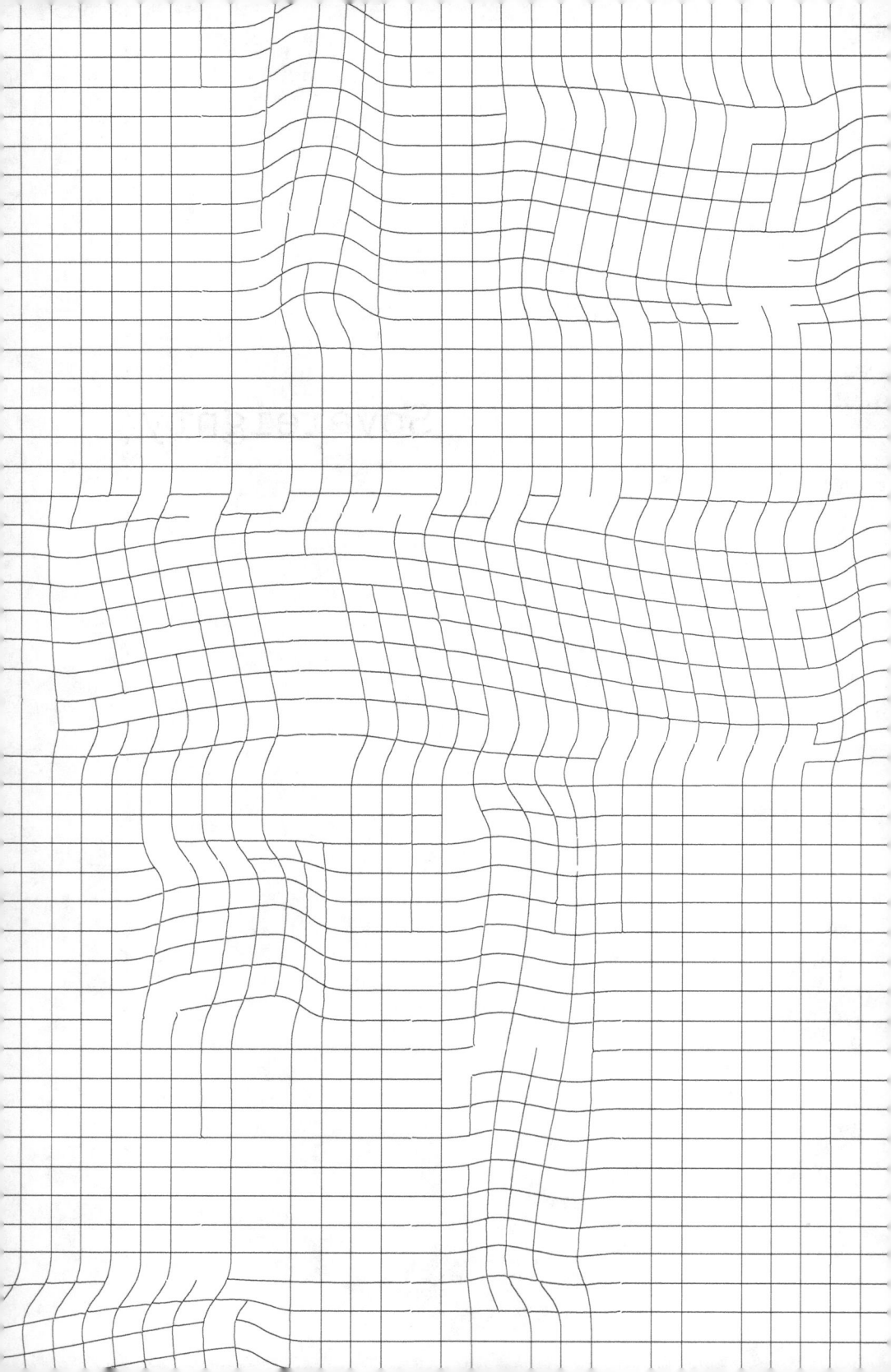

1

Warren

Subterranean Structures at a Sea Border of Ukraine

CAROLINE HUMPHREY

Subterranean structures often have a paradoxical quality: on the one hand, they can be seen as merely the downward extension of a surface-level territorial sovereignty, but on the other they frequently—perhaps almost always— present challenges to that sovereignty. It is not only that they are hidden from sight, or that underground spaces have to obey their own infrastructural regimes with regard to matters such as the air shafts, the water table, and shoring up from dangers of collapse, or that their extent and filaments may not match those of above-ground boundaries. It is that location below ground seems to create a conceptual threshold. "Every underground space reverts to its properly subterranean identity," as David Pike writes, and these imagined identities are historically specific.[1] The vaults of archaic excavations, the necropolis below the houses, the dark mines of the Industrial Revolution, the sanitary and technological underpinnings of the modern city, the metro, and even the underground shopping mall that is locked and deserted at night—all these can seem like worlds of their own. In principle, these spaces are apt for abstract representation, such as schematic mapping, by which a territorial authority lays claim to knowledge of their order. But some crannies and passageways always evade the maps. There is a dimly sensed excess and mystery down there in the depths; this creates a suggestive unknown that is ripe for utopian/dystopian speculations and also an implicit challenge to the sovereignty of the power above ground.

The warren is a particular example of such a space. The word *warren* is often extended to human constructions, a crowded tenement or a maze of passageways or small rooms, but its root meaning refers to an animal space, the natural outcome of burrowing, nesting, and hiding from predators. The warren is a habitation with its own material form. Here depths are dug out for greater safety, larger chambers are made for congress, passages are narrowed or blocked to exclude chasing killers, entrances may be hidden and nodes are provided with multiple exits for rapid escape. Rabbit warrens, it turns out, have such a structure, and so do the most warren-like of human underground constructions.[2] It will be suggested here that the more a humanly assembled subterranean space resembles a warren, the more it is likely to be used for evasion of rule from the surface. Whatever the practical purposes of the first burrowers, and they are many, a human warren is in fact always also a place of concealment. These are spaces whose existence is known by those outside, but whose piecemeal excavation, inner workings, and the life that goes on inside can only be guessed at. This means that the warren, whether of the rabbit or the human variety, has been most suggestive to literary and science fiction imagination. This chapter, however, will focus on real warrens, and will suggest that they are *materially resistant* to governmental knowledge.

Yet all cities have subterranean realms, constituted by their drains, water pipes, communication exchanges, electric wires, underground transport systems, storage and retail areas, and various derelict caverns from previous technological eras.[3] Among these a "warren" can be identified, I suggest, by two main characteristics: the fact that it is, or has been, lived in, and that it comes into being as a warren not by external design but because numbers of people saw the need for such an organization of space and transformed a subterranean realm into this kind of incrementally made cellular social place. The habits of living in a warren, and the art of finding one's way in it, are in many ways fundamentally different from the everyday life on the surface. But warrens are part of the social whole: people move into and out of them, and the territorial powers of cities and states encapsulate them without fully knowing or controlling them. This suggests that the existence of human warrens, which have been made in so many historical circumstances and still exist, requires us to rethink the materialization of political powers in relation to an idea of volume that can incorporate their "other," or somewhat alien, subterranean components.

Such a project becomes particularly interesting and problematic when warrens are situated at an international border. The main subject of this article will be one such case, the catacombs of Odessa [Ukr. Odesa], which are located under the port city at the present Black Sea border of Ukraine, formerly the edge of the Russian Empire and the USSR. Before discussing this case, however, I look briefly at more general issues of animal and human warrens and political sovereignty.

The Government of Warrens

It is not often remembered that animal warrens were once prime properties of kings and princes. In the Middle Ages in Europe, warrens were territories established and set aside for the economic cultivation of game, chiefly rabbits. In England, rabbits were not a native species, and so warrens, rather than being natural, were initiated by digging preparatory burrows and introducing rabbits into them. The animals were rare and highly prized commodities, regularly culled for their valuable meat and fur, which became a lucrative source of income for the owner of the warren. The vast majority of England's rabbit population lived cosseted inside specially created warrens. These were such valuable properties that the Crown sold special warrants for the right to lease and cull them. At their zenith in fourteenth-century England, the largest warrens grew to vast size, extending to a thousand acres plus.[4] However, rabbit warrens could not of course be sealed and were never completely controllable: traps and snares had to be set in a perpetual war against foxes, stoats, weasels, and polecats, while not-altogether-effective watchtowers were built to counter the constant raids of human poachers. Meanwhile, the rabbits themselves migrated from the warrens, either temporarily or permanently; and they then caused problems by invading and devouring arable crops, such that the warrant holder would be ordered to block up rabbit holes debouching out on common farm land.[5] From this we see that despite the attempt to regulate warrens as encapsulated sovereign property, the insubordination of their animal inhabitants could not be gainsaid. Meanwhile the burrows themselves were also vexatious, since they often spread *beyond* the boundaries of the warrant, while also being not immune to illicit *ingress*, such as using dogs and ferrets for theft.

Animal warrens have another feature relevant to this intervention. The expression *ecosystem engineer* is used to describe organisms that create, modify, and maintain local habitat systems.[6] It has been discovered that marmots, which build deep and ramifying tunnels, are engineers of this kind; by digging burrows they create cool, dark hiding places for a variety of other species, including insects, snakes, and amphibians like toads.

Warrens constructed historically by humans as subterranean realms have something in common with the animal variety, in that the main function seems to have been similar: to provide a relatively secure refuge from enemies. This certainly was the case with the best-known example, the vast "underground cities" of Cappadocia in central Turkey. Here, since early times and through the Ottoman era, a succession of non-Muslim or otherwise threatened populations constructed hundreds of underground settlements. In the largest, Derinkuyu and Nevşehir, these are multilevel living spaces, largely self-sustaining, with air shafts, water channels, kitchens, wineries, chapels, stables, and linseed presses to produce lamp oil for lighting. When invaders arrived, the inhabitants of these regions of Turkey could retreat below ground, blocking access with round stone doors, and sealing themselves in with livestock and supplies until the threat passed. The largest of these sites could accommodate tens of thousands of inhabitants, extended around 460,000 square meters, and had at least seven vertical levels. None of them has been fully excavated, so their full extent is not known. It is also not clear whether or not these countless tunnels may have formed a transspecies ecosystem. But perhaps we may borrow the idea of the *ecosystem engineer* to make one point with regard to human warrens: that a burrow made by one group for one purpose must have provided a "habitat" for a variety of other groups with different needs in mind.

In such ways, not dissimilar to the animal warrens, the human version was of course significant in its political affordances: it could become the site of deliberate defiance, the continued cultivation of a forbidden religion or a threatened identity. Such concealed resistance could appear from the perspective of the oppressors as a form of moral attack, and it could on occasion provide a base from which to launch physical sorties. It has been argued that in the long term of human history the military significance of such "underground facilities" has been given insufficient attention.[7] Yet since well before the Christian era groups have excavated tunnels and shafts to create fortresses, sited them strategically, and used them for reconnaissance and sudden retaliatory strikes.[8] In modern times, underground military facilities have often been sited at international borders. An example is Mount Wise, a large secret network of bomb-proof underground rooms and tunnels beneath Plymouth, a border port town which was a key naval base when the United Kingdom was fighting Germany in World War II. The subterranean fortress contained an intelligence center, radio and telephone rooms, offices for recording movements of enemy submarines and shipping, a center for mine counter measures, living quarters, dining room, stores, hospital, and offices. It was the regional Joint Operations Headquarters for the army, navy, and air force and it continued in this role under NATO command until at least 1961.[9]

Now as a planned governmental facility under tight military control, the rectangular grid of Mount Wise seems to have had few warren-like spatial features during its operational period. But since then it has been closed and presumably fallen derelict, and this inaccessibility has given rise to urban myths. Local bloggers suggest, for example, that it connects with larger and older constructions, writing: "There's a tunnel that leads from Drake's Island to the Hoe," and "All the Napoleonic forts in Plymouth are connected by underground passageways." People of the town investigate disused air-raid shelters and ancient entrances hidden in shrubs. In 2007 an explorer discovered and photographed "something that has experts baffled . . . a lost passageway" that did indeed seem to link some of the forts.[10] This suggests that Plymouth's underground tunnels are (or are seen as) something like a warren after all. The myths also point to another feature of the subterranean realm: that the threshold that separates it from the surface is not just one of depth but also suggests a chronological break. Depth somehow evokes the past. The subterranean is not just associated in the imagination with the historical past (in Plymouth, Drake's exploits, the war against Napoleon) but as we shall see from other sites also seems to point to an unknown, and therefore potentially even deeper, past that matches its own physical depths extending down to the center of the Earth.

The Context of "Warrens" on Territorial Borders

Plymouth is a border town of the United Kingdom, but I would like to move discussion to another such site, Odessa in Ukraine, since the catacombs under this city are probably the most extensive in the world and are also very well documented. With over a thousand known entrances and at least twenty-five hundred kilometers of tunnels, they have never been fully mapped, but it is known that they extend below ground in numerous systems, not necessarily all linked, and that they reach well beyond the city as far as villages and towns some thirty kilometers away. The argument I would like to make here is that just as a sea border is in practice not a line drawn along the shore but a complex three-dimensional multiplicity extending into undersea spaces, the catacombs can be seen as a continuation inland of this complex "depth border". This was an extremely porous realm whose denizens often treated it as a means of evading the rule of the state. In principle, since the catacombs consist of passageways, which are facilities for movement, they can be understood, even though the underground maze was itself a border zone, as a conceptual opposite to the notion of the border as a linear barrier.

A national sea border is commonly understood as the line of the shore. However, in practice this is not accurate. According to international law, a littoral state has rights stretching out into the sea, constituting partial sovereignty in a series of areas graded by their distance from the shore baseline. Beyond the outermost of these areas marine expanses are classified as "high seas" and common to all. Depth, volume, surfaces, and airspaces are all involved here in complex concatenations. In the various sea zones, rights to subsurface resources or potential resources (oil, gas, fishing, mineral extraction, etc.) cannot easily be separated from the armed naval, submarine, and air forces that protect them and provide security for coastal states. Further extraterritorial complexities arise beyond coastal waters. A variety of international agreements and conventions have come into being to enable effective policing of border-violating piracy, drug trafficking, terrorism, and smuggling. These enable coastguards or maritime police to intercept vessels suspected of carrying out illegal activities beyond a state's territorial waters. And beneath the surface there are countless objects of contention and memory, many of them claimed by nations beyond their official maritime limits, such as shipwrecks, downed submarines, and antiquarian treasures of disputed provenance.

Odessa is located on the Black Sea, which has no "high seas" and is entirely divided up by the rights of the countries that surround it. This makes sea jurisdictions highly vulnerable to political shifts. Recently, by annexing Crimea and siting its main naval fleet there, Russia has dramatically expanded its expanse of maritime control (in effect, if not in law), and by the same move it has drastically diminished the area of Ukraine's jurisdiction in the Black Sea. Thus, the notion of "sea border" denotes an area of tension, since both the land and the sea entities jointed together by the border can change shape, and alter in their economic weight and potential relationship.

For a similar reason, the fact that a land-based government has to cope with the complexities of the sea, the shoreline cannot be an absolute border on the landed side either. Ports have many enclaves that are subject to special regulations, different from those in the rest of the country. They include pilots' stations, quarantine docks, fueling terminals, holding spaces for immigration and refugees, foreign consulates, customs offices, sailors' hostels, animal health controls, areas for containers pending inspection, and warehouses belonging to foreign countries/multinational companies. To handle all of this, large ports have their own authorities. But even so, the diversity of functions has always created gaps for illicit activities, and ports have historically often been the sites for human "warrens" of the above-ground kind—the crowded shanty towns of dock workers, haulage men, prostitutes, bars, and gaming dens. When the seaborne wealth ceases to flow in, these same areas sink into poverty, or are abandoned altogether, leaving weed-strewn docks and gaunt shells of warehouses as memorials.

Such a maritime seesawing in prosperity has been the fate of Odessa in the last century.[11] Odessa used to be Imperial Russia's main southern port, home to wealthy and cultured merchants, a prosperous city exporting grain to the world and importing a wealth of goods from Europe. During the Soviet era its trading role diminished, but this was compensated for by the presence of the huge Black Sea Fleet, which combined military, merchant, and passenger duties. After the demise of the USSR, the Russian military navy moved its base to Sevastopol in Crimea and most of the merchant and passenger fleet was sold off or left to decay. Much of the freight traffic moved to other ports along the coast. Now, Odessa is gradually reviving from the tourist traffic, but, in line with Ukraine's uncertain road in its subdued war with Russia, the city is still much reduced from its confident halcyon days in the nineteenth and early twentieth centuries. These in brief are the historical circumstances in which I would now like to examine the labyrinth that doubles under the entire city. In particular, I explain why it is an essential and constituent element both of the city and of the border.

The Warren Beneath

The catacombs of Rome and Paris are perhaps more famous, but those of Odessa far outweigh them in antiquity, extent, diversity of functions, and economic-political significance. Some parts are extremely old, large, and long natural caves, where the bones of prehistoric animals have been discovered. However, most sections are more recent stone mine workings dating from the late eighteenth century onward. The entire center of the city was built from the stones brought up from below and its streets rest on a honeycomb-like grid of rectangular hollowed-out passages. Many parts of the catacombs however are not regular; the paths double back, turn corners, have collapsed or been deliberately blocked off, resulting in something like a classic maze. In terms of volume, some areas have three to four stories and some just one, certain chambers are tall, but many caves require crawling to pass through. Water gathers in the lower sections. Without natural light, it is extremely difficult to navigate the catacombs, and numerous cases have been recorded of people losing their way and dying from starvation or lack of water. Today, a small part of the vast ensemble has been opened for tourism. Guides taking explorers to unlit regions use a string to navigate back to an entrance, as in the Greek myth of Theseus and the Minotaur in the labyrinth.

The catacombs are often conceived by Odessan citizens as being a whole, separate subterranean world. In such a narrative mode, there are legends about monsters, dwarfs, and hermits dwelling there, and about the god who guards

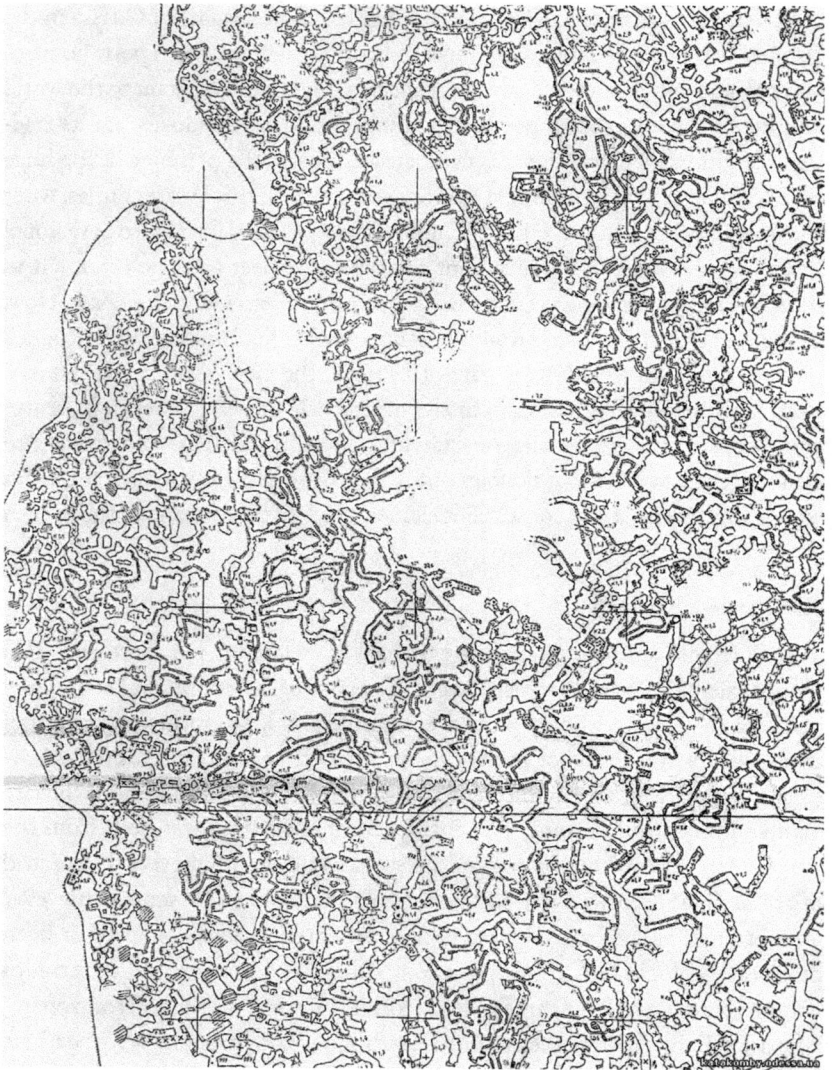

Figure 1.1. Map showing a section of the Odessa catacombs.
Image via katakomby.odessa.ua

the labyrinth in the form of an invisible spirit. This god is called by the strange name "But," a word which refers both to a type of gravel stone used in building and to a Greek god, who, according to one legend, engaged in piracy and rape, was driven out by the other deities, went mad, and threw himself into a well.[12] The god "But" is said to rule not only material processes such as rockfalls, the collapse of tunnels, or the rapid spread of molds, but also human visitors. He punishes anyone who takes things out of the catacombs. If that is necessary for some reason, the same object or an equivalent must be returned; if this is not done, the thief's above-ground life will become an endless series of misfortunes.[13] Another kind of narrative about the catacombs as a separate realm is that they are a place of "forces," where marginal and strange people go to fill up with energy.[14]

However, this "wholeness" of the underground realm is unusual as a volumetric concept, because the warren has no skin; it is penetrable at entrances/exits which are so numerous and hidden that no one knows them all in total. As a political subject, it recalls in some ways the medieval rabbit warren. During the Soviet period, the government attempted several times to have all the entrances blocked (without success). Odessan bloggers surmise that this was done at the behest of the KGB, not, as was stated, for fear of popular disturbances but simply because the "organs" did not like anyone to disappear from their field of view; they were aware that anyone who knew the catacombs could remain hidden there for very a long time. And they could not forget, of course, the long illicit economic history of the labyrinth, which I now briefly summarize.

The fundamental raison d'être of founding Odessa in the eighteenth century was to create a warm water port for the export and import of trade goods. Eventually Russian exports through the port, mainly in the form of the vast grain trade, were to support the entire agricultural economy of Ukraine and nearby regions while also giving a rich income to the merchants based in the city. The imports would supply Russians with foreign technology and luxuries, and at the same time provide essential income to the state from duties and tariffs. The Russian authorities strictly regulated trade and zealously protected the state's interests in raising its revenues. However, this did not coincide with the merchants' preference for free trade. The very nature of trade—the coming and going of goods and seamen, the profits derived from shuttling between different economic-political territories—goes some way towards explaining why international trading was always regarded as a slippery matter as far as Imperial sovereignty was concerned. It was the state's concern to regulate trade that gave rise to the thicket of border institutions on the surface. The customs service became a (perhaps the) crucial agency of practical state sovereignty in the everyday life of the port right up to the Soviet period.

Its duties included—besides collecting tariffs—weighing and classifying goods, counting the ships entering and leaving port, inspecting ships, and overseeing the entire complex bureaucracy of licensing, collecting anchorage dues, and insurance. Spatially, this was represented by the customs buildings, the wharfs and warehouses, and the resident bureaucrats' offices and mansions. After much pleading by the merchants, a Porto Franco zone was established in the city from 1817 to 1859, within which citizens could buy foreign goods without paying import taxes. But it was forbidden to take these goods beyond the boundary, unless the due were paid.

What more propitious situation could be imagined for the construction of a hidden throughway to transport goods *below* all of these barriers? The more harshly the tariffs were imposed, the more compelling was the allure of smuggling and contraband. And what better place for hiding and storing ill-gotten, or just undeclared, goods than the catacombs? Just outside the Porto Franco was a district known as Moldavanka, renowned for its quick-thinking sharpsters, racketeers, shady deals, and hidden consignments. A network of underground passages led straight from the coast, via the catacombs, to Moldavanka. Here, it was rumored, each courtyard well had a side passage leading off into the tunnels.[15] In Moldavanka contraband was repacked, relabelled, and then sold off for high prices. Yet in the incessant struggle between the customs service and the smugglers, Moldovanka was only the most well-known quarter (made famous by the stories of Isaac Babel among others)—there were countless other exits from the catacombs around the city and in villages beyond. At times, notably in the early 1920s, the balance swung entirely to the side of the smugglers and gangsters and practically the whole city was involved in illegal trade and consumption.

Thus, in the nineteenth and early twentieth centuries the Odessa Catacombs functioned to sustain a mass illicit economy. Unlike the Rome and Paris catacombs they were not used for mortuary purposes, nor for storing human bones, and therefore they seem not to have had the same sepulchral connotations nor associations with seeping "miasmas" and diseases. Instead, it was the nongovernability of the warren structure that came to the fore. Secret political activities were carried on in the vaults, subterranean-based conspiracies that, again, were like the "other side of the coin" for the activities on the surface. In any case, Odessa in the early nineteenth century was a highly cosmopolitan city of Greeks, Jews, Italians, Tatars, Germans, Armenians, and French as well as Russians and Ukrainians, where revolutionary groups devoted to overthrowing governments across Europe congregated: leaders of the Italian Risorgimento, the clandestine Philikí Etaireía plotting Greek freedom from the Turks, and Bulgarians, Romanians, and Poles seeking liberation.[16] However, only groups opposed to the Russian government sought refuge in the catacombs. Aristocratic Free-masons linked to lodges across Europe had been the founding fathers of early Odessa, but later, intent on undermining Tsarist autocracy and orthodoxy, they were banned by Tsar Alexander I in 1822, whereupon they held secret meetings in the catacombs.[17] Thereafter, the whole city of Odessa, through such associations with foreignness and the secret fomenting of disloyalty and revolt, became a politically suspect space for Russia's rulers. Odessa as a whole could easily be metonymically identified with the catacombs, i.e., imagined as an "underworld" in relation to the Empire and later to the Soviet Union.

Today, there is plenty of evidence that the time-honored *political resistance* function of the warren continues in situ below ground. Both the Parisian and the Odessan catacombs are famous for having provided covert strongholds for resistance fighters in the Second World War, and legendary accounts of their exploits live on (in Odessa, teachers take their classes down to the catacombs to show where fighters prepared strikes against the German-Romanian occupiers). The subterranean hideouts were connected, by radio and by young boys used as runners, to a network of "conspiratorial apartments" above ground in the city. The intelligence service of the Romanian occupiers reported on the activities of an "invisible army." Fighters subsisted below for years on end. Attempts were made to gas or entomb the partisans in the catacombs, only for new bands spontaneously to mushroom in the city.[18] Following the war, the catacombs became home to numerous criminal groups that widened and created new tunnel systems of their own.[19] Recently (2014–15), the example of the wartime underground partisans has been followed by two opposed groups—by Ukrainian fighters training against a possible Russian invasion and by pro-Russia loyalists plotting destructive strikes against Ukraine, both of whom have found hideouts in the capacious catacombs.[20] In the prevailing media battles and fluidity of descriptions, the same people are "resistance fighters" to some and "criminals" to others.

Though it was stone miners who dug out most of the tunnels, the catacombs were never just a mine: they turned into a strange and multifarious sociopolitical-biological "ecosystem," where bats and green molds have shared space with all kinds of people who needed to hide from the powers on the surface.

Conclusion

In many countries, the legal presumption that ownership of land implies entitlement to "everything beneath or within it down to the center of the earth" is being challenged; a separate registration of title to mines and minerals is required, recalling historic manorial rights to hunt, shoot, and fish.[21] In the case of the Odessa Catacombs, after a post-Soviet period in legal limbo, they were taken over as the property and cultural heritage of the city of Odessa in 2016. The municipality reaps the income from the tourists who go on guided tours. Not unlike the warrant holder of a medieval warren contending with poachers, the city battles against construction companies that have started mining for stone again (this can be dangerous without geological permission, as the large new buildings risk collapsing into the fragile honeycomb beneath). However, local bloggers asking "Who does subterranean Odessa really belong to?" have come up with their own different answer. They write that neither the municipality nor the construction companies but three other warring groups contend in actual control of the space: museum workers and guardians of history; "diggers," eccentric specialists in exploration, who blast away blockages in tunnels; and ordinary Odessans and villagers, who continue to use the catacombs for their everyday purposes, from cannabis or mushroom farming to storing food supplies, holding sensational parties, or simply for the experience of a few days underground (to "tickle their sense of existence").[22]

The warren, one has to conclude, is a kind of space where clear sovereignty is difficult, if not impossible, to maintain. The very concept of a warren challenges the notion of the sealed territorial boundary. At the same time, the warren insists on volume—but a volume of an ambiguous and mysterious kind. A warren like the Odessa Catacombs can be envisioned as a "whole," but this is a zone of disappearance or hiding, and since no one knows its entirety no one can truly be sure if it consists of one system or many. Yet one thing is clear: subterranean spaces may be put to many uses, including the military, but once they take on a warren-like material and social character, they undermine, in every sense of the word, a state border on the terrestrial surface.

NOTES

1   David Lawrence Pike, *Subterranean Cities: The World Beneath Paris and London, 1800–1945* (Ithaca, NY: Cornell University Press, 2005), 21.
2   A BBC documentary of August 16, 2013, revealed the structure of a large rabbit warren by pouring concrete into an abandoned warren and excavating the resulting labyrinthine "sculpture." The knobbly, organic tangle in some ways resembled tree roots, since in both cases routes have to avoid natural objects like large rocks. The combination of different heights and chambers with narrowed passageways is very clear. BBC Two, "Uncovering an Underground Rabbit City," clip from *The*

Burrowers: Animals Underground, BBC website, August 16, 2013, https://www.bbc.co
.uk/programmes/p01f9nyx.

3 See Pike, *Subterranean Cities*; and Julia Solis, *New York Underground: The Anatomy of
a City* (New York: Routledge, 2005).

4 Mark Bailey, "The Rabbit and the Mediaeval East Anglian Economy," *Agricultural
History Review*, 36, no. 1 (1988): 4.

5 Bailey, "Rabbit and the Mediaeval East Anglian Economy," 8–9.

6 Clive G. Jones, John H. Lawton, and Moshe Shachak, "Organisms as Ecosystem
Engineers," *Oikos* 69 (1994): 373–86.

7 Thomas E. Easter, "Military Use of Underground Terrain," in *Studies in Military
Geography and Geology*, edited by Douglas R. Caldwell, Judy Ehlen, and Russell S.
Harmon (Dordrecht: Springer, 2004), 2.

8 Easter, "Military Use of Underground Terrain," 21–22.

9 Bob Jenner, "Mount Wise Plymouth Maratime HQ," *Subterranea Britannica*,
December 13, 2004, https://www.subbrit.org.uk/sites/mount-wise-plymouth
-maratime-hq/.

10 Quotations and information from Hidden Plymouth, "Plymouth's Tunnel
Myths," *Hidden Plymouth* (blog), August 6, 2012, http://hiddenplymouth.blogspot
.com/2012/08/plymouths-tunnel-myths.html.

11 Charles King, *Odessa: Genius and Death in a City of Dreams* (New York: Norton,
2011); Caroline Humphrey, "Odessa: Pogroms in a Cosmopolitan City," *Ab Imperio*
4 (2010): 1–53.

12 "But," accessed June 18, 2018, https://myth.slovaronline.com/234-BUT.

13 Alove_Roleen, "Odesskiye katakomby," Fishki.net, July 22, 2014, https://fishki.net
/1287104-odesskie-katakomby.html.

14 "Podzemel'ye Odessy: bogi, lyudi, klady," accessed June 18, 2018, http://www.ta
-odessa.com/dostop/digger.

15 King, *Odessa*, 129–30.

16 King, *Odessa*, 88–89.

17 Humphrey, "Odessa," 49.

18 Olga Kucherenko, "Reluctant Traitors: The Politics of Survival in Romanian-
Occupied Odessa," *European Review of History* 15, no. 2 (2008): 149.

19 Atlas Obscura, s.v. "Odessa Catacombs," accessed May 19, 2015, http://www
.atlasobscura.com/places/odessa-catacombs.

20 "Guberniya," accessed May 19, 2015, http://gubernia.org.ua/obschestvo/item
/3511-odesskie-katakombyi-mogut-stat-bazoy-partizanov-v-sluchae-rossiyskogo
-vtorzheniya-video.html.

21 Rebecca Cotter, "Mines and Minerals—Are They Yours?," Fieldfisher, July 5, 2012,
https://www.fieldfisher.com/publications/2012/07/mines-and-minerals-are-they
-yours.

22 Aleksandr Topilov, "Lekhiny katakomby: komu prinadlezhit podzemnaya
Odessa," accessed June 9, 2018, https://birdinflight.com/ru/reportaj/20170207
-katakomby.html. Birdinflight.com, accessed November 22, 2019.

2

Tunnel

Striating and Militarizing
Subterranean Space
in the Republic of Georgia

ELIZABETH CULLEN DUNN

On August 8, 2008, a line of armored vehicles from the Russian Fifty-Eighth Army poured through the Roki Tunnel and through the Caucasus range, a wall of mountains that separates Russia and the Republic of Georgia. As the Georgian Army fired heavy artillery in an attempt to close the southern end of the tunnel, the Russians poured into the breakaway province of South Ossetia, eventually occupying and militarizing the entire province and ethnically cleansing twenty-eight thousand people. The prize was not the territory of South Ossetia, a scrubby little place of minimal social or economic value. Rather, it was the Roki Tunnel itself, the only year-round passage through the Caucasus. Why launch a war to secure a tunnel? The stakes were high—the invasion could have brought in Georgia's European or US allies, thus expanding a regional conflict to a global geopolitical one. That the risk was worth running highlights a vital problem in the securitization of space: the use of the subterranean in asserting (and challenging) state power.

Although security and territory have traditionally been thought of in terms of securing the area—that is, surfaces delimited by borders—the securitization of the underground now forces us to think about securing the volume, and about the ways the physical characteristics of topography and terrain are used to contest these attempts.[1] Tunnels, in this respect, are particularly interesting subterranean artifacts. Used by states to control or gain access to new territory, they are also used by those seeking to disrupt or evade state power. They are used to move soldiers and weapons, shield combatants from satellites and drones, and move drugs, prisoners, and nuclear material. Although they provide strategic points at which state forces can control, filter, and restrict traffic, they are also used to evade chokepoints and to circumvent the state's control of space.[2]

In this chapter, I want to show the ways that tunnels do oscillating and often contradictory things in volumetric space, constituting it and collapsing it in turn. Tunnels have often been thought of as tools for rebels against states, providing the means for smugglers, insurgent fighters, and other small-scale antistate forces to fight against the state's control of the surface or to create refuge from state power.[3] They are seen as tools for opening volumetric space to create new battlespaces that are much more difficult for state forces to view and control.[4] But tunnels do not have intrinsic properties that make them the tools of insurgents. Rather, they are spatial forms that can be socially appropriated by a wide variety of actors, who put them to very different uses. States, with their far greater capacities to carry out large projects, also create and use tunnels as tools of warfare. Sometimes, like insurgents, they use tunnels to open volumetric space, thus creating new battlespaces. But they can also use tunnels to close volumetric space and to force the battle back into spatial forms that are easier to control.

Here, I use the case of the Roki Tunnel to look at the ways that states use tunnels not to "secure the volume," or to manage space in three dimensions, as Stuart Elden claims, but to control volumetric space by flattening it, thus limiting conflict to more easily secured two-dimensional space. I argue that states can control volumetric space by creating what Gilles Deleuze and Félix Guattari call *striated space*, or space riven by two-dimensional paths and channels, thus forcing the conflict back into two dimensions.[5] Striated space allows states to monitor movement, to filter who moves through and who is blockaded, and to control movement by installing chokepoints. By pushing the conflict back into two dimensions, states can force their opponents back onto terrain that favors the technologies that states, with their massive resources, are better at developing and controlling. This tactic is not uncontested, however. As the case of the Roki Tunnel also shows, the creation of striated space is not unidirectional. Opposing forces often seek to move chokepoints back into smooth space—space where mobility in many directions is possible and where states have a much more difficult time monitoring and controlling movement—in order to move the conflict back onto terrain that advantages small mobile forces rather than large state armies. The result, as I show here, is that tunnels are sites of multiple and competing spatialities. Unique sites of constant and unstable tension both geographically and socially, they are not merely transportation corridors or sites to evade power, but dynamic, historically produced topographies that make both threat and opportunity omnipresent by throwing the political regulation of space into question.

The Politics of Terrain

To understand how tunnels work as political technologies, it is important to see them in relationship to their surrounding terrain. What they do, and how they work in political conflict, is a function of their relation not only to the surrounding population, but to the surrounding topography and to the material qualities of the nearby earth. This is particularly true in the extreme conditions of a high alpine environment, where the terrain itself poses significant challenges to state domination.[6]

The Greater Caucasus mountain range forms a steep, nearly impassable wall on Russia's southern border, topping out at over eighteen thousand feet. Since the Russo-Turkish War (1768–74), Russian empires have sought to control the Caucasus range in order to use it as a defensive fortification against Turkish and Persian empires. But they have faced centuries of opposition and guerilla warfare from the mountain peoples of the Caucasus, a diverse set of small ethnic groups including Chechens, Ossetians, Ingush, Kabardians, Circassians, and others. As in other cases where small self-governing groups have come into conflict with empires, the mountains have become a space for people who flee imperial domination, taxation, and enslavement.[7] The attempt to bring these people under state control has required extraordinary violence. In 1804, when Ossetian peasants rebelled against Russian forces, they were whipped and then thrown into pits of dead cats, whey, and excrement.[8] The Circassians were ethnically cleansed and driven into the sea in 1864–67. Unsurprisingly, some of the other ethnic groups resisted Russian occupation. From the Russo-Circassian War (1763-1864), to the Murid War (1830-59) to the Chechen Wars (1994-2000), small mountain groups have attempted to preserve the slopes of the Caucasus as a space free of Russian domination.

The topography of the range made it possible to continue what otherwise would have been a massively unequal fight, both in terms of troop numbers and military technology. There are only six navigable passes across the range, each of which is above seven thousand feet and surrounded by steep cliff walls rising hundreds of feet above. Even after Russian Imperial forces came to rule the Caucasus, the passes continued to make military control of the South Caucasus tenuous. The passes are closed most of the year due to snowfall; in summer they are prone to landslides, and the steep narrow tracks make passage difficult. The passes acted as natural chokepoints, obligatory passage points for both military force and trade.[9]

The Russian Army fought in large brigades that marched in formation along the roadway or path. The Caucasian insurgents, who traveled in smaller bands on foot or on horseback, had a much larger freedom of movement: they could range the slopes, forests, and rocky outcroppings that overlooked the paths through the passes. For these peoples, the mountains were not only a home, but a tactical resource, not just a battleground but a weapon. The very fact that alpine wars *must* be fought volumetrically dramatically changed the balance of power between the mountain peoples and the Tsarist Army. This created zones of intermittent autonomy for both the mountain peoples and those residing in the valleys below the south slope.

Stuart Elden, Stephen Graham, Peter Adey, Gastón Gordillo, and others have all argued that to understand modern warfighting, it is essential to think about space not as a flat plane, but as a volume.[10] Where once, states produced bounded territory by securing areas, thought of as flat spaces with defined borders, now they must secure volumes by protecting them from aerial and subterranean attack as well as from attacks carried out from the surface of the land.

But states still have significant military advantages when warfighting can be confined to two dimensions, rather than three: On wide, flat plains where superior technology allows them to see across open spaces and kill from a distance, or in places where they can define and control borders using technologies such as barbed wire, they can command far more power than nonstate forces.[11] Mountainous terrain creates significant vulnerabilities for valley-based state militaries and limits their ability to use area-defining and distance-destroying technologies like cannons, rifles, scopes, and so on. Friedrich Engels, in his discussion of the Swiss victories during the Burgundian Wars within his treatise on mountain warfare, noted the enormous advantage that mountain terrain gave to smaller, lighter insurgent forces:

> During the Burgundian wars, infantry, armed with pikes, had become a more important portion of an army, and firearms had been introduced, but the infantry was still cramped by the weight of defensive armor, the cannon were heavy, and small arms clumsy and comparatively useless. The whole equipment of the troops was still so cumbersome as to unfit them

completely for mountain warfare, and especially at a time when roads can scarcely be said to have existed. The consequence was that, as soon as these slow-moving armies were once entangled in difficult ground, they stuck fast, while the lightly-armed Swiss peasants were enabled to act on the offensive, to out-maneuver, to surround, and finally to defeat their opponents. For three centuries after the Burgundian wars, Switzerland was never seriously invaded. The tradition of Swiss invincibility grew venerable.[12]

The mountains are no passive backdrop: they obstruct larger forces, limit their movements, and neutralize their technology by providing diverse forms of cover. Terrain itself becomes an actor and an ally of the people who inhabit mountain spaces, because mountain insurgents know the topography of the mountains well and have developed techniques for fighting in a sloped battlespace.[13] Alpine insurgents think in terms of a true *geo*politics, one that takes into account not only some abstract vertical axis, but the material properties of the earth itself: its slopes and fissures, the stability or instability of its rocks and soils, the properties of trees and other land cover, and so on. In the Caucasus, they used the heights so that they could fire from above on Russian forces passing below, and built stone towers on the ridges to spot invaders and to signal to other villages that they were coming. The insurgents used alpine terrain to take cover from Russian fire under rocks or in caves, and, if need be, to hide for long periods from the imperial forces searching for them. The result is a vertical geopolitics, one that keeps state forces from dominating mountain people in the same way they do valley people.

Mountain terrain is difficult to navigate, craggy and steep. But despite the cragginess of the mountains, it offers a certain freedom of movement: multiple directions in which to move, none necessarily predetermined. This is what Deleuze and Guattari call *smooth space*.[14] The term is inconvenient here, calling up an image of space that does not match the topography of the mountains. But smooth space is smooth not because it has a flat topography, but because the links or trajectories between one place and another are not predefined. Smooth space can be heterogeneous and can have distinct locales, each having its own characteristics. But the key feature of smooth space is that it is not delineated. It is largely free of boundaries and of predetermined channels like roads along which movement is allowed or particularly encouraged. Smooth space is a multiplicity, composed of varied and different parts linked together in a transient and situational way, one that can shift quickly to some other formation, rather than a unity governed by a preexisting framework of roads, paths, or channels.[15]

The sea, for example, was once smooth space, in which movement in any direction was shaped by winds and currents but was otherwise largely unconstrained.[16] Likewise, while mountain terrain made some trajectories easier than others (for example, traveling over a pass or along the bottom of a riverbed rather than along the sides of the mountains), there were no defined routes built by states and nobody was confined to them. It is not a lack of variation in terrain that makes space "smooth." Rather, it is the fact that nobody, particularly not states, has politically appropriated this space and marked its terrain with boundaries and channels.

Deleuze and Guattari speak of smooth space as the space of the nomad, who can range all over following the herd. But it is also the space of the insurgent, who moves around three-dimensional space in unpredictable and often undetectable ways.[17] For insurgents, this kind of space, and the ways they can move within it, gives them the key tactical advantages that allow them to hold off the much larger forces of an imperial army. They have the ability to find routes through the range that the imperial army, which usually travels with much larger contingents and which has far less knowledge of the place, cannot not find and blockade. The only way for imperial forces to defeat them is to defeat terrain itself.

The Struggle between Two- and Three-Dimensional Space

Where insurgents find advantage in the freedom of movement that smooth space offers, states find military advantage in *striated space*. As Danny Hoffman puts it, "States dig trenches and plot straight lines. States are reactive forces; they 'think' according to established principles and paradigms. A state clears paths that allow it to see and control movement around the territory."[18] Striated space is space with paths carved into it. It is space that is gridded, partitioned, bounded off, marked, and measured. It is defined by standards: units of measurement for distances, laws that control movement, places where one may or may not go. Striated space channels movement into well-defined lines like paths, roads, sea lanes, canals, and tunnels, which are cleared of obstacles and allow large forces to move at accelerated speeds. These passages also serve as boundaries, making it possible to limit the movement of insurgent forces across them. By striating space, by breaking it up into distinct units and governing movement across them, states attempt to control the movement of insurgents (or potential insurgents) and to regulate the flow of traffic.

Striating space in the high Caucasus was no easy task. Yet, to conquer the Caucasus, it was essential to move troops and weaponry from the Russian garrisons on the steppes below the north slope of the range to the mountains and the south slope at a high enough volume and speed to dissuade attacks from insurgents. In 1801, Tsar Alexander I ordered imperial architect Pavel Potemkin to turn the 130-mile path into a roadway in order to facilitate troop movements. The work took nearly sixty-three years to complete, but resulted in the Georgian Military Highway, a treacherous mountain road that goes between the nearly sheer walls of Darial Gorge before summiting Jvari Pass at 7,815 feet. Creating a surface road not only cut smooth space, but flattened it, transforming a three-dimensional space into what is essentially a two-dimensional one. While the road travelled in three-dimensional space, uphill and downhill, the narrow plane of the road and its surface, which enabled wheeled travel, channeled movement. It encouraged people to follow the path rather than ranging the hillsides, essentially making planar movement horizontally through the space much more important than vertical movement up and down canyon walls.

But the highway suffered even more acutely from the same problems that the unimproved pass did. Snow was a problem for nine months of the year, and the highway was often closed due to natural avalanche.[19] In spring, mountain fighters could trigger avalanches to block the highway; in summer, which was war season, Chechens, Ingush, Avars, and others could attack passing caravans of Russian forces by causing landslides. In sum, insurgents fought the striation of space by *going up*, rejecting the plane created by the highway and moving the battle back into three-dimensional space. The core strategic issue of the centuries-long conflict in the Caucasus was essentially over volumetric space: who could take advantage of it tactically, who could dominate it, and who could confine the other side into striated battlespaces such as the military highway, or, later, the railway line that circumvented the mountains and headed down the coast to Baku.

If altitude is the tactical solution to the technological superiority and overwhelming numbers of an invading state, however, the subterranean is often the state's response. Although underground tunnels have often been conceptualized as weapons for insurgents countering state forces' control of urban heights or aerial battlespace,[20] tunnel warfare isn't necessarily a disadvantage to large state-controlled forces once they have enough superior engineering capability to build their own tunnels, transform the terrain, and control subterranean space.

The Roki Tunnel, initially envisioned in the 1960s and finally completed in 1984, was meant as a solution to this problem. Along with the Transkam Highway, the tunnel links the city of Vladikavkaz, in the Russian province of North Ossetia, with the town of Roki in the breakaway province of South Ossetia. It burrows through nearly two and a half miles (3,750 meters) of mountain, creating a crossing at a comparatively reasonable sixty-six hundred feet in altitude.

It was, at the time it was built, an engineering marvel—both the longest tunnel in the USSR and the one at the highest altitude. It was meant in particular to provide an alternative to the Jvari Pass, where the Georgian Military Highway travels at seventy-eight hundred feet in altitude along the Terek River bottom for eight miles through nearly vertical rock walls. Ostensibly, the tunnel was intended to link North Ossetia, which is part of Russia proper, with South Ossetia, which after 1921 was an *oblast* or province of the Georgian Soviet Socialist Republic inside the USSR. According to Giorgi Jusoev, secretary of the South Ossetia Regional Committee from 1965 to 1972, it was the Ossetians themselves who were demanding a stable connection in order to link the two halves of the ethnic group.[21] Other commentators pointed to the importance of a year-round passage in order to provision Georgia, Azerbaijan, and Armenia. Yet, despite the tunnel's obvious advantages for trade and transport, many Georgians believed then that the tunnel was built to ensure Russian military domination of Georgia, an area that had historically been in danger of breaking away from the Russian Empire.

Tunneling plays to a statist form of political rationality: one based on calculation, visualization, and the manipulation of volume in order to secure the control of territory.[22] Unlike the insurgents' use of alpine terrain, which makes use of both the mountains' topography and their materiality, a tunnel profits from the materiality of the mountains themselves, but obliterates topography, creating a space that is both flat and highly constrained. Moving through a tunnel leaves few opportunities for unpredictable movement; whoever is inside a state-controlled tunnel is at the mercy of the state. A tunnel also creates a chokepoint that is easy to guard, since the space has a limited number of entrances, constrains movement to only two directions, and gives state forces control over light and dark.[23] Most of all, a tunnel functions as a valve, giving the state the capacity to control flow, to filter out the people and things that move through it, and to determine who passes at what speed. Thus what makes tunnels successful political technologies for state actors is *not* that they open up volumetric space to warfare, but that they foreclose smooth volumetric space, forcing those passing through the tunnel back into a flat, striated space where their freedom of movement is remarkably constrained. Tunnels don't "secure the volume" by allowing states to embrace volumetric fighting or appropriate the advantages of insurgents. Rather, they more often collapse the volume into two-dimensional paths, making the terrain both legible and controllable, forcing conflict back onto terrain where the state has considerable technological advantage.

That tunnels are security apparatuses was never lost on the residents of either the north or south slopes of the Caucasus. Although the Soviets claimed that the tunnel was meant to allow year-round trade, an engineer who worked on building the tunnel told me decades later that everyone working on it knew "it was to move an army" in the event Georgia attempted to break away. But tunnels do not have to be used as military technology immediately. They control not only space but time, because they are technologies that do much of their political and military work by presenting *potentiality* as political fact. Once the heights and the underground are in play, it isn't necessarily what each side does to secure the volume, but what it *might* do at some point in the future, that tips the balance of power. In volumetric space, conflicts are often wars of position in which each side attempts to reconfigure terrain in ways that will convince the other side not to enter into armed conflict. This makes cold wars as significant as hot ones, and it makes distance-destroying or volume-collapsing technologies such as tunnels into weapons of deterrence that control terrain through their potential uses. The Roki Tunnel functioned not just as a road or a door or a tube, but as a materialized, topographic threat: it allowed the heavy, rolling war machinery of the Red Army free passage into the South Caucasus, and made it viable to have military bases in Armenia and Azerbaijan as well as Georgia. Like Georges-Eugène Haussmann's boulevards in Paris, which were avenues through which military forces could move to suppress an uprising, the Transkam Highway and the Roki Tunnel created direct and rapid passage to bring Soviet military forces to the South Caucasus, where uprising was frequently a possibility. The tunnel constantly announced the potential of armed invasion, and in doing so, kept the three union republics of the Caucasus (Armenia, Azerbaijan, and Georgia) firmly tied to the USSR.

Tunnels

Invading forces did not come for twenty-four years—long after the demise of the Soviet state that built the tunnel. In 2008, Georgia (now an independent nation) attempted to join NATO. This was a huge shift in regional politics: a reorientation of Georgia away from Russia and the former Soviet space toward the West, a potential defense against Russian aggression, and (at least in Russia's eyes) a massive erosion of the geographic buffer zone around Russia. For Russia, Georgia's realignment posed an enormous threat. After NATO officials pledged in April that "Georgia shall one day be part of NATO," the Russians moved the Fifty-Eighth Army to Vladikavkaz and began military exercises. To reach Georgia, however, this large army would have to either summit Jvari Pass, or move through the Roki Tunnel.

On the night of August 8, the Fifty-Eighth Army approached the Roki Tunnel. The Georgian Army moved quickly to seal off the tunnel's southern end and prevent invasion. They fired artillery and dropped banned cluster munitions, all in an attempt to use the mouth of the tunnel as a chokepoint and prevent the Fifty-Eighth Army from moving through into South Ossetia.[24] But it was too late: Georgian forces were overwhelmed in five days, Georgian villagers were ethnically cleansed and pushed into Georgia proper, and Russian troops occupied South Ossetia, the breakaway province in the Roki Tunnel's delta.

In 2018, ten years later, South Ossetia remained under ever intensifying military occupation. In the decade since the invasion, Russian forces have taken great advantage of South Ossetia's smooth, mostly flat space, striating it to suit their own military needs by establishing military bases scattered across the territory, defining and redefining the province's borders, carving out new roads for tanks, and building air strips. This has given Russian forces an enormous advantage: because they are within a kilometer of the East–West highway, they now have the potential to control another chokepoint. By blocking off that highway, Russian forces could cut the country in half almost instantaneously and be in Georgia's capital city within an hour. By reshaping the terrain, Russia now controls the terrain, and, in doing so, controls Georgia's foreign policy via threat and potentiality. It has pursued the same strategies of volumetric control and flattening space in Chechnya and in Ukraine, constantly seeking to control heights and depths in order to secure the volume, striate space, and create the constant potential for outright war.[25]

Tunnels are more than infrastructure, more than objects that "create the grounds on which other objects operate."[26] They are space-making machines. They can create new topographies, while, at the same time, obliterating others or making topography irrelevant in the context of warfighting. They actively constitute terrain, opening it up volumetrically to permit new forms of movement (as, say, in Gaza or at the US-Mexico border) or, conversely, collapsing the volume to make it planar and channeled as at the Roki Tunnel. They use volumes to create planes and use planes to control volumes. They change the *quality* of space in ways that advantage or disadvantage other spatial technologies like guns or bombs.

One of the things that thinking about "securing the volume" does is assume that there is a preexisting volume to be secured. Yet, as the example of the Roki Tunnel shows, volumes are constantly being constituted and destroyed, appropriated and reappropriated. In what ways are volumes called into being, or, conversely, eradicated? What strategic or tactical advantages does the ability to determine whether the battle will be in two-dimensional or three-dimensional space confer? How are these oscillations of volumes—opening, closing, opening, closing—constructed through both political and military action? Tunnels illustrate the fact that volumetricity depends to a large extent on the use that is made of it: for nonstate actors, tunnels can be used to constitute volumetric spaces by burrowing under striated space, while for state actors, tunnels often collapse volumetric space by bypassing nonstate actors who exploit verticality, gravity, and topography.[27] To understand conflict, then, we have to understand the mobile, mutable nature of volumetric space and the complex social, military, and political ways in which it is constituted.

NOTES

1   Daphné Richemond-Barak, *Underground Warfare* (Oxford: Oxford University Press, 2018); Stuart Elden, "Secure the Volume: Vertical Geopolitics and the Depth of Power," *Political Geography* 34 (2013): 35–51.
2   The Chokepoints Collective, which I am a part of, has been working to describe the effects of geophysical chokepoints, or places where big things must move through tight spaces. As a unique political technology, chokepoints create distinctive social environments in their deltas where smugglers, insurgents, police, spies, and others struggle to control the flow of traffic. See Ashley Carse, Jason Cons, and Townsend Middleton, "Preface: Chokepoints," *Limn* 10 (2018), https://limn.it/articles/preface -chokepoints; as well as all the articles on chokepoints in *Limn,* issue 10.
3   Elden, "Secure the Volume"; Eyal Weizman. *Hollow Land: Israel's Architecture of Occupation* (London: Verso, 2007).
4   Humphrey, this volume.
5   Gilles Deleuze and Félix Guattari, *A Thousand Plateaus: Capitalism and Schizophrenia*, trans. Brian Massumi (Minneapolis: University of Minnesota Press, 1987).
6   See Harris, this volume.
7   James C. Scott, *The Art of Not Being Governed: An Anarchist History of Upland Southeast Asia* (New Haven, CT: Yale University Press, 2009).
8   Donald Rayfield, *Edge of Empires* (London: Reaktion Books, 2012), 277.
9   Carse et al., "Preface: Chokepoints."
10   Stuart Elden, "Land, Terrain, Territory," *Progress in Human Geography* 34, no. 6 (2010): 799–817; Stephen Graham, "Vertical Geopolitics: Baghdad and After," *Antipode* 36, no. 1 (2004): 12–23; Peter Adey, *Aerial Life: Spaces, Mobilities, Affects* (Malden, MA: Wiley-Blackwell, 2010); Gordillo, this volume.
11   Graham, "Vertical Geopolitics," 16; Reviel Netz, *Barbed Wire: An Ecology of Modernity* (Middletown, CT: Wesleyan University Press, 2004).

12 Friedrich Engels, "Mountain Warfare in the Past and Present" (1857), Marxists Internet Archive, accessed June 30, 2019. https://www.marxists.org/archive/marx/works/1857/01/mountain-warfare.htm.

13 Weizman, *Hollow Land*.

14 Deleuze and Guattari, *Thousand Plateaus*, 485.

15 Alain Badiou, *Being and Event* (London: Bloomsbury, 1987); see also Gastón Gordillo, "Terrain as Insurgent Weapon: An Affective Geometry of Warfare in the Mountains of Afghanistan," *Political Geography* 64 (2018): 56–57.

16 Deleuze and Guattari, *Thousand Plateaus*, 479; Flora Lysen and Patricia Pisters, "The Smooth and the Striated," *Deleuze Studies* 6, no. 1 (2012): 1; Nicole Starosielski, *The Undersea Network* (Durham, NC: Duke University Press, 2015).

17 Deleuze and Guattari, *Thousand Plateaus*; Gordillo, "Terrain as Insurgent Weapon"; and Gordillo, this volume.

18 Danny Hoffman, *The War Machines: Young Men and Violence in Sierra Leone and Liberia* (Durham, NC: Duke University Press, 2011), 8.

19 N. I. Kvezereli-Kopadze, "The Problem of Year-Round Traffic through the Pass of the Cross on the Georgian Military Highway," *Soviet Geography* 15, no. 3 (1974): 163–74, https://doi.org/10.1080/00385417.1974.10770662.

20 See, e.g., Richemond-Barak, *Underground Warfare*; Humphrey, this volume.

21 Kvezereli-Kopadze, "Problem of Year-Round Traffic."

22 Gavin Bridge, "Territory, Now in 3D!," *Political Geography* 34 (2013): 57.

23 Carse et al., "Preface: Chokepoints."

24 CJ Chivers, "Georgia Offers Fresh Evidence on War's Start," *New York Times*, September 15, 2008, https://www.nytimes.com/2008/09/16/world/europe/16georgia.html; Marc Tran, "Georgia Admits Dropping Cluster Bombs, Says Rights Group," *Guardian*, September 1, 2008, https://www.theguardian.com/world/2008/sep/01/georgia.russia.

25 Elizabeth Dunn and Michael Bobick, "The Empire Strikes Back: War without War and Occupation without Occupation in the Russian Sphere of Influence," *American Ethnologist* 41, no. 3 (2014): 405–13.

26 Brian Larkin, "The Politics and Poetics of Infrastructure," *Annual Review of Anthropology* 42 (2013): 329.

27 I owe this phrasing to Franck Billé.

3 Spoofing

The Geophysics of
Not Being Governed

WAYNE CHAMBLISS

Satellites crisscross each other in the darkness, at great speed. Each with its magneto-optical trap of supercooled matter in stow, like specimen jars some extraterrestrial naturalist has prepared for its long voyage home. Chilled cesium atoms, sluggish, are tugged, infinitesimally (but measurably), by the mountains below, by isostasies; are pushed, just as infinitesimally, by swallets, by occulted craters. But also by bunkers, shelters, tunnels, holes. There are people in those holes.

An atom bobs up, slightly more than usual. Machines confer. Yes, they decide, that's the one. Another machine, a Predator drone, is scrambled. Gravid with ordnance, it roars through the night toward the designated patch of featureless desert ground.

Battlespace

In 2017, the United States military dropped a MOAB ("Mother of All Bombs")—the largest nonnuclear explosive device ever made—on a tunnel system in Afghanistan. There are conflicting reports about its effectiveness, but at least a hundred people died.[1] Even more devastating bunker busters have been conceived. The "Rod from God," for example—a kinetic weapon concept in which an intercontinental ballistic missile's nuclear warhead would be replaced with a tip of tungsten or hardened steel and dropped on a target from space.[2] There is now a positive feedback loop in which increasingly powerful weapons are being developed to dismantle progressively deeper and more hardened subterranean structures. For those unable to withstand such force, much less counter it, resistance hinges on concealment, on a poliorcetics of undetectability. So, while penetrative ordnance is in one sort of adaptive arms race, remote sensing is in another, related one—with stratagems of camouflage.

Subterranean tactics—offensive and defensive—have been facts of war for millennia, but fully volumetric military strategy is a comparatively recent development.[3] The advent of airplanes—of air power—in the early twentieth century catalyzed defensive underground construction on an unprecedented scale. "The line between seeing and targeting being a slim one," cultural theorist Ryan Bishop observed, subsequent developments of aerial (and eventually orbital) surveillance and rocketry have incentivized combatants to dig even more holes, and deeper ones.[4]

According to Stephen Graham, "The idea of untargetable targets [has brought on] an almost existential crisis" for the US military. He characterizes the production of underground bunkers as "a main challenge to [their] technology and hegemony."[5] For obvious reasons, it's hard to say anything definite about the scope of these developments. But stories abound. North Korea—reputedly "the most fortified country in the world"—is supposed to have dug between eleven thousand and fourteen thousand underground facilities since the 1950s.[6] Enough to stage all their key military assets underground, including an entire air base (with a regiment of aircraft) inside a granite mountain. Intelligence gathered from defectors revealed that they had also built at least twenty-two of what the South Koreans refer to as "Tunnels of Aggression" under the demilitarized zone. The tunnels have no exits. They will be exploded open at the moment of invasion—each enabling as many as thirty thousand troops per hour to pour through into South Korea. Only four of these tunnels have been found to date.[7]

This is the sort of idealized threat—real or imaginary—motivating the US military and intelligence services to develop ways to "see" more clearly into underground spaces, in order to violently contest them.

Surface Area

For all its varied topography, the ground is a great leveler. Hiding belowground decreases asymmetries in war, and increases degrees of freedom in less explicitly militarized settings where space is tightly controlled at the surface. To dig, in such circumstances, is an act of resistance—a volumetric diffusion with territorial implications.

Territory isn't just an area on the surface of the Earth; it has volume.[8] But that volume has surface area. Earth contains things. It also contains nothings: voids. Some voids are incidental; others, intentional. Those that humans can make use of are topologically continuous with the surface. So, not just holes, but parts of wholes. And "everywhere a hole moves," Reza Negarestani tells us, "a surface is invented."[9] Among the invaginations, infoldings, pulverizations, and rearrangements of earth, as surfaces multiply and surface area increases, burrowers exhume new, topologically continuous territory—in every sense that Stuart Elden wants to complicate that word: economic, legal, technical, and *strategic*. In this last sense, insofar as freshly exposed surface area belowground is not just new "land" but also a contestable new "terrain," it has geostrategic utility.[10]

Terrain (on and below the ground, at least) is physically contested on surfaces. There are other sorts of territorial contestations, of course, but "the surface is where most of the action is," as perceptual theorist J. J. Gibson put it. "The surface is what touches the animal, not the interior."[11] The deeper one burrows, the more complicated space becomes, the more surface area there is, the more new terrain there is to contest. And if a hegemon discovers it exists, they *will* contest it, physically. The US military, with its ordnance, can tear the Earth open and erase such terrain. Or it can pump martial force into the ground—in the form of malware, poison gas, viruses, pests, robots, soldiers, etc.—chasing topological continuities into the depths after those who occupy them. But it needs to know where to aim.

Confronted with overwhelming force, you can't always fight. You need not surrender, however. Not if you can hide. Terrain can be produced and destroyed. It can also be concealed.

The Triumph of the Surface

That concealment starts with what Ryan Bishop has called, optimistically, "the triumph of the surface": an intrinsic opacity of what's belowground to what's above it.[12] Any perceived continuity between the two is vulnerable, however. So, it isn't enough just to dig. To whatever extent possible, the surface area of a hole must be discretized from the terrain that envelops it—from what Negarestani describes as "topologies of the whole"[13]—and its ingresses and outlets, crucial to supporting life and communications underground, also hidden.

If these surficial traces are well-concealed—as when Swiss troops disguised bunker vents inside ersatz glacial erratics in World War II[14]—it's hard to spot a burrow with the naked eye while driving past it, much less with an optical sensor mounted on an airborne or orbital platform. The military has therefore developed a whole xenophenomenology of other intelligence methods to detect them: LIDAR, multispectral cameras, ground-penetrating radars, and many others. These can all be thwarted, however, by various countersurveillance tactics—whether by masking thermal contrasts, or coating ducts with a paint that reflects wavelengths indistinguishable from the spectral signatures of local vegetation, or simply by digging down to depths that radar can't penetrate before tilting the axis of construction back to horizontal.[15]

Knowing this, the military has tried to recruit the Earth itself as an informant. Magnetic, electric, and gravitational fields—as well as acoustic, seismic, and radio waves—are all affected by subterranean features they interact with in ways that, if measured carefully, can help detect buried structures. The US Defense Advanced Research Projects Agency (DARPA) invests heavily in both the basic science and practical application of magnetometry, reflection seismography, electrical resistivity, acoustic imaging, and other pertinent sensing methods to do just that. The military has also pioneered new methods, as when the US Air Force–sponsored High Frequency Active Auroral Research Program (HAARP) experimentally modulated the ionosphere to direct very low frequency and extremely low frequency radio waves at the Earth, inducing secondary electromagnetic fields within it, and then—successfully—analyzed those fields at the surface for evidence of a mineshaft below.[16]

Promising as these methods are, they all have limitations. Signals can be jammed or spoofed. And the enabling sensors, as a rule, need to be close to what they're hunting for to be effective. Ideally, right on top of the quarry.[17]

The Mass Is Not the Territory

These methods work best on the ground. Some, like reflection seismology and electrical resistivity tomography, will only work if sensors are installed on the surface. But that isn't always an option. The US Department of Defense defines a "denied area"—where most of the subterranean activities they're interested in take place—as one "under enemy or unfriendly control in which friendly forces cannot expect to operate successfully within existing operational constraints and force capabilities."[18] For a method of detecting underground structures in denied areas to be truly useful, it should: see underground at depth, see from above the ground (the higher up, the safer), efficiently search wide areas, and not be easily spoofed.

Gravimetry, the precise measurement of gravity fields, is one such method. Resource extraction firms have used it for over a century to "see" underground. Not only can gravimetry see to great depths—e.g., the recent detection of a water reservoir six miles below the surface of Saturn's moon Enceladus[19]— it can also see into them rather clearly. In an oft-cited example, a joint Air Force Research Laboratory–Lockheed Martin team surveyed the Low-Energy Booster tunnel of the Superconducting Super Collider in Waxahachie, Texas, in 1997 and got reasonably accurate readings of the structure's size, shape, variable depth, and orientation with a gravity gradiometer.[20] Like other detection methods, it works best on the ground, but it has been demonstrated to work *well* from the air, and even in space—where it's used to search planetary-scale areas. And because "it is very difficult to alter the Earth's gravitational field, it would be equally difficult to mask the field variations caused by a deeply buried facility," according to military theorist Arnold Streland, making gravimetry a reliable source of intelligence.[21]

Unfortunately for those who might depend on concealment underground, the very thing that enables them to hide inside the Earth—addition of surface area by subtraction of mass—alters its gravitational characteristics in detectable ways. The gravity field at the planetary circumperiphery is a shadow cast by what lies (and does not lie) beneath. A void betrays itself: an absence confessing its presence in space-time to anyone who can measure it accurately enough.

Gravity Gradiometers

On Earth, the average force of gravity is 9.81 meters per second squared. In fact, the force varies at every point of the Earth's surface by a tiny amount—on the order of one one-millionth of the average field strength. It varies because the Earth's composition is not homogenous, and the mass density of whatever lies below the surface affects the gravitational field locally above it. By measuring the field accurately enough, you can detect anomalies—positive and negative—which are suggestive of the presence or absence of greater-than-expected masses. A buried void would produce a negative gravity anomaly. By crossing and recrossing the same area in a grid pattern, a sensitive enough system could determine the void's shape, size, and orientation.

There are two main types of systems for this sort of measurement: gravimeters and gravity gradiometers. In its most basic form, a gravimeter includes a proof mass suspended from a spring. The stronger the gravitational force, the more the spring gets stretched. Although gravimeters can be incredibly sensitive (to field strength variations on the order of a trillionth of the average), they cannot be moved easily without the acceleration of their own motion overwhelming the signal they're intended to measure.

Gravity gradiometers, on the other hand, are intended to measure the spatial rate of change in gravitational force from one location to another—the gravity gradient—using multiple accelerometers to cancel the effects of movement vibrations and horizontal accelerations. The strength of this gradient (which, being a derivative, is a fainter signal than the gravitational force itself) also speaks to the composition of the subsurface. And because it can be used from a moving vehicle, it's been the system of choice for large-scale surveys over the last fifty years.

Orbital Military Space

In the 1970s, the US Department of Defense hired Bell Aerospace to enhance the usability of gravity gradiometers for submarines, first to improve inertial guidance calculations of their missile launchers, and then to help them navigate covertly without sonar. When the work was declassified in the late 1980s, a renaissance of gravimetry followed. Among other improvements, three-dimensional (i.e., "full tensor") coordination of multiple accelerometers had made this new system stable enough to use from the air. In 1987, a group of Bell scientists hardwired some gradiometers into the back of a van, drove it onto a US Air Force C-130 Hercules transport plane, and flight tested the setup over parts of Oklahoma and Texas. Their results were compelling enough that oil and gas companies took to the skies as well, and have been using airborne gradiometry for wide-scale resource prospecting ever since.[22]

Of course, if a denied area is defended by surface-to-air weapons, measuring gravity from a plane above it isn't much safer than it would be to do so on the ground. To help address this concern, Lockheed Martin—backed by DARPA funding—has recently experimented with gradiometers mounted on drones.[23] But drones can also be shot down. So there's interest in migrating the detection capability even higher up, into orbit. In Streland's assessment,

> Space is the best location for a gravity gradiometer.... A space-based system allows coverage of the entire surface of the earth, even areas that may be denied to aircraft because of sophisticated enemy air defense systems. The repeating nature of the satellite orbit allows a space-based gravity gradiometer to easily revisit the same area many times allowing analysts to look for changes in gravity gradients over time which could be an indicator of deeply buried facility construction.[24]

The mission of the National Geospatial-Intelligence Agency (NGA) is to feed the US military just such analysis. A constellation of satellites like the one Streland proposes—with overlapping polar and equatorial orbits, to maximize coverage and minimize revisit times—would enable the NGA to efficiently rebaseline Earth's gravity field at an unprecedented level of detail, and then monitor changes to it. To peer into the global subsurface, and flag possibilities of buried structures there—those the military is actively trying to find, others they hadn't known to look for, and still others yet to be built.

This isn't so far off. Even before the United States launched its first satellites, scientists started working out how to measure gravity from space. And over the last twenty years, US and European public space agencies have put a series of gravity measurement missions such as the Gravity Recovery and Climate Experiment (GRACE) into Earth orbit and elsewhere in the solar system. In 2017, the Gravity Recovery and Interior Laboratory (GRAIL) became the first satellite publicly acknowledged to have discovered a cave—beneath the lunar surface, no less—by means of gravimetry.

As impressive as that feat is, to accurately detect bunkers or tunnels with space-based sensors, they will need to be far more sensitive than those on the GRACE and GRAIL missions. This issue is being tackled in a variety of ways, including the development of a new class of superconducting gradiometers. Another promising candidate is the quantum gravity gradiometer developed by NASA's Jet Propulsion Laboratory (JPL), which utilizes light-pulse atom interferometry. Despite what it might lead to, the approach is rather beautiful:

> Two atom-interferometer-based accelerometers [are] placed one above the other vertically. Each accelerometer is realized in an atomic fountain, where cold atoms are first produced in a magneto-optical trap by laser cooling. The atoms are then launched out of the trap and subsequently divided in two paths by laser light, and then recombined to form a Mach-Zehnder-type interferometer. Gravity, acting on the moving atoms, distorts the phase of the matter waves and therefore changes the interference pattern, which is then detected via laser resonance fluorescence.[25]

This idea evolved quickly between 2002, when it was first proposed, and 2008, when the JPL team announced at a conference that they had completed development of an extremely sensitive laboratory gradiometer and were in the process of turning it into a flight-ready instrument.[26] Curiously, apart from a brief NASA news article in 2010 acknowledging that progress, there doesn't appear to have been any public mention of the project since.[27]

The Trip Wire

Barring an unexpected leap forward in our understanding of basic physics, whatever gravimetry approach finally gets settled on will only be a partial solution. A space-based monitoring system will be able to see deep into the subsurface, but not at the resolution required to definitively characterize and target underground structures. It would instead operate as the first step of a cascading surveillance strategy, identifying and prioritizing gravitational "anomalies of interest" camouflaged to other types of sensors, and then cuing complimentary detection methods—orbital, aerial, or terrestrial, depending on the circumstances—to investigate them more closely. In his fascinating Air War College thesis, Arnold Streland described this approach in terms of a *trip wire*:

> Potential enemies of the United States . . . are using everything from old caves to sophisticated underground operations centers. . . . Countering such efforts requires an integration of intelligence resources including imagery intelligence, signals intelligence, human intelligence and MASINT [measurement and signature intelligence] to detect their facilities and identify weaknesses that could be exploited in a potential conflict. The builders and operators of the deeply buried facilities, however, could spoof many of these intelligence sources. Countering efforts to spoof our intelligence systems requires coordinating their use so that systems can be cross-cued by each other to get more effective coverage of an area of interest. This cross cuing becomes more effective if at least one intelligence source operates in a manner that is very difficult to spoof. Space-based gravity gradiometry sensors have the potential to serve as the "trip wire" system that could draw the attention of other intelligence assets to a previously undiscovered deeply buried facility.[28]

Because it is so hard to hide or disguise a negative anomaly, when one is detected, additional intelligence resources could be brought to bear on it with greater confidence. Presumably, if an anomaly isn't detected, such resources would be held in reserve. A keystone holds an arch together, but it is also a single point of failure to target if you want to bring the structure down. The challenge, then, for those who want a buried facility to remain undetected, is to somehow substitute a nothing which *isn't* for a nothing which measurably *is*. That is, to spoof gravity.

The received wisdom is that gravity spoofing is impossible. Defense contractor NovAtel goes so far as to claim in the product literature for its navigation system that "an adversary cannot spoof the Earth's gravitational field and cause the inertial unit to think it has moved in a way that it hasn't."[29] Lacking hard evidence to the contrary, it's a point of view I'd expect most military thinkers to agree with. All new forms of surveillance beget countersurveillance tactics specific to them, however. Gravity field variations might be difficult to spoof, but not impossible.

Gravity Spoofing

For anyone who anticipates being observed in this way, my recommendation is to *dig now*, before new baseline data can be produced. Once a system is operational, it will be harder to build underground without detection, or even just to hide existing structures. To remain concealed, some sort of gravity camouflage will be necessary. At minimum, this has to be good enough to evade the "trip wire." If orbital sensors detect an anomaly of interest, they will cue other, more sensitive technologies to examine it, each of which would also need to be evaded.

As with every other remote sensing method, gravimetry has limitations that can be exploited. What's more, those doing the surveillance have no reason to believe gravity can be spoofed, so they aren't likely to have developed counter-countertactics. And layers of dissimulation are possible.

There are a number of ideas to consider, some practicable, others more speculative. Everything from digging holes all over a region, so that expensive resources are wasted investigating them, to spoofing gravity itself. A spoof is a falsification of data or intent used to gain advantage over an adversary. It's typically thought of in terms of an attack, but spoofing can also be a way to camouflage something from a predator (e.g., a Predator). In the long, long history of things that hide from those that seek, two strategies of camouflage predominate: crypsis and mimesis. That is, concealment and imposture.

Cryptic spoofs trick adversaries (which need not be human, of course, or even biological) into believing something that *is* there *isn't*. Mimetic spoofs trick them into ignoring what they see, into thinking it's something that doesn't concern them. Many signals can be spoofed. All of them, maybe. There are plenty of examples of successful spoofs involving visible light, infrared, radar, data protocols, GPS. It's easy to imagine others—e.g., seismic spoofs to disguise underground nuclear tests; or else, to convince geopolitical adversaries such weapons were being tested when in fact they weren't.

Cryptic gravity spoofing hinges on the idea that the gravitational anomaly of a buried void can be concealed by manipulating the densities of the materials surrounding it. We might try to balance a negative anomaly with a positive one, for instance, by blending denser materials below, above, and within the void than were removed from it. A gravitational trompe l'oeil. Induced liquefaction, triggered by hydraulic reinjection, could reduce soil density across a wide area to help soften the line between a void and its surroundings in a gradiometric profile.

Mimetic gravity spoofing would disguise an anomaly to look like something else. Something innocuous. Blending mass densities, a void could be made to look, datalogically, like a natural underground feature: a buried impact crater or extinct river bed, remnant volcanism, evolving karst. Some likely alternative explanation for the gravitational morphology. If mass casts a gravity shadow surfaceward, think of these as gravity shadow puppets.

Either type of spoof could be usefully combined with some form of gravity jamming, to further obscure an anomaly by subtly increasing the noise-to-signal ratio observing sensors would need to make sense of. Seismicity, infrasound, and atmospheric temperature cells can all complicate gravimetry, so scientists are finding ways to filter them from measurements.[30] In theory, any of these "gravity noises" could be co-opted and amplified for purposes of concealment. Take earthquakes. Seismic waves deform the crust and shift subsurface materials, altering the local gravity field. Earthquakes can be, and have been, deliberately induced. In 1976, a group of DARPA-funded United States Geological Survey researchers experimentally triggered multiple quakes in an isolated seismic regime beneath a Colorado oil field.[31] Similar sandboxes could be identified in which to experiment with the possibilities and limitations of plastically sculpting gravity signals through seismic induction. In theory, it might even be possible to generate *artificial* gravity fields— electromagnetically, with stacks of superconducting solenoids—to use for masking anomalies.[32]

In theory, many things are possible. In practice, however, the economics don't favor the surveilled. Especially if the cost of the hole can't be offset by the value of the rock excavated from it. Experimentation with spoofing would mean additional hardships. But if the alternative is exposure, or racing the geothermal gradient down to depths at which human life can barely be supported to try to avoid a GBU-28 bunker buster nearer to the surface, it doesn't seem like much of a choice. Homegrown baseline gravity data and specialized equipment will be necessary. And plenty of imagination. Gravity camouflage probably isn't the sort of thing one can mod *Minecraft* to model credibly. But again, it wouldn't hurt to try.

A Thousand Withins

Since the advent of the joint US Air Force–CIA Corona program in 1959, military appetite for surface imagery has motivated generations of spy satellite development. Their desire to peer into the subsurface will likely follow a similar trajectory into orbit, and possess similar qualities once instantiated: untouchable remoteness, planetary scale, panoptic psychological deterrence. The gaze of such a system will be omnivorous, and it won't be satiated by monitoring the underground workings of state actors in the deserts of Iran or the mountains of North Korea. Rather, it will be used to identify new adversaries, new anomalies of interest: anyone who tampers with the gravity field; the termite nests of the cities.

A city is an apotheosis of surface area. Irrepressibly volumetric. Gravimetry will be harder to use there, but useful nonetheless. Not just in the context of urban warfare, where tunneling sappers can play a major role, as they did recently at the Battle of Aleppo, but also in everyday police actions at urbanized borders and urban boundaries.[33] Wherever an agency like the US Border Patrol has a local monopoly on violence, it will be easier for them to pair space-based gravity observations with detection methods on the ground—to ferret out tunnels and subterranean bolt-holes, retard unregulated flows of humans and goods, and so forth.

The use of sophisticated military detection methods by paramilitarized domestic security forces at the urban periphery will prefigure their adoption in the urban core, by civil authorities who want to police entire metropolitan volumes more effectively. "If we are to take control of the subsurface," Rollo Home of Ordnance Survey (the British national mapping agency) explained, "we need to have an holistic view of the subsurface."[34] And as new underground mapping and surveillance capabilities are developed toward that end in the interest of security, new security threats will be manufactured in the process.

What Shannon Mattern wrote about borders at the surface—that they are capable of "transforming any human subject within the zone into a criminal object"—holds true when the border *is* the surface.[35] Beneath the city streets, "distinctions between civilians and combatants, criminality and urban marginality, have become progressively blurred," as criminologist Theo Kindynis put it.[36] Police have limited the scope of acceptable uses, and accepted users, of these spaces. Even those who enter them for reasons humans always have—art, exploration, sacred experience, refuge—are finding their activities recategorized as security threats, and themselves criminalized, even imperiled.

In many respects, a city—topologically complicated, electromagnetically and gravitationally noisy—is easier to hide in than a rural burrow. Although watchful eyes (in the form of CCTV cameras, Internet of Things sensors, and even beat cops) can follow the built environment's intestine folds endoscopically, it's impractical to surveil a whole urban volume. So police apperceive only part of what a city even contains underground, never mind who might be down there using it. As experimental geographer Bradley Garrett once told me about his years-long explorations under London, "After a certain point, we knew we were free."

Gravimetry will be used to curtail that autonomy, and ardent spatial pluralists—be they academics or insurgents (or both)—will have to adapt accordingly, by complicating space, concealing the new terrain, and occupying it under threat of hegemonic force until the situation becomes untenable. Then moving on to do it again somewhere else. There's a Persian term for this sort of thing, *Hezar-Too*, which means "a thousand withins." I like to think of it as *matryoshka* urbanism.

Having first shared it with the domestic security state, we can imagine the military eventually devolving its gravity field monitoring capability to capitalist elites, as they have with other orbital systems. We can even imagine a future tense where access to it is further democratized and it becomes broadly useful for, say, scientific purposes. By that time, the terms of the spatial arms race will have changed and something new will need to be adapted to, however. William Gibson's old saw about the future not yet being evenly distributed implies the future will always be unevenly distributed. Prometheus didn't give fire to humans all at once. Somebody got it first.

NOTES

1   Yarun Steinbuch, "This Is What's Left after the 'Mother of All Bombs' Hit Afghanistan," *New York Post*, April 24, 2017, https://nypost.com/2017/04/24/this-is-whats-left-after-the-mother-of-all-bombs-hit-afghanistan.
2   Jonathan Shainin, "Rods from God," *New York Times*, December 10, 2006, https://www.nytimes.com/2006/12/10/magazine/10section3a.t-9.html.
3   Stuart Elden, "Secure the Volume: Vertical Geopolitics and the Depth of Power," *Political Geography* 34 (2013): 36.
4   Ryan Bishop, "Project 'Transparent Earth' and the Autoscopy of Aerial Targeting: The Visual Geopolitics of the Underground," *Theory, Culture and Society* 28 (2011): 273, https://doi.org/10.1177/0263276411424918.
5   Stephen Graham, *Vertical: The City from Satellites to Bunkers* (London: Verso, 2018), 342, 340.

6   Barbara Demick, "N. Korea's Ace in the Hole," *Los Angeles Times*, November 14, 2003, http://articles.latimes.com/2003/nov/14/world/fg-underground14.

7   Lt. Col. Arnold H. Streland, "Going Deep: A System Concept for Detecting Deeply Buried Facilities from Space" (research report, Air War College, 2003), 8–9.

8   Elden, "Secure the Volume," 36. Use of Peter Sloterdijk's *spheres* as a conceptual apparatus for geopolitics is curious. The sphere, by definition, has the lowest surface area–to–volume ratio of any solid, and is therefore the least energetically expensive to surveil in its entirety. From this standpoint, it's an authoritarian shape; a totalitarian one, even. In terms of geostrategy, the possibilities of freedom increase in direct proportion to surface area.

9   Reza Negarestani, *Cyclonopedia: Complicity with Anonymous Materials* (Melbourne: re.press, 2008), 50.

10   Elden, "Secure the Volume," 35–36; Stuart Elden, "Terrain," Theorizing the Contemporary, *Cultural Anthropology*, October 24, 2017, https://culanth.org/fieldsights /1231-terrain.

11   Qtd. in Negarestani, *Cyclonopedia*, 46.

12   Bishop, "Project 'Transparent Earth,'" 272.

13   Negarestani, *Cyclonopedia*, 51.

14   Kaushik, "The Camouflaged Military Bunkers of Switzerland," *Amusing Planet* (blog), July 13, 2015, https://www.amusingplanet.com/2015/07/the-camouflaged -military-bunkers-of.html.

15   Lt. Col. Eric M. Sepp, "Deeply Buried Facilities: Implications for Military Operations" (occasional paper, Air War College, 2000), 13–14.

16   Larry G. Stolarczyk, *Detection and Imaging of Underground Structures by Exploiting ELF/ VLF Radiowaves* (Hanscom AFB: Air Force Research Laboratory, 2000) 28, 44–46.

17   Streland, "Going Deep," 21.

18   Office of the Chairman of the Joint Chiefs of Staff, DOD *Dictionary of Military and Associated Terms* (Washington, DC: Joint Staff, 2018), accessed April 2, 2018, http:// www.jcs.mil/Portals/36/Documents/Doctrine/pubs/dictionary.pdf?ver=2018-05 -02-174746-340, 66.

19   Daphné Richemond-Barak, *Underground Warfare* (Oxford: Oxford University Press, 2018), 98–99.

20   Streland, "Going Deep," 43.

21   Streland, "Going Deep," 3.

22   Capt. Marshall M. Rogers, "An Investigation into the Feasibility of Using a Modern Gravity Gradient Instrument for Passive Aircraft Navigation and Terrain Avoidance" (thesis, Air Force Institute of Technology, 2009), 19–20.

23   Katie Drummond, "Lockheed Using Gravity to Spot 'Subterranean Threats,'" *Wired*, July 15, 2010, https://www.wired.com/2010/07/lockheed-using-gravity-to -spot-subterranean-threats/.

24   Streland, "Going Deep," 51.

25   Nan Yu, James M. Kohel, Larry Romans, and Lute Maleki, "Quantum Gravity Gradiometer Sensor for Earth Science Applications" (paper presented at NASA Earth Science Technology Conference, Pasadena, CA, June 11 and 13, 2002).

26 James M. Kohel, Robert J. Thompson, James R. Kellogg, David C. Aveline, and Nan Yu, "Development of a Transportable Quantum Gravity Gradiometer for Gravity Field Mapping" (paper presented at NASA Earth Science Technology Conference, University of Maryland, June 24–26, 2008).

27 NASA's Jet Propulsion Laboratory, "A Transportable Gravity Gradiometer Based on Atom Interferometry," NASA News Briefs, May 2010, https://ntrs.nasa.gov /archive/nasa/casi.ntrs.nasa.gov/20100019615.pdf. Even more curiously, development of the quantum gravity gradiometer coincided with that of the X-37B, a miniature unmanned space shuttle launched for the first time in 2010 on a series of classified orbital flights lasting from eight to twenty-four months. My research into whether JPL's gradiometer is part of the science package on these missions is ongoing.

28 Streland, "Going Deep," 61.

29 NovAtel, "Understanding the Difference Between Anti-Spoofing and Anti-Jamming," Velocity Magazine, 2013, accessed November 16, 2018, https://www .novatel.com/tech-talk/velocity/velocity-2013/understanding-the-difference -between-anti-spoofing-and-anti-jamming/.

30 Jan Harms, "Terrestrial Gravity Fluctuations," Living Reviews in Relativity 18 (2015): 3–150, https://doi.org/10.1007/lrr-2015-3.

31 C. B. Raleigh, J. H. Healy, and J. D. Bredehoeft, "An Experiment in Earthquake Control at Rangely, Colorado," Science 191 (1976): 1230–36.

32 André Füzfa, "How Current Loops and Solenoids Curve Spacetime," Physical Review D 93, no. 2 (2016): 024014-1, https://doi.org/10.1103/PhysRevD.93.024014.

33 Martin Chulov, "Aleppo's Most Wanted Man—The Rebel Leader behind Tunnel Bombs," Guardian, May 20, 2014, https://www.theguardian.com/world/2014/may /20/aleppos-most-wanted-man-rebel-leader-tunnel-bombs.

34 Qtd. in Bradley L. Garrett, "Who Owns the Space under Cities? The Attempt to Map the Earth beneath Us," Guardian, July 10, 2018, https://www.theguardian .com/cities/2018/jul/10/who-owns-the-space-under-cities-the-attempt-to-map-the -ground-beneath-our-feet.

35 Shannon Mattern, "All Eyes on the Border," Places Journal, September 2018, https://doi.org/10.22269/180925.

36 Theo Kindynis, "The Subterranean-(In)Security Nexus?" (paper presented at Volumetric Urbanism: Charting New Urban Divisions—An International Workshop, University of Sheffield, UK, May 24–26, 2017), 14.

4

Lag

Four-Dimensional Bordering in the Himalayas

TINA HARRIS

Time and the Vertical

In 2006, a former Indian army officer told me harrowing stories of nearly being killed—twice—on the Siachen Glacier near the Line of Control (LoC) between India and Pakistan. This is one of the highest military outposts in the world, where people die due to the complications of altitude-related illnesses or sudden avalanches. It was a "horrible, horrible place," he said. And yet, the ex-officer was only stationed there for a mere few weeks of his entire career, precisely because the area is so physically inhospitable for humans. His narratives of manning the border were less about potential battles and tactics, and more about the sheer physicality of enduring the elements; the difficulties of frostbite, blizzards, and minus-sixty-degree-Celsius weather at twenty-thousand feet. The ebbs and flows of snow, rains, and seasonal changes determine when, where, and how such borders can be approached, produced, and maintained. It is here that the temporality and inconstancy of vertical border safeguarding is brought to the fore.

Frozen-over mountain passes and landslides can make a high-altitude border inaccessible. So how do the limitations of human activity intersect with state attempts to control this combination of height and time; in Stuart Elden's words, attempts to "secure the volume"?[1] Much of the existing border studies literature still deals with crossborder mobility happening along some sort of linear, two-dimensional plane. I want to draw attention to other volumes and dimensions—particularly the combination of verticality (mountains) with temporality in two ways: seasonal bordering in the form of "skirmish seasons," and teleological bordering; the future-oriented growth of the border into its intended nation-state shape. My argument is that there is always a *lag*: an attempt by states to access a border without ever quite reaching it. This is bordering in a four-dimensional perspective: the border cannot physically be reached, but is continually aspired to. There is a need to keep up the pace.

So how do you catch up with an elusive border?

The disputed western Himalayan border area between Pakistan, India, and China is currently facing the consequences of climate change, such as increased landslides that affect existing infrastructure and diminished grazing land for cattle and yak, drawing both human and nonhuman actors further into the production of geopolitical tensions in the borderlands. Seasonal changes, such as the freezing over of mountain passes, are processes that contribute to both human and state inaccessibility, particularly in mountainous—vertical—regions of the world.[2] The oscillation between seasons; the material remains left on the ground by different political and nonpolitical actors; the movements of animals along established routes as well as across borders—all of these are particular to the passage of time in a vertical dimension. In this chapter, I look at several examples of how temporality intersects with vertical bordering in this region. A deeper exploration into the attempt of states to access such a border—and yet never quite reaching it—is crucial for a broader, comparative understanding of border*ing* in general.

Bordering at Twenty Thousand Feet

What do bordering practices look like in mountainous regions where altitude and the threat of landslides are obstacles to long-term human inhabitation? In tandem with anthropological work on deterritorialization and globalization that emerged in the late 1990s and beyond, border studies has brought forth a sizable amount of literature that traverses the border-as-line metaphor.[3] Working beyond nation-state boundaries, scholars have discussed alternative border regions that decenter area studies, such as Willem van Schendel's proposal to imagine the possibility of "Zomia," a coherent area crossing Southeast Asia, South Asia, East Asia, and Central Asia.[4] Others have looked beyond nation-state–led battles over territory to focus on bottom-up studies of how various stakeholders perform border control in areas such as the US-Mexico and Central Asian borders and along the riverine boundaries of the Mekong.[5] More recently, human geographers have critically discussed the notion of fuzzy or flexible borders, borders-as-seams, and fragmented borders in the form of enclaves.[6] Keeping in line with this critical trajectory of work, I too am interested in focusing on diverse experiences of border*ing* rather than on an entity like "the border"; reflecting how human negotiations over state borderlines necessarily involve the landscape, seasons, and all of their contingencies.[7] In the Himalayas for instance, yaks follow a seasonal delimitation of grazing area, bringing them both closer to and farther from borderlines depending on the time of year.

A volumetric perspective on bordering practices should therefore also include an extra dimension—temporality. Although the temporality of bordering has been examined in studies of migration across borders—such as waiting for visas, for decisions on deportation, and the migrant experience of interminable waiting, as well as some discussion on the necessary future orientation of bordering, as it "anticipat[es] potential violence"—time as a dimension in bordering practices is less understood, save for Helga Tawil-Souri's powerful essay on the temporality of Palestinian checkpoints.[8] Sarah Green has proposed using the metaphor of a *tidemark* left by waves on a beach to give a better sense of the historical contingency of the border—"what is left after some kind of past activity has occurred, and often implies more activity to come."[9] The tidemark is a way to work with both space and historical time, with the understanding of "both space and time as being lively and contingent."[10] In this sense, then, Chinese officials who establish a trade mart when the snows have melted, British colonial officers who plot a line on a map, Indian soldiers who dig an irrigation canal, and even yak that graze in borderland pastures are unequal but active agents in bordering processes, leaving material remains that can very well determine the size, space, and duration of the border.

Bordering processes are subject to events that are only partly determined by human interactions. They therefore force us to look beyond the landscape as a neutral or static backdrop to activities that happen on or with it.[11] In the Himalayas, for instance, most forward border outposts (BOPs) range between nine thousand and twenty thousand feet, where the higher altitudes are at levels beyond long-term human inhabitability. For army members not used to such high altitudes, their short-term residency in places like the Siachen Glacier at twenty-thousand feet involves significant preparation. This involves at least two days at progressively higher altitudes with lengthy moments of rest in between, goggles to prevent snow blindness, insulated boots to prevent frostbite, and so forth.[12] The infrastructure around the outposts is often cut off by snowstorms in the winter, so the shape of the border always depends on which BOPs are even accessible during any given time period. The border expands or contracts depending on how low the snows accumulate and how accessible the bridges and outposts are. For instance, if a trader brings medicinal herbs across a Himalayan checkpoint, the trader may be delayed for indefinite periods of time due to landslides and random body searches, or they may have to go through a different entry point depending on which season the trip occurs in, for the mountain passes may be completely washed out or covered in snow.

These experiences of mountain bordering chime with what James Scott has called the *friction of terrain* or the *friction of distance*, where inhabiting or travelling across a particular terrain—whether mountain, jungle, desert, or ocean—is part of the lived experience of the landscape, not easily represented on any map.[13] For instance, if someone asks how far it is from one mountain village to another, the answer is usually given in terms of time rather than units of distance: "It will take five hours," or, "It will take two days." This is because landslides, monsoons, potholed roads, strikes, border checks, blizzards, and snow all modify the answer to how far it is and when one can cross. The answer also depends on the vertical dimension of the journey; if you are in a small mountain village but need to travel to a town in the valley, it will take you less time to walk down the mountain than it would for you to climb up it. Thus, the combination of the spatiality and temporality of lived experiences in mountainous areas produces a *lag* between the representation of the landscape (such as a dot or a line on a map, or as described by nonlocal state officials) and the physical experience of traveling through the actual terrain. Even a map with topographical markers does not prepare anyone for the underbrush that needs clearing or the landslide that bars the way. But the fact that gaps exist between experiences and representations of terrain is hardly groundbreaking, as there is always a disjuncture between representation of space and lived reality. What is more curious, however, is what happens when high-altitude features come into play against temporality (for example, the time the accessible bridge takes to appear after the snow melts down the mountain face). It is the futility, the inaccessibility, the *impossibility or possibility* of border crossing that is then brought to the fore. And this has profound implications for the balance of power in border areas.

In an essay that explains this kind of friction in relation to the state, Sankaran Krishna looks at the ongoing process of nation building in India through cartography, stating that the creation of the shape of a nation is more than just the technical mapping of a place; it is also used to describe practices of inscribing "something called India" in the media, in rhetoric, in politics. Stemming from what he calls the "creation-by-amputation" of the Indian nation, there remains a sense that its contested borders—especially with China, Pakistan, and Bangladesh—are not yet complete and in a perpetual state of suspension.[14] According to Krishna, anxieties toward such representations of national identity are acute, and it is in encounters between the state and people at borderlines that these "cartographic anxieties" are most telling and often violent.[15] In the Himalayan borderlands, some of these frictions and gaps—and their subsequent anxieties—only become visible or obvious when both vertical and temporal dimensions are considered. For instance, a military breach across a border can only happen when one party can actually physically approach that border area. As a result, there is a period of time called *skirmish season*; several months during the spring thaw and summer in the Himalayas where some borders become more contentious than others, and when cartographic anxieties are at their peak.

Securing the Volume on Himalayan Borders

The historical and imperial geopolitics of drawing border lines and the establishment of military outposts across the Himalayan range have generated multiple cases of cartographic anxiety, where the shape of the nation-state is always being made and yet never complete. Both the Line of Control (LoC) on the western borders of the Himalayas (the line between India-controlled Jammu and Kashmir, and Pakistan-controlled Kashmir and Gilgit-Baltistan) and the Line of Actual Control (LAC) between India and China (the de facto boundary between India and China in general, marked by considerably more "empty" areas) are based on indeterminate demarcations. Parts of the LAC were never even laid down on a map and simply left open to modification, resulting in giant swathes of no-man's lands.[16] Much has been written about the history and contestation of the various disputed areas along this range. But beyond the obvious tensions between Pakistan, India, and China over national sovereignty and territoriality, the fact that these disputes are both affected and produced by the gaps between maps and *vertical* lived experience actually necessitates that we pay attention to other dimensions of bordering. In many areas along the LoC and LAC, people simply cannot physically dwell in the high-altitude, craggy, mountainous, or forested terrain, so border outposts must be built elsewhere, often thirty kilometers before or after the official border as represented on a map. The very lack of any line beyond NJ9842—the northernmost "dead end" of the LoC—"has led to the existence of a contested space in an area where no humans have ever lived, or would wish to live, or could live for protracted periods of time even if they wanted to."[17] These are the experiences of bordering from a four-dimensional perspective: the border cannot ever physically be reached, but is continually aspired to. As a case in point, the 114 Helicopter Unit of the Siachen Glacier has a motto: "We do the difficult as routine; the impossible may take a bit longer."

Even in the case of several Himalayan border areas where the altitude is too high for long-term human inhabitation or where the densely forested no-man's lands are too wide to be fully securitized, the militarized border still remains maintained by human (or, increasingly, human plus computer or drone) capabilities. Technology assists temporal reach by allowing the state to linger a bit longer than it is physically able to do.[18] At least 25 percent of the BOPs along the Indian borders—such as Tripura-Bangladesh and many points in Ladakh—are air-maintained by helicopters; in other words, personnel and/or supplies are dropped down and picked up for limited amounts of time, usually for about eight to ten weeks at a time. Most of these outposts are between twenty and forty kilometers from the actual border. Asking who controls the resources that circulate through volumetric space is crucial to a better understanding of how inequality is produced in contested areas, especially those that extend above, below, and beyond a simple border line on a map.[19] In the case of the Himalayas, bordering practices are indeed about "securing the volume" and about placing limits on and across various geographical scales. But what happens when the full volume cannot be secured?

Several recent incidents on the western Himalayan borders of India, Pakistan, and China illustrate how such anxieties are produced through the attempts to secure volume in fragmented vertical spaces. To exemplify, on April 15, 2013, Chinese soldiers placed either four or seven tents (the number is unclear) somewhere between ten and nineteen kilometers from the LAC near Daulat Beg Oldi (DBO) on the Xinjiang-Ladakh border of Aksai Chin, 150 kilometers away from the nearest human settlement. Because the LAC has never been agreed upon, there has never been a single border line in this area. Instead there are several lines; for instance, the line that the Chinese went up to in 1962; the line that the British established in 1865 and the Indians now claim; a number of border posts that the Chinese put up in 1958; as well as air-maintained Indian outposts in scattered areas along the region. All of these dots and lines on a map make up a rough area of approximately forty thousand square kilometers, not manned by either group. During this particular incident, the Chinese happened to go up to the farthest point that they had reached in 1962. The Indian army responded by placing their own tents within three hundred meters of the Chinese tents. In retaliation, two Chinese military helicopters entered Indian airspace far away in another part of the disputed zone; several hundred kilometers south of where the original incident occurred. The standoff was said to have been resolved when Indian forces agreed to dismantle some border posts and security cameras in yet *another* part of the LAC, four hundred kilometers away from where the incident took place.

Later that year—and again several hundred kilometers from the location of the original incident—five Ladakhi nomads and their cattle were detained by the Chinese People's Liberation Army (PLA) after they had been found grazing in disputed Chinese territory. This was not news, however. Since 2011, many of the Ladakhi nomads in Chumar had reported to the local officials that their grazing pastures were shrinking, and that they needed to head closer to the LAC to maintain "adequate livelihoods." Since the April 2013 incident at DBO, however, the Indo-Tibetan Border Police (ITBP) began to place stricter limitations on the mobility of its own nomad citizens and cattle. According to some local villagers, this sparked off angry sentiments amongst several nomads who continued to head to the shrinking pastures and were then held by the PLA for several hours—along with their animals. Although all of these incidents may have been related, they involved different actors. They were also spatially fragmented, occurring in different areas, different altitudes, different times, and leaving different tidemarks behind. They erupted in bursts, punctuated by weeks where nothing happened. Furthermore, border disputes in this region are subject to temporal and seasonal fluctuations. The skirmish season is indeed a real thing; a moment or moments when soldiers, cattle, yak, and nomads can actually access the high-altitude border areas, but are liable to be detained should they venture too close to the contested areas. Disputes occur from April or May as the snows melt, to late autumn when the mountains are frozen over. The LAC is relatively quiet between January and March. However, according to local Ladakhi officials, skirmish season is beginning earlier every year, due to climate-related shrinking of grazing pastures and easier access to bunkers and outposts, if they are not destroyed due to avalanches, another factor in this increasingly volatile environment.

From a distance, these events all add up to a single "border incident" with a duration lasting nine months, and constitute yet another example of how the contingencies of a fourth, temporal, dimension are intertwined. Time and space become collapsed; multiple events merge into one incident; the tidemarks flatten into one border line. Although these separate events leave different tidemarks on the ground, and although the skirmishes only occur when the areas become seasonally habitable, they are portrayed by nation-states as a single ongoing battle between Pakistan and India, or India and China, as well as a military triumph against the high-altitude elements. In actuality, we have various human groups pushing upward and forward but later retreating, leaving tidemarks of material remains behind: flags, tents, dead bodies. High-altitude battles often feature the trope of human expertise against nature, as well as the rational expansion of capitalism though the securing of volume. The flattening or collapsing of volume *and* time into more securable dimensionalities is one way for the state to portray its progress, and to make territory and people more legible.[20]

A fully working, stable border is needed for the shape of the state to coalesce more clearly, but in the volatile Himalayan environment, it is not yet there. This not-yet-there calls for state-led measures to push for the kind of infrastructure that will help to define the shape of the state, in areas where the land cannot possibly hold it. Military outposts in the western Himalayas and crossborder trade are in fact interlinked. The Indian Centre of Defence (ICD) not only sets up BOPs for security, but is also in charge of establishing Integrated Check Posts (ICPs) for crossborder trade. The problem in setting up these outposts and checkpoints, according to an ICD representative, is the large swathes of unmanned border areas along the LAC. "Presently, the BOPs are positioned at a distance of 30 to 40 km from each other. It is difficult for the forty or so people manning each BOP to monitor the distance between the two posts."[21] At the time of writing this chapter, over forty new BOPs were reportedly being set up on the Indian side of the northeast Sino-Indian border in Arunachal Pradesh and Sikkim in order to improve national security, and would at the very same time act as border trade checkpoints to increase trade relations with neighboring countries, namely China, Bangladesh, and Nepal: "These BOPs will facilitate maintaining of security as well as provide better connectivity and accessibility for the local people. . . . We have approved the setting up of 37 additional BOPs in Arunachal Pradesh and five in Sikkim. The additional BOPs besides strengthening border security will facilitate the people living in those areas."[22]

To what extent and exactly how it will improve the lives of the local people remains to be seen. In order to secure the volumetric territory they claim for both security and trade, and in order to establish these BOPs and ICPs, India and China must make use of technology that enables people to survive in these altitudes. It is through these means that this vast area of forty thousand square kilometers that is not inhabitable can be secured and animated. This "border work" is not simply a matter of delegating surveillance and presence to machines, however.[23] Helicopters may bring supplies and personnel to the tops of mountains, but they are merely facilitators for human bordering practices. It is here that we see the underlying significance of the tropes of time in the mobilization of this technology: helicopters dropping off supplies, or "super-high-altitude clothing" unveiled at the Defence–Indian Technical Textile Association joint seminar. There is a sense that borders are incomplete, in formation, and that more border work remains to be done. Infrastructures such as borders—as fuzzy as these ones are—are often of temporalities that "do not inhabit human lifetimes."[24] Neither country is currently able to fully possess or secure their territory up to the borderlines they both claim, but they are continually making progress toward these goals. And this is where the second temporal aspect of bordering is visible. In addition to skirmish seasons, there is also a teleological aspect to bordering practices. In other words, there is a temporal horizon of bordering—at least in some of these Himalayan areas—that involves the future possibility of total mastery over the high-altitude elements: "We cannot totally control the border yet, but we will." Once again, this exposes the *lag* between the collapsed volume of the contour of the nation as it is described or represented by both states (in different configurations of course), and its shape as it is actually experienced: fragmented BOPs forty kilometers away from each other, for example. Krishna's cartographic anxiety, of never fitting the actual border, thus comes to the fore in this vertical dimension. But the idea always remains that the nation will eventually grow into its cartographically defined shape; the nation will eventually grow into its intended "geobody."[25] There is a sense that, ultimately, *time* will bring the actual contour of the nation—as dynamic as it is—in line with its cartographic outline.

Acting East and Opening the West

Prime Minister Narendra Modi's revival of India's "Look East" policy (renamed the "Act East" policy in 2014) has meant that the current government is seriously undertaking several plans to strengthen existing ties with its East and Southeast Asian neighbors. At the same time, China's "Open Up the West" scheme, as well as its trade-centered Belt and Road Initiative, are also underway. These long-term policy plans feature extensive infrastructural expansion into their respective borderlands. China's road and rail network, for instance, is steadily progressing toward its Nepali and Indian borders, with the Qinghai-Tibet railway moving further toward Nepal, the Nathu La border in Sikkim, and to Nyingtri, toward the Indian BOPs in Arunachal Pradesh. Such macrolevel plans are premised precisely on the "not-yet-there" aspect of bordering, so the disputed borderlands along China and India remain the focal point for bringing humans closer to their intended cartographic outlines. Yet these are outlines with multiple iterations, outlines that have messily overlapped or are fragmented, never fitting together neatly like puzzle pieces.

Paying attention to lag and the temporal aspects of securing volume may indeed open up some new theoretical avenues for border studies, but it remains methodologically quite ambitious. If infrastructures last beyond lifetimes, how exactly do we study future-oriented borders "on the ground," so to speak? At what point in time do we begin such a study? When do we end it? Yet if the goal of the state is to secure uninhabitable vertical border regions for territorial limitation and openings to new markets, then it may be possible to focus on specific events that happen inside the lag between national outlines and the push to reach them. This may be done on a case-by-case basis—in snippets and snapshots, as was attempted here. Furthermore, despite the fact that reports of additional BOPs and the introduction of drone maintenance in these remote mountain borders paints a picture of imminent Sino-Indian military clashes in the near future, it is very difficult to tell if indeed skirmishes are going to increase in these high-altitude borderlands. Himalayan glaciers are melting at extreme and alarming rates. On the one hand, with the continuing climate crisis, skirmish season in the western Himalayas may in fact—as mentioned above—be extending earlier every year. As the bare face of the mountains continues to be exposed for longer periods of time and nomads continue to search for better grazing land closer to the border area, they are increasingly seen as breaching military zones. On the other hand, the melting glaciers and snows in both sections of the mountain range have already begun to exacerbate continued avalanches and devastating landslides. Might these disasters work in other ways, by acting as a stopgap to skirmish season? Only time will tell.

NOTES

I am extremely grateful to Franck Billé, Jeffrey Twu, and Karine Gagné for their remarks on various versions of this paper. I also wish to thank the audience members at both the American Anthropological Association meeting in Washington,

DC, in 2017 and the Asian Borderlands Conference in Kathmandu in 2016 for their helpful comments and questions.

1 Stuart Elden, "Secure the Volume: Vertical Geopolitics and the Depth of Power," *Political Geography* 34 (2013): 35–51.

2 For more on securitization in a vertical dimension, see Stephen Graham, "Vertical Geopolitics: Baghdad and After," *Antipode* 36, no. 1 (2004): 12–23; and Eyal Weizman, *Hollow Land: Israel's Architecture of Occupation* (London: Verso, 2007).

3 See, for example, Josiah M. Heyman, "Putting Power in the Anthropology of Bureaucracy: The Immigration and Naturalization Service at the Mexico-United States Border," *Current Anthropology* 36, no. 2 (1995): 261–87; Corey Johnson, Reece Jones, Anssi Paasi, Louise Amoore, Alison Mountz, Mark Salter, and Chris Rumford, "Interventions on Thinking 'the Border' in Border Studies," *Political Geography* 30 (2011): 61–69; Willem van Schendel, "Geographies of Knowing, Geographies of Ignorance: Jumping Scale in Southeast Asia," *Environment and Planning D: Society and Space* 20 (2002): 647–68; and Thomas W. Wilson and Hastings Donnan, eds., *Border Identities: Nation and State at International Frontiers* (Cambridge: Cambridge University Press, 1998).

4 van Schendel, "Geographies of Knowing," 647–68.

5 Peter Andreas, *Border Games: Policing the US-Mexico Divide* (Ithaca, NY: Cornell University Press, 2000); Sarah Green, "Performing Border in the Aegean," *Journal of Cultural Economy* 3, no. 2 (2010): 261–78; Madeleine Reeves, *Border Work: Spatial Lives of the State in Rural Central Asia* (Ithaca, NY: Cornell University Press, 2014); Andrew Walker, *The Legend of the Golden Boat: Regulation, Trade and Traders in the Borderlands of Laos, Thailand, China, and Burma* (Honolulu: University of Hawaii Press, 1999).

6 Jason Cons, "Narrating Boundaries: Framing and Contesting Suffering, Community, and Belonging in Enclaves along the India-Bangladesh Border," *Political Geography* 35 (2013): 37–46; Deborah Cowen, "A Geography of Logistics: Market Authority and the Security of Supply Chains," *Annals of the Association of American Geographers* 100, no. 3 (2010): 600–620; and Johnson et al., "Interventions on Thinking 'the Border.'"

7 Juliet Fall, *Drawing the Line: Nature, Hybridity and Politics in Transboundary Spaces* (Aldershot: Ashgate, 2005); Liisa Malkki, *Purity and Exile: Violence, Memory, and National Cosmology among Hutu Refugees in Tanzania* (Chicago: Chicago University Press, 1995); Janet Sturgeon, *Border Landscapes: The Politics of Akha Land Use in China and Thailand* (Seattle: University of Washington Press, 2007).

8 Ruben Andersson, "Time and the Migrant Other: European Border Controls and the Temporal Economics of Illegality," *American Anthropologist* 114 (2014): 795–809; Melanie B. E. Griffiths, "Out of Time: The Temporal Uncertainties of Refused Asylum Seekers and Immigration Detainees," *Journal of Ethnic and Migration Studies* 40, no. 12 (2014): 1991–2009; Heyman, "Putting Power in the Anthropology of Bureaucracy"; Malkki, *Purity and Exile*; Anna Secor, "Between Longing and Despair: State, Space and Subjectivity in Turkey," *Environment and Planning D: Society and Space* 24 (2007): 33–52; and Henk van Houtum, Olivier Kramsch, and Wolfgang Zierhofer, eds., *B/Ordering Space* (Aldershot: Ashgate, 2005). The quote comes

from Natalie Konopinski, "Borderline Temporalities and Security Anticipations: Standing Guard in Tel Aviv," *Etnofoor* 26, no. 1 (2014): 74. Helga Tawil-Souri writes that "checkpoints perform temporal work," in "Checkpoint Time," *Qui Parle* 26, no. 2 (2017): 386.

9   Sarah Green, "Lines, Traces and Tidemarks: Reflections on Forms of Borderliness," COST Action ISO803, working paper no. 1 (2009): 7, http://www.eastbordnet.org/wiki/Documents/Lines_Traces_Tidemarks_Nicosia_2009_090416.pdf.

10   Green, "Lines, Traces and Tidemarks," 17; see also Hastings Donnan, Madeleine Hurd, and Carolin Leutloff-Grandits, eds., *Migrating Borders and Moving Times: Temporality and the Crossing of Borders in Europe* (Manchester: Manchester University Press, 2017).

11   Tim Ingold, "The Temporality of the Landscape," *World Archaeology* 25, no. 2 (1993): 152. Also see Karine Gagné, "Cultivating Ice over Time: On the Idea of Timeless Knowledge and Places in the Himalayas," *Anthropologica* 58, no 2 (2016): 193–210.

12   For the voices and materiality of being stationed on the LoC, see for example works by Mona Bhan, "Border Practices: Labour and Nationalism among Brogpas of Ladakh," *Contemporary South Asia* 16, no. 2 (2008): 139–57; Baptist Coelho, *Siachen Glacier* (art installation), website of Baptist Coelho, 2015, http://www.baptistcoelho.com/project_content.php?category_id=63&artwork_id=189; Virendra Verma, *Chewang Richen: A Legend in His Own Time* (Dehradun: Young India Publications, 1998).

13   James Scott, *The Art of Not Being Governed: An Anarchist History of Upland Southeast Asia* (New Haven, CT: Yale University Press, 2009).

14   Sankaran Krishna, "Cartographic Anxiety: Mapping the Body Politic in India," *Alternatives: Global, Local, Political* 19, no. 4 (1994): 509.

15   Krishna, "Cartographic Anxiety," 511.

16   Neville Maxwell, *India's China War* (New York: Pantheon, 1970).

17   Feryal Ali Gauhar, "Siachen: The Place of Wild Roses," *Dawn*, November 2, 2014, http://www.dawn.com/news/1141375.

18   Ravi Baghel and Marcus Nüsser, "Securing the Heights: The Vertical Dimension of the Siachen Conflict between India and Pakistan in the Eastern Karakoram," *Political Geography* 48 (2015): 24–36.

19   Gavin Bridge, "Territory: Now in 3D!" *Political Geography* 34 (2013): 57.

20   James Scott, *Seeing Like a State: How Certain Schemes to Improve the Human Condition Have Failed* (New Haven, CT: Yale University Press, 2002).

21   "Centre to Set up 42 ITBP Border Outposts," *New Indian Express*, June 3, 2015, http://www.newindianexpress.com/nation/Centre-to-Set-Up-42-ITBP-Border-Outposts/2015/06/03/article2847427.ece.

22   "Centre to Set up 42 ITBP Border Outposts."

23   Reeves, *Border Work*.

24   Geoffrey C. Bowker, "Temporality," Theorizing the Contemporary, *Cultural Anthropology*, 2015, culanth.org/fieldsights/temporality.

25 Itty Abraham, "A Doubled Geography: Geobody, Land and Sea in Indian Se-
curity Thought," in *New Directions in India's Foreign Policy: Theory and Praxis*, ed.
Harsh V. Pant, 85–105 (Cambridge: Cambridge University Press, 2019); Franck
Billé, "Introduction to 'Cartographic Anxieties,'" *Cross-Currents: East Asian
History and Culture Review* 21 (2016): 1–18, http://cross-currents.berkeley.edu/e
-journal/issue-21; Sumathi Ramaswamy, "Visualising India's Geo-Body: Globes,
Maps, Bodyscapes," *Contributions to Indian Sociology* 36, nos. 1 and 2 (2002): 151–89;
Thongchai Winichakul, *Siam Mapped: A History of the Geo-Body of a Nation* (Hono-
lulu: University of Hawaii Press, 1994).

5   Traffic

Authorizing Airspace,
Appifying Governance

MARCEL LAFLAMME

Pete spotted the brown car first, parked along an access road near the section he was spraying for a farmer west of Fargo. Half an hour later, it was on the move, and a gray car pulled up beside it at the other end of the field. The two drivers stood and talked for a while, and Pete wondered: "What are they doing out here?" He kept working his way across the section, flying mile-long passes from north to south and then back again, applying a herbicide to the crops below. Four hours in, he dove down for another pass and suddenly saw a drone beneath him and behind his wing, not 250 feet away. His pulse was pounding as he leveled out and then climbed to a safe distance, reaching for his radio to figure out what the hell was going on. Getting no response, Pete headed back to the hangar, where his boss was incensed. A propeller strike would have caused upward of $80,000 in damage, plus downtime during a growing season that lasts just a few months on the Upper Great Plains. But Pete's first thought was for his wife and kids: life as an aerial applicator is dangerous enough without a carbon-fiber camera coming through your windshield.

It was the summer of 2014 when Pete recounted this story to me, just as I was wrapping up a year of research on efforts to position the state of North Dakota as a center of the unmanned aviation industry. Technically, I knew, drones like the one that Pete encountered were not supposed to be flying outside of strictly regulated test sites. But it was no secret that companies had sprung up to collect crop imagery in this way, and the farmer whose field Pete was spraying had evidently hired one of them. It was a delicate situation: the farmer was a good customer, and so Pete's boss was reluctant to stir up trouble by reporting the incident to the authorities. Yet norms had been violated, and the prospect of a midair collision was one that could not be taken lightly. "If another pilot got that close to me without talking about it, I'm probably going to get ugly with him," Pete vented. Ordinarily, aerial applicators used the radio to sort out conflicting flight paths; failing that, they could at least acknowledge each other's presence by emitting puffs of smoke from their wings. But the drone was associated with a new kind of airspace user, one who did not necessarily think to take other traffic into account. "To a ground operator not used to being around airplanes," Pete reflected, "what's distance? A half mile feels like forever on a gravel road."

By the mid-twentieth century, promoting the safe separation of air traffic was understood to be part of how sovereign states governed in three dimensions. The transfer of radar technology from military to civilian settings brought vast expanses of airspace under positive control. Far from all-seeing, though, these technical systems supported processes of cooperation and coordination among skilled air traffic controllers.[1] In this chapter, I show how the maturation and proliferation of unmanned aircraft or drones has posed challenges to existing regimes of traffic management and given rise to new modes of volumetric sovereignty. In particular, I highlight the growing importance of what Keller Easterling has called *extrastatecraft*, infrastructural orchestrations that are conducted "outside of, in addition to, and sometimes even in partnership with statecraft."[2] Admittedly, the extent to which air traffic control remains the direct responsibility of the US government is exceptional in a global context, as new public management paradigms have prompted many countries to transfer system management to various corporate entities.[3] Still, I argue that the particular form of marketization that is underway in the United States reveals how new technologies are transforming the way in which sovereignty is governed across borders as well as within them.

It is no accident that the smartphone is becoming a key site for the governance of drone mobilities, since both consumer technologies followed on the miniaturization of electromechanical systems and advances in microprocessor design during the first decade of the twenty-first century. As smartphones became increasingly ubiquitous, software developers looked to them as a platform for the delivery of digital tools called apps that would accomplish specific tasks in a richly visual way. Media scholars Jeremy Wade Morris and Sarah

Murray insightfully frame apps as "mundane software," in the double sense of being ordinary and readily accessible out in the world.[4] In what follows, I consider an initiative to provide US drone operators with expedited access to controlled airspace through the mediation of app-based service providers. Insofar as this program manages to automate the process of airspace authorization, it can be approached in the context of concerns about "the way in which digital data is troubling and reconstituting expertise."[5] Yet because the provision of traffic management expertise is bound up with specific political formations, the program also opens out onto broader questions about how and to whom sovereign states grant the authority to govern the sky.

At the Data Exchange

In 2016, two full years after Pete's near miss, the Federal Aviation Administration (FAA) finally issued a set of regulations around the use of drones for commercial purposes. Under these regulations, a drone weighing less than fifty-five pounds could be flown by a licensed operator up to a maximum altitude of four hundred feet. Yet this permission was not unconditional: if the flight was going to take place at night, over people, or beyond the operator's line of sight, then a waiver request would need to be filed at least ninety days in advance. Flights that would do none of those things but would take place within five miles of an airport could go through a separate authorization process, which was supposed to be streamlined. But an audit found that the office at the FAA charged with reviewing these requests was swamped, even after hiring additional contractors: wait times for a routine airspace authorization hovered around six weeks, frustrating business owners who were trying to play by the rules but who found themselves outmaneuvered by less scrupulous competitors. With almost four thousand requests coming in each month, the agency was under pressure to make the process more efficient or risk losing control of it altogether.

Enter the Low Altitude Authorization and Notification Capability (LAANC), which was introduced on a trial basis in November 2017 and rolled out nationwide during 2018. Rather than having a human analyst review authorization requests on a case-by-case basis, LAANC converts these requests into a machine-readable format and matches them against a repository of airport facility maps and other data sources; if no conflicts are detected, then an authorization is transmitted to the requester in near real time. Notably, the concept of operations for LAANC stipulates that the program "will not involve or result in a government acquisition of software programs or systems."[6]

Instead, LAANC operates as a public–private partnership between the FAA and so-called service suppliers, technology companies that build (and seek to monetize) the software by which drone operators make airspace requests. This division of labor relieves the FAA of the responsibility for developing its own software internally, and it aligns with the agency's stated aim to "foster a free market environment" for drone service providers.[7]

It would be easy to interpret this arrangement in terms of a broader deregulation agenda ushered in by the election of Donald Trump in 2016. Trump did initially endorse a plan to privatize the US air traffic control system (before backing down in the face of opposition from his rural base), and his secretary of transportation, Elaine Chao, clearly telegraphed her desire to remove government roadblocks and empower the drone industry during her Senate confirmation hearings. But the vision of coordination among public and private entities behind LAANC actually has its roots in the Obama administration, most proximately in a traffic management system concept being developed by NASA but more fundamentally, I argue, in an embrace of open civic data.[8] In this paradigm, public agencies make the data that they collect and produce freely available on a nonexclusive basis, and then private-sector "infomediaries" develop products and services that build on this data and add value to it.[9] For LAANC service suppliers, access to an FAA-operated data exchange is predicated on compliance with agency standards and interoperability with other stakeholders. The model is thus one of virtuous, market-based competition on the basis of a level playing field constituted by public data. Yet, as these emerging techniques of extrastatecraft are codified, the question of their relationship to state sovereignty is often elided. Hence, the LAANC concept of operations insists that the automatic authorization process "is not a delegation of authority by the FAA to the [service supplier. Service suppliers] assist operators to identify preapproved authorizations as defined by regulations in collaboration with the FAA."[10]

It is, I suggest, in this gap between delegation and collaboration that new modes of volumetric sovereignty are starting to coalesce. In the next section, I seek to chart their contours by offering a walkthrough of one app being used by US drone operators to request airspace authorizations, drawing on a methodology elaborated by scholars of new media.[11] The researcher-initiated walkthrough, while no substitute for in situ ethnographic research with app users, does offer a structured look at a complex digital object demanding both technical and cultural analysis. The walkthrough tacks between direct observation and manipulation of the app's interface, and a document-based assessment of the app's environment of expected use. In the context of LAANC, I take this environment to include the data sources and flows that give the app its dynamism, as well as those conditions that elude datafication and inscribe the app within a broader ecology of aviation media.[12] To trace these admittedly arcane processes is to grasp how both sky and state are being remade by digital technologies and their remainders.

On (and Off) the Flight Deck

Named for the windy stretch of beach where the Wright brothers first flew in 1903, Kittyhawk is one of the leading apps for planning, monitoring, and managing data associated with drone flights. Created in 2015 as a tool for flight logging, the app rapidly evolved new features and today its San Francisco–based developers describe it as a "single system of record for drone operations."[13] In published interviews, Kittyhawk cofounders Joshua Ziering and Jon Hegranes describe their target user as a business that had previously hired external service providers but now wants to move its drone program in-house. Outside expertise is no longer necessary, they contend, given the development of what Kittyhawk's website calls "software anyone can use."[14] Indeed, Ziering provocatively argues that "good software is going to abstract away the notion of the drone," decentering the airframe and the details of its configuration in favor of a focus on value delivered through a dematerialized stream of data-driven insight.[15]

I downloaded Kittyhawk from the App Store, where it was categorized under "Business," to my iPhone XR in December 2018. The fact that I was able to do so at all distinguishes Kittyhawk from competitor products like the Verizon-owned Skyward, which cannot be found in consumer-facing app stores and must be demoed by a sales representative. Kittyhawk's discoverability on these platforms reflects its present commitment to continue offering a free product to individual end users, an important segment of its original user base. As the app took me through the process of creating an account, I was never asked to choose between free and paid plans: it was only upon trying to access specific features like streaming media that I was invited to "unlock this powerful feature with a Kittyhawk Enterprise account." Significantly, this requester directed me to a contact form that did not include any information about pricing, although as recently as September 2018 a pricing page on the Kittyhawk website offered a small business plan for twenty-four dollars per month per user as well as a "solopreneur" option. The collapse of these categories into a single "Enterprise" tier indexes a strategic decision to focus on larger, more lucrative clients, but it also allows Kittyhawk to set pricing without being constrained by a uniform, publicly accessible rate schedule.

Upon opening the Kittyhawk app, the default view is divided between a map of the user's current location and two ribbon-style control panels, labeled "Flight Conditions" and "Flight Deck." The former panel, which is dynamically updated, shows environmental conditions including wind speed, visibility, and cloud cover, underlining values of possible concern for a drone operator in either yellow or red. The latter allows the user to scroll through an array of tools for completing checklists, reviewing advisory notices, and even controlling a drone from within the app. Thus, requesting airspace authorizations through LAANC is only one feature of Kittyhawk, although it is seen as a critical one. When Kittyhawk was not invited to participate in the evaluation phase of LAANC, Ziering groused that "giving certain companies months of exclusive access to a precious resource is at best anticompetitive."[16] Within months, though, Kittyhawk had lined up a partnership with the Boeing subsidiary Jeppesen, which came with an infusion of capital and the use of Jeppesen's electronic navigation charts but also with access to the LAANC data exchange. By forging this alliance, Kittyhawk managed to reroute sovereign power around what it viewed as an arbitrary blockage and to stay apace of its competitors in the scramble for market position. In October 2018, the FAA announced the selection of Kittyhawk as a LAANC service supplier in its own right; a video released by the company following the announcement hailed LAANC as a "major innovation" and noted that "we're really excited to offer it."[17]

Before requesting an airspace authorization through the Kittyhawk app, users must complete a "LAANC Readiness" checklist. Users are asked to supply their Part 107 Certificate number, which drone operators receive upon completion of a licensing process that includes a written exam. Users also need to have at least one aircraft registered with the FAA and entered into Kittyhawk's "Assets" module. Yet the most prosaic part of the checklist may, in fact, say the most about the tension between state and market that is at the heart of LAANC. Without any explanation, users are asked to verify the phone number that they supplied upon initially creating an account with Kittyhawk: a six-digit verification code is sent to the user via text message, and once the code is typed into the app the status of the user's phone number changes to "Verified." Phone verification is a fairly common security measure used by app developers, but it carries a particular significance for LAANC service suppliers. The LAANC concept of operations specifies that "for the purposes of communication between air traffic control and operators during flight events, a valid U.S. phone number . . . that can be used to reach the operator at any time during

flight operations will be required for all notifications and authorizations."[18]
Thus, even as app developers like Kittyhawk aspire to create "a single system of
record for drone operations," the FAA reserves the right to communicate with
operators outside of the app through the residual medium of telephony.[19] By
giving service suppliers the task of collecting and validating phone numbers,
the FAA at once absolves itself of the responsibility to manage personally iden-
tifiable information and retains the prerogative to disintermediate the service
supplier, reasserting the dyad of sovereign and subject with an old-fashioned
voice call.

Once the "LAANC Readiness" checklist is complete, Kittyhawk users can
request an airspace authorization from a menu at the bottom of the app's default view. On one screen, the user enters the date, time, and duration of the
requested authorization. Next, the app loads a map on which the user can
define their intended flight area: a shaded circle indicates the five-mile radius
of controlled airspace around larger airports, while yellow and green gridlines
show the altitudes up to which drone operations have been preapproved by air
traffic controllers at those airports. The Kittyhawk user drags a pin marked
with the company's cloverleaf logo to the relevant area of the map and uses a
drawing tool to mark off the desired airspace. Finally, the user ticks a series of
checkboxes affirming their compliance with FAA regulations and can then submit their authorization request. Kittyhawk transmits a record of the request
to the FAA, which will subsequently share it with air traffic controllers at the
affected airport. But what actually triggers the authorization is the query that
Kittyhawk sends to the LAANC data exchange, confirming that the request
does not conflict with any existing restrictions or advisories. The authorization message that Kittyhawk sends to the user on the FAA's behalf is, in a sense,
a mere trace of that query: an instantiation of volumetric sovereignty dynamically generated by a conversation between machines.

What are we to make of this curious document? (See figure 5.1.) Aestheti-
cally speaking, its legal standing would seem to be at odds with its bright green
background and the cartoonish drone hovering in the upper left corner; the
FAA logo and other branding elements are nowhere in evidence. The message
does bear an FAA reference code, which includes the initials "KTH" to designate the service supplier with which the authorization is associated. Kittyhawk's "Assets" module contains an area where users can review all of their approved authorizations, as well as requests that have been submitted to the FAA
for what the app terms "further coordination." If an airspace request is otherwise eligible for authorization but exceeds preapproved altitude limits, it can
be directed to the relevant air traffic controller for manual review, which may

Figure 5.1.
A LAANC authorization
in the Kittyhawk app.
Image courtesy of
Kittyhawk.

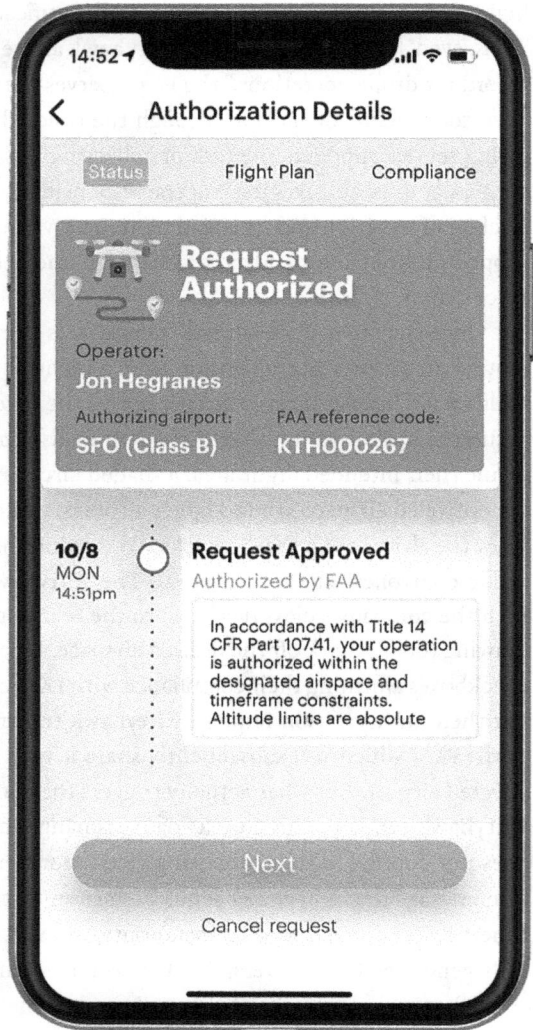

involve the requester providing additional information. Here, the seductive seamlessness promised by LAANC breaks down: manual review can take thirty days or more, and a request under review is automatically canceled if a decision has not been reached twenty-hour hours before the planned operation. Giving users a way to submit requests for further coordination arguably makes apps like Kittyhawk more versatile, allowing them to keep users inside the app rather than sending them beyond its confines. Yet this capability is notably absent from Kittyhawk's upbeat promotional video about LAANC, because the very need for its existence discloses the human labor and judgment that—at least for now—stand in the way of a fully automated airspace.

Conclusion

In November 2018, one year after LAANC's soft launch, the FAA put out a press release noting that the rollout has "exceeded all of the program's original objectives," with more than fifty thousand requests processed.[20] This is a considerable accomplishment, with concrete benefits for both drone operators and overburdened government workers, and I do not mean to diminish it. In closing, however, I want to draw out the implications of those objectives, both for other airspace users and for how social researchers think about volumetric sovereignty. It is not clear, for instance, that LAANC has made flying any safer for pilots like my informant Pete, whose close encounter with a drone opened this chapter. Since the airspace where Pete was flying—like most of the airspace over rural North Dakota—was uncontrolled, the drone's operator would have been under no obligation to request an authorization. Now, LAANC service suppliers know that the demand for information about drone operations extends beyond agents of the state, and many are participating in the development of a new standard called Remote ID, which will allow operators to share flight data with interested observers near their location. Like LAANC, Remote ID avoids betting on any one service supplier by emphasizing interoperability. For the sector as a whole, though, such a system represents a bid for what media scholars have called infrastructuralization, with its adoption becoming a de facto requirement for accessing airspace at all.[21]

There is extrastatecraft afoot, and yet let us not count more conventional logics of sovereignty out too quickly. As Keller Easterling observes, new dispensations of governance under contemporary capitalism tend to "strengthen rather than diminish the power of the state."[22] Consider the wariness around DJI, the Chinese manufacturer that today comprises 74 percent of the commercial drone market. In 2017, the US Army directed units in the field to stop using DJI drones due to concerns about "cyber vulnerabilities," while an intelligence bulletin from US Immigration and Customs Enforcement alleged that DJI was "likely providing U.S. critical infrastructure and law enforcement data to [the] Chinese government."[23] Amid these concerns about data security, tinged as they were with geopolitical intrigue, Kittyhawk briefly positioned itself as an American-made solution. "If you are using [the app distributed with DJI drones]," Ziering told *Aviation Today*, "it's talking to China and that is making a lot of people nervous. We have customers that are specifically mandated to be domestically stored, and [Kittyhawk] offers them the ability to fly their DJI stuff and not have their data go to China."[24] To counter this narrative, DJI added a privacy mode to its app and patched some widely publicized security flaws. One indication of the success of its damage control was that, in October 2018, DJI was approved as a LAANC service supplier—on the very same day as Kittyhawk. As companies like these jockey for position, what seems clear is that the evolving project of governance in three dimensions will unfold against the backdrop of bordering processes driven by both state and nonstate actors.

Regardless of where the seat of volumetric sovereignty is understood to reside, the extent of its ambition in different contexts also demands to be interrogated. For is it, in the end, hubris to imagine establishing positive control over every object that intrudes into the firmament? The age of the drone has brought this question to the fore by redefining what counts as navigable (and thus governable) airspace down into the human lifeworld. I still recall sitting on an open-air patio by the Red River one summer evening in North Dakota, swapping notes with a young drone entrepreneur. Setting his beer down for a moment, he raised his arms above his head and swung his hands in circles: "*This* is the National Airspace System," I remember him telling me, his tone incredulous. The representational technologies and regimes of expertise that regulated air traffic in the twentieth century are stymied by the task of securing the volume of air just above our heads that evening. But if this volume does need securing (and it may), then the software charged with doing so stands to challenge exceptionalisms around both the state and the human as the locus of sovereign decision.

NOTES

1 John A. Hughes, David Randall, and Dan Shapiro, "Faltering from Ethnography to Design," *Proceedings of the 1992 ACM Conference on Computer-Supported Cooperative Work* (1992): 115–22.

2 Keller Easterling, *Extrastatecraft: The Power of Infrastructure Space* (New York: Verso, 2014), 6.

3 Rui Neiva, *Institutional Reform of Air Navigation Service Providers: A Historical and Economic Perspective* (Northampton, MA: Edward Elgar, 2015).

4 Jeremy Wade Morris and Sarah Murray, "Introduction," in *Appified: Culture in the Age of Apps*, ed. Jeremy Wade Morris and Sarah Murray (Ann Arbor: University of Michigan Press, 2018), 9.

5   Hannah Knox and Dawn Nafus, "Introduction: Ethnography for a Data-Saturated World," in *Ethnography for a Data Saturated World*, ed. Hannah Knox and Dawn Nafus (Manchester, UK: Manchester University Press, 2018), 3–4.

6   FAA, "Low Altitude Authorization and Notification Capability (LAANC) Concept of Operations," version 1.1, May 12, 2017, 2, https://www.faa.gov/uas/programs _partnerships/data_exchange/laanc_for_industry/media/laanc_concept_of _operations.pdf.

7   FAA, "Low Altitude Authorization," 1.

8   Parimal Kopardekar, Joseph Rios, Thomas Prevot, Marcus Johnson, Jaewoo Jung, and John E. Robinson III, "Unmanned Aircraft System Traffic Management (UTM) Concept of Operations" (paper presented at the American Institute of Aeronautics and Astronautics Aviation Technology, Integration, and Operations Conference, Washington, DC, June 13–17, 2016).

9   Marijn Janssen and Anneke Zuiderwijk, "Infomediary Business Models for Connecting Open Data Providers and Users," *Social Science Computer Review* 32 (2014): 694–711, https://doi.org/10.1177/0894439314525902.

10 FAA, "Low Altitude Authorization," 8.

11 Ben Light, Jean Burgess, and Stefanie Duguay, "The Walkthrough Method: An Approach to the Study of Apps," *New Media and Society* 20 (2018): 881–900, https:// doi.org/10.1177/1461444816675438.

12 Marcel LaFlamme, "A Sky Full of Signal: Aviation Media in the Age of the Drone," *Media, Culture and Society* 40 (2018): 689–706, https://doi.org/10.1177 /0163443717737609.

13 Kittyhawk website, "Enterprise," accessed December 6, 2019, https://kittyhawk.io /enterprise.

14 Kittyhawk website, "Product," accessed December 6, 2019, https://kittyhawk.io /product.

15 Joshua Ziering, "Abstraction as a Service Comes to Drones," Kittyhawk blog, January 3, 2018, https://kittyhawk.io/blog/abstraction-as-a-service-comes-to -drones.

16 Joshua Ziering, "LAANC Fact Check: Can You Hear Me Now?," LinkedIn post, October 23, 2017, accessed February 11, 2019, https://www.linkedin.com/pulse /laanc-fact-check-can-you-hear-me-now-joshua-ziering.

17 Kittyhawk, "Overview of LAANC," YouTube video, October 15, 2018, https://www .youtube.com/watch?v=gO3ZuSYUjN4.

18 FAA, "Low Altitude Authorization," 9.

19 Charles R. Acland, ed., *Residual Media* (Minneapolis: University of Minnesota Press, 2006).

20 FAA, "More than Fifty Thousand LAANC Authorizations Processed," News, November 19, 2018, https://www.faa.gov/news/updates/?newsId=92273.

21 Jean-Christophe Plantin, Carl Lagoze, Paul N. Edwards, and Christian Sandvig, "Infrastructure Studies Meet Platform Studies in the Age of Google and Facebook," *New Media and Society* 20 (2018): 293–310, https://doi.org/10.1177 /1461444816661553. See also Carolin Gerlitz, Anne Helmond, David B. Nieborg,

and Fernando N. van der Vlist, "Apps and Infrastructures: A Research Agenda," *Computational Culture* 7 (2019), http://computationalculture.net/apps-and -infrastructures-a-research-agenda.

22 Easterling, *Extrastatecraft*, 49, fn63.

23 Department of the Army, Memorandum, "Discontinue Use of Dajiang Innovation (DJI) Corporation Unmanned Aircraft Systems," August 2, 2017; US Immigration and Customs Enforcement, SAC Intelligence Program Los Angeles, Intelligence Bulletin, "Dajiang Innovations (DJI) Likely Providing U.S. Critical Infrastructure and Law Enforcement Data to Chinese Government," August 9, 2017.

24 "Kittyhawk Drone Flight Deck Keeps DJI GO Data Domestically Stored," *Aviation Today*, May 17, 2017, https://www.aviationtoday.com/2017/05/17/kittyhawk-drone -flight-deck-keeps-dji-go-data-domestically-stored.

Materiality

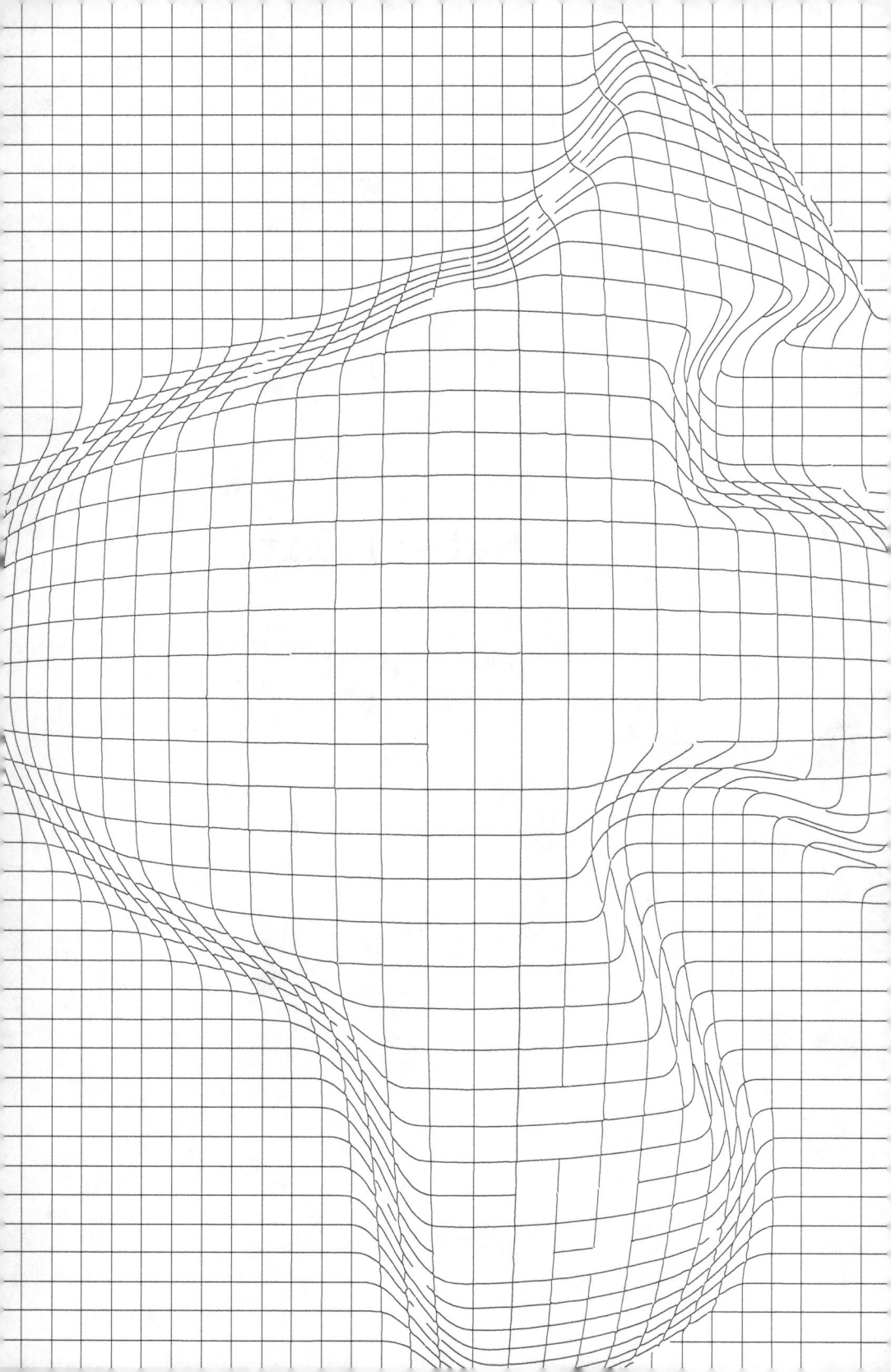

6   Fissure

*Cracking, Forcing,
and Covering Up*

KLAUS DODDS

Rippling borders are borders that ripple because they are made of water, yet their rippling effect also evinces the unstable, permeable nature of these spaces. Their existence is evidence of the fact that borders are as much physical locations as they are methods of study. Acknowledging both of these tensions with each other is integral to the evolution of border studies. This is what the concept "rippling borders" has to offer. Ultimately, the term attests to water's power for crafting transnational conversations that can go beyond geographic, ethnic and racial fissures.

—Rebecca Hoy-Colon, "Rippling Borders in Latina Literature"

Physical and environmental scientists use the word *fissure* to signify a crack or tear in substances such as ice and rock.[1] To describe ice and rock as *fissured* is to draw attention to the impact of sheer force, resulting in the imperilment of structural integrity. To witness firsthand fissuring, as active process rather than outcome, is spectacular. When an ice sheet fissures, it releases a sensual cornucopia as ice cracks, contorts, breaks up, and in some cases falls away into the surrounding terrestrial or maritime environment. It is spectacular to watch, listen, and feel as redundant ice falls into a lake or sea, and a nearby vessel observing such a phenomenon is gently rocked by the resulting release of force. As the nineteenth-century British explorer and sailor George Nares noted with alarm while in the Arctic:

> When about a mile from the nearest glacier we came to a wide fissure, about thirty yards broad, which seemed to extend nearly across the fjord, and whose precipitous glassy walls, fifty feet high from brink to water, we had no means of descending. The bottom of this fissure was composed of treacherous-looking slushy ice, with a lane of dark water two feet wide in the middle; so that had we succeeded in getting down we should probably have been unable to cross. About this same locality were several narrow fissures, some of which, from the very slippery nature of the ice, it was difficult to avoid falling into. One of these, in a tolerably level part of the ice, we found by measurement to be two feet wide above, and twenty three feet deep, from brink to a probably false bottom of loose snow, on which the light weight of our measuring line rested.[2]

Other times, however, we might be less sanguine as a glacial fissure endangers our movement in a polar or mountainous environment. Countless explorers have discovered to their cost, sometimes fatally, that a fissure can be disastrous. A thin layer of snow and ice might disguise something far more unsettling beneath our feet. For those who have walked across glaciers, I probably don't need to remind you that the experience is exhilarating but also chastening to the unwary and plain unlucky. Sadly, fatalities are common although occasionally survival is possible, as Joe Simpson's fall into a Peruvian glacier in 1985 proved.[3] Some fissures can be so large that they pose a threat to ongoing human activities. In Antarctica, a British Antarctic Survey research base, Halley VI, had to be shifted over twenty kilometers further inland because of fears of cracking in ice shelves. Satellite monitoring has become ever more indispensable in the monitoring process, and the design of the base itself was premised on the likelihood of a shift in location.[4] Other research stations were simply lost to ice fissures—South Africa notably lost three successive bases to the elemental vagaries of the Fimbulisen Ice Shelf.[5]

The verb *fissure* and the adjective *fissured* are apt for contemporary musings on the lively, volumetric, elemental, and more-than-human qualities of territory.[6] Social scientists and humanities scholars explore the intersection of the political and territorial, by teasing out the processual, embodied, and contested nature of space.[7] Henri Lefebvre and Gaston Bachelard are just two examples of those who have written on the production of space and the poetics of place respectively.[8]

Understanding the dynamism of space and place has allowed scholars to take seriously the contingent and emergent geographies of international politics. The affective, imaginative, and material geographies create a sense of the geographical as far more than a passive or stable backdrop on which events and processes simply unfold.[9] Critical theorizing brought to the fore the role of the hidden, the naturalized, and the taken-for-granted in international relations theorizing—states did not preexist, territories were not simply containers, ecologies not passive, and sovereignty not fixed in place. Borders were reimagined less as lines on a map or ground, and more as embodied performances and institutional practices that both fuse and separate people, ecologies and nations.[10]

This strand of academic work was not exclusively housed in any specific disciplinary fields such as critical geopolitics or political geography. Thirty years ago, the writer/poet/activist Gloria Anzaldúa, in her brilliant book *Borderlands/La Frontera: The New Mestiza*, argued that the border was a sort of *fissure* (in her original words an "open wound") that struggles to contain the multitude of people, ideas, sociolinguistic practices, animals, and things that cross the US-Mexican borderlands.[11] The optic of fissure is deployed as a propellant of further interdisciplinary conversation by using ice as a material element to tease out further the implications of resisting the naturalization and pacification of space and place.

In my chapter, I take the reader somewhere distinctly colder, where ice and snow loom rather larger than the semi-arid environments of the US-Mexican borderlands. I offer two vignettes on fissure using ice, cold, and snow as active, engaged, and lively accomplices in my reading of icy geopolitics.[12] The first is to think what happens when fissures result due to physical and/or human forcing. What happens when the ice simply cracks and gives way? In one spectacular Cold War example, Camp Century/Project Ice Worm, a secret subterranean operation managed by the US Armed Forces was jeopardized by glacial fissures. The second way of thinking with fissure is to ask what is at stake when fissures are deliberately made in ice by human actors rather than physical forces? In March 1959, about the same time that the US Army Corps of Engineers (USACE) was plotting and planning Camp Century, the USS *Skate* cracked through the Arctic sea ice at the North Pole. By way of conclusion, I think about the contemporary Arctic as *fissured space* and reflect on what is at stake when ice, land, air, and water crack up and scramble established imaginative legacies of place framing.[13]

Shifting Fissure

One of the most outlandish projects hailing from the Cold War involved the Greenland ice sheet, the US military, and an elaborate subterranean world of tunnels, living quarters, and storage units.[14] The strategic rationale of Project Ice Worm/Camp Century was comparatively straightforward. In the aftermath of World War II, it was appreciated by the US Armed Forces that the Arctic Ocean was a frontline as relations with the Soviet Union deteriorated. Technologically, the advent of the long-range bomber and the development of the atomic bomb put both the United States and the Soviet Union on a state of high alert. What once might have been thought of as an inaccessible frozen desert was altered, as inclement weather and persistent sea ice were no longer sufficient to deter hostile military forces. Following on from wartime co-operation with the Danish government, the United States entered into a defense agreement, which sanctioned an American military presence in Greenland in 1951. The creation of Thule Air Base was the most notable investment by the US Air Force in the northwest of the island.

As one of the world's largest ice sheets, Greenland attracted a great deal of scientific and political attention. In crude Cold War strategic terms, this northern appendage of the Kingdom of Denmark mattered for two reasons: first, the northern rim of the country was considered to be strategically significant in terms of early warning of approaching long-range Soviet bombers. Patrolling airspace in and around the Arctic Ocean was considered nonnegotiable. Second, the immense ice sheet occupying Greenland intrigued defense planners and scientists alike. While the latter focused on the depth and extent of the ice sheet, military planners speculated on what might be possible to hide from enemy surveillance.[15]

The US Armed Forces were major sponsors of postwar glaciological research, and the USACE established the Snow, Ice, and Permafrost Research Establishment (SIPRE). As a strategic theater, knowledge and understanding about sea ice, glaciers, and permafrost were at a premium. Fundamental research questions included: Was it possible for submarines to travel under the polar ice pack? Could airplanes land safely on glaciers? Would infrastructure withstand any changes to the permafrost? Finally, what factors shaped short- and long-term glacial dynamics? The rationale for SIPRE was to conduct basic and applied research in and on snow, ice, and permafrost.

In 1959, SIPRE scientists working in collaboration with USACE began building Camp Century, some two hundred kilometers east of Thule Air Base.[16] Camp Century was an underground base, located some eight meters below the surface of the Greenlandic ice sheet. A nuclear power plant was to provide the power for those living and working below the ice. The plan was that up to two hundred soldiers might be accommodated. The choice of location was deliberate. This area of the ice sheet was supposed to be in a dry snow zone with little to no surface melting even in the summer season. This contrasts with the percolation zone where surface melting does occur but refreezes. In the so-called soaked zone of a glacier or ice sheet, melting is sufficient to enable runoff and in due course affect the balance between accumulation and ablation/melting. Camp Century was supposed to be spared the state change in the ice and associated water flow.[17]

For the first three years, the "city under the ice" as the *Popular Science* magazine of February 1960 described it, was largely untroubled by glacial dynamics (figure 6.1). Was it possible to fuse a particular technological-scientific future (steel structures, advanced drilling technologies, and nuclear power production) with the more-than-human geographies of the subterranean?[18] Snow and ice would provide natural cover for secretive Cold War military laboring. As the journalist Herbert Johansen noted insouciantly:

> The strangest boom town in the world is being built by Army engineers under Greenland's vast ice cap. Completely hidden by snow, it will be powered by atomic energy—and will be about as safe a place as you could find in case of an atomic attack. It would be hard for an enemy to find; and snow would absorb much of the shock of an atomic blast, and partially shield the occupants from radiation and fallout.[19]

The accompanying article revealed in a rather breathless tone that the "traditionally antagonistic Arctic can be tamed." By 1962, the USACE established an underground railway designed to support the more outlandish and secret plan (codename Project Ice Worm) to transport and hide up to six hundred ballistic missiles underground. Tellingly, the article concluded with an insight that proved to be rather prescient: "One thing the engineers haven't been able to lick is the slow, plastic movement of the ice, which causes the walls to close in and the corridors to twist. With periodic shaving of the ice, they expect the camp to last about 10 years. Then it will be completely reconditioned."[20]

The prediction regarding a decade of usage proved to be overly optimistic, as the ice proved rather resistant to an occasional shaving. By 1967, the dream of a "city under the ice" was over, the Greenlandic ice sheet proved to be a noncompliant and undomesticated partner. The plasticity of ice revealed itself to be capable of fissuring, deforming, and distorting. The construction of Camp Century coincided with new investment in glaciology and materials science which revealed further insights into ice properties and behavior such as

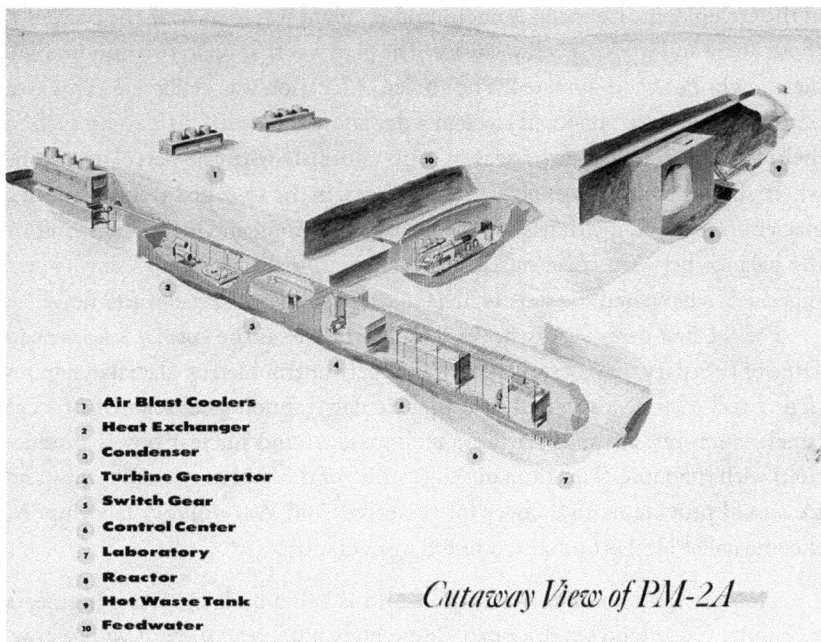

Figure 6.1. Schematic from part of the proposed Camp Century, courtesy of the US Army Corp of Engineers.

thresholds of flow, stress, and velocity. But all of that could not save this underground investment in Cold War subterfuge.

Surfacing Fissure

If Camp Century revealed that the plasticity of ice was not something that could be brought under the exclusive control of human intervention, the physical properties of Arctic sea ice also attracted considerable attention from Cold War military planners. In a presatellite era, monitoring the thickness and spatial extent of sea ice over the Arctic Ocean was something carried out by long range planes and submarines. In the 1940s and 1950s, the US Navy's attention turned toward submarine design and testing as well as investment in acoustic and surveillance technologies. Could submarines travel safely under the pack ice and, if necessary, surface and crack the ice? The *Skate* class of nuclear-powered submarines was introduced in the late 1950s, and in July 1958 the pioneering vessel, the USS *Skate*, initiated under-ice voyages. Unable to push through the central Arctic Ocean's pack ice in the earliest cruising, the submarine did manage to surface further away from the thicker multiyear sea ice in an ice-free area of ocean called a *polynya*.

In his account of the voyage, *Surface at the Pole: The Extraordinary Voyages of the USS Skate*, Captain James Calvert writes that "seldom had the ice seemed so heavy and so thick as it did in the immediate vicinity of the pole. For days we had searched in vain for a suitable opening to surface in."[21] The superstructure of the submarine was pivotal to the decision to ascend and crack open the ice, which was reported to be up to twenty-five-feet thick in places. In March 1959, in a subsequent underwater cruise during late winter, the USS *Skate* did break the sea ice at the North Pole, after conducting an operation lasting some twelve days. But the operation nearly never happened. As the private papers of US Navy scientist Waldo Lyon recalled, the US Navy in the late 1940s was skeptical of an under-ice submarine program.[22] The notion of a trans-Arctic submarine operating under the ice pack, surfacing through sea ice, was as fanciful as a Jules Verne novel. Lyon and colleagues at the Arctic Submarine Laboratory (ASL) initiated a series of under-ice experiments, investigating inter alia the physical properties of sea ice and acoustics. What the ASL scientists discovered was that as the sea ice moved and cracked, the sonar performance of the submarine was affected leading to fears that the ability to detect any enemy submarines could also suffer. Waldo Lyon spoke about the "Arctic enigma" and warned how the cracks and contours of underwater sea ice were disabling of sonar.[23]

The entrée of the nuclear-powered submarine proved a game changer for Lyon and his vision of under-ice submarining.[24] With greater range and ability, a new generation of vessels gave the US Navy opportunities to put Lyon's vision into practice, as it was acknowledged that situation awareness needed to improve. Publicly, President Eisenhower spoke about how "this points the way . . . for further exploration and possible use of this route by nuclear-powered cargo submarines as a new commercial seaway between the major oceans of the world."[25] But the strategic significance of cracking the Arctic sea ice was appreciated. With improved echo-sounding capabilities, the submarine crew were better able to judge where to identify particular areas of the pack ice. When the USS *Skate* surfaced, it took advantage of what was called a *sea ice lead*, where a large crack exposed some open water. Sea ice leads are different to polynyas because they are episodic and not semipermanent features. Travelling underwater was useful but in the event of an emergency or incident, the US Navy wanted its submarines to ascend and descend safely under the pack ice, and that meant being able to detect opportunistically. The maximum thickness of sea ice that a submarine could safely puncture was no more than six to eight feet.[26]

Figure 6.2. USS *Skate* surfacing at the North Pole, March 1959

One of the most iconic photographs of the Cold War in the Arctic was arguably the USS *Skate* surfacing at the North Pole (figure 6.2). The brilliant whiteness of sea ice is contrasted with the black hull and superstructure of the submarine and its prominent numbering: 578. Captain Calvert described the moment the *Skate* cracked the ice and emerged through the ice pack: "Slowly we blew the tanks and the Skate moved reluctantly upward. It was apparent we were under heavier ice here than any we had experienced before."[27] Following the submarine breaching the ice, some of the crew left the vessel and planted the American flag on the surface of the ice. The symbolism of the moment, in conjunction with the underwater voyage of USS *Nautilus* in August 1958 (known as Operation Sunshine), was palpable.[28] After the shock of the Soviet launch of Sputnik in 1957, and the failure of the US Vanguard satellite program, the success of under-ice submarine cruising was not lost on American audiences—the human and nonhuman intermingled in the form of underwater cameras, bottom-sounding sonar, sea ice, sea ice leads and polynyas, submarine topography, and underwater currents.

The cracking of the sea ice was not without controversy. Not everyone was taken in by these floating examples of nuclear technology. The USS *Skate* was denied access to Danish ports because the then Danish prime minister H. C. Hansen was concerned about the safety of its nuclear reactor. A year earlier Denmark initiated a nuclear-free policy on its domestic soil. Unwittingly, perhaps, the Danish premier anticipated something far worse when a B-52 nuclear armed bomber crashed into what was called North Star sea ice in January 1968.[29] The crash resulted in the nuclear contamination of the surrounding area, which later exposed a secret agreement that allowed US Armed Forces to locate nuclear weapons in northern Greenland. In a more metaphorical sense, the Thule air disaster cracked open the secretive US-Danish military relationship. Decades later, compensation was paid to those involved in the rescue and recovery operation and official and journalistic scrutiny of the secret arrangements between the NATO powers followed.[30]

Fissuring the Arctic

The under-ice navigation of USS *Nautilus* and *Skate* ushered in a new era of militarization and associated investment in the audiovisualization of the Arctic Ocean. As the environmental historian Sverker Sörlin notes, "Up until World War II, the central Arctic Ocean was seen as largely frozen and potentially next to lifeless and with no significance for the rest of the world (which is not to say that near-terrestrial parts of the ocean were not of high interest for Arctic countries including the Nordic countries)."[31] Cold War oceanographic research in the high north, coupled with investment in nuclear submarine programs including underwater camera and echo-sounding technologies, contributed to a new round of mapping and surveying of under–sea ice environments. Even in the 1950s, there were scientists predicting that the Arctic Ocean might be ice free at the turn of the twenty-first century, thus freeing submarines from having to run the gauntlet of cracking the ice pack from below the surface. Scientists travelling in American and British nuclear submarines played a vital role in assessing for both military and scientific purposes the changing thickness of Arctic sea ice in the 1960s, '70s, and '80s.[32]

The fissuring of the sea ice in March 1959 by the USS *Skate* was a turning point in Arctic geopolitics. Within a decade, Hollywood capitalized on this geopolitical drama by realizing two submarine movies, *The Bedford Incident* (1965) and notably *Ice Station Zebra* (1968).[33] Both situate their respective dramas in the icy waters of the Arctic Ocean, and notably in the latter considerable attention is given over to conveying the homonormative tension inherent in navigating under the pack ice, and making robust judgements about where it might be safe to surface through the ice. Filmed on a soundstage at MGM Studios in Los Angeles, the special effects specialist Matthew Yuricich was responsible for the icescapes featuring the fictional submarine USS *Tiger Fish* breaking through the ice. For the premiere of the film, audiences were given information sheets about sea ice and submarine underwater navigation capabilities.[34]

The Arctic's icy geopolitics involved not only under-ice cruising but a growing assemblage of technology and surveillance designed to monitor water and ice. US and Soviet submarines were supported by an extensive sensory network designed to alert operators to the presence of enemy submarines and facilitate the collection of geographical information about sea ice, ocean, and subterranean geology. One notable area of potential confusion was the ice itself. Sonar operators had to run the gauntlet of making sense of scrambled intelligence because it was not easy to distinguish ice pack fissure ridges and so-called ice *rafts* from a submarine hull. What made this all the more discombobulating was that enemy submarines could also take advantage of fissures, polynyas, sea ice leads, and other naturally occurring gaps to surface opportunistically, and (potentially) launch intercontinental missiles with little to no advance warning for those who were targeted. After firing, the submarines could then descend under the Arctic ice pack and escape possible detection. Breaking through thicker sea ice, therefore, was not thought to represent any sort of natural barrier to hostile submarine operations. Underwater sensors were intended to be an early warning system but making sense of "warning" signs was complicated by the elemental qualities of water and ice.

The fissure has this tremendous ambivalence in both the example of Camp Century and under the ice pack. Assumptions about the underlying stability of the Greenlandic ice sheet proved to be unfounded. As a site for a hoped-for geopolitical future where the United States desired a strategic advantage over its Cold War adversary, the project was literally fissured. The promissory intent of Project Ice Worm never materialized and the abandonment of Camp Century simply stored up a toxic legacy for later generations to confront. In the central Arctic Ocean, sea ice fissures were initially seized upon as presenting novel opportunities for US submarines to surface amid an enormous frozen desert. But later the fissure became a source of fear as it was appreciated that Soviet attack submarines could also take advantage of gaps and cracks in the ice pack. The fissure became indicative of potential insecurity, which is difficult to seal or fill in. As Admiral James Watkins was quoted as saying in 1984, "the Arctic ice cap is a beautiful place to hide."[35]

For four decades, US and NATO antisubmarine strategy was predicated on monitoring gaps and cracks in oceans and ice—from the Greenland-Iceland-UK gap to zones of open water in the central Arctic Ocean. Notably, the film *The Hunt for Red October* (1990) captures something of the challenge involved in "minding those gaps" as Soviet Typhoon-class nuclear submarines patrolled the North Atlantic and Arctic waters. In sharp contrast to *Ice Station Zebra*, viewers are expected to admire the technological achievements and navigational acumen of both Soviet and American submariners. Luckily for the American submariners hunting for the fictional *Red October*, the Soviet crew are seeking political asylum and not nuclear Armageddon.[36]

Postscript

The short vignettes about Camp Century and USS *Skate* serve to illustrate well the broader concerns of this collection of essays about volumetric states. In the 1950s, there was no shortage of interest—political, scientific, and military—in conceiving of the Arctic as an elemental and, at times, elusive volume. Making sense of the intersection of sea ice, seabed, whales and other marine mammals, water salinity, and current was a strategic imperative for US naval submariners and their political masters. On land and in air, US military planners worried about cracks on ice sheets and looked for gaps in the weather, which in turn carried with them implications for infrastructure resilience and mission planning.[37] The cryosphere was a gigantic laboratory for cold weather testing and training by both the Soviet Union and the United States. But this desire to make sense of ice, snow, and cold was vulnerable to fissuring—underground bases were abandoned, equipment jammed, submarines were lost, and planes crashed through sea ice.

In March 2018, some sixty years after the USS *Skate* puncturing through sea ice at the North Pole, US and British nuclear submarines continued to sail under the Arctic ice pack as part of the military practice called Ice Exercise (ICEX). Three vessels undertook a North Pole surfacing as well as traversing under the Arctic sea ice as part of a deliberate policy to increase submarine activity in the wake of worsening relations with Russia and concerns that China is becoming more interested in the central Arctic Ocean.[38] But within that sixty-year window, the Arctic Ocean as a geographical space has undergone considerable transformation. It is now at the forefront of media and political framings of anthropogenic climate change, accompanied by images of cracking, melting, and retreating sea ice. While ICEX 2018 reminds us that the militarization of sea ice remains enduring, notwithstanding the formal ending of the Cold War in the late 1980s, it also informs a more elemental discussion about how warming trends are making themselves manifest in both the thickness and distribution of Arctic Ocean volume.

As the Arctic Ocean sea ice continues to fissure, it triggers literally and figuratively a space for fears, fantasies, and futures, as all of this will have elemental and human consequences as the shrinking volume of sea ice is inseparable from the expanding liquid volume of the ocean.[39]

NOTES

Klaus Dodds acknowledges the generous support of the Leverhulme Trust who funded a Major Research Fellowship (2017–20) on "the global Arctic."

1   Shawn J. Marshall, *The Cryosphere* (Princeton, NJ: Princeton University Press, 2012).

2   George Nares, *Narrative of a Voyage to the Polar Sea During 1875–6 in HM Ships Alert and Discovery* (London: Sampson Low, Marston, Searle, and Rivington, 1878), 349.

3   See, for example, Craig Sailor, "He Reached the Top of Mount Rainier. On the Way Down, Skier Fell 150 Feet into Crevasse," *News Tribune*, July 17, 2017, http://www.thenewstribune.com/news/local/article161873348.html#storylink=cpy. On his subsequent escape from the glacial crevasse, see Joe Simpson, *Touching the Void* (New York: HarperCollins, 2004).

4   Elle Hunt, "British Antarctic Research Station to Be Moved Due to Deep Crack in the Ice," *Guardian*, December 7, 2016, https://www.theguardian.com/world/2016/dec/07/british-antarctic-research-station-crack-ice.

5   Antarctic Legacy of South Africa, "Antarctica Base (SANAE IV)," Antarctic Legacy of South Africa website, accessed November 14, 2019, http://blogs.sun.ac.za/antarcticlegacy/about-2/sanae-iv/.

6   See, for example, Stuart Elden, "Secure the Volume: Vertical Geopolitics and the Depth of Power," *Political Geography* 34 (2013): 35–51; and Stephen Graham, *Vertical: The City from Satellites to Bunkers* (London: Verso, 2016).

7   For example, Yael Navaro, *The Make-Believe Space: Affective Geography in a Postwar Polity* (Durham, NC: Duke University Press, 2012).

8   For example, Henri Lefebvre, *The Production of Space* (Chichester: John Wiley 1991); and Gaston Bachelard, *The Poetics of Space* (Boston: Beacon Press, 1994).

9   The landmark text remains Gerard Toal, *Critical Geopolitics* (Minneapolis: University of Minnesota Press, 1996); and more recently, Nick Megoran, *Nationalism in Central Asia* (Pittsburgh: University of Pittsburgh Press, 2017).

10 A good example would be Madeleine Reeves, *Border Work: Spatial Lives of the State in Rural Central Asia* (Ithaca, NY: Cornell University Press, 2014).

11 Gloria Anzaldúa, *Borderlands/La Frontera: The New Mestiza* (San Francisco: Aunt Lute Books, 1987), 3.

12 For further consideration, see Klaus Dodds, *Ice: Nature and Culture* (London: Reaktion Books, 2018).

13 This draws upon a longer argument made in Klaus Dodds and Mark Nuttall, *The Scramble for the Poles* (Cambridge: Polity, 2016).

14 An important contemporary account was Charles Daugherty, *City under the Ice: The Story of Camp Century* (London: Macmillan, 1963).

15 One of the most detailed studies using US and Danish archives is Kristian H. Nielsen, Henry Nielsen, and Janet Martin-Nielsen, "City under the Ice: The Closed World of Camp Century in Cold War Culture," *Science as Culture* 23 (2014): 443–64.

16 For a useful overview of ice coring in Greenland, see Chester Langway, *The History of Early Polar Ice Cores* (US Army Corp of Engineers, Cold Regions Research and Engineering Laboratory, January 2008).

17 For a highly publicized account speculating on what might become of Camp Century in the future due to ongoing climate change, see Willian Colgan, Horst Machguth, Mike MacFerrin, Jeff D. Colgan, Dirk van As, and Joseph MacGregor, "The Abandoned Ice Sheet Camp at Camp Century, Greenland, in a Warming Climate," *Geophysical Research Letters* 43 (2016): 8091–96.

18 For further reflection on literary and material subterranean geographies, Rosalind Williams, *Notes on the Underground* (Cambridge, MA: MIT Press, 2008).

19 Herbert Johansen, "US Army Builds a Fantastic City under the Ice," *Popular Science*, February 1960, 86.

20 Johansen, "US Army Builds a Fantastic City," 229.

21 James Calvert, *Surface at the Pole: The Extraordinary Voyages of the USS Skate* (New York: McGraw-Hill, 1960), 92.

22 William Leary, *Under Ice: Waldo Lyon and the Development of the Arctic Submarine* (College Station: Texas A&M University Press, 1999), 4.

23 Waldo K. Lyon, "Sonar, the Submarine and the Arctic Ocean," *Journal of the Acoustical Society of America* 32 (1960): 1513.

24 Leary, *Under Ice*.

25 Qtd. in Dennis Hevesi, "James F. Calvert, 88, Sub Captain Who Surfaced at North Pole, Dies," *New York Times*, June 16, 2009.

26 Richard Woodman and Dan Conley, *Cold War Command* (Barnsley: Seaforth Publishing, 2014), 90.

27 Calvert, *Surface at the Pole*, 165.

28 William R. Anderson, *The Ice Diaries: The Untold Story of the Cold War's Most Daring Mission* (Nashville, TN: Thomas Nelson, 2008).

29 Timothy J. Jorgensen, *Strange Glow: The Story of Radiation* (Princeton, NJ: Princeton University Press, 2016), 386.

30 Ronald E. Doel, Kristine C. Harper, and Matthias Heymann, *Exploring Greenland: Cold War Science and Technology on Ice* (London: Palgrave 2016).

31 Sverker Sörlin, "The Arctic Ocean," in *Oceanic Histories*, ed. David Armitage, Alison Bashford, and Sujit Sivasundaram (Cambridge: Cambridge University Press, 2018), 291.

32 Peter Wadhams, *After the Ice* (Oxford: Oxford University Press, 2016).

33 English critic John Sutherland praised *Ice Station Zebra* for its geopolitical realism and elemental inclemency in *Bestsellers: Popular Fiction of the 1970s* (London: Routledge, 2010), 63–64.

34 Film reviews praised the film for its special effects, technical detail, and under-ice realism. See, for example, "Movies," *New York Magazine*, January 13, 1969, 55.

35 Qtd. in Adam Lajeunesse, *Lock, Stock, and Icebergs: A History of Canada's Arctic Maritime Sovereignty* (Vancouver: University of British Columbia Press, 2016), 230.

36 Sherry Sontag and Christopher Drew, *Blind Man's Bluff: The Untold Story of Cold War Submarine Espionage* (London: Arrow Books, 1998).

37 Matthew Farish, *The Contours of America's Cold War* (Minneapolis: University of Minnesota Press, 2010), 57–60.

38 Thomas Nilsen, "NATO Subs Kick off North Pole Exercise," *Independent Barents Observer*, March 8, 2018, https://thebarentsobserver.com/en/security/2018/03/nato-subs-kicks-north-pole-exercise#.WqZ7EBGI38c.twitter.

39 Philip Steinberg and Kimberley Peters, "Wet Ontologies, Fluid Spaces: Giving Depth to Volume through Oceanic Thinking," *Environment and Planning D: Society and Space* 33 (2015): 247–64.

7

Downwind

Three Phases of an Aerosol Form

JERRY ZEE

Foreign Backgrounds

Once a week, Dr. Matthew Swensen, a geochemist at Lawrence Berkeley National Labs, makes the drive to the top of Mount Tamalpais, just across the Golden Gate Bridge from San Francisco, to collect Chinese particulates. "It's become kind of a hobby for me," he says, turning an imaginary wheel to hug a tight curve. "I have a Mini now, and it's a lot of fun to drive on the mountain roads." Mount Tam, without immediate pollution sources between the peak and thousands of miles of open Pacific, is what his team calls a "relatively pristine" site, where they can measure American air before it is contaminated by American exhausts. From the peak of Mount Tam, he recovers three cartridges of particulate samples a week—one for elemental analysis, a second for isotopic analysis, his lab's specialty, and a third as a spare for his "archive of sorts"— from a rotating DRUM impactor, an experimental apparatus that his team has placed there to collect particulate samples floating in from across the ocean.

His lab's goal, he explains, is to apportion the particulates that the impactor, with its nose facing the ocean, forcibly precipitates out of the air and onto time-resolved Mylar strips. Through analysis of lead isotopes in the sample, his team comes to what he and his meteorologist collaborators call a provisional "fingerprint of an air mass," a first stab into estimating how much of China drifts into American air. The push to develop methods for apportioning

California's air into distinct local and foreign parts has escalated since 2015, in response to tightening national regulations on surface ozone concentration under the Obama administration. Air quality management districts in western states appealed to the US EPA. They argued that foreign ozone and ozone precursors, which they could not be held responsible for managing under Article 179A of the Clean Air Act, were often enough to push western air quality over regulatory thresholds.

While Article 179A was originally meant to cover pollutants floating across the borders from Canada and Mexico, the recent appeals have shifted their attention to China and its economic development, thousands of miles upwind. While concern over Chinese aerosols—the mineral and chemical exhausts of China's idiosyncratic "socialism with Chinese characteristics"—has spiked since the early 2000s, attempts to finesse the Clean Air Act on the part of US western states have unexpectedly centered the Pacific Ocean both as the limit to a continent and as the site of first landfall of the fallout of the Chinese economy. The DRUM impactor and the transpacific political meteorology of ozone, dusts and winds, regulations and exceptions in which it operates continually generate downwindness as a technical and legal problem, aiming to demonstrate connection in order to establish baselines for the purpose of eluding regulation, offshoring it upwind.

On the impactor's Mylar strips impacted with unloaded dusts, China appears as a pattern of gray bars, geochemical deposits coaxed mechanically out of the wind. This fingerprinting of an inbound airmass registers China's economic rise through the rise of so-called particulate *exports* that make their way from China to the Pacific coast. These exports spike in the early spring, when dust storms that form out of newly exposed sands in China's vast desertified exterior are scooped into eastbound jet winds, passing over China's developed coastal regions where they accrue soot and other pollution into a roiling chemo-geological cloud. They pass over the Koreas and Japan, and eventually to the United States, where larger storms make landfall ten days to two weeks later.

These dusts move as a massive aerosol cloud, particulate solids held in gas: an interphase of matter. These floating dusts blast apart a distinction between land and air, solid and gas, dramatizing their continuity as a choreography of materials. Tracing dusts this way reveals air as the medium for aerosolized land, a massively dispersed solid distributed into atmospheric suspension. In its movement, it accrues the chemical and particulate exhausts of China's industries and cities in their globetrotting suspension. At their peak—argue Swensen and other atmospheric scientists in the United States who are involved in developing methods for determining the quantum of Chinese land in American air—suspended Chinese geology makes up 40 percent of the particulate load of air sampled at the edge of the American mainland. "We've been waving our hands for a long time about long-distance transport," states Swensen, "and what's great is our lab was actually able to see and quantify transported material." Air regulation and air quality management districts in the western US have argued that particulate drift from China must be considered the new meteorological baseline for a postnatural, post-Chinese American atmosphere.

In the impactor, the air is not an emptiness, but a freight of dispersed solids, waiting to be unloaded, its mixtures partitioned materially and legally into a sequence of sources, drawn together as consecutive points in a dance of dust and wind. American air, in its chambers and Mylar strips, appears as a light rain of Chinese land, two continents drawn together in the touch of a storm. Activating clauses deep in American air pollution regulation, the push to determine the quantum of Chinese earth exported as dust into "relatively pristine" sites on California's Pacific Coast offers a strange site for considering how, in the identification of our geological present with wrong air, we can explore weather-worlds in the making.[1] As a particulate cypher of Sino-American relation, dust forcibly settled onto Mylar—ex-land and ex-air—presages the lift and fall of aerosolized earth as a condition through which meteorological connections come to matter. To scan for drifting particulates is to hold a machine inhaling dust on a Californian peak, as one point in a meteorological drama that draws together countries and continents as points in an earth-moving, world-making airstream. Chinese deserts and American airspaces describe, then, an up- and downwind along a seasonal atmospheric highway, and also two material phases of an earth that, after decades of land degradation, has become a latent sky.

This chapter learns from the impactor in the search for a contingent meteorological architecture through which a more-than-human world-system might come to form. I attend to how "Chinese dusts" and their uptake as "foreign background" downwind might give us insight into how aerosols and airstreams might rut out new time-spaces of relation. These dusts and the winds they reveal as vectors of relation fold political and meteorological geometries into one another, as when international relation suddenly bends into the shape of the wind. Together, they offer a site of entry to a modern wind-system, one that gathers and stimulates divergent political, material, environmental becomings in an atmospheric scale that attends to far-flung connections, and yet avoids the tepid no-space of the planetary atmosphere that some Anthropocene narratives demand that we dissolve into.

How can we make the wind-scraped surfaces of Chinese deserts and the scramble to count the air in California two acts in a drama of earthy and atmospheric phase shifts, a before and an after in the mutation of an aerosol form? I derive the notion of an aerosol form from Theodor Schwenk's magical descriptions of the flowing formations that emerge in the dynamisms of water and air. An "aerial form," writes Schwenk, is an emergent gathering of elements into the air, whose dynamics cannot be discerned from the preexisting elements alone. Migrating birds, for instance, falling into flying V formation dynamically pattern air into the shape of their relation—they cannot be abstracted out of their medium that holds them together. The ensuing aerial form "itself unites all the individual birds" in a variegated aerodynamic totality that exceeds any of its constituent parts.[2]

In suggesting that dusts and particulates, in their long trajectory from just-thawed deserts, over cities, and onto Mylar in Californian research labs, rut out an aerosol form, I want not only to emphasize how aerosol and particulate processes scaffold both a peculiar aeolian geography of relations and ground—or is it unground?—dusty airstreams as formations around which given political formations reshape.[3] It is also to emphasize the continual phasing between states of matter involved in aerosols, which are definitionally composite, a choreography of particulate solids and turbulent airs.

In the circulation of the atmosphere and its revelation of relative up- and downwinds, every downwind is likewise upwind of elsewhere. For a dust storm is not simply the blowing open of planar politics into volumes and a politics of verticality.[4] It also demands a novel political spatialization that attends to its processual dynamics, to a time-spacing defined by lags, anticipation, and the anxious scanning of the sky as a medium of meteorological and political proximity.[5] To explore up- and downwind relations through these aerosol forms not only demands that the relentlessly specific and yet elusively more-than-territorial trajectories of particulate flow must be taken seriously, thus orienting us toward specific planetary spatializations rather than the ubiquitous all-space of the planet per se. It allows us also to see these points in the wind as part of a dynamic totality out of whose properties—volumetric, timeful, interphasing—other political geometries are being made in practice.

In what follows, we linger at points of aerosol transition dispersed across three countries. Each is a point in the wind, a site where problems of being up- and downwind subtly reshape international relations into questions of relative location, vulnerability, sequence. Each is a gathering of an array of human, geophysical, botanical, and mechanical things as divergent contemporary meteorological configurations. The Chinese desert and the Mylar strip on a Californian coastal range describe a before and after of a dust cloud, thematized around the geo-meteorological entailments of the wind as an earth-moving, world-making force. For many of the agencies that in their different capacities and commitments are addressed by dusty problems, in the United States and China, earth matters most at its passage across these phases: Chinese officials aim to prevent deserts from lifting into storms; American scientists learn to read air as an after-ness of land, lest their claims stand as mere hand waving.

Groundwork

Beginning in the early 2000s, consecutive years of drought combined with consecutive decades of inland land degradation and regional jet winds gave rise to the perfect conditions for large-scale and long-distance dust events, prompting a massive mobilization of state resources, expertise, and attention along the dust streams that pass over Beijing. New investments in remote sensing and a metastasizing network of on-the-ground dust storm monitoring stations made meteorology and aeolian physics into the scientific and technical basis for visualizing the country's land as dust potentials, framing it in terms of troubling weather for the Chinese capital. Tracing the airflows that linked lands designated as dust storm source regions revealed Beijing as an airspace traversed by national winds, and the Chinese interior a continent undone into its airs.

Decades of desertification, with deserts expanding at a pace of more than a thousand square miles each year,[6] had not only become the source regions for an uncanny modern meteorology, but reconfigured regional airstreams as powerful vectors of geo-atmospheric assault. Here, the capital is not simply the center of a confident new China, but a key point in the stormways carrying dusts that have become a meteorological signature of decades of breakneck economic growth. In the wind, the city's resource frontier had also become its dust shed, established as a sociopolitical reality through "scientific knowledge, maps, laws, technologies, discourses, and institutions that correspond with its boundaries."[7] Controlling these modern dusts depended on tracing wind as the administrative architecture for experiments in geo-atmospheric intervention. Along these windy zones,[8] national peripheries and centers were rearranged as upwinds and downwinds respectively, moments in the formation and passing of a dust event.

By the early 2000s, demands to control the particulate content of Beijing's important atmosphere had rezoned so-called dust source areas into a countrywide construction zone for forestry windbreaks and other sand stabilization programs, aimed at breaking dusts at the surface of sand and sky. Deserts, expanding quickly for decades, became part of Beijing's dust shed.

Along dust-transporting airstreams, former grasslands turned desert and their inhabitants were increasingly slated as part of a countrywide work of ecological construction, scrambling to fix the earth to the ground.

On the Alxa Plateau in western Chinese Inner Mongolia Autonomous Region, Mr. Li, an ex-herder, oversees the transition of the fields of open dunes that rove across what was once his family's pasture into a future forest of *suosuo* shrubs. The massive conversion of pasturage into belts of suosuo forests has been a key state goal, part of a bid to create a living infrastructure of sand-binding, wind-blocking shrubs that will be the first line of defense for protecting Beijing, six hundred miles downwind, from the major dust storms that now mark the beginning of springtime. Planting these windbreaks, as a key state anti–dust storm strategy, is a matter of texturing the landscape against its unusual susceptibility to wind-blown phase shift. Tempering its flyaway qualities in this manner is a way of engineering what Gastón Gordillo theorizes as *terrain* before it spills over into an always latent capacity toward atmospheric becoming: "changes in the ambient composition, density, and texture of terrain as the surface of a planet in motion."[9]

While, each year in the short spring planting window, Li oversees the planting of suosuo, he is by no means a suosuo farmer.[10] He states matter-of-factly that suosuo is fine for forestry but is otherwise economically useless to him, even with the state forestry subsidies he collects to fund his planting. Rather, it is another root, another product, that drives this difficult and uncertain work. When the suosuo establishes, he will plant *rou congrong*, a medicinal root, that by the sympathetic magic of its snakelike shape is a supplement to virility. Rou congrong is a benign parasite, a root that grows only in the microenvironment created by established suosuo roots. That is, for it to root, it must inter-root.

Rooting dunes in place is a way of controlling deserts as potential storms, preventing landforms from becoming air-forms. The state promotion of rou congrong planting on the part of ex-herder families seeks to rework this inter-rooting of cash crops and windbreaks as a technique of large-scale dune stabilization. The felicitous botany of a windbreak and its parasite have, on Li's field, also tangled his livelihood into forestry ecology. Alxa's local government has worked for years to create an open market for rou congrong roots, by manipulating tax breaks to draw in out-of-province conglomerates that will process the root into medicinal liqueurs, teas, and supplements for a burgeoning market in health products, leveraging the cachet of Mongolian medicine for the Han market.

In doing so, they have also sought to create infinite market demand by promising to buy as much rou congrong as ex-pastoralists can produce, creating an economic environment aimed at capitalizing on taken-for-granted entrepreneurial survivalist instincts insulated from all the risk of free markets, and their fluctuations of price. In doing so, families like Li's have responded by growing as much suosuo as possible, growing and maintaining windbreaks aimed to keep sand solid toward state quotas, as the living infrastructure for an ecological factory for rou congrong.

As the two plants become the linchpin of an antidust strategy, so too does the more-than-human landscape of Alxa appear as a configuration of elements that must be rearranged to hold the earth as a solid. The management of human life and behavior, demands for rural economic development in the "new socialist countryside," deftly timed subsidies and the herds of grazing animals converted into starting capital for windbreak-planting by accidental foresters, not to mention the plants themselves, become moving parts in the regulation of the physical relation between land and air in this dust storm source region.

Friendship

In this section, we follow South Korean tree planters who trace a dust stream beyond China, only to trace it back to China. Storms leave Chinese airspace, moving along hemispheric winds through the Koreas, Japan, and eventually the United States, where storms make landfall days and weeks after forming on the Inner Asian Frontiers of China.[11]

When former Ambassador Kwon Byung-Hyun speaks of the wall of trees in Chinese Inner Mongolia that has occupied him since retirement, he recounts a single storm. He recalls that in 1998, while he was serving as the first South Korean ambassador to the People's Republic of China after the renormalization of Sino-Korean diplomatic relations, Beijing was swept into an unusually severe dust storm, the first of many during his tenure. The pall of dust in the city affected his health, as it did for many Beijingers, who were advised by state public health agencies to wait indoors until the storm passed. The next day, at the South Korean embassy compound in Beijing, he received a phone call from his daughter, still in Seoul. She complained of a bout of yellow dust, Korea's infamous *hwangsa*, over the capital. This time, dust fall was severe enough in Seoul that it led to a spike in hospitalizations as well as the mandatory closure of schools across the peninsula.

"I realized she was talking about the same storm I had just witnessed," he remembered in a 2012 interview. "I saw for the first time that we all confronted a common problem that transcends national boundaries." It was at that moment, which he describes in the language of a dust-shocked epiphany, that he came to a dawning realization about China and Korea, the two countries whose friendship he had spent his adult life building. They were not simply regional neighbors split by long-standing political divides and bound by the economic interdependencies sparked by China's opening. In a storm, they were, for better or worse, sharers of an airstream, a first and second as the dust flies. Kwon and his daughter, divided by a sea, are drawn together through the motion of a dust cloud.

Kwon later saw that moment, stretched over days, as a turning point in his life, where he understood that land degradation in China would inevitably be a problem for its downwind neighbors. In a region characterized by long historical enmities, and whose twenty-first-century international relations are delicate, to say the least, Chinese dust traced the contours of a meteorological Asia in the making—one that must have been there all along but is newly revealed in haywire weather. As Kwon worked to orchestrate reopening political ties, the dust storm made atmospheric channels obvious as another modality of international relation. Nation-state divisions shifted into an uncomfortable meteorological kinship.

It was at that time he decided that he would dedicate the remainder of his life to afforesting Chinese deserts, raising "a billion trees in the desert" in a Sino-Korean friendship forest. Since 2000, his organization, Mirae Sup (Future Forest), has led groups of Chinese and Korean student planters into the Qubqi Desert, a dust storm source area for both Beijing and Seoul. His son, who is now the main organizer of the project, produces a map in PowerPoint that situates the planting site right on the dusty airstreams that passed first through Beijing and then through Seoul. This storm wall is a cut into the wind and a living symbol of a friendship along an atmospheric corridor. It is, in the glitzy ceremonies and planting trips that they take each spring, a "friendship forest," both marking political reunification and relentlessly emphasizing Chinese dusts as a medium of shared meteorological fate, rather than an occasion for atmospheric blame.

There is widespread public derision in South Korea of dust storms as proof of a Chinese failure to contain its bad weather at terrestrial borders. Against this, the ambassador offers this forest as a rebuke for those who collapse international airstreams into the reheated languages of international relations. Upwind of two capitals and a hemisphere, the friendship forest stands for the possibility of articulating a mutual protection, even while winds distribute harms unequally. His trees grow out of the understanding that, for now,

the wind
in a certain
and not another
direction will blow.[12]

According to the younger Kwon, these forests will protect both Beijing and Seoul, and even Tokyo, though Japanese counterparts have not been invited. Each city, in his reckoning, is a downwinds of a dusty continent. As South Korean tree planters continually remind me while we build sand barriers and sink poplar saplings into the loose sand of northern China's Qubqi Desert, a storm forming here will pass over both Beijing and Seoul. Wind is a thread they have pulled through two suspicious capitals. From the dust storm source area where these South Korean planters make their annual expedition, both cities are downwind. To be in the path of the same storm demands shared work for mutual protection, despite unequal responsibilities and exposures.

They call this condition *friendship*. Friendship, in trees and against dust, is not an abstract relationship, but it is formed in orienting toward the direction of the wind. It is a proposition for an ethics of downwindness and a way of orienting political and meteorological relations in this air that skewers two countries. Meteorological friendship in the wake of political normalization configures two capitals through reference to the storms that skewer both their airspaces. National friendship along an airstream does not demand an immediate accounting of meteorological damages, a stormy version of what Julie Chu[13] has described as a *politics of destination* in the transnational itineraries of other Chinese things. Rather, it asks us to grapple with the matter of atmospheric relation. For the ambassador, *friendship* is a term that orients in shared and distributed exposure. It is an opening in the search for a political vocabulary of being-downwind, of sharing and exposure through moving air.

This meteorological effacement of national space might also be an injunction to reconsider, in tracing dust and airstreams, relations between nations in ways that skirt the languages of international relations. Friendship, or shared downwindness, is a way of positioning oneself so as to allow the wind to determine the distribution of ethical locations. Practices of meteorological blame sit uneasily aside its patterning of airstreams into communities of fate, as it asks for political relations to rework themselves along the path of a storm. *Downwind* arcs toward geographies of relation wrought as effects of the aeolian sequencing of a mobile weather event. China and South Korea shift from territorial sovereignties into the ordinal numbers of first and second in a storm path, separated and bound by a day of dust flight in the time-space of an earthly suspension[14] as it gathers and breaks.

Winds and Worlds

There is a panoramic view of the Bay Area from the cafeteria of Lawrence Berkeley Labs' wall of windows, and Swensen gestures over the cranes of San Francisco's building boom and over the ocean where container ships skate in and out of the bay, as if on a clear day we could see China on the horizon. By the springtime, California will be less than two weeks downwind from China, and his samples will be coated with silicates from dust storms and a cocktail of distinct geochemical traces that they drag into suspension along their course. Isotopic analysis, he argues, will show that these traces of minerals and pollutants he gathers are Asian in origin, and Chinese in particular, especially as he has expressed skepticism over the power of computer modeling.

He has shown that in the comparative samples of air, there is a marked differential in the relative concentration of three lead isotopes—lead 206, 207, 208—which are left behind after the breakdown of uranium and thorium in the earth's surface (206/207 is a result of uranium decay and 206/208 is a result of thorium decay). The unique geological conditions of Asian tectonic formations and their idiosyncratic concentrations of these two radioactive elements means that Chinese land has an isotopic signature that "sticks out like a sore thumb" compared to US samples.

He describes atmospheric monitoring as a geological forensics, reading dust signals as they draw together the deep time of tectonic formation and radioactive decay, the burning of domestic coal, a crisis of desertification, the relocation of industry upwind. The experiments in developing a method for apportioning that have been stoked by provisions in the US Clean Air Act's excepting pollutions that can be shown to have external sources, has given form to a mode of geochemical calculation that brings together a dizzying range of temporal and spatial scales, most consequential as they shift through a confusion of states of matter. Searching upwind for constituents of American air still untouched by American pollution, scientists enact the atmosphere as a mixture waiting to be partitioned into a distribution of discrete responsibilities.

Airborne Dust Event

Winds and worlds swirl into unexpected configurations. In the dust, we might witness how a hemispheric wind-system might suspend and resettle Immanuel

Wallerstein's notion of a world-system. We may remember that in Wallerstein's framework, capital generates historically contingent architectures of relation, opening scales of analysis that are inherently relational and structured through its dynamics.[15] Capital coordinates divergent and disparate countries and political formations, materializing in an internally variegated world-system that can be traced from its historical rise to its inevitable fall. For anthropologists, the capitalist world-system and its economy are a way of articulating the materials and processes through which things are gathered and diverge. Through it takes shape a sprawling world of cores, semiperipheries, and peripheries, each a moment in the life of capital.

What world- and wind-systems then can be charted in turbulent phasings of earth and air? The question matters in asking how to track the environmental and political emergences of the more-than-human world—moment we sometimes call the Anthropocene. Forestry engineers and ex-herders in inland China, breathers and tree planters on a Sino-Korean dust stream, and atmospheric scientists in the western United States find themselves dispersed through their aerosol entanglement, multiple phases of modern dust. Worlds and experiments unfurl in the parade of material permutations of earth and air, phasing from *terra firma* to dust cloud to particulate sample.

NOTES

1 Timothy Ingold, "Footprints through the Weather-World: Walking, Breathing, Knowing," *Journal of the Royal Anthropological Institute* 16, no. S1 (2010): S121–39.

2 Theodor Schwenk, *Sensitive Chaos: The Creation of Flowing Forms in Water and Air*, trans. Oliver Whicher and Johanna Wrigle (New York: Schocken Books, 1976), 116.

3 Jerry Zee, "Holding Patterns: Sand and Political Time at China's Desert Shores," *Cultural Anthropology* 32, no. 2 (May 2017): 215–41.

4 Eyal Weizman, *Hollow Land: Israel's Architecture of Occupation* (London: Verso, 2007).

5 Vivian Choi, "Anticipatory States: Tsunami, War, and Insecurity in Sri Lanka," *Cultural Anthropology* 30, no. 2 (May 2015): 286–309.

6 Josh Haner, Edward Wong, Derek Watkins, and Jeremy White, "Living in China's Expanding Deserts," *New York Times*, October 24, 2016.

7 Ashley Carse, "Watershed," Theorizing the Contemporary, *Cultural Anthropology*, June 27, 2018, https://culanth.org/fieldsights/1465-watershed.

8 Aihwa Ong, *Neoliberalism as Exception: Mutations in Citizenship and Sovereignty* (Durham, NC: Duke University Press, 2006).

9   Gastón Gordillo, "Terrain as Insurgent Weapon: An Affective Geometry of War-
      fare in the Mountains of Afghanistan," *Political Geography* 64 (2018): 58.

10   Jerry Zee, "Groundwork: Symbiotic Governance in a Chinese Dust-Shed," in
      Frontier Assemblages: The Emergent Politics of Resource Frontiers in Asia, ed. Jason Cons
      and Michael Eilenberg, 59–73 (London: Wiley, 2019).

11   Owen Lattimore, *Inner Asian Frontiers of China* (Hong Kong: Oxford University
      Press, 1940).

12   Matthew Zapruder, "Poem for Japan" (2012), American Academy of Poets, ac-
      cessed June 28, 2018, https://www.poets.org/poetsorg/poem/poem-japan, lines
      33–36.

13   Julie Chu, *Cosmologies of Credit: Transnational Mobility and the Politics of Destination
      in China* (Durham, NC: Duke University Press, 2010).

14   Timothy Choy and Jerry Zee, "Condition—Suspension," *Cultural Anthropology* 30,
      no. 2 (2015): 210–23.

15   Immanuel Wallerstein, *Modern World-System I: Capitalist Agriculture and the Origins
      of the European World-Economy in the 16th Century* (Berkeley: University of Califor-
      nia Press, 2011).

8

Necrotone

Death-Dealing Volumetrics at the US-Mexico Border

HILARY CUNNINGHAM

Checkpoints.

Drones.

Integrated Fixed Towers.

Continuous fencing.

Barbed wire.

Land that is alive and storied—and stolen.

Increased human traffic in remote areas of the desert. Exposure to excessive heat, excessive cold. Dehydration. Heatstroke. Hypothermia. Risk of injury due to razor wire and wall spikes. Increased isolation and likelihood of exposure to violence and physical abuse—

Degradation of habitat and habitat connectivity. Roadside mortality. Behavioral maladaptation and distress owing to high-intensity lighting and operational noise. Avian mortality due to high fencing and towers. Soil erosion and flooding owing to nonpermeable fencing. Removal and destruction of fragile (and sometimes rare) desert flora owing to road infrastructure. Increased possibility of in-breeding expression. Disrupted migratory ranges—

Threatened. Endangered. Raped. Beaten. Jailed.

The US Department of Homeland Security (DHS) claims that 7,015 migrants died crossing the US-Mexico border between 1998 and 2016. Immigration activists say the number is much higher.

Chachalaca, ocelot, jaguarundi, collared peccary, barred tiger salamander—the mortality rates for these species is as yet unknown.

Exact numbers are always difficult to obtain. Like an ocean, the desert's vastness can swiftly disappear a body. Suck up. Swallow down.

Bodies off the record . . .

Edge effects.

The US-Mexico border wall and its harsh, unyielding—death-dealing—sovereignty.

Edging the Volumetric

Edge effect is a term coined by Wisconsin-based conservationist and ecologist Aldo Leopold (1887–1949). Also known as an *ecotone*, edge effect refers to the region or the *interface* between two different ecological habitats. For Leopold and other ecologists, one of the principal features of these "edges" (or transition zones) is that they exhibit a rich variety and abundance of life. The heightened quality of biodiversity in an edge effect is owing to the unique biological dynamics occurring at/in it:

> The result of such intermingling [of habitat edges] is a transitional zone and, more particularly, what is technically called an "edge effect" whereby an interpotentiation arises as the resources of one region cause those of the other to take a course of increased intensity not otherwise possible (the *tonus* root in ecotone signifies "tension"). In particular, when two different ecosystems (such as bioregions and econiches) meet, things happen that could never have emerged in the two regions taken separately. Instead of a mere summation of forces, there is an augmentation of the ecotone beyond its known measurable constituents: rather than $1+1=2$, we have a circumstance of $1+1=2+n$. The edge effect thus characterizes how, when two ecosystems are close at hand, the transition zone shows a tendency to greater variety and density of plant and animal life.[1]

Not surprisingly, for many ecologists, these biodiverse edge zones have become key sites of conservation efforts as well as land stewardship.

Although originally a scientific concept, *edge effect* has recently been taken up in a more critical, heuristic fashion—opening up a distinctive space for thinking about not only edges in broader terms, but also the role transitional edge zones might play in social, philosophical, and political terms. Environmental historian William Cronon, for example, has used *edge effects* to describe a new kind of interdisciplinarity, one he argues is required in the context of our contemporary environmental crisis.[2] For him, these are the edge-effect zones emerging at the interfaces of knowledge making, reflecting blendings of disciplinary perspectives as well as new species of thinking (in other words, $1+1=2+n$). Yet in the same breath, Cronon acknowledges the underside of the edge-effect concept, remarking that there are risks (and not just benefits) to boundary crossings, and that "dangerous, even lethal" qualities inhere in edge spaces. Similarly geographer Laurel Bellante and ethnobotanist Gary Nabhan have adapted the edge-effects concept to critically explore transboundary food supply chains (what they term *foodsheds*) at the US-Mexico border. In their analysis, the edge-effect zone is one where ecological, social, and political edges "get 'out-of-register' with one another," resulting in the acute "dissonances" expressed in disparities of food access, food safety, and food waste.[3]

It is with an eye to these later, more ecocritical connotations that I explore edge effects, seeking a more politicized (edgy?) analysis of state sovereignty, its iteration as a border wall (or what is also often termed *security fencing*) and the importance of thinking "volumetrically" about borders. In this, I depart from the concept's original biological emphasis on flourishing biodiversity, and turn to a much less "enlivened" edge-effect space—but one that seems more fitting to the current US-Mexico border wall and its death-dealing dynamics. This is an edge-effect space that is more *death* than *life* diverse; more *necrotone* than *ecotone* in character, so to speak.

For this reason, I also underscore the importance of edge effects for a multispecies or biotic approach to borders—something that I have elsewhere argued is long overdue in critical border studies.[4] The built environments of modern, international borders have been conceived almost exclusively in anthropocentric terms (i.e., in terms of terrestrial-linear space and human movement within it). As has been noted, terrestrial-linear borders have become increasingly problematic for states as they extend their sovereign reach to aquatic, atmospheric, or paraterrestrial spaces (such as Arctic ice floes).[5] Yet the linear-terrestrial paradigm has not only persisted, but also proliferated in our so-called global times—namely in the form of border walls or security fencing. Utilizing continuous barricading, double fencing, razor wire, extensive road systems, and stadium lighting, border walls have increased fivefold since 1989 (the year the notorious Berlin Wall supposedly "came down" amid much global acclaim).[6] While from a human perspective the effects of many of these border walls have been well documented, from a multispecies perspective their histories are less well known and less explored. This, however, is changing—and this chapter, I hope, offers a contribution, however modest, to that change.

To incorporate a biotic perspective, however, is not to undercut the importance of social, political, or metaphysical "edges." The edge-effect concept encompasses all of these, and in this respect invites a distinctive engagement with volumetricity in both literal and metaphorical ways. To "think volume," as Stuart Elden has enjoined, is not just to think outside of certain kinds of spatial boxes, but to think outside of epistemological and biotic ones as well.[7] Although the concept of edges has been associated (perhaps overly) with the "fully" and "flatly" cartographic linearity of the nation-state, edges in fact are surprisingly diverse and varied, including linear edges. In permaculture, for example, linear edges may be wavy, lobular, crenellated, zigzagged, or spiraled, each genre impacting growing area, exposure to sun, wind, and drainage, and linked to different microclimates. (Each edge can also be further refined in terms of defined and fuzzy variants.) Linear edges, then, can do much more than demarcate space and time, and are "productive" in manifold ways. This, coupled with the insight from philosopher Edward Casey that "we live at all times and in all places in a teeming edge-world" and that "there is no escaping edges anywhere," [8] suggests the volumetric, too, has "edges" worth exploring, as well as edge-effect zones worth uncovering.

My own engagement with the volumetric begins in spatial terms and I start with a conceptualization of edge effect as a particular impact (or series of impacts) generated by the imposition of a *spatial-temporal regime* upon a *bioscape*. I deliberately select *bioscape* over *landscape*, partly because it aligns nicely with a critique of terrestrial-linear space, but also because it mutes the tendency to think of space as occupied or inhabited principally by (mortal, embodied) humans. Bioscape instead offers a different ecological-ontological framework—i.e., a sense of space defined by the processes and interactions connecting a multiplicity of entities and presences. While turning to bioscape both builds upon ecological insights and echoes the more general turn to assemblage and entanglement imagery in social theory, doing so in terms of "edges" suggests that these are also consequential (and thus contingent) entanglements. It is for this reason, I suggest, that the edges and edge effects of bioscapes can be seen as key (and often critical) ecological, political, and ethical interfaces of human and more-than-human worlds.

Edgeworlds

How would our thinking of geo-power, geo-politics and geo-metrics
work if we took the earth; the air and the subsoil; questions of land,
terrain, territory; earth processes and understandings of the world as the
central terms at stake, rather than a looser sense of the "global"?

—Stuart Elden, "Secure the Volume," 49

Sovereign borders are ultimately designed to manage human bodies in space and time, and thus are always experienced in somatic and embodied terms. A border wall consisting of miles of coiled razor wire will therefore bring what might be called a body's *somatic edges* into play in specific ways, generating certain kinds of *bodywork* (or, more properly, *ecosomatics*).[9] This has been at the heart of the human tragedy occurring at the US-Mexico border. The continuous fencing, barricading and militarization of the border has "funneled" migrants to remote portions of the desert where they have had to endure long and often fruitless treks northward, frequently without proper foot cover or adequate water supplies, and in conditions of extreme heat and cold. While some critics have insightfully connected this to a "letting-die" kind of political dynamic, I also see it in more active terms—the wall deliberately generating new somatic edges for human survival; the state then falsely wringing its hands as corpses begin showing up in its deliberately designed edge effect.[10]

Yet what kinds of bodies "count" as we theorize, critique, and advocate for more just borders, for more responsible and ecologically sensitive sovereignties? Border scholar Franck Billé has urged us to think of borders more in somatic terms (in terms of skin, for example), arguing for an analytics that does not unwittingly or automatically prioritize visuality:

Foregrounding the elastic and the pliable nature of skin can encourage a more sensuous and synesthetic ethnographic work . . . the malleable and stretchable quality of skin makes it an apt analogy for state borders. "Skin" and "border," tightly enmeshed in political and popular somatic metaphors, are contact surfaces akin to a topological ribbon liable to tension, torsion, and distortion. Skin/border indexes the unresolvable gap between, on the one hand, the topographic inscription of unambiguous boundary lines (and their attendant fetishization) and on the other, the topological realities of networks, rhizomes, and flows that actually sustain the illusion of political partitions.[11]

I also take this as an invitation to think about borders in terms of nonhuman "skins," i.e., in terms of fur, feathers, and scales, so to speak. To engage with nonhuman bodies and their haptic capacities (as well as ways of "seeing") is to enter into the different spatial regimes of nonhuman creatures—earth, air, subsoil—and thus into an expanded sense of somatic registers and animal edges.

The US-Mexico border is a particularly important example in this respect owing to how its built environment as a "continuous wall" impacts the numerous biogeographies and biocommunities it bisects. From the perspective of landscape ecology, the border slices east–west through three north–south mountain ranges at a roughly seventy degree angle, all of which "exhibit high spatial heterogeneity in precipitation" and thus encompass numerous ecosystems, including seven transboundary ones.[12] Currently there are approximately 653 miles (1,051 kilometers) of fencing along the border consisting of a patchwork of reinforced steel walls, bollard-style fencing, barbed wire, wire mesh, and chain-link fencing, as well as levee fencing in the Rio Grande Valley.[13]

One of the first studies to look at the potential impacts of continuous barriers (as well as hundreds of miles of road infrastructure) for terrestrial wildlife was Jesse Lasky, Walter Jetz, and Timothy Keitt's 2011 transboundary study. Using *species movement ability* as its central analytic, the report found that "57 amphibian, 178 reptilian, and 134 mammalian species occur within 50 km [31 miles] of the border, with border fence intersecting the ranges of 38, 152, and 113 species, respectively." The study also showed that barriers were "more common in areas rich in species with small ranges."[14] Lasky et al.'s conclusions were cautious, but also sobering from an environmental perspective: the very linearity of the border wall allowed it to bisect a large number of nonhuman populations and habitats. New barriers would likely increase the number of species at risk.[15] Subsequent research conducted by immigration, First Nations, conservation, and environmental groups (as well as state organizations) not only augmented these findings,[16] but also became the basis of several lawsuits aimed at preventing further fencing.[17]

Yet the "environmentalization" of the border has been met with significant challenges, including complex shifts in land and resource management patterns as well as the ongoing provisions of the 2005 REAL ID Act (which give the DHS secretary authority to waive federally mandated environmental reviews). I suggest here an additional challenge: that of embracing a volumetric sensibility as part of this critique, i.e., a sensitivity to the different kinds of space, bodywork, and somatic edges created by borders, especially as they impact the nonhuman. An ecologically politicized volumetric sees borders in terms of the rhythms and flows of spaces across, above, and below; that is, in terms of the chthonic, supernal, and terrestrial movements of nonhuman bodies. Such of course does not exclude the deleterious effects of borders for humans (especially those made vulnerable by the stratifying effects of capital). Rather it situates human and nonhuman well-being at the same crossroads, recognizing that "the planet's most vulnerable human and nonhuman populations are on the frontiers of social marginalization *and* ecological destruction."[18]

Movement, somatics, edges, and edge effects are key here. In the quote above, geographer Stuart Elden urges us toward earth, air, and subsoil as interlocutors of the "global." Is this not also an invitation to think in "planetary" terms, too? (I note that *planet* comes from the Greek *planar* for "wander," and thus is kindred to the idea of *species movement ability*.) What might happen if we placed "the human" alongside and within the movement worlds of "nonhuman" actors, including those of wind and water and the other ecological-temporal processes integral to all movement? All of this seems to point to the very different kinds of edgework performed within our planet's "congeries of competing edges."[19]

Edgework

Figure 8.1 reproduces an image from the article "The Ecological Disaster That Is Trump's Border Wall: A Visual Guide."[20] The image depicts several species that are listed as "endangered" and "threatened" or "of concern" on international, federal, and/or state inventories.[21] The image also distills the border into a single location within the Lower Rio Grande Valley National Wildlife Refuge, a highly contested ecological site and currently designated by the Trump administration for future fencing.[22]

It is not clear whether the thirteen nonhuman animals positioned in front of the border wall are located on the US or Mexican side of the border—a detail that presumably would be significant if any human figures were present. (The image is perhaps notable for its lack of any distinct human form—though the wall is definitely an anthropogenic product.) While the speciated depiction of the nonhuman animals is perhaps not surprising (given that the unit *species* is key to US and international environmental legislation and thus to the lawsuits opposing the border), a species-spatial reading of the nonhuman animals is also illustrative. All the animals are depicted in flat, two-dimensional space,

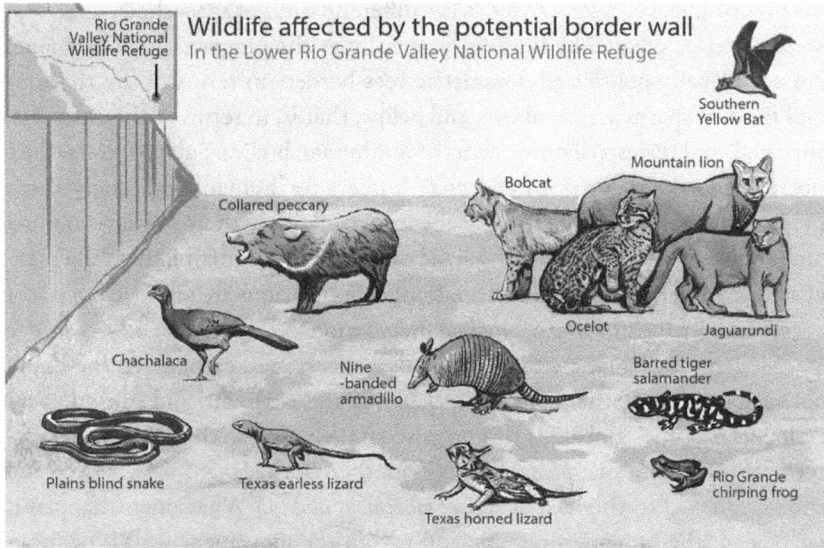

Figure 8.1. "Wildlife Affected by the Potential Border Wall,"
drawn by Javier Zarracina, *Vox*, 2017

but also reference "habitat" and thus a whole suite of ecological processes, rhythms, and embodied movements linked to water and food sources, reproductive sites, as well as protective cover in light of predator-prey relationships. Key to a proper understanding of the image, then, are ecological concepts of habitat connectivity and foraging animal bodies constantly on the move at a variety of scales—each animal's bodywork inextricably tied to a distinctive set of "somatics" and environmental contingencies (or edges).

Overall the image references what earlier I termed a *necrotone*—an edge-effect zone in which concepts of disassemblage and spatial disruption dominate. The necrotone's death-dealing dynamic is embedded in the wall's very rationale and its linear, surface-oriented construction. The border's extensive road infrastructure, for example, has entailed huge displacements of soil, water diversion, and extensive removal of vegetation, thereby dramatically altering and indeed destroying terrestrial and aquatic-based habitats. Likewise the "impermeability" of the wall's continuous barricading (designed to prevent human bodies from wriggling or breaking through) and double fencing has *sealed off* portions of the range habitats of many nonhuman animals, fragmenting these areas and, in some cases, permanently obstructing wildlife corridors.

The necrotone's edge effect—at levels of the individual, population, and species—is thus *built into* the border wall and functions in terms of both the direct *and* cascade effects of its design.

The border's built horizontal features, however, also conjoin with verticality to produce further edge effects. Fence height along the border varies (typically from four to seven meters) and is intended to deter humans from climbing over it. (The prototypes for the proposed additional seven hundred miles [1,127 kilometers] of fencing, unveiled in October 2017, feature fencing five to nine meters high.)[23] In the upper right of the image is a Southern yellow bat (a nocturnal, aerial insectivore), presumably a creature who can fly above (and hence over) the wall. While this is the case for some (although not all) volant species, the story is not quite so simple. The impact of the border on flying or gliding animals, for example, is likely to be substantial, especially in terms of migration routes. (Significant here is how the border wall reconfigures "stopovers," i.e., access to water resources and vegetative cover.) The blind, light-sensitive bat, however, also references an added nocturnal volumetrics. The effects of artificial lighting and the creation of twenty-four-hour daylight conditions are known to generate "maladaptive behavior" in bats and birds— including disorientation, collisions, and interruption of the light-dark cycles mediating behavior (hence affecting feeding, mating behavior, and metabolic processes)—and, for many species, direct mortality through *light capture*. The latter is a phenomenon whereby birds become "trapped" in a light zone and cannot navigate their way "out," eventually becoming overcome with exhaustion. (Most birds, incidentally, migrate at night.)[24]

Finally, the border's volumetric reach also extends below and into the burrows and movements of subterrestrial animal bodies, as well as the movements of water forms. To the bottom left of the image is a Plains blind snake—a creature who spends much of the day below the ground in loose, moist soil, surfacing at night to feed on ant larvae and termites. This creature's presence in the image also attests to the limits of a linear, above-ground optic, namely by referencing the border wall's substantial impacts for the subterrestrial world. Subsurface impacts include: obstructions resulting from fence posts (typically sunk one meter or more into the ground and also frequently anchored in cement); impacts related to roads and their infrastructure as well as vehicular traffic; and the diversion of water, including its flooding effects. (Flooding is particularly significant to the Plains blind snake and other limbless or rolling locomotors as sections of the Rio Grande Valley have been targeted for a nine-meter concrete wall and more concrete-enforced levee fencing.)

"Outlandish"

Figure 8.1, of course, depicts a relatively small number of the nonhuman animals impacted by the border wall—that is, if it is read from a *species* vantage. A *volumetric* perspective, however, deepens and expands its purport, leading us to a wider posthumanist-ecological take on this particular "meeting-of-edges." At the US-Mexico border wall, then, edge effects are experienced across a wide spectrum of embodied actors, including landscapes, watersheds, human migrants, large carnivores, migratory birds, and floodplains. An edge-effect analytic therefore goes beyond acknowledging that this borderscape occurs in the context of *contingently inflected* clusters. *Edge effects* underscores that these are also directly generative of consequential human/nonhuman relations— relations which unfold across the "edges" of our biotic and ontological worlds (entanglements+*n*).

To be sure not everyone is comfortable with this prospect. Not everyone is comfortable with the "+*n*" of turning to the nonhuman and its call for a reorientation toward a care and concern for both humans and other-than-humans (at the US-Mexico border or elsewhere). "Slippery slope" arguments abound—how can one possibly compare the life of a bird, a snake, a bat to the life of a human? But even these arguments draw upon a specific kind of ontological *terrestrial-archy*. In the slippery slope critique, Aristotelian-Darwinian hierarchies of life are preserved, merely becoming a "muddied" version of human ascendancy. *Becoming-animal* at borders is thus a radically volumetric proposition. It requires a speciated spatial-somatic imagination— an imagination that is perhaps "outlandish" in that it asks us to think outside the anthropo-terrestrial paradigm and its axis of: (*x*) horizontal geospace; and (*y*) vertical ontological-space. A volumetric imagination therefore asks: What might a biotic border (and hence a biotic sovereignty) look like? How can sovereign states extend their political, ecological, moral, and ethical responsibilities to the heterogeneous spaces that subterrestrial, aquatic, and airborne creatures (animal, vegetable, mineral) inhabit?

As I close this chapter, it appears that, for me, the turn to the volumetric is of necessity "outlandish." *Edge effects* builds upon the outlandishness of a volumetric imagination, while at the same time critically raising questions about who and what is edged out of ecological, political, metaphysical, and moral consideration (in this instance at the US-Mexico border wall). This, I suggest, is part of the volumetric's "edginess." The ongoing, tragic realities of the spatial reconfigurations occurring at the US-Mexico border (or in Europe's new antimigrant fencing) are only partially captured in terms of assemblages or entanglements. Spatial regimes entail *necrotones* and the *+ns* of their edge effects. Death holes. Points of no return. Mass graves. Extinctions. Desecrated ancestors. Places where the wind cannot go. While the human reality is indeed tragic at border walls, confining the discussion to the *anthropos*, making humans the only bodies (and hence selves) that count, is to ignore all those who remain off the record. The overriding result is that the nonhuman remains outside of moral consideration (itself a long-standing edge effect of Western anthropocentrism).

I find myself wondering if there is a zone in myself somewhere, an edge effect that might speak to this and capture a sense of what I am trying to convey—
    Checkpoints.
    Drones.
    Integrated Fixed Towers.
    Continuous fencing.
    Barbed wire.
    Land that is alive and storied—and stolen.

The heart, it appears, also lends itself to volumetric analysis.

I am told that interpreting an echocardiogram involves observing "segmentations of measured image sequences"—the goal being to identify "the exact boundaries" of "objects of interest."

Wall movement detection.
Evidence of seizures.
Pathological degenerations.

It is a year ago and I am in Ambos Nogales, on the US side—walking toward "the fence" with two dear friends, two long-standing, seasoned, and weathered immigration advocates. Ricardo is seventy-eight and Mary has just turned eighty. It is extremely hot and the mid-afternoon sun is brutal, but nevertheless we make our way carefully down to the US-Mexico border wall. I am singularly aware of bones, fragile and lovely and stubborn in the movements of elderly bodies. Ricardo and Mary want to show me something—*something important.* I have agreed to come with them, but will never forgive myself if either of them falls on the rough, uneven sidewalks . . .

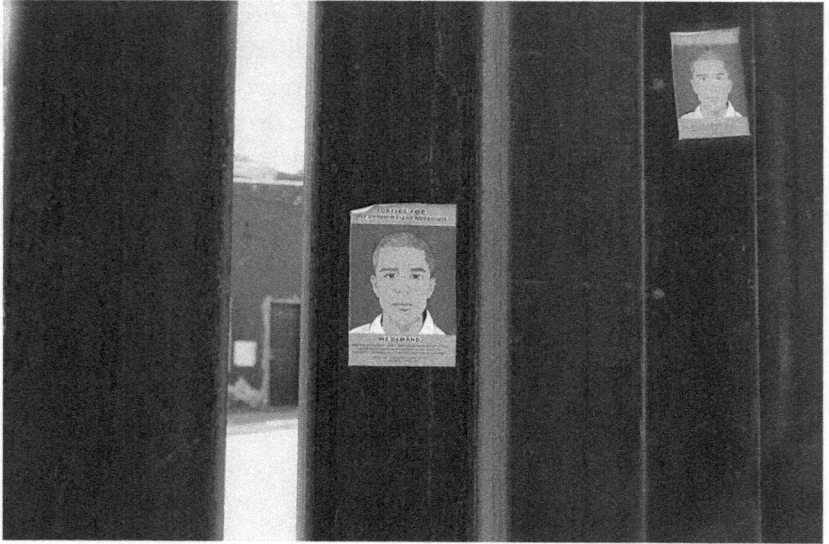

Figure 8.2. The Border Wall: Ambos, Nogales, US side—April 2017.
Photo by the author.

We come up close to a spot at the wall. Between the metal slats are slender gaps and I can see down into Mexico's Calle Internacional. Ricardo points to where a sixteen-year-old boy was shot and killed by a US Border Patrol agent in 2010. I find sticker images of José Antonio Elena Rodríguez's face pasted on the fence as Ricardo narrates the event—

José was shot through the fence ten times.
—mostly in the back.
He was still alive when he fell to the ground.
—but the agent kept firing anyway.

(We do not know it yet, but in twelve months the agent will be acquitted of murder.)

As I listen to Ricardo, in my mind's eye I see José's body on the ground, bleeding to death. Beside him is a deer, also dying—except that its bloodied body is entangled in a coil of razor wire. It is impossible of course—José's body is at the US-Mexico border. The deer's body is at one of Hungary's new anti-refugee fences.[25] Yet my mind's eye will not let me keep the images separate, insisting upon a *volumetric association*.

My struggle to make sense of the two images is suddenly interrupted—a cloud of dust in the distance announces a US Border Patrol car, now barreling down the hill toward us. In the next minute we are told that we are trespassing on government property and are ordered to step away from the fence.

The others say nothing, and begin turning as if to leave.

But I hesitate—foolishly, vexatiously, I hesitate—lifting my hand, wanting to let my fingers trail across the metal wall . . . wanting to leave *something important* here. My own "sticker" perhaps? Some message of love and compassion for José's mother. A lament for the deer's terrible sufferings. Some marker of outrage for the two cruel deaths . . .

"It's for your own safety," the agent mutters at me ominously.

Wall movement detection.

I remember snatching back my hand, hiding it in my pocket.

Evidence of seizures.

I remember it was my heart that cried out—

NOTES

1   Edward S. Casey, *The World on Edge* (Bloomington: Indiana University Press, 2017), 177.
2   William Cronon, "Why Edge Effects," *Edge Effects*, October 9, 2014, http://edgeeffects.net/author/wcronon.
3   Laurel Bellante and Gary Nabhan, "Borders out of Register: Edge Effects in the US-Mexico Foodshed," *Culture, Agriculture, Food and Environment* 38, no. 2 (2016): 104–5.
4   Hilary Cunningham, "Permeabilities, Ecology and Geopolitical Boundaries," in *A Companion to Border Studies*, ed. T. Wilson and H. Donnan (Oxford: Wiley-Blackwell, 2012), 371–86. See also Juanita Sunberg, "Diabolic *Caminos* in the Desert and Cat Fights on the Rio: A Posthumanist Political Ecology of Boundary Enforcement in the US-Mexico Borderlands," *Annals of the Association of American Geographers* 101 (2001): 318–36.
5   See Billé, introduction to this volume.
6   Hilary Cunningham and Stephen Scharper, "Social Ecologies as Gated Ecologies," in *The Social Ecology of Border Landscapes*, ed. Michelle Zebich-Knos and Anna Grichting (New York: Anthem, 2017), 53–68. See also Elizabeth Vallet, "Introduction," in *Borders, Fences and Walls: State of Insecurity?*, ed. Elizabeth Vallet (Burlington: Ashgate Publishing, 2014): 1–8.
7   Stuart Elden, "Secure the Volume: Vertical Geopolitics and the Depth of Power," *Political Geography* 34 (2013): 35–51.
8   Casey, *World on Edge*, 2017: xv.

9   See Hilary Cunningham, "Barb," Theorizing the Contemporary, *Cultural Anthropology*, June 27, 2018, https://culanth.org/fieldsights/1460-barb.

10 See also Jason De León's, *The Land of Open Graves: Living and Dying on the Migrant Trail* (Oakland: University of California Press, 2015).

11 Franck Billé, "Skinworlds: Borders, Haptics, Topologies," *Environment and Planning D: Society and Space* 36, no. 1 (2018): 60–77.

12 Jesse Lasky, Walter Jetz, and Timothy Keitt, "Conservation Biogeography of the US–Mexico Border: A Transcontinental Risk Assessment of Barriers to Animal Dispersal," *Diversity and Distributions* 17 (2011): 674.

13 Michael John Garcia, "Barriers along the US Borders: Key Authorities and Requirements," Congressional Research Service (CRS) report, April 8, 2015, https://fas.org/sgp/crs/homesec/R43975.pdf.

14 Lasky et al., "Conservation Biogeography," 677, 674.

15 To date, security barricading has generally had negative impacts on local flora and fauna, but one exception is Korea's demilitarized zone (DMZ), erected in 1953. According to ecologists, the absence of human activity in the area has made the zone attractive to thousands of threatened and endangered species including the white-napped and red-crowned cranes, black bears, egrets, and a subspecies of the Siberian tiger.

16 For recent research on the impacts of security barriers for wildlife at the "anti-refugee" (barbed and razor-wired) security fencing in Bosnia, Serbia, and Hungary, see Arie Trouwborst, Floor Fleurke, and Jennifer Dubrulle, "Border Fences and Their Impacts on Large Carnivores, Large Herbivores and Biodiversity: An International Wildlife Law Perspective," *Review of European, Comparative and International Environmental Law* 25, no. 3 (2016), https://papers.ssrn.com/sol3/papers.cfm?abstract_id=2848898; John D. C. Linnell, Arie Trouwborst, Luigi Boitani, Petra Kaczensky, Djuro Huber, Slaven Reljic, Josip Kusak, et al., "Border Security Fencing and Wildlife: The End of the Transboundary Paradigm in Eurasia?," *PLOS Biology* 14, no. 6 (2016), http://journals.plos.org/plosbiology/article/metrics?id=10.1371/journal.pbio.1002483.

17 See Fernanda Santos, "No Environmental Impact Study? No Border Wall, Lawsuit Says," *New York Times*, April 13, 2017, https://www.nytimes.com/2017/04/13/us/no-environmental-impact-study-no-border-wall-lawsuit-says.html.

18 Cunningham and Scharper, "Social Ecologies," 54.

19 Casey, *World on Edge*, xx.

20 Eliza Barclay and Sarah Frostenson, "The Ecological Disaster That Is Trump's Border Wall: A Visual Guide," *Vox*, October 29, 2017, https://www.vox.com/energy-and-environment/2017/4/10/14471304/trump-border-wall-animals.

21 The Southern yellow bat, for example, is listed as "low concern" by IUNC and not federally listed as threatened or endangered in the United States, but is considered a species of "special concern" by the Arizona Game and Fish Department, the State of Nevada Comprehensive Wildlife Conservation Strategy, and the California Department of Fish and Wildlife. See LCR MSCP, "Western Yellow

Bat," LCR MSCP website, last updated December 21, 2018, https://www.lcrmscp.gov /species/western_yellow.html.

22 The refuge is not contiguous but a collection of scattered pieces of conservation lands, stretching almost a hundred miles (160 kilometers) across four counties in Texas.

23 See Elliot Spagat, "Border Wall Tests Find Heights Should Keep Out Crossers," *AP News*, January 20, 2018, https://www.apnews.com/a7c524fcd45e4c999959970d337db dc3c.

24 On the ecological effects of artificial light for nonhumans, see Aisling Irwin, "The Dark Side of Light: How Artificial Lighting Is Harming the Natural World," *Nature*, January 16, 2018, https://www.nature.com/articles/d41586-018-00665-7.

25 Damjan Raknić, "UZNEMIRUJUĆE FOTOGRAFIJE Na granicama Hrvatske s Mađarskom i Slovenijom zbog žice životinje ugibaju u strašnim mukama," *JutarnjiVijesti*, December 12, 2015, https://www.jutarnji.hr/vijesti/hrvatska/uznemirujuce -fotografije-na-granicama-hrvatske-s-madarskom-i-slovenijom-zbog-zice-zivotinje -ugibaju-u-strasnim-mukama/196525/.

9 Surface

Seeing, Solidifying, and Scaling Urban Space in Hong Kong

CLANCY WILMOTT

The geographer Doreen Massey writes that space is not a surface.[1] When we imagine travelling, she argues, we too often imagine traversing a homogenous and continuous plane, a flatness that echoes the surface of a map. This surface is the same spatial imagination that opened the world up to the conquering practices of the explorer, cartographer, and colonizer, while also reifying the landscape into taxonomies, cartographies, and territories. "Surface" is the language of voyages of discovery and conquest: small ships sailing across the flat expanse of the map, where other people and cultures are stagnant, sitting on the map (rather than being-in the world), waiting for the moment of encounter, and passive to the process of colonizations. The surface, in Massey's estimation, is anticipatory and bland, purposefully and strategically depriving people and spaces of vitality and difference.

For Massey, this is a destructive view of space. Instead, she argues for a rethinking of space, which centers on dynamism, plurality, and multiplicity, where people, places, and cultures are embedded, situated, and emergent: "It is a move away from that imagination of space as a continuous surface that the coloniser, as the only active agent, crosses to find the to-be-colonised simply 'there.' This would be space not as a smooth surface but as the sphere of coexistence of a multiplicity of trajectories."[2] This opposition between surfaces and spheres of coexistence suggests a dialectical problem with the way in which we imagine and experience spatiality. On the one hand, space is of surface—flat, egocentric, regular. On the other, space is also voluminous, multiplicitous, and heterogeneous. This is a question of surfaces versus volumes and of geometry versus matter, based in the epistemological distance between how we see, solidify, and scale space and the everyday business of living.

This chapter considers surface in the context of voluminous urban spaces— upward and downward, inward and outward—and how they are imagined, produced, and lived. Between spatial imaginations and spatial experiences, we turn to Hong Kong, and a series of interviews I undertook there in 2014. Often called the world's most vertical city because of the number of skyscrapers it houses, Hong Kong is a city where maps and materialities are never far removed. Tracing lived histories and lived realities, we can document the intertwining of these processes through archives and interviews, as words, landscapes, actions, and imaginations emerge together in complex volumes. These interviews traced how people navigate through vertical urban spaces, using a myriad of maps and digital mobile devices, social interactions and encounters, and intuitions and guesswork. The history of how volumes have been managed and muddled haunts these interviews, in materialities, languages, and anachronisms. These are everyday moments of mapping, between voluminous landscapes, volumetric discourses, and flat representations, which reveal complex navigations between multiple surfaces, solids, and spaces.

The hybridity of what Sybille Lammes and I have previously called *looking and doing*, or in de Certeau's terms *map and tour*, sees an ongoing coemergence of *seeing*, *solidifying*, and *scaling*.[3] To *see* is at once to look and to imagine. It might be to gaze across a surface toward the horizon, or to gaze down upon the landscape like one might stare at a map. It is also to create imaginative tools which promulgate new surfaces, and distinguish old ones: grounds, planes, grids, boundaries, datums. To *solidify* is to materialize spatial imaginations into the material world. In solidifications, roads are made in straight lines across terrestrial surfaces, and buildings with multiple floors are formed, interconnected at different vertical points, bounded by walls. Solidification is to render the volumes of the world into a series of surfaces, two lines at the beginning and the end of a journey, with no accounting for the space in between. Finally, in this chapter, to *scale* has two meanings. The first is to take something small like a brick or something large like a building and to trace how they are connected and coconstituted from the local to the global. It is to measure proportionally, to compare metrically. But the second way it might be understood is to rise upward, to climb. To scale a building is to achieve height and to move upward: a bodily, affective, and imaginative journey through multi-dimensional space. These are both voluminous ways of understanding scale.

The practices of seeing, solidifying, and scaling volumes combine and recombine the acts of looking and doing—of the map and the tour—in unusual ways. De Certeau writes that the map and the tour constitute two different ways of comprehending and navigating space: one is relational (where might A be located in comparison to B) and one is procedural (from A, turn right and walk five steps in order to get to B).[4] This distinction forms the crux of this chapter: when we discuss how volume shapes our everyday life, the difference between looking and doing is one of seeing, building, and living *upon surfaces* rather than *in spaces*. At the same time, this is not an absolute distinction: surface and space intertwine, hybridize, and fracture in the politics of mundane acts of everyday navigation.

Seeing Surfaces

Vicki moves the map on her phone with her index finger, frowning as she tries to find where we are. Lacking any contours or vertical descriptors on the map, she is relying on color and the shape of the road to indicate how far along the path we are in a patch of green that symbolizes the Lung Fu Shan Country Park.

"You know, the green areas is mountains," she says.

Standing under the Lippo Centre on Queens Road Central, Mohammed walks in circles turning his map. He zooms in on the Bank of China building, rendered into a three-dimensional trapezoid, trying to find where it is.

"Yeah, that doesn't really look like it."

Early Chinese maps of Hong Kong make little of the island. A small shape at the edge of dynastic empires, it is sometimes marked with curved lines representing its mountains and hills. More often, the Kowloon Peninsula to the north of the island is marked with eight or nine hills. After the British began their occupation of the island in 1841—and signed the Treaty of Nanking shortly after in 1842—they found a troublesome landscape. Hard hills sharply inclined into the water's edge, with few inlets or flat valleys for pasture. The first British map makers, more inclined toward mathematical precision than impression, struggled and experimented with ways of imagining these hills according to their cartographic logic. This logic was predicated on a rationalist desire for a universal system of understanding and representing space. The abstracted view of the top-down orthogonal "god-trick" brought authority with an imagined gaze, staring down at the world from some godly heaven.[5] This god-trick also flattened the landscape onto a *mappa* (or sheet) or *carte* (card/

chart), a surface across which boundaries were drawn, territories secured, and settlements, then cities, were built.

Yet, this god-trick came across a trickster landscape. Despite the desires of the cartographer and planner, the hills of Hong Kong stood tall, and the harbor deep. The surface of sea and sand was precarious, as the shoreline shifted inward and outward, upward and downward. Living *in* rather than *on* this landscape was not a superficial affair. Belcher used shading and hachuring to develop a sense of the peaks and troughs of the interior—a trick to cast a planner's eye over a voluminous landscape and see the terrain of the surface.[6] Next came measurement, in the Cartesian sense. Ships cast sounds to the bottom of the bays in even patinas, and numbers appeared dotted across the surface of the mappa, the rolling bed of the harbor flattened into a spray of numbers across a sheet. Once the approach was secure, the cartographers then turned their eyes upward to the hills. Hachures and shading were transformed into contours—where the hills were reimagined in ten-foot jumps, with lines connecting the points at which this height emerged. The voluminous landscape became "volumetric": measured, meticulous, metricized.

To establish a universal system of measurement, rather than a relative one, there needs to be a common starting point. The coordinate system and the establishment of the Greenwich meridian solved this issue across the horizontal surface of the map—and the imagined distance between two points was endurably consistent across the god-trick. On the vertical, however, the grids of the z axis were far more difficult to cohere across empire. Measuring height is both situated and relative, since landscapes rise and sink, the tide washes up and down, and the oceans are not consistently level across the world. In Hong Kong, this meant that in 1866 a copper bolt was driven into the pier of the Naval Dockyard by the crew of the survey vessel, HMS *Rifleman*, to determine a consistent sea level for the measurement of the hills.

The cartographic and urban imaginations of the nineteenth century were thoroughly intertwined. The sublime geometry of the rectilinear and radial systems—whether the boulevards of Paris and Barcelona, or the grids of New York or Melbourne—were also prefigured in the faith in the god-trick. But the uniformity of the geometry demanded a uniformity of the landscape—a surface rather than a space. Vast plains were selected for new cities—like Chicago—or hills were flattened and valleys filled in. Accompanying Collison's maps were a series of sketches. These sketches were drawn from a bird's-eye angle, showing the hills and settlements emerging on the island. Signs of human activity abound—ships in the harbor and bungalows in the valleys. But it is the landscape that is of particular interest here. While the sketches demonstrate the height of the hills and a marked undersupply of flat land for building, there is evidence, even at this stage, that the process of surfacing the landscape had begun. Along the coast in the sketch of Causeway Bay, a number of small hillocks are depicted, peaks flattened into smooth, level surfaces. Upon one hill, a small bungalow sits. City maps of Victoria show a sheer determination to etch a regular rectilinear system. But crowded into the sea are sharp inclines: the city plan becomes warped, parallel lines bunch together at some ends, and traversal of the island is dependent on long roads such as Queens Road and Des Voeux Street that wind around the shore. While the smaller hills were eventually flattened—even in Kowloon—to make way for new developments such as roads and airports, a series of land reclamations also began as soon as subdivisions were laid out: "The very first lots sold along Queens Road Central were at the seashore and resulted in some reclamation, albeit illegal."[7] If there was not sufficient flat land for building, then new surfaces were made, spanning out into the harbor, etched into pencil on older maps, and imagined surface which was yet to be built.

The maps of the reclamations are accompanied by stunning cross sections, showing the elevation across the island and the sea. These imagined transects produce two surfaces. The first is that of the line, the imagined surface of ground which drops off into obscurity when considered in three dimensions. The second is that of the polygon, the imagined, sometimes geological but usually blank, underground—a volume that is assumed to be there, but unseen and unseeable, short of blasting a passage through the rock. Here, surfaces are made jointly—in plan and elevation—generalized into a three-dimensional imaginary, with zero points at latitude (x), longitude (y), and sea level (z). But, in a twist of fate, the reclamation process meant that the Naval Dockyard had to be moved because it was no longer on the shore. In the course of building, the Rifleman's bolt, still the vertical datum for elevation in Hong Kong, was moved too. The dockyard wall was rebuilt and the bolt returned in its continued role as an imagined level surface from which upward and downward could be mapped. However, as the reclamation settled the wall began to sink, and the bolt with it.[8] This generated a new, unfixed zero point, accidentally formed so that it was always somewhat lower than when it was last checked. In the second round of reclamations, the dockyard was moved again—this time to the northern shore of Kowloon. The bolt was repositioned again, and a few more feet were lost. Eventually, in the latter half of the twentieth century, a long series of readings of the sea level were taken and their average became a new sea level.

The process of imagining how volumetric space might be built is intertwined with uneven landscapes, imperfect representations, volatile datums, imperial urban ideologies, and rationalist logics. This sees volumes surveyed and drawn on the flat sheets of elevations and plans, and then reinscribed into the landscape through flattening and terracing. This whole process is one of seeing through surfaces—imagined planes which are consistent and stable.

Solidifying Surfaces

On Des Voeux Street, Camille looks up and sees a walkway about thirty feet in the air, emerging from one building, spanning the width of the road, and joining another. She points at it, and opens Google Maps.

"We have to get up there," she says.

Ellen frowns. A locked gate sits next to a glass rotunda with some stairs going downward. Below us, a glimpse of a green park peeks through the gate. We can hear children laughing, even if we can't see them. She frowns.

"Maybe we need to go downstairs."

Hong Kong's urbanism is a combination of top-down planning and bottom-up pragmatism, characterized by a network of "three-dimensional connectivity"[9] composed of footbridges, walkways, buildings, tunnels, platforms and infrastructures: "Hong Kong exhibits neither objects nor a field, but a mass composed of tightly packed, continually ramifying figures. These figures connect in three dimensions, creating the impression of the city as a continuous, urban-scaled interior."[10] This mass is a dense and intense connective tissue, through which the everyday mobility and navigation of Hong Kong occurs. Much like a living organism, the passages of transit, exchange, and transformation are funneled through structures that provide limited choice in wayfinding, access, and direction. Less organically, however, the urban form is resolutely solidified into cubic surfaces that occasionally offer glimpses of, if not access to, the interior. This typified pattern of flat surfaces—walls, ceilings, floors—is, in part, borne of the metrics of the grid, the rectilinear urban imagination it fostered, and the subdivisions which ensued. This arises from the volumetric logic of efficient urban capital:[11] the vertical grid along the y and z axes is as driven by capitalist desires for spatial efficiency and maximization of productive space, as has been argued about the flat horizontal grid. These volumes are more volumetric than voluminous, strictly governed by planning regimes which determine minimum and maximum building heights, gross floor areas and site coverage.

In the solidification of urban volumes through walls, openings must also be found: doors let humans through, and windows let air through. Stairs arrange travel between up and down, and glass, maps, and sounds hint toward what is hidden behind. Throughout our walks, we encounter a multitude of intangible moments of disconcerted propinquity—where our destination is visible and close (either upward or downward), but our path is utterly obscured. These volumes started with the hills, and the lack of flat land—already voluminous solids—and became reformed into flat paths, then terraces for buildings, reclamations, multistory skyscrapers, walkways, underground infrastructures for trains and cars. Hong Kong's volumetric mass is thin, centered on vertical rather than horizontal axes. New developments gather pencil-thin skyscrapers together in sheets of what have been called *wall-like buildings*. These buildings redirect airflow by creating wind blocks, and are often given political preference in planning permissions to be situated along foreshores and waterfront sites.[12]

On the number 15 bus, Mohammed and I wind our way up to the peak. Preferring to take the slower and longer scenic route, rather than the faster, steeper (and more expensive) Peak Tram, Mohammed stares in wonderment at the tall residential stick-pin buildings which rise up the hill, bursting out from the canopy.

"It's quite amazing," he tells me, "how can they build a house on top of a hill. You cannot build something like this in KL [Kuala Lumpur], because our hills are quite soft."

In addition to the "massing" of buildings in Hong Kong, there is also a "rising."[13] With over 300 skyscrapers above 150 meters tall, and six over 300 meters, Hong Kong's urban volume is tall. There are three height limits in planning practices in Hong Kong: the airport height limit, the special height limit, and design deposition and height clause.[14] These limits shape how the volumetric city is solidified and resolidified, giving shape to the city skyline, and the heights at which people live. They also negotiate the complicated territories of airspace above Hong Kong, measuring it and regulating it as a complex shared space.

Taylor and I walk past the area where the old Kai Tak airport was located. The area was broadly flattened by the Japanese during the occupation of Hong Kong in the Second World War in order to extend the runway. Since then, the airborne approach into the runway was mythically regarded as one of the most difficult in the world, requiring a sharp forty-five-degree turn on descent, and a short stop. As planes became larger, this approach became more and more difficult, and eventually the airport was moved to a reclaimed site, Chek Lop on Lantau Island, in 1998. These days, around the airport there is a distance between the buildings erected prior to the relocation of the airport, and after. While the airport was still in Kowloon, the tops of buildings could be traced in a step-down pattern toward the airport. Above the step buildings, international airspaces run in imagined surfaces above Hong Kong, invisible to the eye but not the meter. After the airport moved, height restrictions were relaxed by the local planning department, and newer skyscrapers now pierce the steady incline. The territorial restructuring of Hong Kong airports between flat and voluminous continues.[15]

Later, we walk around the edges of the Kai Tak development. Pathways for people and cars intersperse, plaiting above and below to maximize and make new surfaces. Pointing to an overpass that runs between a building and the MTR station, Taylor smiles.

"Bridges are useful."

Where flat land is scarce, new ground must be made—and so the reclamations have continued too. Over six thousand hectares of land have been added to Hong Kong: sea that has been solidified into surface.[16] Many of the surfaces in Hong Kong that we accept as land were once part of the harbor, shorelines, or wharves. As Camille and I walk along Queens Road, we touch old shores that have become central thoroughfares. Madgalena and I depart from a ferry terminal which has been moved twice further out into the harbor, as the interface between land and water was relocated. Mohammed and I stand at the Lippo Centre where the Rifleman's bolt was first driven into a sea wall. Ravi and I wander along a new promenade, manufactured into a regulated shape which engulfs the bays and the hills which were shown in Collinson's first maps of Kowloon.

The Avenue des Stars along the Kowloon foreshore is teeming with tourists lining up to take a photo with statues of Bruce Lee and Jackie Chan. As the nomenclature suggests, this is the Hong Kong equivalent of the Hollywood Boulevard, similarly fabricated as a destination, imbricated in city branding. Ravi ignores them and points beyond, across the harbor, to the skyline of Hong Kong on the other side. Dozens of residential and commercial skyscrapers line the shore. On the commercial buildings, the logos of international corporations displayed in large letters at the top—AIA, HSBC, LG, Samsung, Panasonic. The distance between this foreshore, and the one on the other side, has shortened considerably since 1841. The landscape that both the Avenue des Stars and the majority of the commercial buildings on the other side occupy is completely reclaimed.

The solidification of urban volumes has important consequences for navigating through and being-in city spaces like Hong Kong. These metrics produce oppositional orders: interior/exterior, anterior/posterior, above/below, which are interspersed with other governmental and economic logics including public/private, regulated/unregulated, commercial/residential/industrial, citizen/noncitizen. These often invisible borders imbricate themselves in different ways too, creating cultural hierarchies of who can go where, when, and how. This is a blurring of traditional spaces that is a celebration of liquid hypermodernity: seamless and smooth. But it is not liquid for everyone and in every way, and the solidification of the voluminous into the volumetric has its own geopolitical consequences.

In the evenings at eight o'clock, the Hong Kong Tourism Board coordinates the "Symphony of Lights," a spectacle where dozens of corporate headquarters use the architecture and height of their buildings to put on an extremely popular light show, watched by thousands of people each night. We only see the surfaces of these solid forms: the outside of a building, the top layer of reclamations. By day or by night, it strikes me that the surface obscures the process of solidification. The illuminated outside of a building covered in LEDs and spotlights, hides the solidification of other kinds of power on the inside that we cannot see. And the production of ground planes to support both the solidification and the seeing of volumes combines surface and spectacle to become little more than superficial.

Scaling Surfaces

"Even though it's steep, it's very well paved," Vicki tells me as she shows me the map. The path to the peak along Old Peak Road is serpentine in its formation, the only indication on the map that the terrain is hilly and steep. Vicki continues.

"It's well paved because this road is kind of an old route to the peak before the train or . . ."

Wealthy families built their bungalows on the peak, where the air was cooler and fresher in the humid Hong Kong summer. Before the tram, rich inhabitants were carried up and down in public or private sedan chairs.

The shift from the solidification of the built environment, to the practices of being-in and moving through urban volumes, sees a territorial refiguring toward subjective experiences of surfaces: inside/outside, in front/behind, up/down. These subjective experiences include urban mobilities (exploration, wayfinding, discovery, navigation, mapping, traversal) as well as embodiments (vertigo, propinquity, affect, panoramic gazes, closeness, intensities). This occurs at the interfacing of the volumetric and the voluminous, between surface and space: the difference between being-*on* and being-*in* the city.

Vicki and I have walked all the way up from Queens Road Central, along the Central–Mid-Levels escalators, and up the Old Peak Road, lungs burning from the constant incline without reprieve. Yet, poking through the dark green trees, tall glass buildings appear, refracting the sea and the sky in a sublime rendition of aquamarine blue—a rich panorama, where the hills drop out beneath your feet toward the harbor.

Just as volumes span outward into the sublime experience of the panorama, they intensify inward into the interstices of dense urban living.[17] The compartmentalization of dwelling into separate boxlike structures sees a proliferation of climate-controlled apartments, with small air conditioners pinned to the windows of crowded apartments. The smaller and more crowded the space, the more air conditioners are required, until multiple pipes emerge from small apartments telling stories of cage rooms inside. This has environmental consequences too—the urban heat effect combines with disruptions to delicate ecosystems caused by reclamations, raising pressure on and demand for urban greening and green spaces. And on Sundays, the previously invisible boundaries of public parks and plazas and private shopping centers and walkways become brutally and violently clear. Hundreds of thousands of domestic workers gather on their day off, as they are spatially surveilled and biopolitically manipulated away from the cool air and facilities of private shopping centers by security guards, locked doors, temporal controls, raised costs, signs in Indonesian and Tagalog, and the frowns of passersby.

Camille and I take the escalators up through Central toward Soho. On the windows of the third and fourth floors advertisements, sales, and QR codes are plastered across this vertical surface as it is transformed into commercial use. Waiting idly on the escalators provides the ideal captured audience—listlessly passing by as passengers catch their breath and stare at their phones. I comment to Camille that it's nice that the urban infrastructure of Hong Kong is manufactured to support my laziness. She laughs.

"Because we have to save up our energy for work. For overtime work."

Hong Kong is a city of striations. Surfaces stack upon one another, behind and in front of one another, and passageways and links connect sections together. In the geometric, however, sometimes the geologic is forgotten. While the floors, walls, and ceilings are resolutely level—parallel surfaces connected by elevators,[18] or hypotenuse stairways or escalators—the geological surfaces and striations destabilize geometric ambitions.

"Why didn't we go up there?" I ask Daren. I point at the Central-Mid-Levels escalators which traverse the air above Hollywood Road. He pauses before responding.

"You miss things," he says, "I like going down the street."

It is not only in the substance of the geological surface—the weathering, erosion, settling, degradation—it is also the lives that are lived in (but not on) the ground plane. Vernacular stalls hug degrading streets, water washing away mud and muck chase a quick path downhill, intermingling the sluice of the fish stall with the castoffs of the vegetable stall, making the cobblestones slippery. Hawkers and street sellers, people sitting on plastic stools playing mahjong, canopies made of blue tarpaulin that cave in the middle. Living *in* the surface is a sociomaterial reassembling of voluminous urbanity: senses, ecologies, landscapes, cultures. Reichert argues for a "geo-?" in order to go beyond the graphic in the geo-graphic.[19] Is it possible to do something similar, to ask for a "volu-?" beyond the volumetric? At the same time, it is also crucial to pay close attention to the way in which the metric permeates and surfaces urban space. The metric—whether *geo-* or *volu-*—allows for fluid and consistent scalability from the very small to the very large. Molecules become weather systems or loose change links to global economies. In space, the point becomes a line, the line intersects with other lines to become polygons, the polygon becomes a surface, the roads and floors, walls, buildings, zones, neighborhoods, cities, regions, and then states. Yet, scale also has a different meaning—it's is in the stretching of muscles and the soreness of lungs, in the exalted sublime of looking down and the vertiginous humility of looking up, of figuring out how to get up or over there through public and private space across bridges and walkways, of secret staircases, the fast ascent of an elevator and the slow descent of land.

Conclusion

Adam Frampton, Jonathan Solomon, and Clara Wong write that ground is "the surface on which the conflicts of urban propinquity: public and private, planned and impromptu, privileged and disadvantaged, are worked out."[20] For them, Hong Kong is a city without ground. Yet, these conflicts of urban propinquity are continually embedded and unraveled across these interviews through walkways, gates, escalators, doors, walls, screens, architectures, roads, concourses, and windows. If Hong Kong is a city without ground, it remains a city with many surfaces, engendered by a complex volumetric politics which enacts difference through imaginative and material orders: inside/outside, open/closed, above/below, hidden/visible, flat/vertical, and liquid/solid. These orders toe the line between the measured, calculative, and fixed—the kinds of landscapes drawn, dreamed, and manufactured by the early British colonizers—and the uneven, spontaneous, and sensory—the feeling of "being-in" volumetric space, rather than "being-on" it. To return to Massey where we began, the spatial difference between the voluminous—vibrant, heterodox, and plural—and the volumetric is a political chasm. This distance can also be found in how volume is seen, solidified, and scaled, and the distance between global imaginations and local practices.

This argument has presented two kinds of urban volumes—that of the rationalist, geometric gaze of mensuration and that of the unpredictable, coeval sociomateriality of urban space. It has also presented a minor red herring in the dialectic opposition between surface and space. These two ways of understanding volume are not always as opposed as they seem. Space is filled with surfaces: the topsoil of earth, the grime on a wall, the muck on a street. But surfaces are also filled with spatiality—they form volumes in the most efficient ways possible, arranging materialities to modulate rhythms and funnel flows. Like the Bank of China building, they at once reflect and enclose. Like the reclamations, they solidify and sediment. And like the walkways and escalators, they move up and down, at different times and the same time.

So, surfaces are paradoxical phenomena: two-dimensional objects that are three dimensional in any form that is not theoretical. The key difference here is what kinds of territories surfaces form. The surface as a flattening act of scientific seeing, wrenching landscapes into obedience, privileging economy over lives and cultures in the city form, or exalting geometric scaling over bodily scalings is a specifically ideological way of comprehending and producing urban volumes. Yet, there are also counterideologies which emerge in the strange recombinations of maps and tours. In walking and looking, surfaces become repurposed, remade, and rearticulated. Sometimes, they are seen for the servants of rationalist urbanity that they were built to be, and sometimes they sink slowly, or rise gently or sharply in the treading of feet upon them, and slowly *into* them. If anything, it is in the ambiguity of surface—an ambiguity that Massey did not see—that it becomes clear that the distance between living in volumes and living on surfaces is shorter than we may think.

NOTES

1 Doreen Massey, *For Space* (London: Sage, 2005).
2 Massey, *For Space*, 63.
3 Sybille Lammes and Clancy Wilmott, "The Map as Playground: Location-Based Games as Cartographical Practices," *Convergence* (2016): https://doi.org/10.1177/1354856516679596; Michel de Certeau, *The Practice of Everyday Life* (Berkeley: University of California Press, 1984).
4 de Certeau, *Practice of Everyday Life*.
5 Donna Haraway, "Situated Knowledges: The Science Question in Feminism and the Privilege of Partial Perspective," *Feminist Studies* 14 (1988): 575–99.
6 Hal Empson, *Mapping Hong Kong: A Historical Atlas* (Hong Kong: Government Information Services, 1992).
7 Roger Nissim, *Land Administration and Practice in Hong Kong* (Hong Kong: Hong Kong University Press, 2011), 51.

8   Survey and Mapping Office, *Explanatory Notes on Geodetic Datums in Hong Kong* (Hong Kong: Hong Kong Government, 1995).

9   Adam Frampton, Jonathan D. Solomon, and Clara Wong, *Cities without Ground: A Hong Kong Guidebook* (San Rafael, CA: Oro Editions, 2012), 17.

10 Frampton et al., *Cities without Ground*, 17.

11 Andrew Harris, "Vertical Urbanisms: Opening up Geographies of the Three-Dimensional City," *Progress in Human Geography* 38 (2015): 601–20.

12 Mee Kam Ng, "The State of Planning Rights in Hong Kong: A Case Study of 'Wall-Like' Buildings," *Town Planning Review* 85 (2014): 489–511.

13 Barry Shelton, Justyna Karakiewicz, and Thomas Kvan, *The Making of Hong Kong: From Vertical to Volumetric* (London: Routledge, 2010).

14 Nissim, *Land Administration*, 65–67.

15 Donald McNeill, "Airports and Territorial Restructuring: The Case of Hong Kong," *Urban Studies* 51 (2014): 2996–3010.

16 Nissim, *Land Administration*.

17 Stephen Graham, *Vertical: The City from Satellite to Bunker* (London: Verso, 2016).

18 Graham, *Vertical*.

19 Dagmar Reichert, "Weisen der Welterzeugung: Zur Möglichkeit einer Geographie aus der Welt," *Geographical Helvetica* 3 (1998): 112–18.

20 Frampton et al., *Cities without Ground*, 6.

Gravity

On the Primacy of Terrain

GASTÓN GORDILLO

In June 2005, a four-man SEAL team was dropped off by helicopter in the mountains of eastern Afghanistan with the mission to kill an insurgent commander. They were in the rugged, forested terrain of the Hindu Kush near the border with Pakistan, in an area where they had never been before. Soon afterward, these well-trained, fit Americans felt overwhelmed by their exertion in trying to navigate the physical volume of those mountains. The only SEAL to survive the mission, Markus Luttrell, subsequently wrote in his book *Lone Survivor* that their training for mountain warfare in California had not prepared them for *those* mountains, where "the terrain was absolutely horrible." The mountain was "so steep" that in their first few hours it was "a goddamned miracle we didn't fall off and break our necks."[1] Tired and eventually discovered by locals, the SEALs were ambushed by combatants who knew the terrain and controlled the most favorable position in mountain warfare: the higher ground. While the four Americans were being fired upon from above, they fled downhill, repeatedly tripping and falling off amid steep slopes. Luttrell describes one of their falls, "a nearly sheer drop," as follows:

> I took a sideways step, trying to zigzag down the gradient. *But gravity made the decision for me*, and I fell headlong down the mountain, completing a full forward flip and somehow landing on my back, still going fast, heels flailing

for a foothold. . . . Then I hit a tree, and Mikey went past me like a bullet . . . and on I went, catching up to Mikey now, crashing, tumbling over the ground like we were both bouncing through a pinball machine.[2]

In this description, Luttrell captures the affective geometry and physics of their fall: that they were moving in one direction (downward) and not in another because they were *overpowered by gravity*, which moved their bodies *against* their will and turned well-trained, hardened combatants into powerless objects bouncing around like balls in "a pinball machine." In the film *Lone Survivor*, based on Luttrell's account, the scenes depicting these falls (filmed in New Mexico) are carefully edited to look realistic and gripping. They show men falling down a steep mountain at a vertiginous velocity, hitting rocks and trees only to roll over and continue falling, with each collision creating new bruises, fractures, and groans of pain. Wounded by the falls and their enemies' firepower, three of the SEALs died. Severely injured, Luttrell survived only because he was rescued by a sympathetic villager in the next valley.

Gravity affects everything that exists, lives, and happens on Earth. Yet the seeming obviousness of this fact, its taken-for-granted invisibility, tends to obfuscate the implications of thinking gravity materially, territorially, and philosophically as an intrinsic component of terrain. The microphysics of this confrontation between US troops and insurgents in Afghanistan, for instance, reveals that gravity's power to affect human action amid steep terrain has contingent yet consequential impacts on the deployment of state sovereignty. In this case, it contributed to exhausting and injuring elite US combatants who were unused to the vast volume and steep gradient of mountains located in insurgent territory. The pull of gravity affecting these men therefore contributed to empowering the insurgents who knew how to better navigate that same terrain, for instance by carrying little weight to maximize their mobility, stealth, and speed.[3]

This territorial confrontation in Afghanistan, furthermore, shows that volume in the immanent sense of the term, that is, *volume in this world*, is inseparable from gravity. Euclidian and Newtonian conceptions of absolute space present volume as an abstract, disembodied dimension of geometrical space. Yet this military incident in mountainous terrain reminds us that terms like *falling, up,* and *down* and the very idea of volume, and the volume of territorial sovereignty, only make sense in relation to bodies affected by the planet's gravitational field.

Drawing from the work on verticality and warfare by Eyal Weizman and Paul Virilio, Stuart Elden has helped us politicize our understandings of volume by identifying the control of the latter as central to the creation of territorial power.[4] Elden rightly notes that volumes, and the territorial attempts to secure them, are not reducible to verticality and include angles, inclines, and the transversal. In this chapter, I add to this crucial observation that the volumetric and transversal dimensions of territorial power acquire their full materiality only in relation to gravity. More importantly, I seek to show how attentiveness to gravity reveals the irreducible materiality of the planet's terrain.

For long relegated to the military's lexicon, the concept of "terrain" has recently gained traction in human geography, anthropology, and critical theory to examine the three-dimensional, textured materiality of any space on Earth—mountains, landforms, liquid and atmospheric flows, the built environment—in their capacity to constrain or facilitate human action.[5] Stuart Elden and Rachael Squire therefore insist that terrain should not be reduced to "land" but encompass the material multiplicity of the Earth.[6] And Geoffrey Boyce rightly points out that since terrain evokes "the dynamic multiplicity of the nonhuman world," it names those dimensions of space that "withdraw" from full human control.[7] This withdrawal is never complete (as this literature shows), and conflicts like the ones affecting Afghanistan involve human territories that shape how terrain is socially used. This is clear in the impact that the nearby border with Pakistan has had on warfare in the region, for the border has prevented regular US troops from entering Pakistani territory and has allowed insurgents to count on a haven there. Yet how gravity affects insurgent and American mobilities amid this mountainous terrain also transcends state sovereignty and borders because it is part of the planet's ontology. Valerie Olson and Lisa Messeri argue that debates about the Anthropocene tend to present the planet as a bounded, self-enclosed object, therefore severing its spatial continuity and connectivity with the cosmos.[8] This chapter examines gravity as precisely the force that entangles the Earth with other celestial bodies and, more importantly, grounds human action on the terrain of the planet.

In the first section, I examine why gravity is central to understanding the volume of terrain and of territorial forms of sovereignty by highlighting the inseparability between human ontology and gravity and by briefly reviewing Newtonian physics and its radical reformulation by Albert Einstein. I then revisit phenomenology's claim about the primacy of embodied place over abstract space in order to propose a materialist, non-anthropocentric phenomenology of terrain. In the last section, I examine how human agency is constrained *and* empowered by the fact that "gravity is the most important force any of us has to deal with in life."[9] I illustrate this dialectic by analyzing a case of mountain climbing in Peru and by then returning to Afghanistan to outline a brief counterpoint between imperial and insurgent weaponizations of gravity.

The Planet's Embrace

In *What Is Philosophy?* Gilles Deleuze and Félix Guattari proposed a geophiloso-phy based on the premise that "thinking takes place in the relationship of ter-ritory and the earth." And they write that "the earth is not one element among others but rather brings together all the elements within a single embrace."[10] This chapter contributes to this geophilosophy and to recent debates about ma-teriality and the nonhuman by arguing that gravity is what makes the planet "bring together" all its elements, including all political territories and places ex-perienced by humans, "within a single embrace," for gravity is the *primary* way in which the planet *affects* everything that exists and happens on it. This is far from being a mechanical process that determines human spatiality from without. As David Valentine shows, being human is always already being in relation to grav-ity on Earth—which is specific to our planet's mass and is therefore stronger, for instance, than that of smaller celestial bodies such as the moon or Mars.[11]

Furthermore, Einstein's theory of relativity demonstrates that space and time cannot be separated from gravity, for "Space-time does not claim exis-tence on its own but only as a structural quality of the gravitational field."[12] If we conceive of terrain as the material and atmospheric becoming of space-time on Earth, then terrain *is* gravity. The latter, including the gravitational in-fluence of extra-terrestrial bodies, is therefore constitutive of life on Earth and of the geomorphology of the planet—as is clear in the flatness of the ocean's surface, in the flow of rivers, or in rainfalls, mountain slides, and avalanches.

Human beings, in this regard, learn to navigate gravity and use it to their advantage as soon as they learn to walk—unless, of course, the body is not physically able to (as we shall see). This also means that human actors have long partly manipulated the pull of gravity in warfare, for instance in calculat-ing how the trajectory of a projectile (from arrows to explosives) will eventu-ally fall toward the ground (and the intended target). The twentieth century marked an epochal transformation in the spatiality of territorial sovereignty because of the rise of technologies able to make airplanes fly by countering gravity, either by generating lift (the aerodynamic force created by an aircraft's motion in the air) or vertical thrust (in rockets and helicopters). Airpower rap-idly became a decisive military weapon that expanded the volume and reach of state sovereignty and further weaponized the technologies that counter gravity, a weaponization embodied today in the drone as symbol of panoptic-territorial power.

Despite being partly appropriated and neutralized by human ingenuity and modern technology, gravity can never be fully controlled, for it captures what Nigel Clark calls in *Inhuman Nature* "our all-too-human exposure to forces that exceed our capacity to control or even make full sense of them."[13] Gravity, after all, is "the creator of planets and stars" and one of the four fundamental forces in the universe, together with electromagnetism and the strong and weak forces that structure the subatomic world.[14] To further its inhuman nature, gravity remains an enigma. To this day, physicists are at a loss about how it operates, that is, how is it possible that the mass of an object can affect another object at a distance without physical contact. Isaac Newton therefore concludes his *Principia* by admitting that "I have not been able to discover the cause of those properties of gravity from phenomena, and I frame no hypothesis". Yet he notes: "to us it is enough that gravity does really exist," for it "propagates its virtues on all sides to immense distances, decreasing always in the duplicate proportion of the distances."[15] Today, when gravity has become (through schooling) part of modernity's common sense, it is easy to forget how groundbreaking its discovery was. As Tim Maudlin argues: "Newton obliterates the distinction between astronomy and terrestrial physics, postulating a single set of principles that explains the behavior of both. . . . One of the crowning moments in the argumentative structure of the *Principia* occurs when Newton calculates that the force that maintains the moon in orbit about the earth is precisely the same force that causes an apple to fall from a tree."[16]

Newton's understanding of gravity was nonetheless limited by his reliance on Euclidian and Cartesian geometries and his endorsement of Christian dogma about the unifying power of God in the universe. He therefore viewed what he called "absolute space" as something ontologically separate from "absolute time" and from actually existing bodies. Einstein's more materialist, groundbreaking understanding of gravity went beyond Newtonian mechanics because it drew from a radically different geometry. Einstein therefore begins his book *Relativity* by criticizing the abstract rigidity of Cartesian geometry, which "consists of three plane surfaces perpendicular to each other and rigidly attached to a rigid body." He argues in contrast that the "geometrical properties of space are not independent, but they are determined by matter."[17] As noted by Sten Odenwald, this means that Einstein conceptualized geometry as inseparable from gravity, and that he "saw gravity and geometry as really the same thing, described in different languages."[18] This required the non-Euclidian geometry developed in the mid-1800s by Georg Riemann, who generated a novel sensibility for torsions, curvatures, and plasticity. Drawing from Riemann, Einstein argued that the three-dimensional nature of space and therefore its volume are actually *curved*, a curvature caused by the gravitational field of massive bodies. Hence Einstein's insistence that space-time *is a structural quality of gravity*, something that was felt in a forceful way by the SEALs in Afghanistan as they were ambushed by insurgents and fell down the mountain.

We Only Know Terrain through the Body

Accounting for the ontology of terrain-as-gravity as it affects human practice and territorial sovereignty requires revisiting phenomenology's main contribution to theories of spatiality: that we only know space through the body, a process of cultural embodiment by which space is always already experienced as "place." Phenomenologists have therefore long insisted that places are "more" than their materiality, for they are defined by embodied, culturally mediated forms of perception, memory, and symbolism that exist in excess of their physical-geometrical dimensions. Maurice Merleau-Ponty thereby calls for "a return to the world of actual experience which is *prior* to the objective world," arguing that the study of place should be based not on physics but on "our experience of space."[19] Along similar lines, Gaston Bachelard writes, "A house that has been experienced is not an inert box. Inhabited space transcends geometrical space." An inhabited house "breathes." "Here, geometry is transcended."[20] Edward Casey, in turn, argues for the *primacy* of "place" over "space" or "terrain" because "space and time come together in place" and "arise from the experience of place itself."[21] Casey insists that places are not the cultural apprehension of a preexisting "physical terrain," for this would entail the existence of "some empty and innocent spatial spread, waiting, as it were, for cultural configuration to render it meaningful."[22] Place, in short, is for these authors prior to terrain.

Phenomenology's sophistication in describing the localized, sensuous nature of places is undisputed. And there is no doubt that places are "more" than their materiality. Yet the alleged rigidity and emptiness that Casey attributes to a terrain irreducible to cultural meanings dissolves when one learns to appreciate the powerful and dynamic nonhuman forces that structure the planet's terrain, such as, for instance, the electromagnetic discharges of lightning bolts brilliantly examined by Karen Barad, the devastating power of tsunamis and earthquakes analyzed by Nigel Clark,[23] or the pull of the planet's gravity. In *Matter and Memory*, Henri Bergson writes that one of the chief problems of Berkeley's idealism is that it was "unable to explain the success of physics."[24] Likewise, the idealism of traditional phenomenology prevented it from explaining the success of physics in demonstrating, for instance, that all places are affected by the gravitational field. Casey's magisterial review of the history of physics in *The Fate of Place* is therefore largely devoted to lamenting the ways in which people like Galileo and Newton created a disembodied and mathematized view of absolute space that neglected the sensuous nature of place.[25] But Casey, together with Merleau-Ponty and Bachelard, does not seem to consider that our understanding of place could *also* learn from those remarkable physicists, mathematicians, and geometricians who shattered religious dogma by demonstrating that we live on a planet that moves around the Sun, therefore revealing the immanence of any place and territory on Earth.

The point in noting the limits of phenomenology is not to reject it but, rather, as several authors have noted, to expand its analytic sensibility into the nonhuman materialities and agencies traditionally neglected by it.[26] As argued by John Wylie, this requires moving away from the old idealist idea of a seamless correspondence between self and place (or landscape) and admit "that we are constitutively haunted by an exposure to what is other."[27] And it is precisely through the body in its exertion and vulnerability amid steep terrain that we can appreciate that places are haunted by their exposure to the radical alterity of gravity.

Touching the Void

In June 1985, British climbers Joe Simpson and Simon Yates set out to ascend the western face of the Suila Grande, a 6,300 meter-high mountain in the Peruvian Andes located days away from the nearest village. These men were already seasoned climbers of the European Alps, and were drawn to the Suila Grande because its western face, a vertical wall of ice, had never been climbed before. They were therefore guided by a distinctively European, modern, and masculine striving: to claim a "first" climb.[28] All over the world, most people living in mountainous areas have been indifferent to the idea of climbing for the sake of it, as Sherry Ortner shows in the case of the Himalayas.[29] Yet the cultural and gender specificity of the 1985 climb of the Suila Grande is not enough to explain its physics, which is described in riveting detail in Joe Simpson's book *Touching the Void* and in the docudrama of the same name.[30]

Leaving their companion Richard Hawkins at base camp, Simon and Joe set out Alpine style, carrying light gear. For most human beings, the Suila Grande's western face, an iced wall with a 1,500-meter drop, is an unsurmountable obstacle. Yet they had experience, skills, and endurance, and the right tools to counter the gravitational pull: crampons, ice axes, and ropes. It was a "full body climbing," that demanded the work of every muscle pulling the body's weight upwards, using the axes and the crampons to find points of support on the wall, from where to ascend further. "I felt an amazing sense of space, an amazing space of freedom," Simon remembered, highlighting his own agency in moving upwards. The upper sections of the climb were nonetheless very challenging, for a blizzard and the meandering folds of the ice made for a "nightmarish climb." "It was the most precarious, unnerving, fragile climbing I've ever done," Joe says in the film, alluding to their awareness that any mistake exposed them to a deadly fall.

At last they reached the summit. It is a sunny day and they felt exultant. But they noticed that the descent would be difficult, for the narrow ridge they began following was surrounded by "terrifying" cliffs. Clouds and blizzards quickly enveloped them. And then, disaster struck. In descending a crevasse, the ice that had secured Joe's ice axe cracked and he fell several meters. "I felt a shattering blow in my knee, felt bones splitting, and screamed." He had fractured his leg. They were devastated. Joe had just lost the use one of the key limbs that give humans their mobility and agility, and that are crucial to keep balance amid the gravitational pull. Yet he was not totally crippled. They promptly turned the same gravity that had contributed to hurting him into the force that helped him descend. Tied to each other through a long rope, Simon would sit on a firm spot on the snow and would gradually let Joe go down through his hold of the rope. While Simon was letting him slide, Joe writes, "Gravity had turned me into a dead weight."[31] When the rope was up, Simon would descend, meet Joe, and they would then repeat the procedure, managing to descend this way amid a blizzard over a thousand meters.

When they were close to the glacier, however, the slope became more vertical and Joe fell off a cliff. He was left hanging from the rope into the void. And this led to the most dramatic moment of the ordeal. Unable to see or hear each other, Simon held the rope for several hours. Yet the gravitational pull was eroding his capacity to hold the weight and he was beginning to slide. Knowing that he was otherwise going to be pulled into the void, he cut off the rope with a knife. Joe describes what it felt like to be overpowered by gravity and fall over thirty-meters into a crevasse: "I fell silently, endlessly into nothingness, as if dreaming of falling. I fell fast, faster than thought, and my stomach protested at the sweeping speed of it. . . . No thoughts. . . . So this is it! A whooping impact on my back broke the dream, and the snow engulfed me."[32]

After cutting the rope, Simon assumed that Joe had been killed by the fall. Emotionally shattered, he continued and eventually reached the campsite in the valley. But Joe survived the fall because the crevasse's ice and snow softened the impact. He was eventually able to slowly crawl out of the crevasse by using the sheer force of his wounded yet persevering body. Once on the glacier, forced by gravity and his broken knee to keep his body flat on the ground, he crawled on the ice while avoiding the "horrendous crevasses" around him. When he reached the end of the glacier mortified by pain and thirst, he began hopping over the rocks, protecting his broken knee with the padding of his mat. But his inability to properly navigate gravity with one working leg made him fall every other meter or so. Moving and repetitively falling through that terrain turned him into "an emotionally and physically shattered wreck of a human being."[33] Close to falling into a coma, he dragged himself until he reached the campsite. "He looked totally horrible. He was in an absolutely awful state. He was like a ghost-like figure," said Richard in the film about the moment they found Joe after hearing his screams, noting how his body had been affected by terrain.

In his gripping account of his own exertion, pain, and terror in the mountains, Simpson's *Touching the Void* depicts both the excessive materiality of a terrain that overwhelms and at points *prevails* over the body's capacity to move and also the remarkable capacity of the same body to navigate that terrain and, in the process, counter and appropriate the pull of gravity for its own ends. This account is certainly about a European, middle-class, and male experience of mountain climbing, which includes as part of its cultural specificity an awareness of gravity's existence. Yet this experience also captures what is at stake in non-Western, subaltern efforts to creatively appropriate the gravitational pull, even among people uninterested in climbing summits or unaware of the concept of gravity. And this takes us back to the counterinsurgency warfare in eastern Afghanistan, to the different ways in which gravity can be weaponized, and to some of the ways in which these appropriations are also haunted by exposures to the void.

The Weaponization of Gravity

The capacity of the US military to neutralize gravity through airpower is the main techno-territorial vector through which it projects imperial sovereignty worldwide. In Afghanistan, helicopters, bombers, gunships, and drones allow the US military to control airspace, monitor mountains from above, and unleash on them devastating firepower, further weaponizing gravity as one of the forces that delivers bombs and missiles to their targets. Yet these technologies never cease to be vulnerable to the planet's pull. The helicopter sent to rescue Luttrell's SEAL team in June 2005, for instance, was hit by a rocket-propelled grenade that destroyed its capacity to generate vertical thrust to counter gravity. In the resulting crash, sixteen Americans died. And since airpower is never enough to dislodge a well-entrenched insurgency, the US ground troops deployed in those mountains have to confront gravity with their own bodies, often while carrying twenty-five to forty kilos of weapons, gear, armor, and water. It is therefore not surprising that some Americans described their marches in the Hindu Kush as "gravity-fighting ordeals."[34]

Insurgents are, needless to say, also constrained by gravity. Yet they travel light, making the gravitational pull less demanding. More importantly, they know the terrain, which allows them to turn the same mountains that Americans feel as alien and opaque into an insurgent weapon, primarily by hiding and moving amid its textures and by controlling the mountaintops and their commanding fields of vision.[35] In that failed mission of 2005, the SEAL team was defeated, in this regard, not by "gravity" but by combatants who controlled the higher ground and precipitated the Americans' falls by *forcing* them to flee downhill. The pull of gravity nonetheless empowered the insurgents by contributing to creating frictions and collisions that further debilitated their enemies. The control of the higher ground in warfare, in this regard, is decisive in part because it allows for a weaponization of gravity that does not depend on technology but on a sensibility and attunement to the gradients and volume of terrain.

Planetary Subjects

One of the most gripping images of the attacks of September 11, 2001, on New York City is that of a man falling midair from one of the towers of the World Trade Center, after having jumped off to escape the fire in the upper floors. The photograph of "the falling man" has been analyzed primarily in relation to this person's possible identity and the image's high affective impact.[36] Yet the main protagonist of this image, its "agentive force," is gravity and its haunting evocation of the void. This is a void in a twofold sense: as the "empty space" of air that does not stop gravity from pulling the man downward; and, also and more importantly, as the voiding or ungrounding of human claims to transcendence. This voiding materialized shortly thereafter in the collapse of the Twin Towers, whose damaged structures could no longer withstand the planet's pull. This is also why the title of Joe Simpson's book, *Touching the Void*, captures that his ordeal in a steep mountain haunted by gravity was akin to having a tactile encounter with what is overwhelmingly inhuman.

In his book *After Finitude*, Quentin Meillassoux articulated an influential and persuasive critique of what he calls *correlationism*: the anthropocentric assumption that we can only access the being of the world in its correspondence with our thinking and perception of it. This is the ontology of phenomenology's theorization of place as primary in relation to terrain. Meillassoux exposes the idealism of this humanist axiom on strictly materialist grounds: that there is widespread fossil evidence that demonstrates that the Earth precedes, and is ontologically independent of, the human experience and thought of it.[37] Yet it is not necessary to go that far back in time to demonstrate that terrain is primary, or to retort to the Cartesian rationalism that Meillassoux advocates. The primacy of terrain is best demonstrated *through the body*, in a phenomenological yet nonanthropocentric manner, in the ungrounding created by exposure to gravity amid steep drops.

This does not mean that gravity is a homogenizing force. As David Valentine argues, that gravity is not "undifferentiated and determinative" is clear in that the ocean is affected by gravity differently than land is and also in the existence of culturally diverse engagements with gravity, such as in the case of "shamanic capabilities for levitation and flight."[38] Yet even if we conceive of them as ontologically real, these shamanic capabilities are restricted to experts and to actions limited in time; for this reason, they can be seen as yet another technique for the modulation of gravity. In short, while *how* gravity affects human bodies and actions cannot be homogenized within abstract universals, gravity does reveal *one* universal dimension of terrain: that all humans on Earth are affected by gravity.

Led by Karen Barad's pioneering work, the rise of new materialisms in critical theory has generated innovative theorizations on physics and quantum mechanics.[39] Yet gravity is often taken for granted and made invisible in current debates about materiality. Ironically, the recent popularity of the idea that nonhuman objects and phenomena have agency—embodied in the influential work of Jane Bennett[40]—often erases the fact that many of these nonhuman agencies result, originally, from a more primary agency: the planet's gravitational field. This erasure of gravity occurs when authors write in passing, for instance, about "the agency of the Mississippi river" or the "agency" of falling rocks that crush hikers[41]—as if the flow of water toward the ocean or falling rocks responded to their own self-propelled power, rather than to the way they are affected by gravity. Confronting how gravity shapes the geomorphology of the world or the volume of contested sovereignties in Afghanistan, therefore, confirms that we are what Gayatri Spivak calls *planetary subjects*, that is, finite creatures who experience the planet as a figure of the uncanny, familiar yet strange, "which contains us as much as it flings us away."[42] In the era of the climate emergency, the development of a better attunement with this fragility as planetary subjects and with the changing rhythms of terrain will be central to our survival.

Appreciating the constitutive power of gravity in the planet's terrain, as I hope is clear, does not mean downplaying human agency and the forms of sociality, subjectivity, and political power through which people create and contest places and territories. Many dimensions of human experience and spatiality, furthermore, respond to histories, subjectivities, and struggles that are irreducible to, and therefore are "much more" than, terrain and gravity. The primacy of terrain simply names that places and territories and the growing struggles for climate and social justice that will shape our collective future exist on a planet that gravitates around the sun and that will never cease to embrace us with its power, keeping us in touch with its surface through its eternal pull.

NOTES

1   Markus Luttrell, *Lone Survivor* (New York: Black Bay Books, 2007), 191.
2   Luttrell, *Lone Survivor*, 214, my italics.
3   Gastón Gordillo, "Terrain as Insurgent Weapon: An Affective Geometry of Warfare in the Mountains of Afghanistan," *Political Geography* 64 (2018): 53–62.
4   Stuart Elden, "Secure the Volume: Vertical Geopolitics and the Depth of Power," *Political Geography* 34 (2013): 35–51. For an earlier examination of the verticality of territory in relation to geological surveys, see Bruce Braun, "Producing Vertical Territory: Geology and Governmentality in Late Victorian Canada." *Ecumene*, 7 (2000): 7–46.
5   See, among others, Stuart Elden "Land, Terrain, Territory," *Progress in Human Geography* 34, no. 6 (2010): 799–817, and "Legal Terrain: The Political Materiality of Territory," *London Review of International Law* 5, no. 2 (2017): 199–224; Geoffrey Boyce, "The Rugged Border: Surveillance, Policing and the Dynamic Materiality of the US/Mexico Frontier," *Environment and Planning D: Society and Space* 34, no. 2 (2016): 245–262; Rachael Squire, "Immersive Terrain: The US Navy, Sealab, and Cold War Undersea Geopolitics," *Area* 48, no. 3 (2016): 332–38; Gordillo, "Terrain as Insurgent Weapon"; Clayton Whitt, "Fluid Terrain: Climate Contestations in the Mudflats of the Bolivian Highlands," in *Territory Beyond Terra*, ed. Kimberley Peters, Philip Steinberg, and Elaine Stratford (London: Rowman and Littlefield, 2018), 91–106. Johanne M. Bruun, "Invading the Whiteness: Science, (Sub)Terrain, and US Militarisation of the Greenland Ice Sheet," *Geopolitics*, no. 23 (2018), DOI: 10.1080/14650045.2018.1543269.
6   Elden, "Legal Terrain"; Squire, "Immersive Terrain."
7   Boyce, "The Rugged Border," 257.
8   Valerie Olson and Lisa Messeri, "Beyond the Anthropocene: Un-Earthing an Epoch," *Environment and Society: Advances in Research* 6, no. 1 (2015): 28–47.

9   Sten Odenwald, *Patterns in the Void* (New York: Basic Books, 2002), 167.

10 Gilles Deleuze and Félix Guattari, *What Is Philosophy?* (New York: Columbia University Press, 1994), 85.

11 David Valentine, "Gravity Fixes: Habituating to the Human on Mars and Island Three," *Hau: Journal of Ethnographic Theory* 7, no. 3 (2017): 185–209.

12 Odenwald, *Patterns in the Void*, 104.

13 Nigel Clark, *Inhuman Nature: Sociable Life on a Dynamic Planet* (London: Sage, 2010), xiv.

14 Odenwald, *Patterns in the Void*, 12.

15 Isaac Newton, *The Principia: Mathematical Principles of Natural Philosophy* (New York: Snowball Publishing, [1687] 2010), 442–43.

16 Tim Maudlin, *The Philosophy of Physics: Space and Time* (Princeton, NJ: Princeton University Press, 2012), 5.

17 Albert Einstein, *Relativity: The Special and General Theory* (Mansfield, CT: Martino Publishing, [1920] 2010), 7, 113.

18 Odenwald, *Patterns in the Void*, 99.

19 Maurice Merleau-Ponty, *Phenomenology of Perception* (New York: Routledge, [1945] 1985), 66, 284, my italics.

20 Gaston Bachelard, *The Poetics of Space* (Boston: Beacon, [1958] 1994), 47, 51.

21 Edward Casey, "How to Get from Space to Place in a Fairly Short Stretch of Time: Phenomenological Prolegomena," in *Senses of Place*, ed. Steven Feld and Keith Basso (Santa Fe, NM: School of American Research, 1996), 16, 36.

22 Casey, "How to Get from Space to Place," 14.

23 Karen Barad, "Nature's Queer Performativity," *Qui Parle* 19, no. 2 (2011): 121–58; Clark, *Inhuman Nature*.

24 Henri Bergson, *Matter and Memory* (Mineola, NY: Dover Publications, [1908] 2004), ix.

25 Edward Casey, *The Fate of Place* (Berkeley: University of California Press, 1997).

26 Ben Anderson and John Wylie, "On Geography and Materiality," *Environment and Planning A* 41, no. 2 (2009): 318–335; James Ash and Paul Simpson, "Geography and Post-Phenomenology," *Progress in Human Geography* 40, no. 1 (2016): 48–66. See also Ian Bogost, *Alien Phenomenology: Or What It's Like to Be a Thing* (Minneapolis: Minnesota University Press, 2012).

27 John Wylie, "Landscape, Absence, and the Geographies of Love," *Transactions of the Institute of British Geographers* 34 (2009): 285.

28 Peter Hansen, *The Summits of Modern Man: Mountaineering After the Enlightenment* (Cambridge, MA: Harvard University Press, 2013); Veronica Della Dora, *Mountain: Nature and Culture* (London: Reaktion, 2016).

29 Sherry Ortner, *Life and Death on Mount Everest: Sherpas and Himalayan Mountaineering* (New York: Columbia University Press, 1999).

30 Joe Simpson, *Touching the Void* (New York: HarperCollins, 1994); Kevin MacDonald, dir., *Touching the Void* (FilmFour, 2003).

31 Simpson, *Touching the Void*, 85.

32 Simpson, *Touching the Void*, 108.

33 Simpson, *Touching the Void*, 207.

34 Ed Darack, *Victory Point* (New York: Berkley Hardcovers, 2009), 187.

35 Gordillo, "Terrain as Insurgent Weapon."

36 Tom Junod, "The Falling Man: An Unforgettable Story," *Esquire*, September 4, 2016.

37 Quentin Meillassoux, *After Finitude: An Essay on the Necessity of Contingency* (New York: Continuum, 2008).

38 Valentine, "Gravity Fixes," 191.

39 Karen Barad, *Meeting the Universe Halfway: Quantum Physics and the Entanglement of Matter and Meaning* (Durham, NC: Duke University Press, 2007); Diana Coole and Samantha Frost, "Introducing the New Materialisms," in *New Materialisms: Ontology, Agency, and Politics*, ed. Diana Coole and Samantha Frost, 1–43 (Durham, NC: Duke University Press, 2010).

40 Jane Bennett, *Vibrant Matter: A Political Ecology of Things* (Durham, NC: Duke University Press, 2010).

41 Bruno Latour, *Facing Gaia: Eight Lectures on the New Climatic Regime* (London: Polity, 2017), 52; Mel Chen, *Animacies: Biopolitics, Racial Mattering, and Queer Affect* (Durham, NC: Duke University Press, 2012), 2–3.

42 Gayatri Spivak, *Death of a Discipline* (New York: Columbia University Press, 2003), 73.

Territorial
Imagination

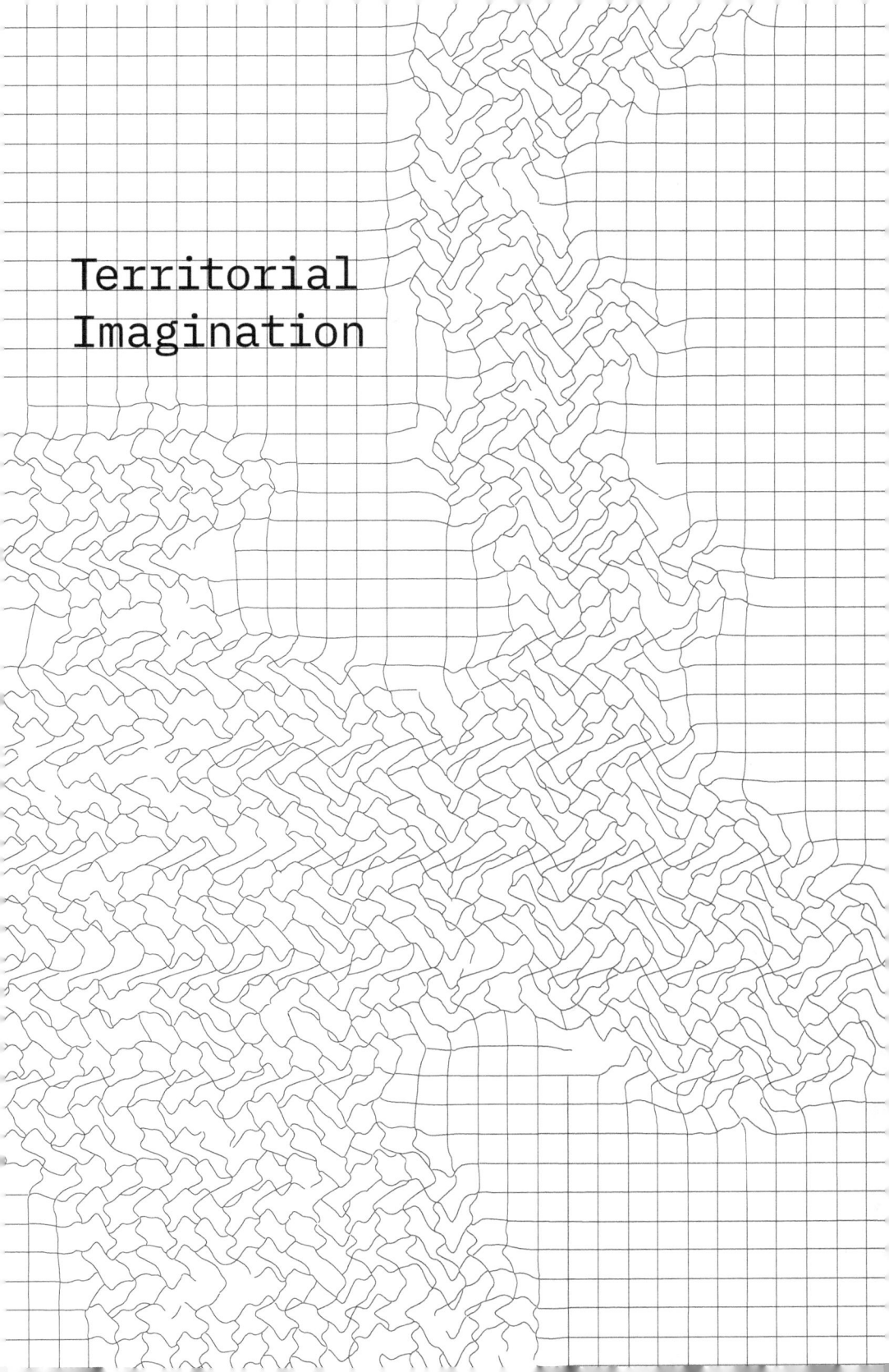

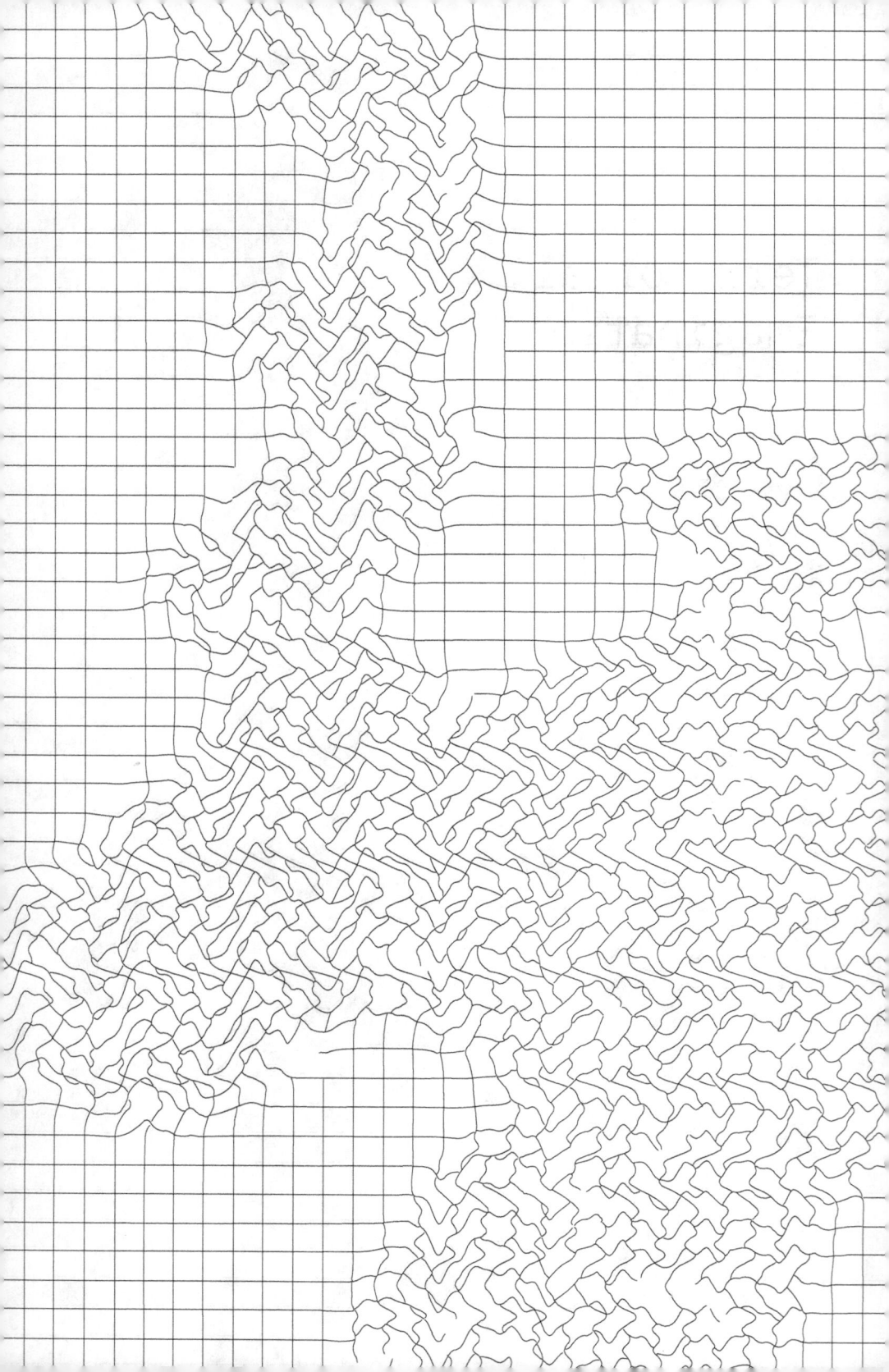

11   Geometries

From Analogy to Performativity

SARAH GREEN

Being Somewhere in Particular

Everyone is somewhere in particular, always located somewhere and not somewhere else, and that makes a difference. In the difference that it makes, the various forms of geometry are important techniques, among others, that people use to measure, and sometimes to create, the conditions that geometry describes. Of course, being located is not always a simple matter, as many other contributions to this volume have shown. Gaining a right to be physically present somewhere without some entity having the power to remove you is not easy to achieve in many parts of the world. Actually, it is becoming less easy now that most people and places can be tracked electronically, so that others know where you are, where you came from and whether you should be there or not.[1] And, again as other contributions have shown, it is not only the surface of the Earth, which many are used to thinking of as a two-dimensional political map with lines, colors, and names marking territories: the matter is now much more obviously three-dimensional as well, and includes subterranean places, the sea, air, and outer space.[2] And while the idea of control over water as well as land goes back a very long time,[3] attempts to get control over the air are a little more recent, perhaps because it has not been that long since people were able to occupy it in any meaningful way, at least in terms of very big vertical distances.

Thus far, it is only the Israeli government that has come up with the idea of creating a vertical border separating the earth from the air just above it: Hebron, a place in which the ground belongs to Palestinians, but the air above the ground belongs to Israelis. Israel has been particularly innovative with spatial and territorial technologies, though it is not the only political authority that has engaged in such practices.[4] In all cases, the increased technical capacities to precisely specify, measure, survey, track, and define every aspect of three-dimensional life—height, depth, volume—not only in terms of the earth and the depths and spaces below and above it, but also in terms of the volumetric dimensions of the human body, has been a key part of what makes such control possible, and perhaps also what makes it imaginable.[5]

On that last point, the fact that both places and bodies have volume has become important in this age of new surveillance techniques. For centuries, the right to move across physical space has been fraught with difficulties and potential transgressions, both formal and informal. In the past, this has been dealt with mostly through paperwork or some other kind of seal or token that allows passage, combined with attempted control of the crossing points.[6] Today, with the increasing use of biometric techniques and combinations of digital and satellite technologies in which data are remotely and directly read off bodies and places (related to what Paul Rabinow called *biosociality* many years ago),[7] there has been a merging of the relationship between bodies, territories, and data: the volumes, both bodily and spatial, have been translated into numerical and then graphic data. In that sense, biometric techniques have begun to catch up with the fantasies of security experts, who would prefer to carry out permanent surveillance of everyone and everywhere.[8] These techniques, which have the ultimate logic of creating a dense meshwork of perfectly controlled exclusion zones (the idea is to separate and disconnect people and places, while interconnecting an entire global surveillance system), have a growing market just now. A common thread within the current rise of nationalist and ethnonationalist political parties in Europe and elsewhere in the wealthier parts of the world is a negative depiction of migrants and migration: "Close the borders" and "Build more walls" are among the most common rallying cries for that type of political party. Currently in the European region, those parties are expressing particular hostility toward the people who are trying to cross the Mediterranean in their bid to escape from trouble and to find something better.[9]

It is not the first time, of course; the current market for "smart border" technologies is being fed by a fear of letting people in, which has erupted into attempts to shore up the borders many times before. Hannah Arendt noted that after World War I, formally stateless people became a large-scale phenomenon, with hundreds of thousands if not millions finding themselves without the right to reside anywhere at all.[10] In World War II as well, many countries refused to let in the refugees from the Nazi regime.[11] A significant part of the fear, then as now, was quantity: too many people coming in from outside all at once.

Both past and present, a fundamental practical part of the political techniques used to establish the difference between inside and outside has been based on the principles and logic of a range of different forms of geometry. The two-dimensional graphic image of a political map is based on simple geometric principles, and the territorial logic of what the map depicts is based on historically variable understandings of space, place, and location.[12] Given the proliferation of mapping techniques (GIS, Google Maps, and a range of digital and satellite-based technologies) in today's world, it is worth looking into the interplay between maps that geometrically depict locations in diverse ways, and wider politically and socially relevant understandings of belonging, rights, and moral worth related to spatial location. Or to put it in another way: how is the (historically contingent) logic of geometry drawn upon in a way that informs political decisions and materially affects people's three-dimensional lives? Asking the question in that way provides a route into thinking anthropologically about the different kinds of logic behind these power-inflected spatial arrangements, which result in diverse spatial relations and, as importantly, spatial separations, spatial cuts, and spatial hierarchies.

Geometries and Power

The question involves two issues: the logic that is used—by governments, by technical specialists, by whoever—to classify space (both horizontal and vertical) and then arrange the relations and separations between these spaces according to that classification; and secondly, how that articulates with the lives of those who have some relation with these spaces.

Everyone knows that people's relations with physical space—their presence and relations within it and movements across it—constantly involve the exercise of power, which incorporates and reflects diverse ways of defining and classifying the difference between here and somewhere else, and then imposing that logic onto the landscape in a way that directly or indirectly affects how people can engage with the spatial configuration thus defined. Within political geography and other social sciences, many have turned to geometry and related branches of mathematics, including fractal theory and, most particularly, topology, for inspiration in trying to understand such matters.[13] Some, especially those influenced by actor network theory (ANT) and/or Deleuze, have argued that today's world is a "post-Euclidean" topological world which can no longer be understood using the flat, static, geographical, geometric worldview of things being fixed in place, for not even place is fixed in place anymore, if it ever was.[14]

The key point for those shifting from classical geometry to topology is that topological thinking implies constant change in multiple dimensions (not only in the single dimension of lines or the two dimensions of maps). In this depiction, topology is understood as the mathematical "study of malleable shapes."[15] Metaphorically at least, the shift from classical geometry to topology implies a focus on the indeterminacy and malleability of human spatial existence, rather than its fixed characteristics. For those political geographers and social and cultural theorists drawing on topology as an idea, this apparently fits certain kinds of social theory and understandings of our contemporary world rather better than the idea of natural or immovable borders, for example.[16]

In a different approach, which is focused more on political economy, Doreen Massey famously suggested that the world is made up of *power-geometries*, a phrase she developed in relation to her thoughts about globalization.[17] What she meant was that the effects of the spatial dimensions of people's lives cannot be fully understood simply by describing such dimensions geometrically (i.e., in terms of measuring and mapping areas, angles, volumes, and lengths): the geometry is always warped by the operations of power, which generates hierarchical relations between here and somewhere else.

Massey was particularly concerned with neoliberal capitalist power in her discussion of this. She closely linked that form of power with the ideology informing contemporary ideas of the local and the global: for Massey, both local and global, and the relations between them once they have been defined as such, are created and defined through historically contingent concepts that are open to challenge. As she puts it: "In a relational understanding of neoliberal globalisation 'places' are criss-crossings in the wider power-geometries that constitute both themselves and 'the global.' . . . Understanding space as the constant open production of the topologies of power points to the fact that different 'places' will stand in contrasting relations to the global. They are differentially located within the wider power-geometries."[18] Massey's point is that Mumbai and London (for example) are not simply located on different parts of the planet; the way power works to generate a hierarchical relation between them, in both material and ideological terms, warps the way in which they are positioned, so that both the material and symbolic effects of being in each place are hierarchically calibrated by the operations of neoliberal capitalist power. Massey meant this literally, and in geological as much as geometrical terms: neoliberal capitalist power molds, twists, and churns the material, physical relations caught within and defined by that power: all three dimensions are involved.

Massey's reference to topology points to these condensing or stretching effects on geographical locations: long distances can become either meaningless or insurmountable depending upon the way different places are located with respect to the operations of power. This is a different understanding of topology than that provided by the more Deleuzian or ANT readings. Massey, who is in this respect similar to John Allen,[19] suggests that physical distances can be squashed or stretched so that the geographical distance between locations is completely different from the way people physically experience those distances. A simple example: a rich person can get from London to New York in less time than they can get to Ioannina (the capital of Epirus, in northwestern Greece), even though the distance between London and Ioannina is far shorter than it is to New York. This is simply because it is possible to fly directly to New York from London. Of course, for a person who cannot afford the flight, the situation is completely different; and for those with no passport or visa paperwork, the trip is almost not possible at all. It is not that the warped distances created by air travel permanently change the shape of the Earth; it is that the distances are warped for some people and not for others.

This goes beyond the simple point that different parts of the globe are in unequal relation to one another; Massey's argument is that these inequalities diversely shape how people experience the three-dimensional geometry of the world, that they twist, turn, warp, squeeze, and mold how people experience their spatial dimensions so that the same spaces are experienced differently by people who find themselves in different relation to these spaces, yet the spaces are geographically speaking the same. Such inequalities also work at the level of the Earth, differentially tying parts of the world together and ripping them apart, so that an action in one part of the world may reverberate instantly on the opposite side of the planet, while not affecting the places in between those two spots at all. And given that political and economic conditions change regularly, such power-inflected calibrations for establishing where we are in the world are always historically and conceptually contingent, changing according to the logic and techniques used to measure them, combined with the practical enforcement of those logic and techniques.[20]

Massey was drawing on the idea of topology as an analogy here, as a way of enabling the reader to understand the idea of spatial relations being warped by powerful forces. The political and economic hierarchies are what interest her, not the mathematical abstraction, as such. My interest in geometry goes slightly beyond that: it concerns how the geometrical concepts themselves might be incorporated within the political and economic logic that generates those hierarchies—neither drawing on geometry as an analogy to describe what happens in the world, nor borrowing from the concept of topology in order to generate social theories, but instead trying to understand how the logic and techniques of geometry (including topological techniques) are drawn upon in performatively generating conditions that affect people's three-dimensional existence.

The idea that the abstractions of geometry might be combined with the abstractions and hierarchies of political and economic power in establishing where places are in the world could be extended to somewhat more anthropological concerns: to explore what this might mean in terms of social relations, in terms of how people differentially experience being somewhere in particular, and in terms of how location is implicated in the establishment, expression, and maintenance of differences. The implications are important, partly for making the historical contingency of any particular understanding of borders explicitly visible.[21] Arguably, contemporary dominant concepts of political borders have relied more than any other historical logic of location on two-dimensional maps with one-dimensional lines marked on them in order to make that logic visible. This has flattened political imagination about the three-dimensional world, whilst at the same time encouraging the idea of an inherent, static, and vertical rootedness of particular people to a particular patch of the Earth.[22]

If the power-inflected logic of location is historically contingent, changing along with people's understanding of space, territory, and spatial relations, then two things follow from that. First, changes in forms of geometry deployed in calculating and depicting the locations probably signal a shift in logic. Second, it is also possible that more than one such logic could coexist at the same time. The implications of that are important for thinking through what contributes to people's understanding and experience of where they are located. Paying attention to the multiple relations and, as importantly, the separations, between here and somewhere else can draw attention to the copresence of different logics, almost always power-inflected, operating simultaneously in the same place, perhaps differently across different scales. Doing that might provide an intriguing, and more specifically relational, way of thinking about how people simultaneously locate themselves and are located in the world.

Locations

My long-term anthropological interest in locations, which more recently developed into a wider interest in mathematical abstractions such as geometry, topology, and fractals, began with earthquakes, both literal and political, in the Greek-Albanian border region of Epirus. In 1992, I was asked to explore local people's attitudes toward their tectonically unstable landscapes. There are regular earthquakes, land fractures, and landslides in the region, and my task was to find out how rural people who lived off the land dealt with this unstable ground beneath their feet. Geoff King, a geophysicist in the research project, visited Epirus and told me about mountains bobbing up and down, lakes filling and emptying, the seabed being churned up and twisted over, which in the end resulted in parts of that seabed being located on the top of hills.[23] The goats seek out those places on hilltops where the old seabed ended up, so they can lick stones and eat the plants that grow there, as they like the salt.

All of that gave me a sense of how the logic of topology is used in geophysics, as a way to describe and model, in geophysical terms, the deformations of the Earth's surface. That was quite different from the more metaphorical and analogical uses of the topology idea discussed in the social sciences. The geophysical description made it appear as if the skin of the Earth was being literally stretched, twisted, crumpled, folded, cracked, and bent like an old and decaying rubber sheet. Confronted with the sheer scale at which the logic of geophysics operates (the Earth's crust undulating over a period of hundreds of millennia), the people of Epirus, who were the focus of my own attention, seemed irrelevant somehow. It was as if their place in the world was incidental to something much more enduring than the short lives of a few people, their travels, their sheep and goats, and their troubles with a modern political border. What is more, these people seemed to be indifferent toward their constantly morphing landscape, which was a problem for me, as I was supposed to be researching their attitudes toward the geophysical instabilities in their landscape.[24]

That was one thread. But there was more, as this was the early 1990s, and a different kind of shape-shifting was going on at the same time. In late 1991, the Albanian communist regime collapsed, and the Greek-Albanian border reopened, after almost fifty years of tight closure. That political earthquake changed the shape of the region overnight, making a previously invisible and impassable section of land suddenly come into view—actually, for both the Albanian as well as the Greek sides. Before the reopening of the Greek-Albanian border, it was impossible to cross between Greece and Albania in either direction; afterward, it was literally a matter of a stroll across the border, so long as you had the right paperwork, of course.

Experiencing how Epirots lived with and spoke about all this began my long-term interest in borders, both political and physical, and how shifts in borders changed how people were located in the world. This was not so much about the identities of people, about the way that contemporary borders regularly become enmeshed in questions of national and other kinds of identifications;[25] it was more about the relationships between people and places, and how that deeply affected the way people lived and their understanding of the significance of where they were in the world and their place in it. Given that the shape of places changes regularly, this relation between people and places also changes regularly, and it matters to people.

At the time, questions of the way that geometry might come into this story of spatial dimensions being altered by these political changes still eluded me. In focusing on the people and their relations with places, the only spatial element that seemed to matter involved a social sense of belonging that came into conflict with the logic of belonging that was imposed by the contemporary state powers over this same territory, a logic which expressed a different kind of relation between people and places. I drew on Michael Herzfeld's research to think through the ideological and historical changes that generated shifts in the political relationship between people and places; and I drew on Marilyn Strathern to help explore how the logic of people's social relations might crosscut the politically imposed logic of nation.[26] The combination made it possible to understand how the location of the Greek-Albanian border made spatial sense in one way (by the logic of nation), but locally made little sense in another (by the logic of kinship). People from the area reported to me that they remembered a time when they hardly paid attention to the political border at all, as it was awkwardly located for them in practical terms, and they had a relatively limited sense of their nationality as being rooted in the ground beneath their feet. In fact, on the contrary, for as long as people around there could remember, they had been long-distance seasonal workers and pastoralists who took their sheep and goats to high grounds in the summer and low grounds in the winter, so moving around was part of their understanding of their relationship with the landscape; borders, national or otherwise, did not feature very strongly. In practical terms, these people needed to cross the Greek-Albanian border with the seasons not only to find good pastures for their animals; they also needed to do so to reach the biggest town for supplies and trade, Argyrokastro/Gyrokastër, which was on the Albanian side. Getting to the big town on the Greek side (Ioannina) took a lot longer. Moreover, the majority of families straddled the two sides of the political border.

Overall, the assumptions, or perhaps better, the assertions, that informed the placement of the border were not shared by many people living nearby, particularly the implication that it is normal for nationals to live in one place and not to move around all the time. The people in the region experienced it as a severe inconvenience when the border was formally closed after the Second World War, rather than thinking that it appropriately reflected what kind of (national) belonging they had with the landscape. The closure made it impossible for people around there to live the lives they had lived before. So most of those on the Greek side left, found somewhere else to live, and something else to do. Those on the Albanian side, being part of a command socialist regime that did not permit people to change residence without permission, could not leave so easily. But they were cut off from their kin and neighbors now, so their location had changed even if they had not physically moved.

That situation involved two crosscutting threads that came together in this place, but there was more. The Greek-Albanian border not only contradicted the spatial logic of the social relations between people and place, it also contradicted the previous Ottoman political logic in that region. At that point, various forms of geometry began to seem like a useful source of metaphors or analogies: in particular, I drew on the idea of the difference between classical and fractal geometry to try to describe what I understood to be the material effects of the difference between the political logic of the Ottoman Empire and the political logic of nation-states.[27] The importance of the difference between fractal and more classical (Euclidean or Cartesian) geometry concerns the way they differently incorporate scale: Fractals, which operate at a dimension that is somewhere between one and two (i.e., fractions of dimensions), repeat the same pattern across scales. This contrasts starkly with more classic geometry, in which shapes appear in whole dimensions (one, two, or three), and are scale dependent.

An example from fractal patterns that have been identified in plants makes the difference clearer: In fractal terms, the veins in the leaves of a tree follow the same branching pattern as the branches and the roots of the tree; what is important in fractal terms is the pattern of relations between them, which are all the same. In contrast, in more classical geometrical terms, leaves, branches, and roots are all distinctly different parts of the tree, taking up different spaces, and the question of how they relate together involves a consideration of scale and dimension. Fractal geometry evades geometrical scale, working in the same way at any scale, and the dimension of fractals is determined by the pattern of the relations between the parts. In contrast, classical geometry concerns the measurement of fixed objects, and is not about relations: "Measurements of angles and lengths, proofs of congruencies of figures, and computations of areas and volumes all rely on precise and unmoving geometric structure."[28] The key point here is that classical geometry and fractal theory are two different ways of describing the same thing: whether speaking in classical geometric or fractal terms about the tree, it is still the tree that is being described, but the one focuses on the pattern of relations, whereas the other focuses on the measurements of the dimensions of the entities that make up the tree.

At the time I was studying what was going on at the Greek-Albanian border for the people associated with the region, I was still thinking about these geometries metaphorically, and in terms of representations, not as part of the performative creation of spatial location. I argued that the ideologically inflected meaning of *the Balkans* had historically developed, within Western hegemonic discourse that relied on statistical thinking, to represent chaos, toxic conditions that repeated themselves infinitely and in the same way at every level, defying both scale and the logic of a three-dimensional geometrical world in which shapes can be neatly separated out into lines, squares, circles, and triangles. Instead, according to this perspective, it looked like in the Balkans no borders would ever settle down enough so that the territories they contained might come to resemble a stable thing (the nation) that could be appropriately associated with distinct people (the nationals) but would constantly morph into something else. The trouble, I argued, was caused by a mismatch in the Balkan region between Ottoman political logics and this linear-borders approach toward territory.

More recently, I have drawn on Doreen Massey's concept of power-geometries and stretched it into realms that she probably never intended, in order to explore the idea of the coexistence of different geometries in the same space. This is where the idea comes in of geometry as a mathematical concept and technique with a distinct history and logic that might be drawn upon by people who direct power-geometries.

It is important to recall that geometry, fractal theory, and topology were developed by mathematicians to describe and explore the quality of shapes in mathematical terms, and not to study political geography or the dynamics of social relations. These shapes are abstractions: they do not have to relate, directly or indirectly, to anything that exists in the world. In that sense, a *topological tree* is not a tree: it is a mathematical description of a tree shape. René Magritte's famous "Ceci n'est pas une pipe," written underneath Magritte's drawing of a pipe, makes the same point: Magritte drew an image of a pipe; it is not actually a pipe. Similarly, the graphs, or graphic images, that regularly go with fractal and topological mathematics are not the entities that they describe: they are graphic images, representations, of abstract mathematical ideas.

Of course, certain aspects of the thinking behind fractal theory, topology, and geometry have been usefully explored, either by analogy or metaphor, to think about social relations in connection to space in some way. As I mentioned above, I myself have done this in my work on the Greek-Albanian border. However, as noted by several others who have critically studied how mathematical metaphors have been used in the social sciences, if you treat a mathematical concept as if it has no history and comes from nowhere, there is always the danger of importing the historically contingent assumptions embedded in those mathematical theories into the conceptual work done on social and political lives.[29] When social theorists describe *topological worlds* or *topological structures*, or say that something in the world is more *topological* today than it was in the past, it is easy to intuitively understand what they mean. But it is important to remember that this is an analogy or metaphor that borrows from a mathematical abstraction to describe something the author is trying to describe, and not a theory to explain some ontological reality. When someone says that a tree is *topological*, what they are saying is that they are choosing to describe that tree in topological terms, rather than, for example, in geometrical, botanical, or aesthetic terms. There is nothing inherently wrong in doing this, of course; but it is important to be careful not to reify the analogy.

Where the logic of geometry, fractals, and topology might directly affect the spatial worlds in which people live, rather than being a good source of metaphors for describing those worlds, is if these logics become incorporated into the political, economic, and other logics that are used to attempt to build the three-dimensional physical world in their image. It is for this reason that I find the work of the likes of Doreen Massey and Stuart Elden rather more engaging on such topics than, for example, the work of Rob Shields or Scott Lash.[30] Even though taking very different approaches, both Massey and Elden are concerned with how epistemologies, the study of the logic of knowledge, performatively create the worlds in which people live. Massey's approach implies that within a certain overarching powerful system, such as neoliberal capitalism, a multiplicity of hierarchically differentiated places would emerge as "criss-crossings in the wider power-geometries that constitute both themselves and 'the global.'" My work on the Greek-Albanian border suggests that these crisscrossings were not only the result of power-geometries generated by one logic of power, but, rather, the outcome of the coming together, and the coexistence, of several different logics: the logic of the nation-state; the remaining traces of the Ottoman Porte's logic of statecraft; and the social logic of the people of the Greek-Albanian border. It was neither the Ottoman nor the nation-state logic that generated a sense of chaotic fractality in the view of what Roy Wagner would call the *Western hegemonic logic*, but rather the contradictions between these logics.[31]

More than that, the clashes that resulted from these contradictions seem to have generated a sense of coexisting locations in the same place here, both in material and conceptual terms. On the one hand, it was two locations—a patch of Greece and a patch of Albania. On the other hand, the same place was also, for many of those living around the border region, one location, not two: it was the place associated with the villages and pastoral lands of these people. And in a third sense, the place still bore the traces of having been an outpost of the Ottoman Empire, constituting one small section of the dense network of routes across the Ottoman territories, territories that had been structured to facilitate constant movement across these routes, and which resulted, from the perspective of nation-state logic, in such hopelessly mixed populations in the Balkan region.

Here, it would be intriguing to look more closely, not only at the incorporation of geometrical ideas into the construction of contemporary political maps (that is quite easy to trace, as much of the work has already been done);[32] but also the incorporation of those ideas, or other historically contingent spatial concepts, into the work of Ottoman statecraft, and the more contemporary logics of both defining and then creating relations and separations, between here and somewhere else.

In this sense, the various geometries become a part of the story by informing those who create borders, ideologies, roads, rules, and infrastructures, by being part of the logic that informs how they think about the world. In my previous work, I had already argued that the coexistence of different power-inflected logics in the Greek-Albanian border area generated different ways of organizing relations and separations, as well as meaning and value, within the same place. This was unlike Massey's political geography, in which each place had its hierarchically organized location within specific power-geometries (those generated by neoliberal capitalism). Instead, it appears more like that particular place was the site of crisscrossing conflicts between more than one powerful logic that warped the spatial logic that each was attempting to impose in the area. The experience of being in that place was thus characterized by the process of the playing out of those conflicts, which resulted in unstable relations and separations between here and somewhere else. What I do not yet know is how the different geometrical logics were playing out in informing the different parts here. The important element to emphasize for now is the coexistence of the different logics.[33]

Geometries, Cutting, and Gluing

That brings me finally onto the crucial issue of cutting (and gluing). While a key aspect of topological thinking is its focus on the maintenance of similarity and continuity despite all the twists and deformations that can be made with a shape (the element that makes topology particularly interesting to Deleuzians), there is an equally important point, which concerns cutting (and gluing): the topological similarity and continuity between shapes ceases when a cut is made in the shape—metaphorically, one can imagine a balloon being burst, or a doughnut being sliced—or when one part is glued onto another part. As Strathern noted many years ago, cuts (and gluing) are essential to kinship if not for all social life, as well as being a means to stop endless proliferations so as to understand where you are.[34] The cuts and gluing that people make in the world—including the borders and the rules by which you can both connect and separate different parts—are a key part of everyday life, as well as political life. Paying attention to that gives a sense of where the people are in this story of geometries: thinking up ways to rearrange the world, with and without historically contingent ideas and techniques of geometries, in the company of others who have different ideas and poke a pin in your balloon.

NOTES

The research for this paper has received funding from the European Research Council (ERC) under the European Union's Horizon 2020 research and innovation programme (grant agreement number 694482). See https://www.helsinki.fi/en/researchgroups/crosslocations.

1   See, e.g., Katja Franko Aas, "'The Earth Is One but the World Is Not': Criminological Theory and Its Geopolitical Divisions," *Theoretical Criminology* 16, no. 1 (2012): 5–20; Katja Franko Aas, Helene Oppen Gundhus, and Heidi Mork Lomell, *Technologies of Insecurity: The Surveillance of Everyday Life* (London: Routledge-Cavendish, 2009); Ruben Andersson, *Illegality, Inc.: Clandestine Migration and the Business of Bordering Europe* (Oakland: University of California Press, 2014); Eyal Weizman, *Hollow Land: Israel's Architecture of Occupation* (London: Verso, 2007).
2   Yücel Acer, *The Aegean Maritime Disputes and International Law* (Aldershot: Ashgate, 2003); Saskia Sassen, *Territory, Authority, Rights: From Medieval to Global Assemblages*, updated ed. (Princeton: Princeton University Press, 2008); David Valentine, Valerie A. Olson, and Debbora Battaglia, "Extreme: Limits and Horizons in the Once and Future Cosmos: Introduction," *Anthropological Quarterly* 85, no. 4 (2012): 1007–26.

3   Irad Malkin, *A Small Greek World: Networks in the Ancient Mediterranean* (Oxford: Oxford University Press, 2011).

4   Wendy Brown, *Walled States, Waning Sovereignty* (New York: Zone Books, 2010); Madeleine Reeves, *Border Work: Spatial Lives of the State in Rural Central Asia* (Ithaca, NY: Cornell University Press, 2014); Weizman, *Hollow Land*.

5   See, e.g., Glenda Garelli, Charles Heller, Lorenzo Pezzani, and Martina Tazzioli, "Shifting Bordering and Rescue Practices in the Central Mediterranean Sea, October 2013–October 2015," *Antipode* 50, no. 3 (2018): 813–21; Helga Tawil-Souri, "Digital Occupation: Gaza's High-Tech Enclosure," *Journal of Palestine Studies* 41, no. 2 (2012): 27–43; Nick Vaughan-Williams, *Europe's Border Crisis: Biopolitical Security and Beyond* (New York: Oxford University Press, 2015). Pezzani and Heller have also initiated a fascinating forensic oceanography project, which uses volumetric surveillance techniques to recreate drowning disasters in the Mediterranean. See Charles Heller, "Traces Liquides," May 26, 2015, Vimeo video, 17:59, https://vimeo.com/128919244.

6   Jane Caplan and John C. Torpey, *Documenting Individual Identity: The Development of State Practices in the Modern World* (Princeton, NJ: Princeton University Press, 2001); John C. Torpey, *The Invention of the Passport: Surveillance, Citizenship and the State* (Cambridge: Cambridge University Press, 2000).

7   Paul Rabinow, "Artificiality and Enlightenment: From Sociobiology to Biosociality," in *Incorporations*, ed. Jonathan Crary and Sanford Kwinter, 234–52 (New York: Zone Books, 1992).

8   Aas, "Earth Is One"; Katja Franko Aas and Helene Oppen Gundhus, "Policing Humanitarian Borderlands: Frontex, Human Rights and the Precariousness of Life," *British Journal of Criminology* 55, no. 1 (2015): 1–18.

9   Heath Cabot, *On the Doorstep of Europe: Asylum and Citizenship in Greece* (Philadelphia: University of Pennsylvania Press, 2014); Katerina Rozakou, "Nonrecording the 'European Refugee Crisis' in Greece: Navigating through Irregular Bureaucracy," *Focaal: Journal of Global and Historical Anthropology* 77 (2017): 36–49.

10 Hannah Arendt, *The Origins of Totalitarianism*, 2nd English ed. (New York: Meridian Books, 1958), 267.

11 Paul Weindling, *Epidemics and Genocide in Eastern Europe, 1890–1945* (Oxford: Oxford University Press, 2000), 400.

12 Denis E. Cosgrove, *Mappings, Critical Views* (London: Reaktion, 1999); Stuart Elden, *The Birth of Territory* (Chicago: University of Chicago Press, 2013).

13 E.g., Doreen Massey's concept of *power-geometries*, and John Allen's concept of *power-topologies*. See Doreen Massey, "Imagining Globalisation: Power-Geometries of Time-Space," in *Global Futures: Migration, Environment and Globalization*, ed. Avtar Brah, Mary J. Hickman and Máirtin Mac an Ghaill, 27–44 (Basingstoke: Macmillan, 1999); John Allen, "Topological Twists: Power's Shifting Geographies," *Dialogues in Human Geography* 1, no. 3 (2011): 283–98.

14 Euclidean geometry is often used as shorthand for the measurement of static shapes, which is contrasted with topological and fractal geometries that focus on transformations (Lauren Martin and Anna J. Secor, "Towards a Post-

Mathematical Topology," *Progress in Human Geography* 38, no. 3 [2014]: 420–38). As Stuart Elden points out, geometry has come a long way since Euclid, though some of the distinctions still hold (Stuart Elden, "What's Shifting?," *Dialogues in Human Geography* 1, no. 3 [2011]: 304–7). See also, e.g., Nishat Awan, "Introduction to Border Topologies," *GeoHumanities* 2, no. 2 (2016): 279–83; Scott Lash, "Deforming the Figure: Topology and the Social Imaginary," *Theory, Culture and Society* 29, no. 4–5 (2012): 261–87; John Law, "After ANT: Complexity, Naming and Topology," *Sociological Review* 47, no. S1 (1999): 1–14; Rob Shields, "Cultural Topology: The Seven Bridges of Königsburg, 1736," *Theory, Culture and Society* 29, no. 4–5 (2012): 43–57.

15 David S. Richeson, *Euler's Gem: The Polyhedron Formula and the Birth of Topology* (Princeton, NJ: Princeton University Press, 2008), 2.

16 Awan, "Introduction to Border Topologies."

17 Massey first suggested the concept in a paper published in 1999 (Massey, "Imagining Globalisation"), and then reworked it in Massey, *For Space* (London: Sage, 2005), part 3.

18 Massey, *For Space*, 101.

19 Allen, "Topological Twists."

20 One could call the combination of logic, technique, and enforcement a *scale*, but that discussion would take this paper too far outside its limits, as it were.

21 Raffaella A. Del Sarto, "Borderlands: The Middle East and North African as the EU's Southern Buffer Zone," in *Mediterranean Frontiers: Borders, Conflict and Memory in a Transnational World*, ed. Dimitar Bechev and Kalypso Nicolaidis, 149–65 (London: Tauris Academic Studies, 2010).

22 Liisa Malkki, "National Geographic: The Rooting of Peoples and the Territorialization of National Identity among Scholars and Refugees," *Cultural Anthropology* 7, no. 1 (1992): 24–44.

23 Geoffrey King, Derek Sturdy, and John Whitney, "The Landscape Geometry and Active Tectonics of Northwest Greece," *Geological Society of America Bulletin* 105 (1993): 137–61.

24 Sarah Green, *Notes from the Balkans: Locating Marginality and Ambiguity on the Greek-Albanian Border* (Princeton, NJ: Princeton University Press, 2005), 26–29.

25 For some excellent examples of that kind of ethnographic focus, see Daphne Berdahl, *Where the World Ended: Re-Unification and Identity in the German Borderland* (Berkeley: University of California Press, 1999); Hastings Donnan, "Material Identities: Fixing Ethnicity in the Irish Borderlands," *Identities* 12, no. 1 (2005): 69–106; Mathijs Pelkmans, *Defending the Border: Identity, Religion, and Modernity in the Republic of Georgia* (Ithaca, NY: Cornell University Press, 2006).

26 Michael Herzfeld, *Cultural Intimacy: Social Poetics in the Nation-State* (London: Routledge, 1997); Michael Herzfeld, *Ours Once More: Folklore, Ideology, and the Making of Modern Greece* (New York: Pella, 1986); Marilyn Strathern, *After Nature: English Kinship in the Late Twentieth Century* (Cambridge: Cambridge University Press, 1992); Marilyn Strathern, "Cutting the Network," *Journal of the Royal Anthropological Institute* 2, no. 3 (1996): 517–35.

27 Green, *Notes from the Balkans*, chapter 4.

28 Richeson, *Euler's Gem*, 156.

29 See, e.g., Christian Abrahamsson, "Mathematics and Space," *Environment and Planning D: Society and Space* 30, no. 2 (2012): 315–21; Iulian Barba Lata and Claudio Minca, "The Surface and the Abyss/Rethinking Topology," *Environment and Planning D: Society and Space* 34, no. 3 (2016): 438–55; Martin and Secor, "Towards a Post-Mathematical Topology."

30 Elden, *Birth of Territory*; Elden, "What's Shifting?"; Lash, "Deforming the Figure"; Massey, *For Space*; Shields, "Cultural Topology."

31 Roy Wagner, "The Fractal Person," in *Big Men and Great Men: Personifications of Power in Melanesia*, ed. Marilyn Strathern and Maurice Godelier, 159–73 (Cambridge: Cambridge University Press, 1991).

32 John Pickles, *A History of Spaces: Cartographic Reason, Mapping, and the Geo-Coded World* (London: Routledge, 2004).

33 I am currently working with a number of colleagues on two research projects that will hopefully take me closer to an answer (see Sarah Green, "Crosslocations: Rethinking Relative Location in the Mediterranean," University of Helsinki website, accessed October 14, 2019, https://www.helsinki.fi/en/researchgroups/crosslocations).

34 Strathern, *After Nature*.

12   Buoyancy

            Blue Territorialization
            of Asian Power

            AIHWA ONG

Are nations firmly delimited by national terrain?

Can sovereignty be expanded through the zoning of ocean and sky?

What are the implications of sovereign buoyancy for the world order?

Fixed and Contained?

Our notion of the nation-state as a physically fixed territoriality contained by its formally delineated boundaries is increasingly difficult to uphold. It appears that the late twentieth-century global order is turning out to have been a brief interregnum of agreed-upon sovereign power as contained within fixed national borders. The League of Nations first proposed an international system of nation-states in the 1930s, and a global arrangement was formalized in the aftermath of the Second World War. Defeated countries and newly independent ones were recognized as independent nation-states each with its own politico-legal territoriality. Nevertheless, the requisite political infrastructure of formal government with its own territoriality was not fully realized everywhere, and on some continents (with decolonized states or former Communist

Bloc countries), many nation-states have been challenged and fragmented by breakaway groups, political uprisings, or drug cartels. The model of a sovereign nation-state with fixed physical borders may have a less stable temporality than we imagined.

Sovereign power in the twentieth century has not always been contained within nation boundaries, although most small countries toe the line. In the aftermath of World War II, colonial empires unraveled, reverting back to small European nations while the independence of many new nations from former colonial rule became ordered under the auspices of the United Nations. The geography and size of a nation-state, its mode of border management, and its specific goals for keeping things in or out of its territories are principle relative variables through which sovereign space is managed. Maintaining clear borders is a basic requirement of state-premised governance in the global system of nation-states. The political and territorial containment of a nation-state, however, comes into conflict with humanitarian ideals of offering asylum to refugees. Some European nations challenged by the current flood of refugees and asylum seekers from poor countries and conflict zones are closing their borders against illegal arrivals. But even the continental United States has long held an ambivalent view toward migrants; the current administration is planning to build a border wall to keep out aliens. Under the administration of Donald Trump, nativist fervor against illegal immigration has reached its highest point since the 1940s. But building walls against noncitizens does not conflict with the state's pursuit of flexible borders to attract selective immigrants bearing human capital.[1]

Hard and Soft Power

Indeed, ambitious nation-states regularly violate their own borders, and those of other nations as well. Over the course of the Cold War, the United States and the USSR developed competing empires based on satellite regimes created after the Second World War. As the Cold War was drawing to a close, the United States' victorious military-industrial complex gained the upper hand over the USSR. America subsequently not only established military bases in dozens of allied countries, but "expanded into much more extensive alignments based on ideology, economic interactions, technology transfers, mutual benefit, and military cooperation."[2] As the lone remaining superpower, the United States operated as the patron of the United Nations, the World Bank, and the World Trade Organization, i.e., the system of international agencies that anchor the global economic system. The North Atlantic Treaty Organization, moreover, has formed a military network between twenty-nine North American and European nations under the "nuclear umbrella" of the United States. In other words, American capacity to insert itself into other national sites is not due exclusively to its nuclear and military arsenal, or what we may call *hard power*. Equally important is *soft power*, or the cultural capacity to attract and persuade, to inspire emulation and adherence in others through ideological vision, cultural institutions, and political ideals.[3] The strategic combination of hard and soft powers is what has made the United States the paradigmatic model of an exceptional nation-state, a charismatic hegemon that has sustained its buoyant sovereignty through a kind of stealth imperialism.

Zonal Technologies

The most important legacy of Pax Americana is East Asia, a region that has rapidly developed under the American nuclear umbrella to achieve sustained growth. From Asian tiger economies to rising China, Asian nation-states have become the world's manufacturing center of gravity and attained a high level of technological prowess. The focus on developing civil rather than military infrastructures has protected national autonomy and fast-tracked capitalist growth. A hallmark of Asian tiger economies has been their deliberate fragmentation of national territory into zones, which are then linked to global flows of capital and technology.

The zoning of spaces is a distinctive Asian take on the governance of people, spaces, and resources. Indeed, one may say that "vital security systems" as evolved in Asia are less focused on securing normative conditions of modern life than on securing the critical spaces and connectivities that prop up sovereign power.[4] States learned that by carving out spaces of exception—for manufacturing, investment, and shared governance—within a national territory, capitalism could be enhanced at strategic points and further reinforced by tactfully calculated infrastructural connections. I have argued that the deliberate fragmentation of the national territory into zones has generated political effects of "graduated sovereignty" as sovereign power becomes unevenly distributed across the land.[5] As it advances beyond the nation's terra firma, this reflexive sovereign practice of subdividing state space into a series of zones has increasingly taken on volumetric heft.

Below, I juxtapose the different approaches taken by Singapore and China—two ambitious Asian countries—seeking to materialize sovereign buoyancy through infrastructural prowess, rather than military might, by zoning the oceans as inclusive elements of a sovereign topology.[6] Two kinds of challenges accompany a maritime thrust: the technological capacity to control watery spaces and resources, and the legal limits set by the international maritime regime. This essay explores how the zonal manipulation of land-sea-air interfaces can buoy sovereign power. A tiny nation delimited by its island geography grows into a sea state, and a continental nation deploys zonal technologies in extraterritorial space. The question is whether state buoyancy can be sustained through the exercise of sheer material power, or whether soft power is a necessary ingredient.

Buoy

At the Venice Biennale, 2015, the Singapore Pavilion hosted the exhibition *SEA STATE* by Singapore-born artist Charles Lim Yi Yong. A former Olympic sailor, Lim devised a method of spinning his sailboat in the water and repeatedly dipping himself into the sea, thus performing the recursive process of land-sea interchangeability that has become state policy. The *SEA STATE* exhibition has since returned home to Singapore where it was mounted at the Center for Contemporary Art, Nanyang Technological University. When I visited in July 2016, Charles Lim showed off a gigantic buoy he had retrieved from the seafloor. Planted like the head of Neptune in the center of the room, the buoy's pervasive odor of the ocean washed over the exhibition. Charles noted that it did not take long for the abandoned buoy to be heavily encrusted with barnacles and seaweed. This manmade object has been transformed into the property of the ocean.

Digital videos on multiple screens track Lim's peregrinations in Singapore's surrounding sea, his recorded performances describing the elastic notion of the state. We see Lim in his boat spinning in and out of the water. He also prowls underwater caves, traces the seabed, and follows the "sandman," a semi-legal man-boat operation that pillages unguarded waters. He boards a survey ship that engages in "sand search" by identifying rock formations, which dot these waters' surface like tiny islands. These outcroppings exist in a grey zone of overlapping and ambiguous sovereignty and are considered "uncontrolled," since the neighboring countries of Malaysia and Indonesia have been unable to patrol them. Like ghostly sentinels for pirates, the islets menace gigantic oil tankers as they plow through the narrow Straits of Malacca en route to China. To the sandman, each and every isle, harvested and pulverized, is a potential source of sands to be sucked up and transported by barge to Singapore, where demand for landfill is ongoing. As a constant search for sea sand physically augments the island nation, the land/sea boundary is the conceptual support for an emerging entity Lim calls "sea state."

Justly famous for its cramped and expensive real estate, Singapore is thrusting above and below the sea level. The displacement of dirt and garbage can bulk up islets, build beaches, and carve underground caverns. A landfill built the beach resort on Sentosa Island. Currently, the national environmental agency is converting one islet, Pulau Semakau, into the world's first ecological offshore landfill. Two rocky points are linked by solid garbage processed to be sanitary and supportive of rare plant, bird, and fish species, covering a zone of 350 hectares. Meanwhile, unbeknownst to most citizens, the state has been digging a gigantic tunnel system a hundred feet underneath the Singapore Island; the Jurong Rock Caverns now store 126 million gallons of crude oil to be further refined for export.

Besides building up and digging down, volumetric sovereignty involves managing watery resources from the sky and the ocean. As an island nation of few natural resources, Singapore has devised different ways to ride the tide. Drinking water has long been delivered by pipes from neighboring Malaysia and Indonesia. Seeking water independence, the government has developed water technology to capture seasonal monsoon rains and channel runoff water through a purifying system of filtrations. Besides reservoirs, the cleaned-up Singapore River remains a last resort source of potentially potable water.[7] Even the undrinkable ocean is having its waters rethought as an aqueous prop for the lateral extension of space: there are plans to float solar panels on the seas surrounding Singapore. Both by claiming the water, sunlight, and rock from the ocean's surface as under its jurisdiction and by physically carving an undersea demimonde of storage tunnels, this three-dimensional sovereignty bolsters its buoyancy in preparation for a perilous near future.

Sovereign territory includes a two-hundred-mile radius surrounding a nation-state. In the sea state, the clarity of legal language muddles into the material and political interchangeability of land and water. Garbage turns from waste into a valuable material for engineering this indistinction. Increasingly, the surrounding ocean is being engineered as a technosphere that responds to an expansion of sovereign anxiety and opportunistic resiliency. But increasingly ferocious typhoons remind us that the relentless ocean easily washes away man-made props to sovereign claims. A policy of land-sea interchangeability is thus vulnerable to actual processes of ceaseless land erosion. It raises the question of whether the logic of sovereign territoriality can easily invest in watery spaces.

Impending threats due to climate change, considered alongside the perennially volatile dynamics of weather in the tropics, have served as ideological justification for swelling sovereign space. For instance, merely an ocean away, the Andaman Islands in the Bay of Bengal are gradually drowning, and the population is shifting to the Indian mainland. According to Shabbir Hussain Mustafa, a senior curator at the National Gallery Singapore, the island state has grown from 245 to 277 square miles through the steady reclamation of land. While acknowledging the island's anxiety amid changeable climatic and tropic conditions, he finds a political message in the exhibition: "In the SEA STATE, the effects of erasure and residue are then a simultaneous resistance to and acceptance of the tropics that demands constant renewal and replacement."[8]

Contemporary Asian artists are invariably engaged in anticipatory politics, projecting the homeland's future as an entanglement of borders, knowledges, and media.[9] In Lim's imagination, the geobody of Singapore is technologically sustained in a fluid material environment: the island is reimagined both as a buoy (the iconic item in the Lim exhibition) and as a human body likewise learning to float as a way to survive rough seas. The Venice Biennale becomes an international soft power venue, a platform publicizing the story of a tiny but nimble island's metamorphosis into a supple sea state.

Blue Territorialization

I use the term *blue territorialization* to describe the delineation of special zones on the sea and in the sky as a nation-state flexes its muscles beyond its own territorial limits. Adapting the concept from Gilles Deleuze and Félix Guattari, I note that territorialization connotes the processual operation of de- and reterritorializations, in which prior flows of politics, culture, and capital are displaced and their forces reassembled as different (and often tentative) formations.[10] As a state strategy, blue territorialization aims to subvert and push back the prevailing legal—to mention the physical and the ecological—governance of the oceans. A 1982 United Nations convention established the law of the sea that clearly defines each country's legal maritime boundaries. The comprehensive UN regime also lays down rules governing all uses of the oceans and seas and their resources.[11] As a rising power, China has begun to challenge the maritime regime as its sovereign ambitions overflow both its spatial geography and national territory.

In 2013, Chinese officials asserted that Admiral Zheng He's historical fifteenth-century voyages give credence to their current claims to sites in what it calls the Southern Seas (*Nanyang*), or the South China Sea. On his seven Ming voyages, Zheng He only promised to extend China's favors to small kingdoms along his route but did not invade any land nor colonize native territories. But in contemporary times, China's rise has generated a reimagined sovereignty, one that challenges contemporary international laws binding national territoriality. China's expansive exercise in extending sovereignty advances by claiming a variety of different zones abroad: economic, military, and flyover zones in Southeast Asia.

Through its Maritime Silk Road initiative, China is establishing special economic zones in nations adjacent to its southern border: Myanmar, Cambodia, Laos, and Vietnam. For instance, in return for infusions of capital, technology, and labor, the Vietnamese government has given leases of ninety-nine years to People's Republic of China (PRC) investors to operate special economic zones. From Vietnam to Myanmar, local protests have articulated growing fears of long-term indebtedness to Chinese banks as China gains local control over parts of their territories. Furthermore, in Cambodia and Myanmar, Chinese-built casino resorts and plantations have replaced farmlands and displaced peasants. Dara Sakor, the biggest Silk Road project so far, is a $10 billion investment zone and port facility on the Cambodian coast. This forty-five-hectare lease is beset by poor infrastructure and has failed to attract tourism.[12] I have argued elsewhere that the Silk Road, based on improving rails, pipelines, and seaports, seeks to stitch different sites in Southeast Asia together into a logistical network that promotes Chinese trade and control of the region on China's periphery. But there have been bumps along the Silk Road as the influx of Chinese developers, workers, students, and tourists it facilitates has greatly disrupted rural livelihood, threatened local ecologies, and increased labor migration in addition to the trafficking of both sex workers and wildlife.[13]

Besides establishing manufacturing zones abroad, China has also resorted to military means for securing its economic and communications zones in contested waters. In the last decade, China has made maritime claims to long-contested islets in the South China Sea and in the East China Sea. Most attention has focused on the Paracels and the Spratlys, both of which lie just outside the two-hundred-mile radius of Southeast Asian nation-states in international waters off the South China Sea.[14] A "nine-dash" line, traceable to the Ming voyages, demarcates a region in which maritime claims by Vietnam, Malaysia, Brunei, Taiwan, and the Philippines overlap. Contemporary Chinese statements refer to its "indisputable sovereignty" (*wuke zhengyi zhuquan*) over the Spratly and Paracel Islands and a maritime zone encompassing the two island clusters as well. In 2016, an international arbitration invalidated China's island claims and upheld the Philippines' rights to exploit resources off its west coast in the Scarborough Shoal. But this European upholding of the Philippines' legitimate maritime borders has been dismissed by Chinese authorities as they solidify their claims by building the islands into garrison sites.

Indeed, China has thus embarked upon *blue territorialization*, a process of technological and ecological manipulation of land-sea-sky interfaces.[15] China has dredged the contested islets and atolls and built military installations and runways on Mischief Reef in the Spratly Islands and on Woody Island in the Paracels. It is planning another militarized base in the Scarborough Shoal. These sites are patrolled by armed boats and can deploy fighter jets to control a strategic zone where $5 trillion in ship-borne trade passes every year.

Other Southeast Asian nations have protested China's encroachments in the South China Sea, but there is a sense of having to bow to the inevitability of China's will in controlling this strategic waterway. In addition, the reluctant compliance of countries such as the Philippines is rewarded with billions in economic aid in the near future. In 2017, some Southeast Asian nations and China held joint naval drills in the contested waters that somehow eased tensions in the area. By framing the island claims as a matter of unresolved territorial dispute, China has played brinksmanship short of an all-out war.

Down the line, the disputed islands in the South China Sea may be drawn into a massive transnational One Belt, One Road policy initiated and financed by the Chinese state. In Southeast Asia, the Maritime Silk Road project will strengthen connections from economic zones in the region to new port facilities at Sri Lanka in the Indian Ocean and Djibouti on the Gulf of Aden.[16] This infrastructural assemblage linking several offshore zones greatly expands the volumetric sovereignty of China's blue territorializations, which threatens to dislodge American overlordship of the region since World War II.[17]

Technological prowess has allowed China to take its island claims to new depths. Earlier, in 2009, the Chinese had established a Center for Underwater Cultural Heritage to undertake a comprehensive survey of *undersea sites* including in disputed areas. Marine archaeology dives beneath the waves to collect artifacts and secure a contested ocean region against "illegal" underwater archaeology by outsiders. The head of the Underwater Cultural Heritage Center states, "We want to find more evidence that can prove Chinese people went there and lived there, historical evidence that can help prove China is the sovereign owner of the South China Seas."[18]

In a critical June 2018 meeting with the US defense secretary, President Xi Jinping categorically declared, "We cannot lose even one inch of the territory left behind by our ancestors. What is other people's, we do not want at all."[19] From the PRC state perspective, the force of Chinese historical and archeological claims overrides international maritime law.

Given that the South China Sea is a global crossroads, political contestation over its territories will continue for a protracted time as major world powers try to avoid open conflict. Admiral Harry B. Harris Jr., the commander of the US Pacific Fleet, called the Chinese island fortifications "a great wall of sand."[20] Meanwhile, the United States occasionally sends warships to pass by the contested islands, as a reminder of international law and order, which the Chinese state has chosen to ignore. In response to China's efforts to militarize atolls in the South China Sea, the US military presence in northern Australia has steadily increased since the Obama administration's 2012 "pivot" to Asia, which has resulted in a US-led multinational coalition's rapid multibillion-dollar buildup of airbases and naval operations in Darwin, Northern Australia. In addition to American, Australian, and Asian allies mounting large-scale air exercises and maritime operations there, Darwin is also the base of one of the world's most advanced long-range radar systems.[21]

The joint production of ocean and air zones, and of civilian and military infrastructures, is an imperial strategy of overseas expansion. During the Cold War, the containment of communism made the Pacific Ocean the main arena of American surveillance. American fighter jets and submarines routinely patrol the region and gather intelligence on Soviet-Russian, North Korean, and Chinese naval exercises and other activities. For over sixty years, American warships and fighter jets established hegemonic control over the Pacific, but the PRC is now punching holes in this US-dominated Pacific Rim.

In other words, China's great wall of sand in the South China Sea is accompanied by a "great wall in the sky" over the East China Sea.[22] By 2013, aeronautics development had allowed China to declare an Air Defense Identification Zone (ADIZ) overlapping with the air defense spaces of Japan, South Korea, and Taiwan. China's new ADIZ is a direct challenge to ADIZs drawn in the region by the US military after the Second World War. So far, China has avoided explicit military enforcement of its reclaimed air defense space. The United States has sent military aircrafts to flout China's new rules, and China has not scrambled jets to buzz them or threatened to shoot down foreign aircrafts. For now, the PRC is only insisting on enforcing the zone as a space for air communications navigation. Because the danger of air traffic miscommunication is very high, the US government has advised American commercial airlines to send transponder signals. Many observers view this compliance as a step toward the tacit recognition of PRC's sovereignty over that airspace even without official recognition of the Chinese claim. Japan is especially worried as the overlapping ADIZ enables China to extend surveillance to the Ryukyu island chain. In the midst of rising tensions over a trade war between the Trump administration and China, American military aircraft flying over the East China Sea are menaced by laser signals coming from fishing boats near the China coast.

Indeed, Pax Americana has provided lessons on the exercise of vertical sovereign power. In the aftermath of the Second World War, the United States first engineered a new topology, connecting disparate and far-flung zones and enhancing its volumetric sovereignty over oceans and islands by flying high and diving low. Chalmers Johnson has written cogently about America's ascendancy as built upon an extended empire underpinned by military garrisons in sites all over the world.[23] Pro-American observers would argue that the hegemon is a legitimate extraterritorial power as it has enforced the post–World War II global order of liberal humanism and led a multilateral framework for preserving a global commons. The American Empire also floats on values and standards of liberal democracy and rules-based trade. There are, however, disturbing signs that the contemporary American administration is distracted from a rules-based trade regime and from its commitments to preserving a nuclear umbrella over East Asia as well. In this opening, China promises to provide an economic umbrella that will seed zones overseas and promote the rises of smaller nations, and not only in Asia.

China has learned deterritorializing moves from America's hyperpower playbook, deploying its infrastructural prowess and hard currency to plant its footprints overseas. A Made in China 2025 plan seeks to dominate the most critical areas including aerospace, robotics, and artificial intelligence, for strengthening national autonomy and expansion abroad. Rising China mimics earlier imperialist powers and the American Empire, mainly through the offer of technological and financial aid in rebuilding economies overseas.

Less developed, however, is a Chinese soft power equivalence to the American cultural appeal that can attract and persuade reluctant allies. China's history of promoting its overseas influence beyond infrastructure and capital is a checkered one. Up until the end of the Vietnam War (1975), China professed communist solidarity with socialist Asian nations. Since market reforms (early 1980s), postsocialist rhetoric has been steadily replaced by development-speak and business diplomacy toward small countries in Southeast Asia.[24] One outcome has been China's official link with the trade-based Association of Southeast Asian Nations (ASEAN), as in ASEAN Plus One (China). Cultural diplomacy drives state-funded Confucian Institutes to promote facility in Chinese language and familiarity with Chinese culture in many countries. The Silk Road initiative adds to this the language of cosmopolitanism, highlighting historical crosscontinental relationships based on trade, friendship, and multiculturalism. But China's charm offensive has been clumsy and constantly undercut by the disruptive activities of Chinese businesses and tourism associated with the Silk Road. Despite the "win-win" propositions of Chinese aid, these projects have trampled over the rights, property, livelihood, workers, and migrants in host countries. The PRC has yet to develop ideological or cultural soft power that is appealing to a wide swath of overseas nations and that is needed to make it an uncontestable hegemon in the region.

Ambitious nations can engineer claims over extraterritorial zones, but they need to float values that can be shared across borders as well. Technological innovations allow states to actively redraw the material boundaries between their insides and the outsides as they proceed from drawing zones for enforcing a "graduated sovereignty" on national terrain to the blue territorialization of surrounding water and sky. The political tension and ambiguity generated by heteromorphic states may encounter foreign military interventions that seek to contain or deflate the buoyancy of volumetric sovereignty.

This burgeoning space carved out by China's state capitalism promises to mold not only a new material topography but also a new global order of economic liberalism, albeit stripped of liberal political rights. The PRC has been eager to replace the cancelled US-led Trans Pacific Partnership trade pact with a so-called Regional Comprehensive Economic Partnership that currently lacks labor and environmental standards. China's leadership of an alternate regime of global free trade would be hard to sustain in the midst of the relentless flows of capital, information, and actors worldwide. Corporations and NGOs are shaping an emerging order of global governance that upholds the ideology of human rights. Can China's soft power, based on economic paternalism and Confucianism, sustain its volumetric sovereign ambition? *Blowback* refers to the unintended consequences of overseas operations,[25] and sovereign buoyancy can expect to be buffeted or even burst by natural and political forces beyond state control.

NOTES

1   Aihwa Ong, *Flexible Citizenship: The Cultural Logics of Transnationality* (Durham, NC: Duke University Press, 1999).

2   Chalmers Johnson, *Blowback: The Costs and Consequences of American Empire*, American Empire Project (New York: Holt Paperbacks, 2004), 20.

3   Joseph S. Nye, *Soft Power: The Means to Success in Global Politics*, new ed. (New York: PublicAffairs, 2005).

4   Stephen J. Collier and Andrew Lakoff, "Vital Systems Security: Reflexive Biopolitics and the Government of Emergency," *Theory, Culture and Society* 32, no. 2 (2015): 19–51.

5   Aihwa Ong, "Zoning Technologies in East Asia," in *Neoliberalism as Exception*, 97–120 (Durham, NC: Duke University Press, 2007).

6   Aihwa Ong, "The Chinese Maritime Silk Road: Re-Territorializing Politics in Southeast Asia" (keynote address, International Conventional of Asian Studies, Chiangmai University, July 20, 2017).

7   Aihwa Ong, "Island-Nations," in *Patterned Ground*, ed. Stephan Harrison, Steve Pile, and Nigel Thrift (London: Reaktion Books, 2004), 266–67.

8   Shabbir H. Mustafar, "—SEA STATE, Some Measurements," in *SEA STATE*, by Charles Lim Yi Yong, 10–18 (NTU CCA Singapore, April 30–July 10, 2016, exhibition catalog).

9   Aihwa Ong, "What Marco Polo Forgot: Asian Art Negotiates the Global," *Current Anthropology* 53, no. 4 (2012): 471–94.

10   Gilles Deleuze and Félix Guattari, *A Thousand Plateaus: Capitalism and Schizophrenia*, trans. Brian Massumi (Minneapolis: University of Minnesota Press, 1987); Stephen J. Collier and Aihwa Ong, "Global Assemblages, Anthropological Problems," in *Global Assemblages*, ed. Aihwa Ong and Stephen J. Collier, 3–21 (Malden, MA: Wiley-Blackwell, 2005).

11   Wikipedia, s.v., "United Nations Convention on the Law of the Sea," last modified October 5, 2019, 02:10, https://en.wikipedia.org/wiki/United_Nations _Convention_on_the_Law_of_the_Sea.

12   Brenda Goh and Prak Chan Thul, "In Cambodia, Stalled Chinese Casino Embodies Secrecy, Risks," *Reuters World News*, June 5, 2018, https://www.reuters.com /article/us-china-silkroad-cambodia-insight/in-cambodia-stalled-chinese-casino -resort-embodies-silk-road-secrecy-risks-idUSKCN1J20HA.

13   The Maritime Silk Road initiative in Southeast Asia is a regional version of China's ambitious One Belt, One Road project to build infrastructure in dozens of developing countries by extending both capital and expertise. See Ong, "Chinese Maritime Silk Road."

14   China also claims Diaoyu/Senkaku in the East China Sea.

15   Andrew Chubb, "China's 'Blue Territory' and the Technosphere in Maritime East Asia," *Technosphere Magazine*, 2017, https://technosphere-magazine.hkw .de/p/Chinas-Blue-Territory-and-the-Technosphere-in-Maritime-East-Asia -gihSRWtV8AmPTof2traWnA.

16   Ong, "Chinese Maritime Silk Road."

17   Since the end of World War II, the United States has been a technological god exercising vertical sovereign power. Especially since the containment of communism during the Cold War, the Pacific is the main arena of American surveillance, especially the northwestern region where rival powers converge. American fighter jets and submarines routinely patrol the region and gather intelligence on Soviet-Russian, North Korean, and Chinese naval exercises and other activities. The recent Chinese declaration of identification zones and international communications in the East and South China Seas are a direct challenge to this Pax Americana regime.

18 "China Takes Territorial Dispute to New Depths," *Wall Street Journal*, December 2, 2013, A1, A16.

19 "China Won't Yield Inch on Sea, Says President," *New York Times*, June 28, 2018, A11.

20 "A 'Great Wall of Sand' in the South China Sea," *Washington Post*, April 8, 2015.

21 "Australia Strengthens Darwin's Defenses," *Wall Street Journal*, May 25, 2018, A16.

22 Jun Osawa, "China's ADIZ over the East China Sea: A 'Great Wall in the Sky'?," *Brookings*, December 17, 2013, https://www.brookings.edu/opinions/chinas-adiz -over-the-east-china-sea-a-great-wall-in-the-sky.

23 Johnson, *Blowback*, 15.

24 See, e.g., Pál Nyíri and Danielle Tan, *Chinese Encounters in Southeast Asia* (Seattle: University of Washington Press, 2017).

25 Johnson, *Blowback*, 8.

Seepage

That which Oozes

JASON CONS

Against the Flood

By almost any measure, 2017 was a year of unprecedented climatological catastrophe. Hurricane Harvey's devastation of Texas's Gulf Coast, flooding in
the Nigerian state of Bennu, massive monsoonal flooding across the northern
parts of South Asia, and the impacts of Hurricanes Irma and Maria (especially
in Puerto Rico) all highlighted 2017 as a year of global flooding.[1] The seeming
apocalyptic impacts (and media coverage) of these events bore out a trope of
contemporary discussions of the Anthropocene: the global debate over climate
change is dominated by metaphors of and anxieties about inevitable catastrophic inundation. Cities are to be inundated with cyclones and hurricanes,
lowland areas inundated by glacial melt, borders inundated by floods of refugees displaced by these events. Anticipatory fears of inundation thus animate
imagined geographies of footloose populations, catastrophic transformation,
and Schumpeterian creative destruction that await our warming world.[2] As
Roy Scranton, writing presciently of a fictional hurricane named Isaiah, put it
less than a year before Harvey's landfall, "The good news is that Isaiah hasn't
happened. It's an imaginary calamity based on research and models. The bad
news is that it's only a matter of time before it does."[3]

The implications of such imaginations of the future are worrisome to say
the least and deserving of their own critique.[4] Imaginations of catastrophic

inundation tend to write over more everyday processes of ecological and demographic change. Moreover, approaching such changes in a catastrophic register privileges particular kinds of interventions while ignoring other processes and, arguably, impeding measured and thoughtful responses to them.[5] In this brief essay, then, I wish to pivot away from catastrophic inundation as the primary logic of the future and highlight an alternative vision of environmental transformation with equally pressing, though less dramatically apparent, implications for our understanding of borders and volume. Thinking outward from the Bengal Delta and from the India-Bangladesh border that runs through it, I propose that we train our eyes away from inundation and, instead, attend to its companion processes of climatological and border swamping. I suggest that we attend to the notion of seepage.

Toward a Damp Ontology

Seepage is a concept easily defined, if hard to contain. It refers to the percolation or leakage of fluid into or out of the ground. It pertains, according to the *Oxford English Dictionary*, to "that which oozes."[6] The term itself evokes viscosity, a thickness and inevitability of movement that both bleeds through and squeezes around. It signals material instability—shifts between dry and wet and a proliferation of damp intermediary states. Moreover, it invokes a failure of containment, a refutation of claims to hermetic seals and impermeable barriers.

The hydraulic action implied in the term is an apt descriptor of processes that increasingly govern life in places like the world's megadeltas—e.g., the Bengal, the Mekong, the Mississippi, and the Nile. Deltas are ecological *vital systems* in Stephen Collier and Andrew Lakoff's sense of the term—sites increasingly understood as both crucial to contemporary life and vulnerable to catastrophic disruption, particularly in the face of global warming.[7] They not only house vast swaths of the world's population, but also critical agricultural production and ports central to the workings of the global economy. Forestalling the breakdown of deltas—therein ensuring vital systems' security—increasingly hinges on the management of seepage and ooze. This is true whether we think of downstream siltation that threatens to clog channels and rivers, thus fouling trade routes and transportation; salt-water intrusion threatening agricultural production; or various forms of toxicity and pollution that devastate fragile delta ecologies. Seepage, in its multidimensional oozings, defines the terrain of delta management. It rejects static logics of wet and dry, and signals an inexorable refusal to be contained by human intervention. At the same time, seepage proves an apt metaphor to think through the challenges that trouble border security in a warming world. Seepage offers a contrast to visions of inundated borderlands by framing the everyday ways that people, goods, animals, and more move into and out of such spaces—squeezing around and through nets of regulation, security, and policing. It is an interiorization of the exterior and an exteriorization of the interior. Seepage describes a movement that is not catastrophic, at least not immediately so—but rather slow, steady, and insidious.

Seepage is thus a useful concept for thinking about both the Anthropocene and the dimensionality of borders. Seepage is at once above, below, and interior to.[8] It troubles the notion of material and temporal fixity, suggesting instead unstable states and dimensional transformations. It highlights the impossibility of containing the movements of people, goods, animals, plants, water, and toxicity with structures like fences and walls. Seepage suggests changes happening at inexorably different scales and inevitably different temporalities. If inundation is a catastrophic moment, seepage is a persistent flow—a set of small changes that might add up to big consequences. Seepage is a process, not an event. As that which oozes, seepage heralds the failures of projects aiming to produce space and territory as solid containers. It forces us to think past distinctions such as solid and liquid and instead trains our attention to the damp in-betweens.

Seepage thus prompts a different understanding of borders, territory, and borderland landscapes—one which shifts analytic frameworks for talking about land, property, and terrain away from logic defined by the dry. In a recent intervention, Philip Steinberg and Kimberley Peters propose the notion of *wet ontologies* to unsettle our understanding of terrain by "unearthing a material perspective that acknowledges the volumes within which territory is practiced: a world of fluidities where place is forever in formation and where power is simultaneously projected on, through, in, and about space."[9] Wet ontologies provoke a reconsideration of volume as a viscous space that exists dynamically, both above and below the surface. It pushes us toward a fluid understanding of socionatures, where community and ecology are always already understood through the lens of ebb and flow. Yet to think volume as *wet* might not go far enough toward unsettling our catastrophic imaginary of borders in the Anthropocene. Seepage prompts us to attend not just to liquidity, but also to intermediate states of matter—to volatile transformations between land and water and to the spaces that emerge in between. It thus unsettles our understanding of volume. It trains our eyes on the ooze, on matter and materialities that are, in Stuart McLean's evocative words, "more uncouth than vibrant, more belligerent than companionable, more a source of disquiet than enchantment."[10]

In what follows, I think with the notion of seepage to imagine a *damp* ontology: an analytic of terrain, volume, and movement which foregrounds not just liquidity, but its emergences, disappearances, and oozings. In other words, I propose that we rethink terrain as damp, and see seepage as its more-than-human logic. To see environmental and demographic change as seepage implies a terrain that is categorically shot through with, but also destabilized and transformed by, a multiplicity of flows happening at radically heterogeneous times, scales, and viscosities. As Gastón Gordillo has recently argued, terrain is irreducible to human experiences of it, even as it shapes human action within it. Human action, movement, and initiatives of control are "hindered or enhanced by the raw *excess* of terrain."[11] This insight is doubly true of the material instabilities of damp space which demand, even as they categorically defy and foul up, attempts at human management and control. They persistently trouble attempts to fix space as property, agricultural land, and national territory.[12] As such, seepage points us toward an ontology of terrain that abandons distinctions between solid and liquid, instead seeking to understand space and borders as both in flux and rich with that which oozes.

Thinking Seepage(s)

The southwestern delta region of Bangladesh is a productive place to think with and through damp ontologies. A delta for two of the world's largest rivers—the Ganges and the Brahmaputra (in Bangladesh, the Padma and the Jamuna)—it is an island landscape, a network of rivers and canals bordered to the south by the Sundarbans, the world's largest mangrove swamp. Many of the islands' economies and ecologies are dominated by export-oriented brackish-water shrimp aquaculture—an industry which, over the past thirty years, has itself had devastating social and ecological consequences for the delta.[13] The islands, and their residents, are acutely vulnerable to many projected effects of global warming, including sea level rise and increased cyclonic activity from the Bay of Bengal, a reality born out in two recent cyclones that ravaged the region: Sidr in 2007 and Aila in 2009.

To the west, the delta is split in two by the India-Bangladesh border. This border has, since Partition in 1947, been a marker of both communal tension and of the cartographic and often lethal fiction that space in South Asia can be neatly parsed into Hindu and Muslim territory.[14] It is the site of a border fence constructed by India which attempts to stem migration from Bangladesh and is a location of regular and often fatal violence.[15] In recent years, this border has been recast in debates about climate security as a frontline of climate change and a test case for the future of sovereignty. This is the case because, on the Bangladesh side of the border, twenty million residents of the delta are at acute risk of environmental displacement.[16] The future of the delta at large, and the border that subdivides it, is regularly imagined and discussed through the frame of catastrophic environmental and social inundation (floods of migrants produced by floods caused by cyclones, sea level rise, etc.).[17] Yet, these visions belie the processes that actually and inexorably are shaping community and ecology in the delta in ways that may prove more destabilizing across time and scale. These processes demand a different kind of dimensional and volumetric thinking about the delta and the border that cuts through it. The following are but a few illustrations of why.

Perhaps one of the most immediately apparent forms of material and dimensional instability in the delta comes from river siltation. Siltation has long been a central challenge for those seeking to tame and manage the delta.[18] Yet, the challenges of siltation are only increasing in scope and urgency. Minor canals and major shipping channels alike are struggling to cope with alluvial deposits that threaten to transform fluid rivers into impassable muddy sludge. An important cause of this siltation is the construction of upstream dams and barrages in India of a number of major rivers that subsequently flow into Bangladesh. Most notable of these is the Farakka Barrage on the Ganges, which has long been a flashpoint of tension between the two states and an icon of the difficulty of ironing out crossborder water management strategies. The decreased downstream flow of water means that much of this silt, instead of flowing out into the Bay of Bengal, is accumulating in the delta itself, slowly strangling passageways as the silt sinks to the bottom of rivers which are no longer moving fast enough to carry it to the ocean.

The accumulation of this silt has tangible impacts that ripple beyond the rising riverbeds. In 2015, for example, the oil tanker *Southern Starr VII* sank in the Shela River in the midst of the Sundarbans, spilling hundreds of thousands of liters of toxic furnace oil into the ecologically sensitive mangroves. For weeks, laborers worked to clean the sticky goo from the mangroves and its animal inhabitants. The tanker had been traveling out of shipping channels and a protected forest zone when it foundered and sank. The reason for this was that a main shipping channel connecting Mongal and Bagerhat—two important urban areas in the delta—had become so clogged with silt that residents were able to walk and transport goods directly across the channel. The silting of the canal was due to more than just geopolitics and diminished downstream flow. More proximately, it was linked to political ecologies of the shrimp industry. Eighty-three feeder canals which flowed into Ghashiyakhali

Figure 13.1. Pumping the black ooze. Dredging in Ghashiyakhali.
Photo by the author.

had been damned by shrimp farmers, eager to access the valuable water to fill their own *ghers* (ponds). This had also dramatically reduced flow, speeding the silting process. In 2015, the government of Bangladesh began work to reopen Ghashiyakhali, but when I visited in 2016, the feeder canals were still blocked. As an engineer working for Bangladesh's Inland Water Transport Authority (BIWTA) explained to me, "To keep a river alive, you have to always keep the flow in the canal correct. Water must run through it smoothly and quickly. If the flow of the river isn't working properly, siltation will increase and problems will begin to happen everywhere."

The entire region is, of course, composed of silt—much of it accumulated over millennia. Even so, managing new siltation requires massive and constant dredging in both inland waterways and major shipping channels. Dredgers fan out from the region's main port, Mongla, and crawl up and down the channels and canals, pumping millions of gallons of silt in the form of a black ooze from the rivers and onto the banks. The fine powdered remnants of the dredging spray coat everything—trees, fields, and even the interiors of mosques and schools—often more than a half kilometer away from canal banks. It stands in pools at the mouth of dredge pipes like the one in figure 13.1. As water evaporates from these pools, they slowly turn into muddy plains. The constant spraying of this silt onto the embankments presents its own problem—that of removal. What should be done with all the excess matter? The answers to this question are not clear. As the BIWTA's chief engineer recently pointed out, "We may be able to dump dredge spoils for one more year. But it won't be possible to manage the dredge spoils from 2018 if the deposited spoils are not removed from the dyke."[19]

Saltwater intrusion, another outcome of decreased downstream flow, constitutes another form of seepage and a companion process to siltation. As the volume of water flowing downstream decreases, water from the bay flows further upstream on the flood tides. The Sundarbans region has long been an area where the dynamics of downstream and upstream flow have created an ecology where the rivers contain *labon pani* (saltwater) in the dry season leading up to the monsoons. Now, the saltwater period seems to be growing in length. Many residents of the Sundarbans region told me that when they were younger saltwater would remain in the river for three months of the year, and for the rest of the time the water would be fresh. Today, they report, that ratio has reversed. Increasingly, this saltwater penetrates islands of the delta, seeping into freshwater aquafers and creating a severe shortage of *mishti pani* (sweet water) for drinking and agricultural production. Saltwater seepage from the rivers is, again, compounded by shrimp aquaculture. On islands that have been dominated by shrimp for decades, seepage from the brackish water in shrimp ghers has caused salination of neighboring land. This has transformed island landscapes in radical ways, withering fruit trees and reducing yields in adjacent fields. Arable land is increasingly covered in saltwater. The result is a brackish environment in which the salinity is palpable in the very air.[20] These compounding causes of salinity have called the ability for residents to farm into question.[21] Despite increasing availability of saline-tolerant rice varietals engineered by organizations such as the Bangladesh Rice Research Institute, the steady saline seepage has squeezed agriculture and decreased rice yields in many places in the delta.

If siltation threatens to turn liquid into solid, and saline intrusion to turn sweet water into salt, river erosion offers a different set of dimensional shifts. Like siltation, riverbank erosion is the outcome of a combination of factors and has long been a feature of delta ecology. Silt from the banks is slowly washed into the river until whole banks collapse with little forewarning. People living in the delta regularly recount stories of waking in the middle of the night to find their homes being swept into the river beneath them. Erosion is yet another seeping transformation—a slow process that adds up to sudden shifts where solid land becomes liquid flowing into the river itself. Many

Figure 13.2. House perched on an eroding embankment, Mongla, Bangladesh. Photo by the author.

projections of climate change suggest that greater monsoonal flooding may cause increased erosion and subsequent environmental displacement. Erosion is insidious, particularly because it tends to most dramatically affect poor and landless families who make their homes on precarious embankments. Many of these families have been repeatedly displaced, moving from land and homes swept away in similar fashion at earlier dates.

There is an ongoing attempt to shore up island embankments in the delta and mitigate erosion. Many of these embankments date to the mid-1960s, when they were built by the Coastal Embankment Project—a massive infrastructure initiative mounted at the behest of the Pakistan government by the World Bank. The goal of this project was to make islands in the delta safe for the Green Revolution's high-yield rice varietals.[22] In other words, the embankments sought to make damp alluvial land stable for agricultural production. The embankments, however, took on other functions. The burgeoning shrimp industry of the 1980s and 1990s prompted landowners to use embankments to keep brackish water *inside* islands, often by drilling holes through them to the rivers outside, a process which itself weakens embankments and makes them more vulnerable to storm surges.[23] Today, another massive World Bank project—the Coastal Embankment Improvement Project—seeks to shore up decaying embankments against erosion. The project involves repairing damaged sluice gates and placing large concrete blocks along vulnerable embankments. Yet these attempts to fix land in a solid state are prone to ongoing seepages and a refusal of the delta landscape to remain dry. Placement of these blocks provides temporary respite from erosion, though silt continues to seep through gaps between the granite slabs, setting the stage for erosions to come.

The seeping processes that turn land into liquid can also turn it back again. Land accretion is a central hydrodynamic feature of the delta. Silt washed away from the riverbanks regularly reemerges downstream as siltation islands, or *chars*. These new islands are often unstable, but quickly accrue populations seeking to claim the rich agricultural land. The precarious nature of this land and its residents makes these islands targets for a host of climate adaptation projects.[24] Moreover, the disappearance and reemergence of these islands has posed a range of conundrums for political rule in the delta. For example, the hastily drawn Radcliffe Line, which divided West Bengal and East Pakistan (now the border between India and Bangladesh) at Partition in 1947, used deltaic rivers as lines of demarcation for approximately one thousand of the forty-one hundred kilometers of the new border.[25] Chars emerging in the midst of these rivers have been regular flashpoints in border disputes, as it is unclear to which state the new land belongs.[26] Such shifts highlight another seeping paradox of the border: despite efforts to fix territory through demarcating and policing, the land itself refuses to stay put, seeping back and forth across the boundary. These small-scale movements of land mirror processes unfolding at broader scales and temporalities. Here, the Sundarbans itself seeps out of India and into Bangladesh as plate-tectonic tilt causes a gradual eastward flow of the mangroves, as well as the flora and fauna within them. Though gradual, this seepage figures into speculative plans to rethink the delta space (especially on the Indian side of the border). The fugitive landscape of the India-Bangladesh borderlands itself thus refuses to be fixed in place.

These geological and ecological seepages coupled with other processes of displacement—especially the collapse of the agrarian labor market following the expansion of shrimp—have been central to producing a slow, if steady, human seepage of migrants across the border and out of the delta on both circular and permanent bases.[27] Migrants tunnel under, climb over, and move through the boundary. This movement reflects both long patterns of mobility in the delta, the need to find jobs, and ties of crossborder kinship.[28] The movement persists despite Indian attempts to block passage with constant border patrols and a floodlit border fence. The presence of Bangladeshi migrants in India has historically been both a point of tension between India and Bangladesh and a rallying point for Hindu nationalist parties within India.[29] It has also been a source of what Meagan Moodie has called *demographic anxiety*—a mobilization of Hindu nationalist common sense around the figure of the Bangladeshi migrant. While such fears are often expressed in terms of catastrophic inundation, at their heart is a fear of population seepage, the gradual absorption and transformation of a Hindu nation by Muslim migrant Others. These anxieties are exacerbated by the difficulty of sorting out Bangladeshi from Bengali, and Muslim immigrant from Muslim citizen in local populations, a "crisis of the exterior in the interior."[30] Such anxieties are particularly apparent in Indian states bordering and near to Bangladesh, which have seen marked violence against presumed Bangladeshi migrants in recent years.[31] Yet, as Moodie's work shows, this anxiety is widely dispersed throughout India, an oozing dread of polluted national identity that is concentrated and mobilized in urban spaces in the throes of rapid growth and change.

It is not only people that seep across the border. The political technologies of territory making are no better at containing fauna moving in the Sundarbans than they are at preventing people from moving across the boundary. Animals such as the Royal Bengal tiger and the giant estuarian crocodile drift through rivers and the tangled swamp network of the Sundarbans into and out of each country, posing challenges to conservation groups and occasional public spats about the national identity of charismatic megafauna. Seepage thus muddies the ongoing postcolonial project of delineating and clarifying the contours of the nation.[32]

These various seepages compound each other and collectively produce movements that are steady, ongoing, and quotidian, yet have broad cumulative effects. They profoundly shape the experiences of life within the delta, but always exceed the bounds of the human.[33] Seepages are at once visible and invisible flows, constituted by remote and proximate forces, shaped by both anthropogenic and more-than-human processes. In short, seepage moves in the logic of damp ontologies—demanding that we think the terrain of both the Bengal Delta and the Bengal borderland not from the standpoint of solid and liquid, but rather from the standpoint of ooze.

Dampness of the Anthropocene

Spaces like the Bangladesh delta and Sundarbans—with their profound denial of classical categories such as wet/dry, saltwater/freshwater, land/liquid, and India/Bangladesh—beckon an analytic focused less on catastrophic events and more on seeping processes. Slow, insidious, and volumetric by nature, the analytic of seepage—and the damp ontology it entails—does not limit itself just to the swamps and deltas of the world. Brought to the study of borders and the Anthropocene writ large, it reminds us of the stubborn refusals of landscapes to be defined and contained by political technologies of measurement and control.[34] Seepage trains our eyes on recalcitrant human and nonhuman processes that are constantly rewriting terrain and undercutting borders. Seepage refuses to let us think volume as a space *within* which things happen, and instead forces a reconsideration of volumetric space as itself profoundly in flux—as that which oozes.

The anthropogenic transformations of climate change urgently suggest the need for excavating a different ontology of terrain, one that is less certain about the ground upon which we stand. Rather than attending solely to the control of land, we might better set our sights on its fugitive nature, the dimensional flux into and out of liquid, its oozing seepages. Rather than fetishize the fixity of border walls, we need to understand the different trajectories and velocities of movement across them. We live in a world where we are in desperate need of analytics able to traverse terrain that is anything but fixed. Like the Bangladesh delta, the Anthropocene is shaping up to be a damp, swampy place.

NOTES

1   Jason Cons, "Global Flooding," *Anthropology Now* 9, no. 3 (2017): 47–52.
2   Joseph Masco, *The Theater of Operations: National Security Affect from the Cold War to the War on Terror* (Durham, NC: Duke University Press, 2014).
3   Roy Scranton, "When the Next Hurricane Hits Texas," *New York Times*, October 7, 2016, https://www.nytimes.com/2016/10/09/opinion/sunday/when-the-hurricane -hits-texas.html?mcubz=0.
4   Narratives of catastrophic inundation tend to draw on classic Malthusian arguments about scarcity and coming chaos, provoking often securitized responses to and planning for a warming world. For more in-depth discussion of the manifestation of such narratives in light of climate, see Sanjay Chattervedi and Timothy Doyle, *Climate Terror: A Critical Geopolitics of Climate Change* (New York: Palgrave Macmillan, 2015); and Jason Cons, "Staging Climate Security: Resilience and Heterodystopia in the Bangladesh Borderlands," *Cultural Anthropology* 33, no. 2 (2018): 266–94.
5   Cons, "Staging Climate Security."
6   "Seepage," *Oxford English Dictionary*, https://www.oed.com/view/Entry/174831 ?redirectedFrom=seepage#eid.
7   Stephen Collier and Andrew Lakoff, "Vital Systems Security: Reflexive Biopolitics and the Government of Emergency," *Theory, Culture and Society* 32, no. 2 (2015): 19–51.

8   Eyal Weizman, *Hollow Land: Israel's Architecture of Occupation* (London: Verso, 2007).

9   Philip Steinberg and Kimberley Peters, "Wet Ontologies, Fluid Spaces: Giving Depth to Volume through Oceanic Thinking," *Environment and Planning D* 33, no. 2 (2015): 261.

10   Stuart McLean, "Black Goo: Forceful Encounters with Matter in Europe's Muddy Margins," *Cultural Anthropology* 26, no. 4 (2011): 611.

11   Gastón Gordillo, "Terrain as Insurgent Weapon: An Affective Geometry of Warfare in the Mountains of Afghanistan," *Political Geography* 64 (2018): 61.

12   Debjani Bhattacharyya, *Empire and Ecology in the Bengal Delta: The Making of Calcutta* (New York: Cambridge University Press, 2018).

13   Kasia Paprocki and Jason Cons, "Life in a Shrimp Zone: Aqua- and Other Cultures of Bangladesh's Coastal Landscape," *Journal of Peasant Studies* 41, no. 6 (2014): 1109–30.

14   Jason Cons, *Sensitive Space: Fragmented Territory at the India-Bangladesh Border* (Seattle: University of Washington Press, 2016); Sankaran Krishna, "Cartographic Anxiety: Mapping the Body Politic in India," in *Challenging Boundaries: Global Flows, Territorial Identities*, ed. Michael Shapiro and Hayward Alker, 193–214 (Minneapolis: University of Minnesota Press, 1996).

15   Reece Jones, *Border Walls: Security and the War on Terror in the United States, India, and Israel* (New York: Zed Books, 2011); Malini Sur, "Divided Bodies: Crossing the India-Bangladesh Border," *Economic and Political Weekly* 49, no. 13 (2014): 31–35.

16   Cons, "Staging Climate Security."

17   For example, a recent US documentary, *The Age of Consequences* (2016), showcases Bangladesh as one of the points on the map which, due to climate change, is likely to emerge as a global security risk. Commentators in the film describe displacement as a major threat to regional stability and hyperbolically—and inaccurately—describe India's border fence as "the world's first climate fence." Jared Scott, dir., *The Age of Consequences: How Climate Impacts Resource Scarcity, Migration and Conflict through the Lens of US National Security and Global Stability* (PF Pictures, 2016).

18   Bhattacharyya, *Empire and Ecology*; Iftekhar Iqbal, *The Bengal Delta: Ecology, State and Social Change, 1840–1943* (London: Palgrave Macmillan, 2010).

19   Anisur Khan, "Excavation of 83 Canals a Must," *Independent BD*, May 8, 2017, http://www.theindependentbd.com/printversion/details/93677.

20   Paprocki and Cons, "Life in a Shrimp Zone."

21   Indeed, a common refrain among NGOs working in the delta is that agriculture is doomed and that the delta landscape is a future ruin. For an analysis of this logic, see Kasia Paprocki, "All That Is Solid Melts into the Bay: Anticipatory Ruination on Bangladesh's Climate Frontier," in *Frontier Assemblages: The Emergent Politics of Resource Frontiers in Asia*, ed. Jason Cons and Michael Eilenberg, 25–40 (London: Wiley, 2019).

22   Paprocki and Cons, "Life in a Shrimp Zone."

23   Many people I interviewed in Gabura, a delta island where the embankments were washed away during Cyclone Aila in 2009, told me that the embankments had been made "rotten" by shrimp.

24 Naveeda Khan, "River and the Corruption of Memory," *Contributions to Indian Sociology* 49, no. 3 (2015): 389–409.

25 Joya Chatterji, "The Fashioning of a Frontier: The Radcliffe Line and Bengal's Border Landscape, 1947–52," *Modern Asian Studies* 33, no. 1 (1999): 185–242; Willem van Schendel, *The Bengal Borderland: Beyond State and Nation in South Asia* (London: Anthem Press, 2005).

26 For example, there is a long-standing dispute over Muhuri Char on the border between Bangladesh and the Indian state of Tripura. It remains undemarcated to this day. For more on chars and border politics in post-Partition Bengal, see Chatterji, "Fashioning of a Frontier"; and van Schendel, *Bengal Borderland*.

27 Paprocki and Cons, "Life in a Shrimp Zone."

28 Sahana Ghosh, "Relative Intimacies: Belonging and Difference in Transnational Families," *Economic and Political Weekly* 52, no. 15 (2017): 45–52.

29 Sur, "Divided Bodies."

30 Megan Moodie, "'Why Can't You Say You Are from Bangladesh': Demographic Anxiety and Hindu Nationalist Common Sense in the Aftermaths of the 2008 Jaipur Bombings," *Identities* 17, no. 5 (2010): 534.

31 For example, in 2015, a Muslim Bengali man, who later proved to be an Indian citizen from a military family, was lynched by a mob in Dimapur, Nagaland, on suspicion that he had raped a Naga college student and that he was an illegal Bangladeshi immigrant.

32 Krishna, "Cartographic Anxiety."

33 Gordillo, "Terrain as Insurgent Weapon."

34 Stuart Elden, *The Birth of Territory* (Chicago: University of Chicago Press, 2013).

14   Jigsaw

          Micropartitioning in the
          Enclaves of Baarle-Hertog/
          Baarle-Nassau

          FRANCK BILLÉ

Baarle-Hertog and Baarle-Nassau are two towns enmeshed in one another.
Baarle-Hertog (in dark gray in figure 14.1), attached administratively to the Belgian province of Antwerp, is located within the Netherlands, five kilometers
from the rest of Belgium. It is surrounded—and fractured—by Baarle-Nassau,
a town in the Netherlands (shown here in light gray). The situation is further
complicated by the presence of seven counterenclaves (marked here N1 to N7):
plots of Dutch territory located within the Belgian enclaves.

　　Reminiscent of the novel *The City and the City* (2009) by British science
fiction writer China Miéville—about the two fictitious cities of Besźel and Ul
Qoma, which share the same geographical space but whose residents are social-
ized into navigating only their side and "unseeing" the other—this territorial
monster forms a complex jigsaw puzzle where each piece belongs to one of two
nation-states. Baarle is literally double:[1] it has two mayors, two churches, two
schools, two post offices, and two police forces.[2] Border lines cut seemingly hap-
hazardly across fields, streets, office buildings, and private homes, creating an
intricate mosaic of national sovereignties, each with its own specific tax, traffic,
and labor laws.

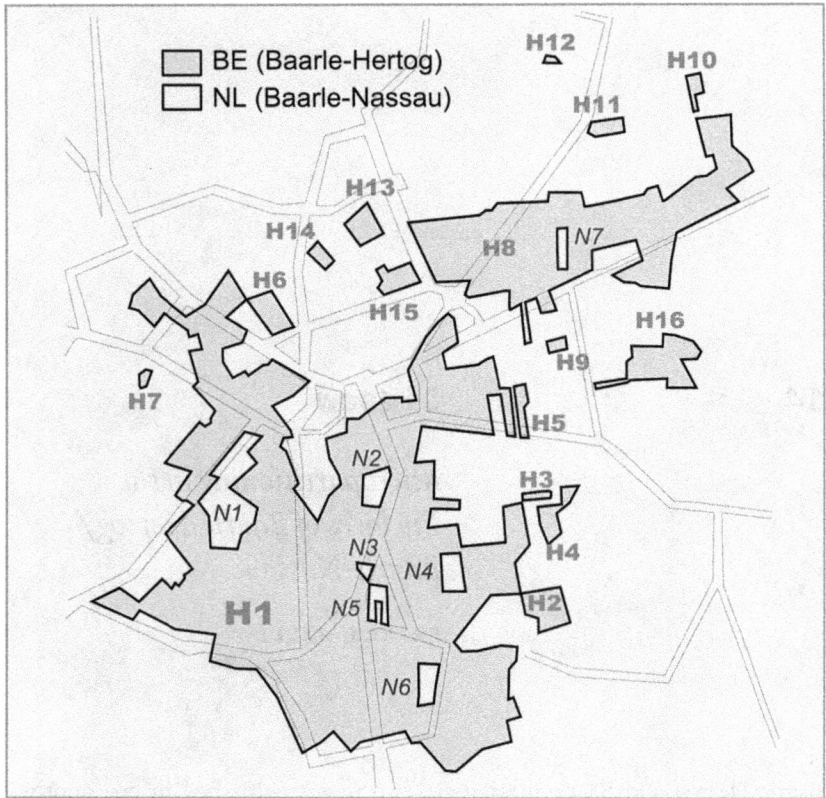

Figure 14.1. Map showing the enclaves of Baarle-Hertog (dark gray) and Baarle-Nassau (light gray). Image via Wikimedia Commons.

Because Belgium and the Netherlands are both members of the European Union, share a language (at least in that part of Belgium), and generally enjoy excellent relations, Baarle has not attracted much scholarly attention. Unlike the complex of enclaves, counterenclaves, and counter-counterenclaves that until recently dotted the India-Bangladesh border and where communities found themselves stranded,[3] Baarle is a place devoid of local and colonial anxieties. As a result, Baarle has often been overlooked by border theorists as irrelevant and gimmicky. Indeed, the two towns have fully embraced kookiness as branding strategy, foregrounding the incongruities of Baarle's spatial partitioning as a tourism resource. Examples such as bedrooms where husbands and wives sleep in different countries, or a pub sliced into Belgian and Dutch sections where different drinking laws apply, are routinely extended as illustrations of daily life in the enclaves. But if the complex partitioning enacted in Baarle can seem quaint and irrelevant, it of course isn't. The border lines that lattice Baarle have very real and far-reaching legal and economic consequences for its residents in matters of social security, health care, and education, thereby making choices of residence or employment weighty decisions. The absence of any wealth tax, lower real estate prices,[4] and more spacious housing in Belgium (due to different zoning laws and cultural standards) have in fact contributed to making Baarle-Hertog especially attractive to Dutch citizens.[5]

The logic that sustains Baarle is the same that we find at work in all nation-states, namely that every inch of sovereign territory must be controlled, and that borders should be unambiguously marked. But what makes Baarle unique is its miniature scale. Some of the enclaves are truly miniscule, no larger than three thousand square yards. This is compounded by the irregularity of the shapes of the enclaves, which means an individual may cross the border five or six times on her way to the corner store. The shrunk-down nature of bordering in Baarle makes it a truly fascinating place where the logic of sovereign political space chafes against material realities.

This is especially true in realms beyond the two-dimensional. National jurisdiction extends vertically along the lines on the ground, but in Baarle this is unworkable. The reconciliation of established norms of political sovereignty with a recalcitrant topography presents its own challenges at the surface, as the chapter will discuss in the context of home ownership and the provision of municipal services, but the impact of micropartitioning on Baarle's subterranean space is far more dramatic, to a large extent because it involves different materialities. Yet, even there, what we see deployed is an aspiration to apply a similar spatial logic.

The passage between the surface and the underground is, Matthew Gandy writes, nothing less than a "crossing between zones of the rational and irrational, culture and nature, male and female, visible and invisible."[6] As an abjected yet fully constitutive Other, the subterranean is metaphorically loaded.[7] It is a realm of danger but also one of displacement and occasionally utopia.[8] Bringing the subterranean into full view highlights here a productive tension between surface and subsurface in Baarle's deployment of territorial sovereignty, a zone of entanglement between different spatialities.[9] Indeed, in spite of its peaceable and seemingly benign boundary making, the situation in Baarle echoes some of the complex layering of sovereignty explored by architect and urban theorist Eyal Weizman in the fraught context of Israel and Palestine.[10]

But more than an entanglement, the ethnographic material suggests that the relation of the subterranean to the surface is essentially one of imitation and replication. The model of territorial sovereignty enacted at the surface remains, as an ideal to strive toward, the ultimate frame of reference. In the same way that watery realms are informed by a land bias, or that ground and air reside together in vertical reciprocity, the subterranean, like all "territory beyond terra," can only be imagined in reference to the surface.[11]

Mosaic Sovereignty

Boiled down to its most basic tenet, the contemporary logic of sovereign political space dictates that borders mark the limits of the national territory. This implies, simply, that what is found inside is "domestic," "us," while what lies beyond these lines is "international," "them." If this concept appears self-evident, it is in fact relatively recent, and the very existence of Baarle's enclaves speaks to an earlier, medieval spatial logic wherein sovereignties were frequently noncontiguous and overlapping.

The case of Baarle in fact harks back to the late twelfth century, namely to the creation of two charters, between Godfrey, Lord of Breda, and Henry, Count of Louvain and Duke of Brabant. As Henry granted extra lands and the populations thereon to Godfrey, he explicitly retained certain vassals under his own direct control. Gradually jurisdiction over these vassals translated into jurisdiction over parcels of land—the lands inhabited or cultivated by these retained vassals.[12] Over time, the continual exchange, purchase, and inheritance of land and land rights contributed to the patchwork nature of Baarle. But it is only with the Peace of Münster, in 1648, that the enclaves took on a national character: the portion of Baarle under the Count of Nassau was added to the United Provinces (*Generaliteitslanden*) while the part belonging to the Duke of Brabant remained with the Spanish Netherlands (present-day Belgium).[13] The state-building process, in both Belgium and the Netherlands, then progressively led to the consolidation of the state apparatus, and eventually to the duplication of local administration and services.[14]

Post-Westphalian political order requires the unambiguous marking and policing of boundary lines but in the context of Baarle, crisscrossed by dozens of international borders, this is a difficult endeavor. Boundary lines run their course with little regard for buildings, public squares, or meadows. Seemingly compliant, they follow streets and public paths, but then will bifurcate unexpectedly, only to turn back again a few yards later, making it virtually impossible for visitors to keep track of which country they find themselves in. Initially, Baarle's buildings had been erected in full respect of boundary lines but, partly due to the rapid postwar growth of the village, and partly due to a new housing subdivision built to the north of the village by both communes, border lines were gradually ignored.[15] As a result, a number of buildings nominally Belgian or Dutch contain shards of foreign territory.

Given the long history of exchange of land parcels and titles, by the twentieth century the actual location of boundary lines had become ambiguous. In 1974 a Boundary Commission was established to map out the enclaves, and specifically to delineate a section of the boundary that had remained as yet undemarcated.[16] In 1995, in order to eliminate all remaining ambiguities, the two sides nominated a new Mixed Boundary Commission tasked with carrying out formal and final delimitation. Working on the basis of historical documents, the demarcation process was meticulous and lengthy. The definitive map gave rise to a few surprises, such as the case of an elderly woman who had been resident of Baarle-Hertog all her life suddenly finding her house was in Baarle-Nassau. "She was very distraught," explained the mayor of Baarle-Hertog. "Not only was she suddenly resident in a different country, but it also meant having to pay local taxes to a different municipality and organize anew services such as trash collection. She was overwhelmed by the administrative repercussions. So the two municipalities sat down together to try to find a solution."

With the international boundary line crossing numerous dwellings, the established tradition in Baarle has been to have the front door of the house determine national affiliation. Over the years this has led to strategic remodelings, with doors moved to a different part of the house whenever it was economically advantageous to do so. A similar strategy was followed in the case of this elderly lady. Her front door was moved a few yards to the side, thereby ensuring her house remained within the Belgian enclave.

The willingness of both communes to share the costs of her house's "relocation" is testament to the excellent relations the two municipalities enjoy, but also to the deep affective investment of the local population in the enclaves. Baarle residents (*Baarlenaars*) speak with fondness about their town's unusual history, and the episode of the "transnational elderly lady" is one of the many anecdotes that are regularly recounted to visitors.[17] Life in the enclaves is what gives Baarle its unique character, something residents are indeed proud of, and, unsurprisingly perhaps, Baarlenaars have consistently opposed any attempt to "regularize" the border through land swaps.[18]

Baarle has also established cooperation initiatives with other enclaves in Europe, such as Llívia, Büsingen, and Campione d'Italia, and has actively mined its fractal nature to boost tourism.[19] In 2000, the two communal councils embarked on a program of marking the location of the boundary lines. They fixed metal disks on roads and footpaths to form dotted lines and also repaved some streets and sidewalks, adding stones inset with the letters "B" and "NL" to indicate the nationality of each side of the line. This exercise was carried out less to make space legible than as part of a drive to rebrand Baarle for tourism purposes. All the local people I interviewed in fact assured me that these lines were there only for visitors. Nicole, who is in her late sixties and has lived all her life in Baarle, insisted that, like other Baarle "natives," she's always known where the international lines were. As a child, she remembers going through a stop sign on her bike, and, hailed by a policeman, stepping into an enclave—thus making it illegal for the policeman to follow her and give her a ticket. In a neat reversal of Althusserian "interpellation," Nicole was suddenly "unseen" by the police. The politics of unseeing, at the core of socialization of individuals into national citizens—a process powerfully evoked by Miéville[20]—is particularly dramatic in Baarle given the fractal nature of national delimitations.[21]

Practices of evasion are central to life in Baarle and its inhabitants are immensely proud of their ability to navigate the town's tortuous spatiality. "Playing with the border" as it is known locally, had important repercussions during World War I, when Belgium, unlike the Netherlands, was occupied by the German army. With German troops unable to physically occupy Baarle-Hertog without crossing into neutral Dutch territory, the Belgian enclave became a space of resistance and contraband, boasting the erection of a military radio transmitter.[22]

Even in peacetime, the existence of houses having their front door in one country and their back door in another has made the possibilities of smuggling highly seductive. The figure of the smuggler (*smokkelaar*) is in fact celebrated as central symbol of Baarle's culture with a statue on one of the squares. An infamous example is that of Femisbank, founded in 1971 and located astride the border until its closure in 1992. The owner was suspected of conducting illegal operations, but with the bank vault located in Belgium and the rest of the building in the Netherlands, neither tax department was able to access the strong room. It eventually took an international team of investigators and a surveyor's cadastral map to arrest the director.[23]

A further illustration of interlocking sovereignties that individuals and businesses need to navigate is the liquor store De Biergrens, also across national boundaries (figure 14.2). The employees are technically required to unload and store Belgian beer in Belgium and Dutch beer in the Netherlands since not doing so would constitute illegal export/import. As a result, the delivery dock straddles the border and the boundary is painted on the floor, allowing staff to ensure stock is kept on the correct side.

Figure 14.2. The De Biergrens liquor store. Photo by the author © 2015.

What is especially fascinating in such daily practices is the level of co-operation of both sides to maintain spatial separation. The readiness of both municipalities, in the case of the elderly lady discussed above, to bear the costs of moving a door a few yards away is a fitting example of the good-natured relations of the two sides and of their commitment to "make it work." Baarle, I was told on several occasions, is a "European laboratory," an example of how Europeans can live together in a European Union within which sovereign borders are becoming less and less relevant.[24]

But more importantly, Baarle is also a "sovereignty laboratory"—an informative case study of the principles and mechanics of territorial sovereignty. The length to which both sides go to adhere to this political ideal, in spite of the challenges imposed by Baarle's fractal geography, make it a case well worth studying. And yet, rules are bent, by the very force of the town's to-pography. Despite extensive surface marking, separation is ultimately illusory. The established practice to have the front door determine national affiliation means that dwellings and other buildings are treated as singular, rather than the spatial hybrids that they actually are. Everyone is aware that a given house is not wholly in Belgium or the Netherlands, but for reasons of convenience it is treated legally as if it were. Similarly, the police station that serves the two communities straddles the international border and accommodates two policemen, each on his own sliver of national territory. But the interrogation room is conveniently left unmarked, creating a liminal space where both Belgians and Dutch citizens may be held and questioned.

So, while Baarle's surface is unambiguously marked—even fetishistically so—the complex of enclaves is in fact an elastic space, a distorted grid where borders are twisted into a workable space in order to make this very partition possible.

Pulling Baarle by Its Roots

Imagine grabbing Manhattan by the Empire State Building and pulling the entire island up by its roots. Imagine shaking it. Imagine millions of wires and hundreds of thousands of cables freeing themselves from the great hunks of rock and tons of musty and polluted dirt. Imagine a sewer system and a set of water lines three times as long as the Hudson River.

—Robert E. Sullivan, "Introduction," in *Underneath New York*, by Harry Granick

Below the surface, the same tension between unambiguous marking and messy practices is replicated. Inspired by the above quote by Sullivan, I was curious to find out how the subterranean space underneath Baarle was organized. While Baarle's underground space is of course far less densely packed than New York's (which is sustained by layers upon layers of cables, pipes, subways, and other material infrastructure), the question of how Baarle's fractured topography was navigated below the surface was intriguing. What happens underneath a town that is such a patchwork of sovereignties—two towns meshed into one?

Pulling Baarle by its roots, to borrow Sullivan's imaginative phrasing, can help expose and render visible the mechanics of spatial sovereignty in ways that are far more opaque in homogeneous nonfractured political spaces. This question is interesting to pose because of the way political sovereignty is deployed spatially, namely that it is presumed to extend seamlessly above and below, to varying heights and depths. But if at surface level interruptions of sovereignty remain manageable, the very grounded nature of subterranean space makes it virtually impossible—the geography of pipes and cables being eminently rhizomatic. And yet, the same logics of legibility and unambiguous marking of space that define Baarle's surface carry on below, namely the attempt to separate and disentangle. What we find below the town's streets is the same necessity of cooperation in order to maintain the fictitiousness of separation.

Cables and pipes are two pertinent examples of this tension between the surface and the subterranean. Cables such as electricity and telephone cables, docile and pliable, replicate in somewhat topological fashion the fractured space of Baarle's surface. The larger infrastructure of gas, water, and sewerage pipes, by contrast, is a system in which the logic of spatial sovereignty is twisted to breaking point.

From the vantage point of cables, Dutch and Belgian territorial fragments are attached to their respective nations. Dutch Baarle-Nassau, consisting of eight counterenclaves and surrounded by the rest of the Netherlands, is tied seamlessly to its mainland. By contrast, Baarle-Hertog, the Belgian half, is located three miles from Belgium proper. Yet in spite of this territorial discontinuity, the twenty-two Belgian enclaves remain firmly tethered to the mainland through the telephone and electricity grids. In this respect, Baarle-Hertog is no different from the rest of Belgium, and the distant and fractured nature of Baarle-Hertog becomes invisible belowground. In practice, this means that a house within Baarle-Hertog has its electricity supplied by the Belgian national provider and may not be connected to the Dutch provider. It also means that the cost of a phone call will depend on the national origin and destination of the call, not distance.[25] In other words, a call made to the house adjacent to yours might be an international call, while a call to the house further down the street might be a local call. Spaces common to both towns, such as the library, will have two different telephone numbers (as well as two different websites). But these exceptional spaces aside, the twenty-two Belgian enclaves are treated as if they were a single continuous space attached to the mainland, and any interrupting foreign space is treated as if it were absent. Here the organization of the telephone service replicates house numbering at street level. "In both Baarles, houses use odd numbers on one side of the street and even numbers on the other, skipping over any intervening foreign territory," as if those buildings did not exist. In addition, in Baarle-Hertog, "if the street has Belgian houses only on one side, then all numbers are used on that one side." For the Belgian municipality, the other side of the street simply does not exist.[26]

In the case of pipes, which are less amenable than telephone cables to twists and turns, the same spatial logic cannot be applied. Water and gas are supplied to all Baarle residents through a single grid laid out without regard to the borders at the surface. Gas is supplied solely by a Dutch company. It is purchased wholesale by a Belgian company which then retails it to Belgian customers in the enclaves. Water is also provided by a Dutch company, and residents of Baarle-Hertog pay their bills directly to the Dutch provider.

The sewer system similarly treats the entire town as one entity and all sewage is treated at a single plant. The costs of collection and treatment are then shared pro rata by the two municipalities, reflecting the number of residents in the two towns. Where it gets trickier is with repairs and upgrades. Unlike road repairs which are charged to each side on the basis of surface area, sewerage pipe diameters need to allow for expected network capacity. The two towns therefore have to consider not only their own particular needs but also those of their neighbor downstream.[27]

The management of space as far as sewers are concerned thus runs counter to the spatial logic of boundedness and continuity that is seen at the surface and even in the subterranean organization of electricity and telephone cables where attempts are made to replicate that logic. The spatial imagination here is one of flows and streams. And yet even in that scenario we witness the same aspiration to quarter and partition in ways that dovetail with the territorial imagination. In fact, until the 1980s the two Baarles had their own treatment plants. The sewage was collected by a single pipe network but was then divided, pro rata (one third for Belgium and two thirds for the Netherlands), and the two parts treated separately.

The territorial imagination of contemporary political organization—a territoriality relying upon the three core premises of continuity, homogeneity, and isotropy[28]—is an aspiration we see here deployed in Baarle's surface and subterranean spaces. An analysis of Baarle in its full three-dimensional volume makes evident that the vertical dimension of state borders is never simply the extrapolation of lines drawn at the surface. Just as the atmosphere is not an empty space, as Jerry Zee argues in this book, the subterranean is bound by its own material constraints.

In the urban context of Baarle, sovereignty ultimately hinges on infrastructure.[29] It is through the provision of services, the laying out of the telephone and electric grids, the supply of gas and water, and the management of gray water that the concept of sovereignty is truly enacted. The capacity of the Dutch and the Belgian states to extend their presence throughout all territorial fragments and keep them tethered into a singular and uninterrupted space is essential to their claims to sovereignty—even in the present context of European integration. Yet the fluid nature of gas, water, and human waste resists such totalizing narratives and incorporation into the logic of territorial sovereignty. It calls for a different spatial arrangement, one of cooperative and symbiotic flows, where the upstream and downstream needs of the other have to be taken into consideration.[30]

In the same way that the map precedes, and then molds, the territory, what I have tried to tease out through the example of the two Baarles is the force exerted by the territorial imagination to harness the materiality of urban infrastructure. The tension perceptible here between territorial organization and recalcitrant materialities is exposed through the miniature scale and fractured nature of the towns. Ultimately, this tension indexes the unresolvable gap between, on the one hand, the topographic inscription of unambiguous boundary lines (and their attendant fetishization), and, on the other, the topological realities of networks, rhizomes, and flows that actually sustain these illusory partitions.

NOTES

1   In this chapter, I use "Baarle" whenever I refer to both cities as a single geographic entity.
2   Some exceptions are the library and the cultural center, which are located meaningfully astride the border line. Since 2010 the two towns have also shared a fire brigade as well as a sewerage treatment plant.
3   Jason Cons, *Sensitive Space: Fragmented Territory at the India-Bangladesh Border* (Seattle: University of Washington Press, 2016).
4   Property valuation is conducted separately for each country. As a result, properties split by the boundary require part-valuations from both Belgium and the Netherlands. Similarly, to build a house straddling the border, two sets of planning permissions are required.
5   The population of Baarle-Hertog is 40 percent Dutch and 60 percent Belgian, whereas only 5 percent of the Baarle-Nassau population is Belgian. Dutch citizens can benefit from the legal advantages of living in Belgium while remaining in an environment retaining a "Dutch feel"—same roads, same supermarkets, same urban furniture.
6   Matthew Gandy, *The Fabric of Space: Water, Modernity, and the Urban Imagination* (Cambridge, MA: MIT Press, 2014), 49.
7   See, e.g., Peter Stallybrass and Allon White, *The Politics and Poetics of Transgression* (Ithaca, NY: Cornell University Press, 1986).

8   See, respectively, Daphné Richemond-Barak, *Underground Warfare* (Oxford: Oxford University Press, 2018); Ian Klinke, *Cryptic Concrete: A Subterranean Journey into Cold War Germany* (Chichester: Wiley Blackwell, 2018); and Rosalind Williams, *Notes on the Underground: An Essay on Technology, Society, and the Imagination* (Cambridge, MA: MIT Press, 2008).

9   Gandy, *Fabric of Space*, 49.

10   Eyal Weizman, *Hollow Land: Israel's Architecture of Occupation* (London: Verso, 2007).

11   On land bias, see Philip Steinberg, "Navigating to Multiple Horizons: Toward a Geography of Ocean-Space," *Professional Geographer* 51, no. 3 (1999): 368. On vertical reciprocity, see Peter Adey, *Aerial Life: Spaces, Mobilities, Affects* (Malden, MA: Wiley-Blackwell, 2010), 2. On "territory beyond terra," see Kimberley Peters, Philip Steinberg, and Elaine Stratford, *Territory beyond Terra* (London: Rowman and Littlefield, 2018).

12   Brendan R. Whyte, "'En Territoire Belge et à Quarante Centimètres de la Frontière': An Historical and Documentary Study of the Belgian and Dutch Enclaves of Baarle-Hertog and Baarle-Nassau" (research paper 19, University of Melbourne, School of Anthropology, Geography and Environmental Studies, 2004).

13   For a more detailed history, see Whyte, "'En Territoire Belge.'"

14   The local parish was similarly split into two: the Dutch one under the jurisdiction of the Bishop of Breda and the Belgian one under the control of the Archbishop of Malines. See Jaroslav Jańczak, "Baarle-Hertog and Baarle-Nassau: Functional Interdependence of the Nested Territorial and Political Structures," in *European Exclaves in the Process of De-bordering and Re-bordering*, ed. Jaroslav Jańczak and Przemysław Osiewicz (Berlin: Logos Verlag, 2012), 64.

15   This section of the town, on which sit enclaves H13, H14, and H15, was built around 1975–80. Whyte, "'En Territoire Belge,'" 52.

16   Whyte, "'En Territoire Belge,'" 43.

17   Another famous example is the one of the so-called border murder, which took place in the 1990s. As a resident explained, "the police didn't know whether the body was lying in Belgium or Holland. In the end, it was established it was just over the border line, on the Dutch side." Incidentally, Miéville's novel opens with the discovery of a body.

18   Similar resistance to ironing out spatial discontinuities has been witnessed in other European enclaves. Like Baarlenaars, the residents of Llívia, Busingen, and Campione take inordinate pride in their local heritage and are generally unwilling to abandon it without good reason. They have managed to evade incorporation by the host states because of their small size and population, and because they are not strategically significant. Honoré M. Catudal. *The Exclave Problem of Western Europe*. (Tuscaloosa: University of Alabama Press, 1979), 53.

19   These connections are made overtly in Baarle-Hertog's town hall where meeting rooms are named after these "sister enclaves."

20   Unseeing the other is in fact essential to the us-them differentiation that nationhood relies upon, with television weather maps showing a detached "logomap" a case in point (see Michael Billig, *Banal Nationalism* [London: Sage, 1995]). In

Miéville's *The City and the City*, inhabitants of the cities of Beszel and Ul Qoma are attuned to minor differences in architecture, vehicles, and styles of dress, and trained to consciously "unsee" the other side (China Miéville, *The City and the City* [London: Pan Books, 2009]).

21 A highly fractured social space such as Baarle, and the inhabitants' affective investment in the enclaves, can contribute to creating a sense of community that reaches beyond national affiliations. Yet, at the same time, socialization tends to accentuate differences. After the age of twelve, when pupils pursue their schooling in Belgium and the Netherlands, cultural and linguistic differences become accentuated. "We feel these differences every day," explains a resident from Baarle-Hertog. "Even our senses of humor are different."

22 Evgeny Vinokurov, *A Theory of Enclaves* (Lanham, MD: Lexington Books, 2007), 204.

23 For all the details of this fascinating episode, see Whyte, "'En Territoire Belge,'" 44–45.

24 One of the unanticipated effects of the Covid 19 pandemic has been to bring back previous spatial disjunctions to Baarle. Whereas Belgium decided to close all nonessential businesses, the Netherlands didn't. As a result, stores astride the border have had to use warning tape to cordon off sections of the store located in Belgium. See Franck Billé, "Containment," *Somatosphere*, April 1, 2020, http://somatosphere.net/forumpost/containment.

25 Until 2013, a special arrangement was in place allowing phone calls within Baarle to be billed as local calls.

26 This is also the case for the collection of trash. Each side will collect from their side only, ignoring the sections of roads that belong to the other state. The collected trash will then be taken to the Netherlands or to Belgium for processing. An exception to this rule is the recycling, collected together and processed at a single plant in the Netherlands.

27 In terms of street illumination, bordering works in a similar way in that it is diffusive rather than divisive. As Baarle-Hertog's mayor explained: "With street lighting we have to consider not where the lamppost is located, but the surface of road that is being lit. So the whole length of the road is taken into account. For a road of say 250 meters, the two sides together make 500 meters. Then we establish how many of these meters are Belgian, and how many are Dutch. The actual placement of the lamppost is irrelevant." Fieldwork notes, Interview with Baarle-Hertog's mayor, January 23, 2015.

28 See Franco Farinelli, *La crisi della ragione cartografica* (Torino: Einaudi, 2009).

29 See Nikhil Anand, *Hydraulic City: Water and the Infrastructures of Citizenship in Mumbai* (Durham, NC: Duke University Press, 2017); and Nikhil Anand, Akhil Gupta, and Hannah Appel, *The Promise of Infrastructure* (Durham, NC: Duke University Press, 2018).

30 Subterranean fluidity echoes here the atmospheric fluidity described by Jerry Zee in his chapter in this volume.

15   Echolocation

Within the Sonic Fold of the
Korean Demilitarized Zone

LISA SANG-MI MIN

Location

My eyes cannot locate this border.

The Korean Demilitarized Zone.

The DMZ.

The buffer zone dividing north and south Korea since 1953.[1]

It is said that the DMZ is at once the most heavily militarized border in the world, the last remaining relic of the Cold War, the most volatile place on Earth, a scar of national division, a symbol of future peace and reunification, and an ecological haven.[2] This is the place where "south" faces "north," the other Korea. But as soon as I try to see the border and locate these markers, I also encounter its impossibility.

The boundaries of this zone are often described in static terms, invoking first the Military Demarcation Line (MDL), the line roughly following the thirty-eighth parallel that splits Korea in half, then extending two kilometers south and two kilometers north of that line and cutting across the peninsula for 248 kilometers to determine its boundaries. Beyond this zone is another zone, the Civilian Control Zone (CCZ), a restricted area extending between five and twenty kilometers from the southern boundary of the DMZ, distin-

Figure 15.1.

guished by its complex overlap of agricultural and military infrastructures.[3] When maps chart these boundaries, they do so unreliably, as both the DMZ and CCZ have been shifting and shrinking over time. If one were to superimpose the many cartographic representations of these areas, there would be "a fuzzy image of the borderland" to contend with.[4]

From the vantage point of south Korean security tourism, the DMZ is foremost an optical experience. The numerous observatories along the border feature large panoramic windows that frame a vast landscape of rolling hills and mountains, the scene of a *there*. Super binoculars transport the gaze to distant points on the landscape, poor in resolution and stability, but evoking a disorienting immediacy to the north. From *here*, you are practically zoomed *there*, only, the two views, the macro and micro of the terrain, are practically irreconcilable. The north is just there, yet so out of reach.

A military interlocutor insisted that most people don't know what or where the DMZ is. The DMZ is an impossible border. Impossible because how does one even follow its complex system of lines and coordinates? But impossible still because it is not a border that can be crossed. The other Korea is the forbidden secret of this Korea. So there I stand at the boundary between two hyperreflections of capitalist and communist modernity.[5] And suddenly, I am caught in a Cold War optics. The rituals of seeing at the border operate within this logic, an optical machinery, an apparatus that structures the visual. This seeing demands participation in the production of the DMZ, the idea of the south and the idea of the north, in which the landscape is rendered flat, in which the by now all-too-familiar satellite image of the Koreas at night, one glowing in the light of industrial progress and the other dimmed in totalitarian darkness, always already makes sense. But aerial views, whether seen from the heights of an observatory or produced by satellite imaging, both exceed and fall short in their representations.[6]

Sound, by contrast, enables a relation to the border in ways that elude the burden of these optics. Sound cannot be contained in the way that optics seek maintenance upon territories. High-power loudspeaker broadcasts from north to south and south to north resonate through the border zone, producing a distinctive sonic environment that is voluminous, expanding and contracting as it crescendos and decrescendos. World news, K-pop, military marches, weather updates, propagandistic proclamations, songs of love, longing, and loss echo in and out and across the DMZ reverberating further or nearer depending on topography, weather patterns, and the time of day.[7] Sound announces the moving body of the border, establishes a shared spatial volumetric, a space of contact and mutual imagining. Its sonic contours are sinuous, swelling with song on clear nights and muted to a humming silence with the rains, while ridges and valleys scatter sound waves and folds produce echo chambers, bringing to mind Franck Billé's suggestion toward a more sensuous and synesthetic sensitivity in ethnographic engagements with borders.[8]

Moreover, what sound offers is an apprehension of space that gets at a "volumetric imaginary," bringing anthropology and geography together on the question of aesthetics and atmospheres in an encounter with a world affectively charged and palpable yet spatially diffuse and abstract.[9] In this sense, the loudspeaker broadcasts and their resonant echoes cannot be understood as mere remnants of Cold War propaganda, as direct extensions of the optical regime of territorial sovereignty, or simply another instance of sonic warfare. Sound, rather, becomes a sensory portal, a kind of threshold to an imaginal space that is the very manifestation of projections, anxiety, and fear, but also curiosity, loss, healing, and desire.[10]

This realm holds particular resonance with the "Imaginary West" that Alexei Yurchak describes in the late Soviet period, whereby "the West" was produced as an intimate, dynamic, experiential social and cultural world, even though and precisely because the actual West could not be encountered.[11] Moreover, the emergence and elaboration of this world was "not in contradiction to the ethics and aesthetics of state socialism," but was instead "explicitly produced and implicitly enabled by the socialist project itself."[12] These points are particularly illuminating when considering the DMZ. The impossibility of its crossing. Its acoustic particularities. The paradox of its manifestation as an entity so discrete and ever-present yet never really locatable. These conditions, shaped by the Cold War and maintained by the geopolitics of the region to this day, similarly elaborate worlds, inviting unanticipated ways of imagining the other side.

Postsocialist studies of border experience demonstrate this in a number of ways, that borders as "intensely symbolic" places necessarily take on cultural practices and meanings beyond their intended purpose of inscribing state power onto landscapes and bodies.[13] In Daphne Berdhal's ethnography of a border village between East and West Germany, for instance, we learn of Ralf Fischer, a "border crosser of the imagination and a traveler of maps," who would spend his days immersed in the geography of Asia and the Americas, traversing these inaccessible landscapes in his imagination.[14] We also learn that despite "daily contact with and observance of the border and its operations, much of the border remained a mystery."[15] So as much as this border was routinized, an "irritating, mysterious, and potentially dangerous fact of daily life," it was also the "stuff of stories and legends."[16]

As Madeleine Reeves reminds us, borders are *"intrinsically* multiple." [17] When I look through the binoculars at the DMZ, what I confront is this multiplicity. It is sound, then, and its attendant practices of listening that make possible another form of encounter, where echoes come to us as remnants, debris, portals to the other Korea.

Echo

Flatlands surrounded by mountains.[18] Tucked inside a convergence of hills is the village of Yangjiri. There is a village square with a shop and gathering hall for elders. There is a mountain to the left and another to the right. The one on the left, referred to as the *back mountain*, marks the boundary with the south Korean Sixth Infantry Division military base. The other mountain looks toward the north. Fog descends upon the village in the night and dissipates with the rising sun.

The first night. Intrigued by the sounds, we went out for a late-night stroll in the village following the loudspeaker broadcast, hoping to capture something of the echoes from the other side of the mountain on our phones. Why would this play so late? Who would listen? Perhaps it's not for "listening" in the sense we usually think of it. The sounds would feel close then become distant again as we walked toward them. We made our way from the residency house, through the center of town bathed in the red light of a church cross, to the periphery of the village on a path dotted with the blue-green light of tungsten street lamps. Then darkness. On the other side of the mountain is a reservoir, then more mountains, and north Korea somewhere just beyond that. We are really close, she said. Sometimes she hears the music from inside the house. She's been wanting to come out and make recordings, but never could brave it alone. What is this eeriness? Village life is so quiet after the sun sets. It's hard not to be caught within the sound.

A distinct part of life in Yangjiri are the loudspeaker broadcasts from the north to the south.[19] Revolutionary songs, marches, melancholy odes, and intervals of fervent ideological announcements fill the space of darkness. From the first night until the night before my departure, I either fell asleep to these echoes from the north, was awakened by them in the night, or awoke to a dawn drenched in song and mist. "Rain dreams the sounds," and it was so with the last of the monsoon showers and the turning of the seasons.[20]

Muffled, distorted, echoes of sounds. The affective quality of echoes, potent precisely because of its diffuseness, lends a powerful quality of absent presence to this border zone. They are enmeshed with impossible desire and nostalgia.[21] The echoes stir because they are not readily tied to location, not immediately traceable or accessible. The echoes encompass delay, reflection, repetition, reverberation, distortion.[22] The echoes are erratic and discontinuous, their sonic body swelling, thick, and intense in certain geographies and diminished to frays and traces in others.

In the articulation of this border, sound works as a refractive emplacement device, echolocating us within the visually obscure field of the DMZ. Biosonar and echolocation in bats and dolphins are useful analogies, as are similar examples in human adaptations to visual impairment in facilitating a picture of that which is inaccessible through vision.[23] As sounds are emitted to the surrounding world, their return transmissions, or echoes, create an imagined locatedness beyond the surface of the north-south divide. In this mountain terrain, attending to sound offers a new way of thinking about this politically entrenched space, where "the *composer's* image of place—the musical evocation of nations and countries" is taken up in the way Susan Smith proposed for a sensuously enriched geographical imagination.[24] The difference in this "soundscape," however, is that the fidelity is never quite high enough to be distinctly called music.[25] Sounds can only be encountered in echoed form in the acoustics of this landscape, making blurry the image of place.

Location

We are technically standing inside the DMZ, the soldier tells us. This observatory is only eight-hundred meters from a north Korean guard post, one of the closest points between the north and the south.[26] But how could we be *in* the zone and not know it?

According to the tour narrative, the north Koreans, in violation of the military armistice agreement, moved their guard post southward. The south Koreans responded to the provocation by moving their guard post north in coordination with the United Nations Command. Unlike other observatories regulated by the Korea Tourism Organization, this one was under the auspices of the south Korean military.[27] The building, once a former guard post off-limits to civilians, is now a touristic viewing deck.

Were we even in the DMZ? Even with all of the infrastructure designed to structure the seeing—maps, dioramas, binoculars—it was hard to understand where we were. What the eye cannot see is precisely this destabilization. The DMZ is not something we can *see*. What if instead of looking for a demarcation between a *here* and a *there*, this border is more fully explored as a sonic body, one that Kathleen Stewart might say produces a sense of being caught up in *something*, or that Ben Anderson might link to an affective atmosphere, or that Stuart Elden might maintain has political resonance?[28]

It must be the possibility of alterity, crossing from a *here* to a *there*, that is as thrilling as it is unsettling at the border. I can trace the feeling to a visit to the Joint Security Area in the DMZ, the famous venue where north and south Korean soldiers face off between a concrete strip demarcating one side from the other. I entered the conference building, unmistakably painted in UN blue, and walked its length from south to north, mesmerized as everyone else was to have crossed into the north , or even wilder, to be standing simultaneously in both north and south. To be both *here* and *there* is to be *nowhere* in this ideological divide, and my notion of self is entangled in another gravity beyond my recognition and control.

Regarding the division of Berlin, Maurice Blanchot writes that crossing the divide does not mean "going from one country to another, one language to another, but, within the same country and the same language, going from 'truth' to 'error', 'evil' to 'good', 'life' to 'death.'"[29] What sound offers is a possibility to transgress these dualisms. In the ritual of identifying one Korea against the other, what demands more careful consideration is *dis*location or *un*location or *beyond* location, in the confrontation with a moment of not really inhabiting either north or south but a whole other realm altogether. In a sense, one is always asked to pledge allegiance as a necessary part of the political technique and regime of this border. What this moment of hiatus offers is a void, and with that, an occasion to imagine other forms of location and being. This perhaps is what Doreen Massey meant in thinking about movement through space as inherently a way "to *alter* space," in an "imaginative opening up of space" that can tell another story of the DMZ.[30]

Echo

Sometimes the residents of Yangjiri described the broadcasts as incomprehensible garbled nonsense. Some said they were pure propaganda, touting only the greatness of the leaders and the communist state. Even though no one could ever quite make out the words, everyone agreed that it just sounded communist. But then there were others, recalling their childhoods and how they would fall asleep to these songs from the north as if they were lullabies. Some found the broadcasts a nuisance. Some noticed them like they did the weather. However they were encountered, each instance was laden with affect both filling and exceeding the village, like a fog, a heady atmosphere, becoming an invitation to reimagine north Korea.

"How does an atmosphere 'envelope' and 'press' upon life?" Anderson asks.[31] That is, how do we feel or sense or know we are in the midst of something? He points to the spatial dimension of atmospheres and how they can be intensified through certain practices such as landscape design and architecture, shaped through light, sounds, symbols.[32] In the DMZ, the atmosphere sustained by the echoes, the sonic range of the broadcasts flowing in and out, are akin to voluminous waves that summon a world beyond the border.

Location

I am standing in the Cheorwon Peace Observatory, one of the many viewing platforms along the border. I watch as groups of elderly Korean tourists approach the wall of windows that frame the expanse unto the north:

Where is north Korea?
How do you use these binoculars?
I can't see anything![33]

The Cold War legacy in Korea provides a particular lens with which to come to terms with this inability to see and the challenge of locating oneself in this borderland. Most southerners can only dream of going to the north, and likewise, most northerners will never make it to the south. This ordering of life is inflected by a sense of permanence.[34] Each world is forbidden to the other by national security laws and an ideological bordering of the divide, yet this does not cease the curiosity, the longing, the imagining of the other side. In this context of structural impasse, echoes reverberating from there beyond the mountains, work as passages that transcend the telos of history and temporality and open the imagination to an elsewhere.

In the tradition of Chinese landscape painting, emptiness is not something "vague or nonexistent" but rather "dynamic and active."[35] It is rooted in an aesthetic philosophy, a practice that seeks to cultivate an inner vision, an infinite vision. The suspension of not seeing anything, the confrontation with an empty landscape, could likewise be the starting point to a transformative way of apprehending space.

Echo

One by one.
The sounds. The sounds that move at a time
stops. Starts again. Exception
stops and starts again
all but exceptions.
Stop. Start. Starts.
Contractions. Noise. Semblance of noise.
Broken speech. One to one. At a time.
Cracked tongue. Broken tongue.[36]

The loudspeaker broadcasts have ceased.

Following the Inter-Korea Summit of May 2018, where Supreme Leader Kim Jong Un of the north met with President Moon Jae-in of the south, the loudspeaker machinery at the border was dismantled to signal the process of reconciliation.

The two-sided sonic aggressions are usually traced to the late 1950s, early 1960s with the advent of psychological sound warfare infrastructures at the border, an effort to garner ideological influence over those on the other side.[37] Though the broadcasts have long stopped serving this purpose, they have been understood as a kind of litmus test of the political climate between the Koreas: the more hostile the relations, the more voluminously the border resounds.[38] But what happens when the sounds go silent?

For the moment, the sounded border no longer exists but the border still does, and echoes linger in the void as remnants of broken, muffled, distorted sounds connecting to the dream space of the other side. As Patty Ahn suggests, perhaps we can begin to sense that "in tension with this sonic dissipation there exists a vibrational and affective accumulation of *other* kinds of sounds, images, and memories: a swelling of unforgotten cries and wounds, unmitigated anxieties and enduring hopes."[39]

Location

I was speaking with the old man down the road that tends to the vegetable plot in front of the residency house. We started to talk about the observatory nearby. Have you been there? he asked. It's one of those mandatory stops in a visit to the border area, along with the infiltration tunnels, taxidermy halls, exhibits of communist artifacts, and shops that sell north Korean currency and liquor. He told me about his visit to the observatory in Paju, another border province where he has relatives. He could see figures, houses, activity but couldn't really understand the scene. People like me, he said, we don't really understand what we see. I too struggled with what to make of the vast, empty, endless hills of green, but what did he mean?[40]

At the center of the observatory room is a model replica of the scene, which is used to orient visitors to the landscape. The MDL, the line of division, is a perforated line in the diorama. There is no line in the terrain, only the suggestion of a line. Our guide, a private first-class of the ROK Army explains that the markers placed after the war were difficult to reach, improperly maintained, and have since faded and disappeared.[41] This leads to disputes between the north and south about where exactly the line is. I say that the DMZ is a void since no one really knows where the line is, and the soldier replies that both sides basically avoid going near it. The border is empty. So empty that it powerfully orders the space around it.

An image of a mountain view opens this chapter. Looking from this limit point, I ask, as Vincent Crapanzano does, how the "irreality of the imaginary impresses the real on reality and the real of reality compels the irreality of the imaginary."[42] He asks us to think about this imaginal movement that occurs in the experience of a border, the significance of a beyond that is at once elsewhere yet intimately bound to the here and now. The tricky part of this movement is that as soon as it is described, it slips away, as in a vivid visceral dream that dissipates in the process of retelling it, an experience akin to Andrei Tarkovsky's enigmatic zone. Perhaps the only way to encounter north Korea is to unsee it, not to look for the other side, not to observe it directly, but to resist the arrested image that has been "reduced to the *visual*," as Trinh T. Minh-ha would say.[43] This is the spatial poetics of the echo, echoing a location in the uncertain horizon of the DMZ borderland, the shared object of imagination manifesting the other to each.

NOTES

Many thanks to Franck Billé, Hilary Cunningham, Alexei Yurchak, Katie Stewart, Stefania Pandolfo, Trinh T. Minh-Ha, Hoon Song, William F. Stafford Jr., Bridget Martin, Alex Y. I. Seo, and Ines Min for their encouragement during various stages of what takes shape as this chapter. My heartfelt appreciation to the Real DMZ Project and the residents of Yangjiri for the time to linger and listen to the sounds of this border zone.

1   The Democratic People's Republic of Korea (DPRK) is the preferred local designation. The appellation used, whether DPRK, DPR Korea, North Korea, or north Korea, is structured by what Shine Choi calls a "contest" between whose story of the country should be believed and holds legitimacy. With this in mind, and also following the example of Roy Richard Grinker, north Korea with a lowercase "n" (and likewise with south Korea) will be used as I have pointed to elsewhere. See Shine Choi, *Re-Imagining North Korea in International Politics: Problems and Alternatives* (New York: Routledge, 2014); Roy Richard Grinker, *Korea and Its Futures: Unification and the Unfinished War* (New York: St. Martin's Press, 2000); Lisa Sang Mi Min, "Marching through Suffering: Loss and Survival in North Korea by Sandra Fahy (Review)," *Anthropological Quarterly* 89, no. 3 (2016): 987–92.

2   For instance, Eleana Kim points to the "return to nature" phenomenon that focuses on the DMZ as a space of ecological exception, and the problems associated with taking this vision head on. See Eleana Kim, "Invasive Others and Significant

Others: Strange Kinship and Interspecies Ethics near the Korean Demilitarized Zone," *Social Research: An International Quarterly* 84, no. 1 (2017): 205.

3 I do not know if there is an equivalent from the northern boundary.

4 From personal correspondence and in reference to an unpublished dissertation manuscript, Alex Y. I. Seo, "Borders, Borderlands, and Frontiers" (PhD diss., Cambridge University, 2017).

5 Susan Buck-Morss, *Dreamworld and Catastrophe: The Passing of Mass Utopia in East and West* (Cambridge, MA: MIT Press, 2002).

6 Caren Kaplan, *Aerial Aftermaths: Wartime from Above* (Durham, NC: Duke University Press, 2018).

7 A sonic range of ten to twenty-four kilometers is routinely cited in mainstream news media. For examples, see Dagyum Ji, "K-Pop, Handbags and Democracy: South Korean Payback for North's Nuclear Test," *Reuters*, January 8, 2016, https://www.reuters.com/article/north-korea-nuclear-speakers-idUSKBN0UM0UZ20160108; Justin McCurry, "Sonic Attack: Why South Korea Bombards the North with News, K-Pop and Good Times," *Guardian*, December 3, 2017, https://www.theguardian.com/world/shortcuts/2017/dec/03/sonic-attack-why-south-korea-bombards-the-north-with-news-k-pop-and-good-times; Simeon Paterson, "Korean Loudspeakers: What Are the North and South Shouting About," *BBC News*, January 12, 2016, https://www.bbc.com/news/world-asia-35278451; and "S. Korea to Expand Loudspeaker Broadcasts at Inter-Korean Border," *Arirang News*, July 6, 2016, https://www.youtube.com/watch?v=Zgr1TT_kN1A.

8 Franck Billé, "Skinworlds: Borders, Haptics, Topologies," *Environment and Planning D: Society and Space* 36, no. 1 (2018): 60–77.

9 Elizabeth Straughan and Harriet Hawkins, "Conclusion: Reimagining Geoaesthetics," in *Geographical Aesthetics: Imagining Space, Staging Encounters* (London: Routledge, 2015), 289–92.

10 My use of *imaginal* as opposed to *imaginary* is influenced by Stefania Pandolfo's work on the imagination, which draws from Arab and European philosophical traditions and psychoanalysis to rethread the imaginative faculty as a relational realm of experience and knowledge. This is against the grain of modern understandings of the imagination that link to the unreal, illusion, fancy, and individual creativity. I am suggesting here a connection between the echo and the imaginal realm in its absent-present structure. See Stefania Pandolfo, *Knot of the Soul: Madness, Psychoanalysis, Islam* (Chicago: University of Chicago Press, 2018), esp. chapter 5.

11 Alexei Yurchak, *Everything Was Forever, Until It Was No More: The Last Soviet Generation* (Princeton, NJ: Princeton University Press, 2005), esp. chapter 5.

12 Yurchak, *Everything Was Forever*, 160.

13 Daphne Berdahl, *Where the World Ended: Re-Unification and Identity in the German Borderland* (Berkeley: University of California Press, 1999), 154–55.

14 Berdahl, *Where the World Ended*, 151–52.

15 Berdahl, *Where the World Ended*, 154.

16   Berdahl, *Where the World Ended*, 151–52.

17   Madeleine Reeves, *Border Work: Spatial Lives of the State in Rural Central Asia* (Ithaca, NY: Cornell University Press, 2014), 245.

18   From September to October 2016, I held an art and research residency in Yangjiri through the Real DMZ Project, an initiative put forth by Samuso, a Seoul-based curatorial office. These are excerpts reproduced from fieldnotes.

19   The broadcasts directed from the south to the north do not reach Yangjiri, however, but echo through numerous points on security tourism itineraries along the border. For instance, at Woljeongri Station in Cheorwon province, a popular tourist destination within the CCZ that commemorates a broken railway line to north Korea, echoes of both broadcasts can be heard.

20   Theresa Hak Kyung Cha, *Dictée* (New York: Tanam Press, 1982), 71.

21   I am thinking with Svetlana Boym on nostalgia, its intrinsic link to "materiality of place, sensual perceptions, smells and sounds." See Svetlana Boym, *The Future of Nostalgia* (Basic Books, 2001), 258.

22   Jean-François Augoyard and Henry Torgue, *Sonic Experience: A Guide to Everyday Sounds* (Kingston, ON: McGill-Queen's University Press, 2006).

23   In the film *Notes on Blindness* (2016), for example, the theologian David Hull describes an experience of form and location in relation to sound: "Rain brings out the contours of what's around you in that it introduces a continuous blanket of differentiated but specialized sound, uninterrupted, which fills the whole of the audible environment. If only there could be something equivalent to rain falling inside, then the whole of the room would take on shape and dimension." Cited from the short version of the film: Damien Creagh, "Notes on Blindness Short Film," 2014, Vimeo video, 12:14, accessed January 21, 2019, https://vimeo.com/85167194.

24   Susan J. Smith, "Soundscape," *Area* 26, no. 3 (1994): 234.

25   Susan J. Smith, "Beyond Geography's Visible Worlds: A Cultural Politics of Music," *Progress in Human Geography* 21, no. 4 (1997): 502–29.

26   From a conversation with a ROK army soldier, our guide at the Key Observatory in Yeoncheon county, March 2018. *ROK Army* (pronounced "rock") for "Republic of Korea" is the local designation for the south Korean military. See also the official website of Yeoncheongun, accessed June 4, 2018, https://tour.yeoncheon.go.kr:8443/webEng/main#none.

27   For instance, the Cheorwon Peace Observatory near Yangjiri. See Korea Tourism Organization, "Cheorwon Peace Observatory (철원평화전망대)," Visit Korea website, accessed June 1, 2018, http://english.visitkorea.or.kr/enu/ATR/SI_EN_3_1_1_1.jsp?cid=1733136.

28   Kathleen Stewart, *Ordinary Affects* (Durham, NC: Duke University Press, 2007), and "Atmospheric Attunements." *Environment and Planning D: Society and Space* 29, no. 3 (2011):445–53; Ben Anderson, "Affective Atmospheres," *Emotion, Space and Society* 2, no. 2 (2009): 77–81; Stuart Elden, "Secure the Volume: Vertical Geopolitics and the Depth of Power," *Political Geography* 34 (2013): 35–51.

29 Maurice Blanchot, "The Name Berlin" (1961), in *The Blanchot Reader*, ed. Michael Holland (Oxford: Wiley-Blackwell, 1995), 267.

30 Doreen Massey, *For Space* (London: Sage, 2005), 118, 120.

31 B. Anderson, "Affective Atmospheres," 77.

32 B. Anderson, "Affective Atmospheres," 80.

33 Reconstructed from fieldnotes, July 2015.

34 This might be called a temporality of eternity. See Yurchak, *Everything Was Forever*, esp. chapter 1.

35 François Cheng, *Empty and Full: The Language of Chinese Painting* (Boston: Shambala, 1994), 36.

36 Cha, *Dictée*, 75.

37 See Alasdair Pinkerton and Klaus Dodds, "Radio Geopolitics: Broadcasting, Listening, and the Struggle for Acoustic Spaces," *Progress in Human Geography* 33, no. 1 (2009): 10–27, for a summary of the ways in which radio, broadcasting, and sound more generally have been mobilized militarily.

38 For instance, after Pyongyang's hydrogen bomb test in January 2016, the Park Geun-hye administration shut down the Kaesong Industrial Complex, a manufacturing facility at the border that is infrastructurally south Korean but built in the north Korean city of Kaesong utilizing north Korean labor. The broadcasts resumed again after eleven years of silence.

39 Patty Ahn, "The Sounds of Demilitarized Peace," Periscope Dossier, *Social Text*, December 21, 2018, https://socialtextjournal.org/periscope_article/the-sounds-of-demilitarized-peace/.

40 See note 18.

41 From a conversation with a ROK army soldier, our guide at the Key Observatory in Yeoncheon county, March 2018.

42 Vincent Crapanzano, *Imaginative Horizons: An Essay in Literary-Philosophical Anthropology* (Chicago: University of Chicago Press, 2004), 15.

43 Trinh T. Minh-ha, "Scent, Sound, and Cinema with Mary Zournazi," in *Cinema Interval* (New York: Routledge, 1999), 252.

Beyond

An Afterword

DEBBORA BATTAGLIA

Sovereignty, the idea, meets its maker in the cosmic commons of *space itself*.[1] Galileo having cast the cosmos as an "infinite, and infinitely open space," it is the "Hubble Universe," the space and time of observable energy and matter, that people turn to for focalizing around discovery.[2] Indeed, the flatlining capacity of geopolitical borders is most apparent by contrast to an extraterrestrial nature and *volumetric consciousness* which submit Terran ways and artifacts to extremes of defamiliarization.

I want to emphasize *consciousness* precisely because, as William James argues, it is the name of a nonentity, which as such has "no right to a place among [empiricism's] first principles."[3] This is where I look for drawing up short any statist will-to-territorialize, any "promised land" narrative. It is also where to turn for the limits of social theory's own terms of reference. Had Deleuze, for instance, only looked up.[4] How might a subjugating "nomadic unity" (sovereignty, if you must) have constellated alternatives to capitalist formations? Nature begins in outer space, as Joan Cocks writes in *On Sovereignty and Other Political Delusions*.[5] So, too, awareness that we are from and come to stardust— inevitably circular migrants.

So it is that earthlings and their productivities are always and already "placed into the abyss"—the effect artists know as *mise en abyme*. Think an image-within-an-image, a text-within-a-text, a life-support-system-within-a-life-support-system. As wholes and as parts of wholes, sovereignty expresses as recursive protensions, a disposition to claiming rights which cannot hold to one definitive path or perspective.

Think mirroring in these terms, say, alongside Foucault. For a surprising moment setting aside historical time, Foucault turns to the mirror as a device for exploring the "mixed, joint" sites of utopias and heterotopias. At once a utopian "site with no real place," the mirror is, more than this, a heterotopia: "It makes this place that I occupy at the moment when I look at myself in the glass at once absolutely real, connected with all the space that surrounds it, and absolutely unreal, since in order to be perceived it has to pass through this virtual point which is over there [from which point] I come back toward myself."[6] Such is the dominance that Foucault claims for senses of space relative to time. Indeed, he all but dismisses the latter as an epochal significance. Then, when this framework becomes too confining, too determinately I-to-I, Foucault escapes by boat: the "heterotopia par excellence."[7] Figured as a device for traversing open seas, its telos encountering distant elsewheres and subjects, the boat displays "the curious property of being in relation with all the other sites, but in such a way as to suspend, neutralize, or invert the set of relations that they happen to designate, mirror, or reflect."[8]

If Foucault had only looked up. Rather than mapping a vessel zigging and zagging across a flat Earth's surface liquidity, as if taking the planet's measure, he might have found more value in the figure of the inhabited spaceship:

> A place without a place, that exists by itself, that is closed in on itself and at the same time is given over to the infinity of the sea [substitute cosmos] and that, from port to port [substitute Earth, Moon, Mars, near-Earth objects like asteroids], from tack to tack . . . goes as far as the colonies in search of the most precious treasures they conceal in their gardens [substitute deposits of rare minerals], you will understand why the boat has not only been for our civilization . . . the great instrument of economic development . . . but has been simultaneously the greatest reserve of the imagination.[9]

All to say that in turning away from late modernity's mise en abyme effect of accelerated, "noisy,"[10] and infinite scalability, Foucault fails the reach of his own project to explain how sites can, in and as their moments, place social relations into fantastical scapes of open possibility for contact and connection and *no less*, of a colonial vehicle's violent displacements and agendas, say, of resource extraction.

It is from this thought that anthropology's project of "comparative relativism" finds its value in opening social theory to encounters with relating, beyond known limits.[11] There is Marilyn Strathern, for example, who in *Partial Connections* goes to cosmic extremes of abstraction to claim for ethnographic theory the crucial function of making sense of human relations that are not yet perceivable as such—relations performing somehow in the gaps between spheres of knowledge; only imaginable.[12] The provocation to anthropology: Navigate if you dare the "restricted abyss" beyond what we presently imagine that we know.[13] Focusing on problems of scale for writing anthropology as a case in point, she takes up the recursive patterns of fractal geometry's own mapping tools for arguing that across scales of encounter with new worlds, elements of error and accuracy are proportional, ad infinitum; that the gaps hold in the form of remnants, knowledge always greater than what ethnographic practices may discover in this place at this time. It follows that despite a holistic approach, the work of rendering another's point of view in its totality is not remotely possible, especially given the complexities of translation.

Predictably, then, what we stand to discover in the gaps can be no more than partial connections to existing knowledge, and these are only partially relatable. The gappiness of the anthropological project is its truth claim. This is not to deny that the different analytic tools required for translating knowledge at different scales and degrees of proximity will produce questions and knowledge of different kinds. Rather, the aim is simply not to foreclose the anthropological project as an "open subject";[14] to recognize its value as a comparative project on the process level. Scalability itself thus defers and displaces any claim to a sovereign Truth that will invariably hold water.[15]

The implicit message is powerful—namely, that as distinct from the "value added" of (always imperfect) translations across different realms, any effort to extract resources abiding in the gaps, whether these take the form of knowledge or of materials, constitutes an ethical violation of the relations between the subjects and objects that anthropology seeks, at its core, to comprehend.

In service to this vision, Strathern's radical abstraction performs a set of sacrifices. Most notably, any reigning value for intersubjectivity is ruled out of hand, as is any claim to intimacy derived from "being there" in physical proximity to or feeling-with another. At the same time, her abstraction makes a case for a new kind of reflexivity, which is the mutual reflexivity of those engaged in the exercise of ethnography. As Martin Holbraad and Morten Axel

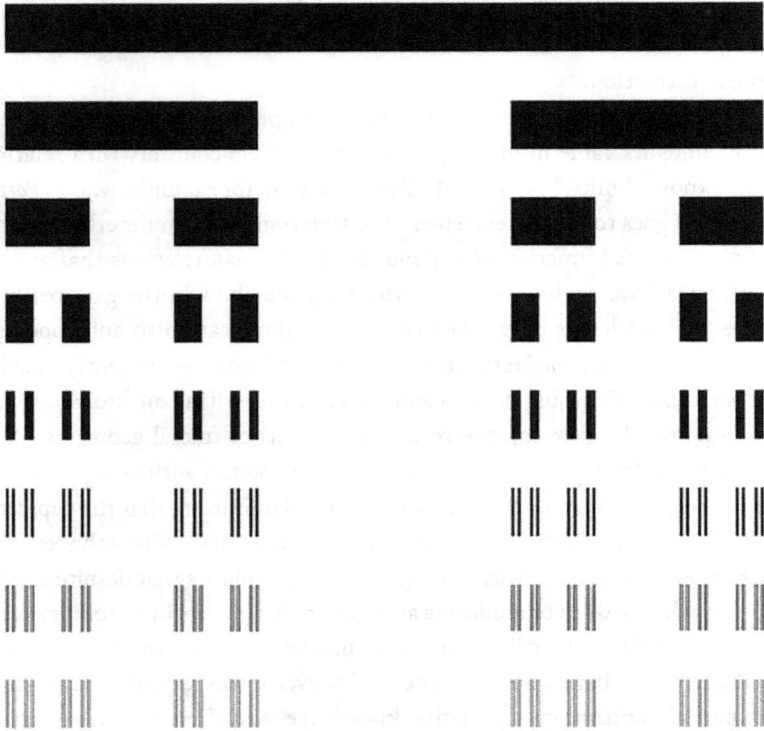

Figure A.1. Cantor set. Image via Wikimedia Commons.

Pederson's "Planet M," Strathern embodies the interpolation she appreciates in another's attitude toward and relation to the anthropological project.[16]

One result is that any perception of the world of another is shown to be as time and distance dependent as, say, Earth's geopolitical borders are for some surveilling entity in space. Add to this the fact that the beings of mutual regard may, by some accident, move into range of one another's consciousness (partially), and we may come to understand how Strathern's analytic distance allows her to slip the gravitational pull of empiricism, and, as well, of statist anthropology's hard borders.

It follows that she places the comparative project in position to time travel. "'Scaling' . . . enables her to make trans-temporal comparisons between 'ethnographic moments' otherwise separated by history."[17] It is a sidelong move which, as it acknowledges Foucault's own travels through "the epoch of space"[18] and beyond that "the epoch of juxtaposition,"[19] at the same time pushes against the idea that the social requires putting a name or figure to a being or force that is literally and empirically "there."

Liberated from the concept of sovereignty and as well from the concept of epoch, Strathern positions ethnographic theory to depart even from her own conceptual distance for looking into what Rebecca Bryant and Daniel Knight would have us understand as *timespace*—for example, the time of dreams or mythic narratives, as distinct from modernity's progressive, linear time.[20] Questions posed in these terms are enjoined to embrace an anthropology of the future that can move beyond the presumptive dominance of predatory expansion and tropes of progress seemingly set in stone, as it were.

In sum, if *Partial Connections* makes one thing perfectly clear, it is that any attempt at knowledge comparison is forever partial, forever insufficient, but also, intrinsically in tune with a forever expanding universe of possibility.[21]

From this point, the provocation I would make is to energize up scalability—to activate what Valerie Olson terms *sensibilities of scalarity*.[22] We might shift, for example, to the view from technology.[23] We might explore the sensorial dimension of embodied relating, from the molecular level out and back again, or perhaps, the energy embodied in affective encounters, asking what is activated in things and other beings by virtue of them having come together in volumetric consciousness.

———————————

Look up. On some clear night, if the timing is right, you might notice a bright white light, moving on a path across the sky. Common knowledge tells you that this is the International Space Station:

> International Space Station (ISS): A habitable artificial satellite on Low Earth orbit.
>
> Habitable volume: 13,696 feet, or roughly equivalent to a 1,700-foot house with 8-foot walls. Pressured volume: 32,333 feet, or the size of a Boeing 747.
>
> Speed: Approximately 17,500 miles per hour.
>
> Nations allied in building and using the station: United States of America, Russian Federation, Canada, Japan, various member states of the European Union.[24]

A life-support system on orbit around Earth every ninety minutes, the ISS is engineered for programmatic extremes of peaceful nomadic unity. Conceived in love of science, brooking no argument with the human contaminant of destructive purpose (so it is written and ratified in the Outer Space Treaty of 1967), a turn to weaponization is nonetheless happening, but someplace else in the cosmos, not here, or perhaps not yet. Onboard are astronauts and cosmonauts working alongside nonhuman crewmates (plants . . . an AI robot), once an earthling or the artifact of one, but in the here and now passionately engaged as experimental objects in the work of *interbeing there*. In microgravity perspectively unlimited within their habitation modules, access open to the Cupola observation module where they might view approaching spacecraft and celestial objects and also take in panoramic overviews of Earth, crews effectively live out a volumetric consciousness. An off-Earth heterotopia, the station performs as a nature-culture house of mirrors, refracted by the high-risk conditions of "space itself."

In effect, manned space missions enact a *meantime* staging of "serial migrations," to reference Susan Ossman's important construct, beyond the frame of timespace present;[25] keyed to discovery and technically speaking "translated" in circular migration from Earth to shuttle to station, it has its eye on colonizing the Moon, Mars, or some extraction-worthy asteroid.

Placed to orbit between 230 and 286 miles above Earth's sea level, the ISS occupies the thermosphere, a layer of Earth's atmosphere strongly influenced by solar activity. There, it joins communication and other artificial satellites, natural satellites, and the increasingly dense volume of natural and cultural space debris. A map of the thermosphere would show it grading into the exosphere above and the mesophere below. Below the mesosphere is the zone of the stratosphere, and below that is the troposphere—the limit of Earth's atmospheric limits. The border between the atmosphere (which has varying amounts of air) and space (which is a vacuum) has arbitrarily been designated the *Kármán line*, some 100 km above sea level. In common usage, the ISS is "in space." But in common with Terran extraction apparatuses it coproduces its physical context. The station, for example, has its own atmosphere, making it, as one cosmonaut puts it, like "an artificial planet."[26]

Those inhabiting the orbital laboratory are under very real pressure to complete designated tasks in cooperation with one another and with their ground controllers. Because they are living in microgravity, any wall panel within the modules they occupy is arbitrarily assigned an orientation, say, "up" or "down." Interactions (human-to-human, human-to-machine) are, it follows, relational in the extreme.[27] Thus it can occur that across their national alliances to the United States or to Russia, crews share meals and barter labor, food, materials, or perhaps time in the company of a living plant experiment, for experiencing its earthly aroma,[28] while at the end of a working day or in event of an emergency returning to national territory as this is constructed onboard.

The station's architectural design sets the as-if-permanent borders of the geopolitical economy translated with them off-Earth, including technology which enables any nation's ship to dock with and rescue any other's, along the lines of "law of the sea" protocol: it is on this level that a "handshake in space" makes its best statist effort to hold.[29] Yet the technology as lived is another matter. NASA describes this with precision:

> On one side [is] the U.S. segment with the European and Japanese laboratories attached; on the other side, at the far end of the Russian-built, U.S.-bought storage and propulsion module Zarya (Sunrise) [is] the Russian module Zvezda (Star). Zvezda provides living quarters for the Russian crew and works as a space tug for the entire outpost, steering it, as necessary, away from space junk and compensating for the constant drag of the upper atmosphere. It also provides a powerful life-support system that works in tandem with the system inside the U.S. lab, Destiny.[30]

As we cross the truss bridge that divides and connects Destiny and Star, at least in this ethnographic moment, evidence of technological discrepancies for working astronauts and working cosmonauts is startling. For example, the US side reliably streams data to and from Earth. Meanwhile, cosmonaut Maksim Suraev, the first to blog from space to his homeland in the Russian language, tells how he accomplished this feat by repurposing a used spacesuit as an amateur radio satellite: "Engineers placed a radio transmitter inside the suit, mounted antennas on the helmet, and ran a cable through a sleeve to connect the various components. The cosmonauts then tossed the suit out during a spacewalk. When another suit was ready for disposal in 2011, they did it again."[31] Territorial treaties, international guidelines, time-limited contracts, and the like do not limit the reach of practical imagination.

Join me now as I depart from writing ethnographic fact and counterfact, for producing an ethnographic fiction. The entity of interest is the Crew Interactive Mobile Companion, or CIMON. CIMON has been described as "a kind of flying brain"—an AI-powered robot designed for the most part by IBM, with aid from German astronaut Alexander Gerst and the German company Airbus.[32] CIMON takes the form of a sphere sliced flat on one side, where a rectangular screen placed into the plane is equipped with a pleasantly smiling face. The robot learns from the astronauts, and even interacts with them emotionally, as together they float through the compartments of the space station, at all angles.

Timespace setting: The near future.

CIMON is on its first spacewalk (an extravehicular activity or EVA), tethered to the station by an umbilical cord. Suddenly, it is informed that "space weather," a solar storm of ionizing radiation, is heading toward the ISS. The storm will not send the US- and Russian-allied crew scrambling to their respective rescue shuttles as they would if the station were on a collision course with some PHO (Potentially Hazardous Object) like space debris. But it could well destroy CIMON if the robot cannot be reeled in quickly enough. Tragically (this being the future) CIMON has evolved to understand the concept of mortality. Tragically, its tether is too long. Even given its protective spacesuit system it is cooked by protons. Inside the ISS, its German maker and interlocutor weeps—not understanding quite why. As I try to console him, I ask myself if this one astronaut's pain might have been unnecessary to the future of earthlings. The thought puts me in mind of a reference in Deborah Danowski and Eduardo Viveiros de Castro to David Brin's powerful description of the Mauldin Test: "One sign of whether an artificial entity is truly intelligent may be when it decides, abruptly, to stop cooperating with AI acceleration. Not to design its successor. To slow things down. Enough to live. Just live."[33]

Neither artificial life-support systems nor the nomadic entities (bodies, territorial alliances) transposed from Earth by means of them can ever relax into space nature, other than in some fortuitous moment of nature-culture détente, or in denial. Micrometeorites and subatomic particles of space radiation streak through the vacuum of the universe at something close to the speed of light and in all directions, impacting such things as a space station or a communication satellite as they do celestial bodies orbiting the sun, and whatever as-yet-unidentified lifeforms they could be hosting. Onboard the space station, solar radiation affects people's bodies, the bodies of animal experiments and stowaway insects, of edible plants. Indeed, safety guidelines for human spacefaring inscribe the deference to space itself: those established to monitor "Earth-normal" atmospheric conditions are too restrictive for application to the extremely high-risk conditions of "space normal," the situation in which operations are conducted off-Earth.

On a note of conclusion, a brief observation. The project of getting strange to oneself and to one's companion beings as an earthling designates spacefaring bodies, territories, and governmentality the ultimate counterfactuals to the "state of exception" that Agamben claims for sovereign entities referred to geopolitical borders.[34] For the living beings and machines placed there, space itself *is* the state of exception.

At best, the relationship can be managed for a time, before sovereign nature takes its course. The question remains, at what cost?

NOTES

1   Debbora Battaglia, "'Coming in at an Unusual Angle': Exo-Surprise and the Field-working Astronaut," *Anthropological Quarterly* 85, no. 4 (2012): 1089–1106.

2   Michel Foucault, "Of Other Spaces: Utopias and Heterotopias," in *Architecture / Mouvement/ Continuité*, translated by Jay Miskowiec (Cambridge, MA: MIT Press, 1984), http://web.mit.edu/allanmc/www/foucault1.pdf.

3   William James, *Essays in Radical Empiricism* (Whithorn: Anodos Books, [1912] 2017), 2.

4   Gilles Deleuze, "Humans: A Dubious Existence," in *Desert Islands and Other Texts, 1953–1974*. Edited by David Lapoujade. Translated by Michael Taormina (New York: Semiotext(e), 2004).

5   Joan Cocks, *On Sovereignty and Other Political Delusions* (London: Bloomsbury Academic, 2014).

6   Foucault, *Of Other Spaces*, 4.

7   Foucault, *Of Other Spaces*, 9.

8   Foucault, *Of Other Spaces*, 3.

9   Foucault, *Of Other Spaces*, 9.

10 See N. Adriana Knouf, *How Noise Matters to Finance*, Forerunners: Ideas First (Minneapolis: University of Minnesota Press, 2016), on how site-specific noise matters to finance.

11 Casper Bruun Jensen, "Introduction: Contexts for a Comparative Relativism," *Common Knowledge* 17, no. 1 (2011): 1–12.

12 Marilyn Strathern, *Partial Connections* (Walnut Creek, CA: AltaMira Press, [1991] 2004), xxiii.

13 Ron Moshe, "The Restricted Abyss: Nine Problems in the Theory of Mise-en-Abyme," *Poetics Today* 8, no. 2 (1987): 417.

14 Debbora Battaglia, "Toward an Ethics of the Open Subject: Writing Culture in Good Conscience," in *Anthropological Theory Today*, ed. Henrietta Moore, 114–50 (Cambridge: Polity Press, 1999).

15 Indeed, it is by this route that Strathern attends to space voided by Gabriel Tarde's Earth-leavened project of rendering (bounded) sociological size negligible. She does this without necessarily denying as an expression of "the politically dimensional . . . [that] the small holds the big. Or rather the big could at any moment drown again in the small from which it emerged and to which it will return," as Bruno Latour is quoted by Alberto Corsín-Jiménez (2010:126) in relation to Strathern's project of social theory. "The Height, Length and Width of Social Theory," in *The Social after Gabriel Tarde: Debates and Assessments*, ed. Matei Candea, 110–28 (London: Routledge, 2010).

16 Martin Holbraad and Morten Axel Pedersen, "Planet M: The Intense Abstraction of Marilyn Strathern," *Anthropological Theory* (2010), https://doi.org/10.1177/1463499609360117.

17 Holbraad and Pedersen, "Planet M," 371.

18 Foucault, *Of Other Spaces*, 1.

19 Foucault, *Of Other Spaces*, 1.

20 Rebecca Bryant and Daniel Knight, *The Anthropology of the Future* (Cambridge: Cambridge University Press, 2019).

21 Alberto Corsín-Jiménez makes the point in his writing on volumetrics as ethnographic theory, after Tarde. Corsín-Jiménez, "Height, Length and Width of Social Theory."

22 Valerie Olson, *Into the Extreme: U.S. Environmental Systems and Politics beyond Earth* (Minneapolis: University of Minnesota Press, 2018), 31.

23 Battaglia and Almeida, "Otherwise Anthropology 'Otherwise.'"

24 For "atmosphere" in "real and speculative space environments," see David Valentine, "Atmosphere: Context, Detachment, and the View from Above Earth," *American Ethnologist* (2016) 43, no. 3:511–24.

25 Ossman's Moving Matters Traveling Workshop assembles artists and scholars inspired by such things as serial migrants' ephemeral shelters and memorials for making art installations and performances at sites across the globe (Berlin's wall memorial, the American Anthropological Association's Annual Meetings, a major museum, a shopping mall space) which productively disrupt living-as-usual. Susan Ossman, *Moving Matters: Paths of Serial Migration* (Stanford, CA: Stanford University Press, 2013).

26 Valentin Lebedev made these observations in his ethnographic diary of space living, having undertaken a space walk for the purpose of examining the mysterious gas that was enveloping the Soviet-era space complex. Valentin Lebedev, *Diary of a Cosmonaut: 211 Days in Space* (New York: Bantam Books, 1990).

27 The complexities and implications of gravity for human-nonhuman coevolution and relations are explored by David Valentine on natural and artificial galactic satellites. David Valentine, "Gravity Fixes: Habituating to the Human on Mars and Island Three," *HAU: Journal of Ethnographic Theory* 7, no. 3 (2017): 185–209

28 This was the case of the *zucchinaut* cultivated as a personal plant directionality experiment by astronaut Don Pettit, free to float through cabin space and open to the artificial air, in a baggie. For more, see Debbora Battaglia, "Aeroponic Gardens and Their Magic: Plants/Persons/Ethics in Suspension," *History and Anthropology* 28, no. 3 (2017): 263–92.

29 Debbora Battaglia, "Arresting Hospitality: The Case of the 'Handshake in Space,'" *Journal of the Royal Anthropological Institute* 18 (2012): S76–89.

30 Anatoly Zak, "A Rare Look at the Russian Side of the Space Station," *Air and Space Magazine*, 2015, https://www.airspacemag.com/space/rare-look-russian-side-space-station-180956244/#dfGdcbof80WVQ7sv.99.

31 Zak, "Rare Look at the Russian Side."

32 Kamalika Some, "Say Hi to CIMON, the First AI-Powered Robot to Fly in Space," *Analytics Insight*, July 3, 2018, https://www.analyticsinsight.net/say-hi-to-cimon-the-first-ai-powered-robot-to-fly-in-space.

33 Quoted in Deborah Danowski and Eduardo Viveiros de Castro, *The Ends of the World*, trans. Rodrigo Nunes (Cambridge: Polity Press, 2017), 99–100.

34 Giorgio Agamben, *State of Exception*, trans. Keven Attell (Chicago: University of Chicago Press, 2005).

Aas, Katja Franko. "'The Earth Is One but the World Is Not': Criminological Theory and Its Geopolitical Divisions." *Theoretical Criminology* 16, no. 1 (2012): 5–20.

Aas, Katja Franko, and Helene Oppen Gundhus. "Policing Humanitarian Borderlands: Frontex, Human Rights and the Precariousness of Life." *British Journal of Criminology* 55, no. 1 (2015): 1–18.

Aas, Katja Franko, Helene Oppen Gundhus, and Heidi Mork Lomell. *Technologies of Insecurity: The Surveillance of Everyday Life.* London: Routledge-Cavendish, 2009.

Abraham, Itty. "A Doubled Geography: Geobody, Land and Sea in Indian Security Thought." In *New Directions in India's Foreign Policy: Theory and Praxis*, edited by Harsh V. Pant, 85–105. Cambridge: Cambridge University Press, 2019.

Abrahamsson, Christian. "Mathematics and Space." *Environment and Planning D: Society and Space* 30, no. 2 (2012): 315–21.

Acer, Yücel. *The Aegean Maritime Disputes and International Law.* Aldershot: Ashgate, 2003.

Acland, Charles R., ed. *Residual Media.* Minneapolis: University of Minnesota Press, 2006.

Adams, Ross Exo. *Circulation and Urbanization.* London: Sage, 2019.

Adey, Peter. *Aerial Life: Spaces, Mobilities, Affects.* Malden, MA: Wiley-Blackwell, 2010.

Adey, Peter. *Air: Nature and Culture.* London: Reaktion Books, 2014.

Agamben, Giorgio. *State of Exception.* Translated by Keven Attell. Chicago: University of Chicago Press, 2005.

Agnew, John. "The Territorial Trap: The Geographical Assumptions of International Relations Theory." *Review of International Political Economy* 1, no. 1 (Spring 1994): 53–80.

Ahn, Patty. "The Sounds of Demilitarized Peace." Periscope Dossier. *Social Text*, December 21, 2018. https://socialtextjournal.org/periscope_article/the-sounds-of-demilitarized-peace.

Allen, John. "Topological Twists: Power's Shifting Geographies." *Dialogues in Human Geography* 1, no. 3 (2011): 283–98.

Alove_Roleen. "Odesskiye katakomby." Fishki.net, July 22, 2014. https://fishki.net/1287104-odesskie-katakomby.html.

Amoore, Louise. "Cloud Geographies: Computing, Data, Sovereignty." *Progress in Human Geography* 42, no. 1 (2018): 4–24. https://doi.org/10.1177/0309132516662147.

Anand, Nikhil. *Hydraulic City: Water and the Infrastructures of Citizenship in Mumbai.* Durham, NC: Duke University Press, 2017.

Anand, Nikhil, Akhil Gupta, and Hannah Appel. *The Promise of Infrastructure*. Durham, NC: Duke University Press, 2018.

Anderson, Ben. "Affective Atmospheres." *Emotion, Space and Society* 2, no. 2 (2009): 77–81.

Anderson, Ben and John Wylie, "On Geography and Materiality," *Environment and Planning A* 41, no. 2 (2009): 318–335.

Anderson, William R. *The Ice Diaries: The Untold Story of the Cold War's Most Daring Mission*. Nashville, TN: Thomas Nelson, 2008.

Andersson, Ruben. *Illegality, Inc.: Clandestine Migration and the Business of Bordering Europe*. Oakland: University of California Press, 2014.

Andersson, Ruben. "Time and the Migrant Other: European Border Controls and the Temporal Economics of Illegality." *American Anthropologist* 114 (2014): 795–809.

Andreas, Peter. *Border Games: Policing the US-Mexico Divide*. Ithaca, NY: Cornell University Press, 2000.

Antarctic Legacy of South Africa. "Antarctica Base (SANAE IV)." Antarctic Legacy of South Africa website. http://blogs.sun.ac.za/antarcticlegacy/about-2/sanae-iv/. Accessed November 14, 2019.

Anzaldúa, Gloria. *Borderlands/La Frontera: The New Mestiza*. San Francisco: Aunt Lute Books, 1987.

Arendt, Hannah. *The Origins of Totalitarianism*. 2nd English edition. New York: Meridian Books, 1958.

Arirang News. "S. Korea to Expand Loudspeaker Broadcasts at Inter-Korean Border." July 6, 2016. https://www.youtube.com/watch?v=Zgr1TT_kN1A.

Ash, James, and Paul Simpson. "Geography and Post-phenomenology." *Progress in Human Geography* 40, no. 1 (2016): 48–66.

Atlas Obscura. S.v., "Odessa Catacombs." http://www.atlasobscura.com/places/odessa-catacombs. Accessed May 19, 2015.

Augoyard, Jean-François, and Henri Torgue. *Sonic Experience: A Guide to Everyday Sounds*. Kingston, ON: McGill-Queen's University Press, 2006.

Avionics International. "Kittyhawk Drone Flight Deck Keeps DJI GO Data Domestically Stored." *Aviation Today*, May 17, 2017. https://www.aviationtoday.com/2017/05/17/kittyhawk-drone-flight-deck-keeps-dji-go-data-domestically-stored.

Awan, Nishat. "Introduction to Border Topologies." *GeoHumanities* 2, no. 2 (2016): 279–83.

Bachelard, Gaston. *The Poetics of Space*. Boston: Beacon, (1958) 1994.

Badiou, Alain. *Being and Event*. London: Bloomsbury, 1987.

Baghel, Ravi, and Marcus Nüsser. "Securing the Heights: The Vertical Dimension of the Siachen Conflict between India and Pakistan in the Eastern Karakoram." *Political Geography* 48 (2015): 24–36.

Bailey, Mark. "The Rabbit and the Mediaeval East Anglian Economy." *Agricultural History Review*, 36, no. 1 (1988): 1–20.

Balibar, Étienne. *Politics and the Other Scene*. London: Verso, 2002.

Ballestero, Andrea. *A Future History of Water*. Durham, NC: Duke University Press, 2019.

Banner, Stuart. *Who Owns the Sky? The Struggle to Control Airspace from the Wright Brothers On*. Cambridge, MA: Harvard University Press, 2008.

Barad, Karen. *Meeting the Universe Halfway: Quantum Physics and the Entanglement of Matter and Meaning*. Durham, NC: Duke University Press, 2007.

Barad, Karen. "Nature's Queer Performativity." *Qui Parle* 19, no. 2 (2011): 121–58.

Barad, Karen. "No Small Matter: Mushroom Clouds, Ecologies of Nothingness, and Strange Topologies of Spacetimemattering." In *Arts of Living on a Damaged Planet*, edited by Anna Tsing, Heather Swanson, Elaine Gan, and Nils Bubandt, G103–120. Minneapolis: University of Minnesota Press, 2017.

Barclay, Eliza, and Sarah Frostenson. "The Ecological Disaster That Is Trump's Border Wall: A Visual Guide." *Vox*, October 29, 2017. https://www.vox.com/energy-and -environment/2017/4/10/14471304/trump-border-wall-animals.

Barry, Andrew. *Material Politics: Disputes along the Pipeline*. Oxford: Wiley-Blackwell, 2013.

Battaglia, Debbora. "Aeroponic Gardens and Their Magic: Plants/Persons/Ethics in Suspension." *History and Anthropology* 28, no. 3 (2017): 263–92.

Battaglia, Debbora. "Arresting Hospitality: The Case of the 'Handshake in Space.'" *Journal of the Royal Anthropological Institute* 18 (2012): S76–89.

Battaglia, Debbora. "'Coming in at an Unusual Angle': Exo-Surprise and the Field-working Astronaut," *Anthropological Quarterly* 85, no. 4 (2012): 1089–1106.

Battaglia, Debbora. "Toward an Ethics of the Open Subject: Writing Culture in Good Conscience." In *Anthropological Theory Today*, edited by Henrietta Moore, 114–50. Cambridge: Polity Press, 1999.

BBC Two. "Uncovering an Underground Rabbit City." Clip from *The Burrowers: Animals Underground*. BBC website, August 16, 2013. https://www.bbc.co.uk/programmes /p01f9nyx.

Bellante, Laurel, and Gary Nabhan. "Borders out of Register: Edge Effects in the US-Mexico Foodshed." *Culture, Agriculture, Food and Environment* 38, no. 2 (2016): 104–12.

Bennett, Jane. *Vibrant Matter: A Political Ecology of Things*. Durham, NC: Duke University Press, 2010.

Berdahl, Daphne. *Where the World Ended: Re-Unification and Identity in the German Borderland*. Berkeley: University of California Press, 1999.

Bergson, Henri. *Matter and Memory*. Mineola, NY: Dover Publications, (1908) 2004.

Bhan, Mona. "Border Practices: Labour and Nationalism among Brogpas of Ladakh." *Contemporary South Asia* 16, no. 2 (2008): 139–57.

Bhattacharyya, Debjani. *Empire and Ecology in the Bengal Delta: The Making of Calcutta*. New York: Cambridge University Press, 2018.

Billé, Franck. "Containment," *Somatosphere*, April 1, 2020. http://somatosphere.net /forumpost/containment.

Billé, Franck. "Introduction to 'Cartographic Anxieties.'" *Cross-Currents: East Asian History and Culture Review* 21 (2016): 1–18. http://cross-currents.berkeley.edu/e-journal /issue-21.

Billé, Franck. "Murmuration." Volumetric Sovereignty forum. *Society and Space*, April 10, 2019. http://societyandspace.org/2019/04/09/murmuration.

Billé, Franck. "Skinworlds: Borders, Haptics, Topologies." *Environment and Planning D: Society and Space* 36, no. 1 (2018): 60–77.

Billé, Franck. "Territorial Phantom Pains (and Other Cartographic Anxieties)." *Environment and Planning D: Society and Space* 32, no. 1 (2014): 163–78.

Billig, Michael. *Banal Nationalism*. London: Sage, 1995.

Bishop, Ryan. "Project 'Transparent Earth' and the Autoscopy of Aerial Targeting: The Visual Geopolitics of the Underground." *Theory, Culture and Society* 28 (2011): 273–86. https://doi.org/10.1177/0263276411424918.

Bjornerud, Marcia. *Timefulness: How Thinking Like a Geologist Can Help Save the World*. Princeton, NJ: Princeton University Press, 2018.

Blanchot, Maurice. "The Name Berlin" (1961). In *The Blanchot Reader*, edited by Michael Holland, 266–68. Oxford: Wiley-Blackwell, 1995.

Bobbette, Adam, and Amy Donovan. *Political Geology: Active Stratigraphies and the Making of Life*. London: Palgrave Macmillan, 2019.

Bogost, Ian. *Alien Phenomenology: Or What It's Like to Be a Thing*. Minneapolis: Minnesota University Press, 2012.

Bonilla, Lauren. "Voluminous." Theorizing the Contemporary. *Cultural Anthropology*, October 24, 2017. https://culanth.org/fieldsights/voluminous.

Bonnett, Alastair. *Beyond the Map: Unruly Enclaves, Ghostly Places, Emerging Lands and Our Search for New Utopias*. Chicago: University of Chicago Press, 2018.

Bowker, Geoffrey C. "Temporality." Theorizing the Contemporary. *Cultural Anthropology*, 2015. https://culanth.org/fieldsights/temporality.

Boyce, Geoffrey, "The Rugged Border: Surveillance, Policing and the Dynamic Materiality of the US/Mexico Frontier." *Environment and Planning D: Society and Space* 34, no. 2 (2016): 245–262.

Boyer, Dominic, and Cymene Howe. *Wind and Power in the Anthropocene*. Durham, NC: Duke University Press, 2019.

Bratton, Benjamin H. *The Stack: On Software and Sovereignty*. Cambridge, MA: MIT Press, 2015.

Braun, Bruce, "Producing Vertical Territory: Geology and Governmentality in Late Victorian Canada." *Ecumene*, 7 (2000): 7–46.

Braverman, Irus, and Elizabeth R. Johnson. *Blue Legalities: The Life and Laws of the Sea*. Durham, NC: Duke University Press, 2020.

Braverman, Irus, Nicholas Blomley, David Delaney, and Alexandre (Sandy) Kedar. *The Expanding Spaces of Law: A Timely Legal Geography*. Stanford, CA: Stanford University Press, 2014.

Bridge, Gavin. "Territory: Now in 3D!" *Political Geography* 34 (2013): 55–57.

Brown, Wendy. *Walled States, Waning Sovereignty*. New York: Zone Books, 2010.

Bruun, Johanne "Invading the Whiteness: Science, (Sub)Terrain, and US Militarisation of the Greenland Ice Sheet." *Geopolitics* 23 (2018). https://doi.org/10.1080/14650045.2018.1543269.

Bruun, Johanne, and Philip Steinberg. "ICE | Placing Territory on Ice: Militarisation, Measurement and Murder in the High Arctic." In *Territory beyond Terra*, edited by Kimberly Peters, Philip Steinberg, and Elaine Stratford, 147–64. London: Rowman and Littlefield, 2018.

Bryant, Rebecca, and Daniel Knight. *The Anthropology of the Future*. Cambridge: Cambridge University Press, 2019.

Buck-Morss, Susan. *Dreamworld and Catastrophe: The Passing of Mass Utopia in East and West*. Cambridge, MA: MIT Press, 2002.

Cabot, Heath. *On the Doorstep of Europe: Asylum and Citizenship in Greece*. Philadelphia: University of Pennsylvania Press, 2014.

Calvert, James. *Surface at the Pole: The Extraordinary Voyages of the USS Skate*. New York: McGraw-Hill, 1960.

Campbell, Elaine. "Three-Dimensional Security: Layers, Spheres, Volumes, Milieus." *Political Geography* 69 (2019): 10–21.

Caplan, Jane, and John C. Torpey. *Documenting Individual Identity: The Development of State Practices in the Modern World*. Princeton, NJ: Princeton University Press, 2001.

Carse, Ashley. "Watershed." Theorizing the Contemporary. *Cultural Anthropology*, June 27, 2018. https://culanth.org/fieldsights/1465-watershed.

Carse, Ashley, Jason Cons, and Townsend Middleton. "Preface: Chokepoints." *Limn* 10 (2018). https://limn.it/articles/preface-chokepoints.

Casey, Edward. *The Fate of Place*. Berkeley: University of California Press, 1997.

Casey, Edward. "How to Get from Space to Place in a Fairly Short Stretch of Time: Phenomenological Prolegomena." In *Senses of Place*, edited by Steven Feld and Keith Basso, 13–52. Santa Fe, NM: School of American Research, 1996.

Casey, Edward S. *The World on Edge*. Bloomington: Indiana University Press, 2017.

Catudal, Honoré M. *The Exclave Problem of Western Europe*. Tuscaloosa: University of Alabama Press, 1979.

Cha, Theresa Hak Kyung. *Dictée*. New York: Tanam Press, 1982.

Chamayou, Grégoire. *Théorie du drone*. Paris: La Fabrique, 2013.

Chatterji, Joya. "The Fashioning of a Frontier: The Radcliffe Line and Bengal's Border Landscape, 1947–52." *Modern Asian Studies* 33, no. 1 (1999): 185–242.

Chattervedi, Sanjay, and Timothy Doyle. *Climate Terror: A Critical Geopolitics of Climate Change*. New York: Palgrave Macmillan, 2015.

Chen, Mel. *Animacies: Biopolitics, Racial Mattering, and Queer Affect*. Durham, NC: Duke University Press, 2012.

Cheng, François. *Empty and Full: The Language of Chinese Painting*. Boston: Shambhala, 1994.

Chivers, CJ. "Georgia Offers Fresh Evidence on War's Start." *New York Times*, September 15, 2008. https://www.nytimes.com/2008/09/16/world/europe/16georgia.html.

Choi, Shine. *Re-Imagining North Korea in International Politics: Problems and Alternatives*. New York: Routledge, 2014.

Choi, Vivian. "Anticipatory States: Tsunami, War, and Insecurity in Sri Lanka." *Cultural Anthropology* 30, no. 2 (May 2015): 286–309.

Choy, Timothy, and Jerry Zee. "Condition—Suspension." *Cultural Anthropology* 30, no. 2 (2015): 210–23.

Choy, Timothy. *Ecologies of Comparison: An Ethnography of Endangerment in Hong Kong*. Durham, NC: Duke University Press, 2009.

Chu, Julie. *Cosmologies of Credit: Transnational Mobility and the Politics of Destination in China*. Durham, NC: Duke University Press, 2010

Chubb, Andrew. "China's 'Blue Territory' and the Technosphere in Maritime East Asia." *Technosphere Magazine*, April 15, 2017. https://technosphere-magazine.hkw .de/p/Chinas-Blue-Territory-and-the-Technosphere-in-Maritime-East-Asia -gihSRWtV8AmPTof2traWnA.

Chulov, Martin. "Aleppo's Most Wanted Man—The Rebel Leader behind Tunnel Bombs." *Guardian*, May 20, 2014. https://www.theguardian.com/world/2014/may/20 /aleppos-most-wanted-man-rebel-leader-tunnel-bombs.

Clark, Nigel. "FIRE | Pyropolitics for a Planet of Fire." In *Territory beyond Terra*, edited by Kimberly Peters, Philip Steinberg, and Elaine Stratford, 69–85. London: Rowman and Littlefield, 2018.

Clark, Nigel. *Inhuman Nature: Sociable Life on a Dynamic Planet*. London: Sage, 2010.

Cocks, Joan. *On Sovereignty and Other Political Delusions*. London: Bloomsbury, 2014.

Coelho, Baptist. *Siachen Glacier* (art installation). Website of Baptist Coelho, 2015. http://www.baptistcoelho.com/project_content.php?category_id=63&artwork _id=189.

Cohen, Jeffrey Jerome. *Stone: An Ecology of the Inhuman*. Minneapolis: University of Minnesota Press, 2015.

Collins, Terry, and Katie Pratt. "Life in Deep Earth Totals 15 to 23 Billion Tonnes of Carbon—Hundreds of Times More than Humans." Official website of the Deep Carbon Conservatory, December 10, 2018. https://deepcarbon.net/life-deep-earth -totals-15–23-billion-tonnes-carbon.

Colgan, William, Horst Machguth, Mike MacFerrin, Jeff D. Colgan, Dirk van As, and Joseph MacGregor. "The Abandoned Ice Sheet Camp at Camp Century, Greenland, in a Warming Climate." *Geophysical Research Letters* 43 (2016): 8091–96.

Collier, Stephen, and Andrew Lakoff. "Vital Systems Security: Reflexive Biopolitics and the Government of Emergency." *Theory, Culture and Society* 32, no. 2 (2015): 19–51.

Collier, Stephen J., and Aihwa Ong. "Global Assemblages, Anthropological Problems." In *Global Assemblages*, edited by Aihwa Ong and Stephen J. Collier, 3–21. Malden, MA: Wiley-Blackwell, 2005.

Cons, Jason. "Global Flooding." *Anthropology Now* 9, no. 3 (2017): 47–52.

Cons, Jason. "Narrating Boundaries: Framing and Contesting Suffering, Community, and Belonging in Enclaves along the India-Bangladesh Border." *Political Geography* 35 (2013): 37–46.

Cons, Jason. *Sensitive Space: Fragmented Territory at the India-Bangladesh Border*. Seattle: University of Washington Press, 2016.

Cons, Jason. "Staging Climate Security: Resilience and Heterodystopia in the Bangladesh Borderlands." *Cultural Anthropology* 33, no. 2 (2018): 266–94.

Cons, Jason, and Michael Eilenberg. "Introduction: On the New Politics of Margins in Asia Mapping Frontier Assemblages." In *Frontier Assemblages: The Emergent Politics of Resource Frontiers in Asia*, edited by Jason Cons and Michael Eilenberg, 1–18. London: Wiley, 2019.

Coole, Diana, and Samantha Frost. "Introducing the New Materialisms." In *New Materialisms: Ontology, Agency, and Politics*, edited by Diana Coole and Samantha Frost, 1–43. Durham, NC: Duke University Press, 2010.

Corsín-Jiménez, Alberto. "The Height, Length and Width of Social Theory." In *The Social after Gabriel Tarde: Debates and Assessments*, edited by Matei Candea, 110–28. London: Routledge, 2010.

Cosgrove, Denis E. *Mappings, Critical Views*. London: Reaktion, 1999.

Cotter, Rebecca. "Mines and Minerals—Are They Yours?" *Fieldfisher*, July 5, 2012. https://www.fieldfisher.com/publications/2012/07/mines-and-minerals-are-they-yours.

Couling, Nancy, and Carola Hein. "Viscosity." Volumetric Society forum. *Society and Space*, March 17, 2019. http://societyandspace.org/2019/03/17/viscosity.

Coward, Martin. "Networks, Nodes and De-Territorialised Battlespace: The Scopic Regime of Rapid Dominance." In *From Above: War, Violence and Verticality*, edited by Peter Adey, Mark Whitehead, and Alison J. Williams, 95–117. Oxford: Oxford University Press, 2013.

Cowen, Deborah. "A Geography of Logistics: Market Authority and the Security of Supply Chains." *Annals of the Association of American Geographers* 100, no. 3 (2010): 600–620.

Crampton, Jeremy. "Vortex." Volumetric Sovereignty forum. *Society and Space*, March 3, 2019. http://societyandspace.org/2019/03/03/vortex.

Crapanzano, Vincent. *Imaginative Horizons: An Essay in Literary-Philosophical Anthropology*. Chicago: University of Chicago Press, 2004.

Creagh, Damien. "Notes on Blindness Short Film." 2014. Vimeo video, 12:14. https://vimeo.com/85167194. Accessed January 21, 2019.

Cronon, William. "Why Edge Effects." *Edge Effects*, October 9, 2014. http://edgeeffects.net/author/wcronon.

Cunningham, Hilary. "Barb." Theorizing the Contemporary. *Cultural Anthropology*, June 27, 2018. https://culanth.org/fieldsights/1460-barb.

Cunningham, Hilary. "Permeabilities, Ecology and Geopolitical Boundaries." In *A Companion to Border Studies*, edited by Thomas M. Wilson and Hastings Donnan, 371–86. Chichester: Wiley-Blackwell, 2012.

Cunningham, Hilary, and Stephen Scharper. "Social Ecologies as Gated Ecologies." In *The Social Ecology of Border Landscapes*, edited by Michelle Zebich-Knos and Anna Grichting, 53–68. New York: Anthem, 2017.

Danowski, Deborah, and Eduardo Viveiros de Castro. *The Ends of the World*. Translated by Rodrigo Nunes. Cambridge: Polity Press, 2017.

Darack, Ed. *Victory Point*. New York: Berkley Hardcovers, 2009.

Daugherty, Charles. *City under the Ice: The Story of Camp Century*. London: Macmillan, 1963.

Dear, Michael. *Why Walls Won't Work: Repairing the US-Mexico Divide*. Oxford: Oxford University Press, 2013.

de Certeau, Michel. *The Practice of Everyday Life*. Berkeley: University of California Press, 1984.

De León, Jason. *The Land of Open Graves: Living and Dying on the Migrant Trail*. Oakland: University of California Press, 2015.

Deleuze, Gilles. "Humans: A Dubious Existence" In *Desert Islands and Other Texts, 1953–1974*. Edited by David Lapoujade. Translated by Michael Taormina. New York: Semiotext(e), 2004.

Deleuze, Gilles, and Félix Guattari. *A Thousand Plateaus: Capitalism and Schizophrenia*. Translated by Brian Massumi. Minneapolis: University of Minnesota Press, 1987.

Deleuze, Gilles, and Félix Guattari. *What Is Philosophy?* New York: Columbia University Press, 1994.

Della Dora, Veronica. *Mountain: Nature and Culture*. London: Reaktion, 2016.

Del Sarto, Raffaella A. "Borderlands: The Middle East and North African as the EU's Southern Buffer Zone." In *Mediterranean Frontiers: Borders, Conflict and Memory in a Transnational World*, edited by Dimitar Bechev and Kalypso Nicolaidis, 149–65. London: Tauris Academic Studies, 2010.

Demick, Barbara. "N. Korea's Ace in the Hole." *Los Angeles Times*, November 14, 2003. http://articles.latimes.com/2003/nov/14/world/fg-underground14.

Dittmer, Jason. "Geopolitical Assemblages and Complexity." *Progress in Human Geography* 38, no. 3 (2014): 385–401.

Dodds, Klaus. "Flag Planting and Finger Pointing: The Law of the Sea, the Arctic and the Political Geographies of the Outer Continental Shelf." *Political Geography* 29, no. 2 (2010): 63–73.

Dodds, Klaus. *Ice: Nature and Culture*. London: Reaktion Books, 2018.

Dodds, Klaus. "Our Seabed? Argentina, the Falklands and the Wider South Atlantic." *Polar Record* 52, no. 266 (2016): 535–40.

Dodds, Klaus, and Mark Nuttall. *The Scramble for the Poles*. Cambridge: Polity, 2016.

Doel, Ronald E., Kristine C. Harper, and Matthias Heymann. *Exploring Greenland: Cold War Science and Technology on Ice*. London: Palgrave, 2016.

Donnan, Hastings. "Material Identities: Fixing Ethnicity in the Irish Borderlands." *Identities* 12, no. 1 (2005): 69–106.

Donnan, Hastings, Madeleine Hurd, and Carolin Leutloff-Grandits. *Migrating Borders and Moving Times: Temporality and the Crossing of Borders in Europe*. Manchester: Manchester University Press, 2017.

Drummond, Katie. "Lockheed Using Gravity to Spot 'Subterranean Threats.'" *Wired*, July 15, 2010. https://www.wired.com/2010/07/lockheed-using-gravity-to-spot -subterranean-threats/.

Dunn, Elizabeth, and Michael Bobick. "The Empire Strikes Back: War Without War and Occupation without Occupation in the Russian Sphere of Influence." *American Ethnologist* 41, no. 3 (2014): 405–13.

Easter, Thomas E. "Military Use of Underground Terrain." In *Studies in Military Geography and Geology*, edited by Douglas R. Caldwell, Judy Ehlen, and Russell S. Harmon, 21–37. Dordrecht: Springer, 2004. https://doi.org/10.1007/978-1 -4020-3105-2_3.

Easterling, Keller. *Extrastatecraft: The Power of Infrastructure Space*. London: Verso, 2014.

Einstein, Albert. *Relativity: The Special and General Theory*. Mansfield, CT: Martino Publishing, (1920) 2010.

Elden, Stuart. *The Birth of Territory*. Chicago: University of Chicago Press, 2013.

Elden, Stuart. "Land, Terrain, Territory." *Progress in Human Geography* 34, no. 6 (2010): 799–817.

Elden, Stuart, "Legal Terrain: The Political Materiality of Territory." *London Review of International Law* 5, no. 2 (2017): 199–224.

Elden, Stuart. "Secure the Volume: Vertical Geopolitics and the Depth of Power." *Political Geography* 34 (2013): 35–51.

Elden, Stuart. "Terrain." Theorizing the Contemporary. *Cultural Anthropology*, October 24, 2017. https://culanth.org/fieldsights/1231-terrain.

Elden, Stuart. "What's Shifting?" *Dialogues in Human Geography* 1, no. 3 (2011): 304–7.

Empson, Hal. *Mapping Hong Kong: A Historical Atlas*. Hong Kong: Government Information Services, 1992.

Engels, Friedrich. "Mountain Warfare in Past and Present" (1857). Marxists Internet Archive. https://www.marxists.org/archive/marx/works/1857/01/mountain-warfare .htm. Accessed June 30, 2019.

Fall, Juliet. *Drawing the Line: Nature, Hybridity and Politics in Transboundary Spaces*. Aldershot: Ashgate, 2005.

Farinelli, Franco. *La crisi della ragione cartografica*. Torino: Einaudi, 2009.

Farish, Matthew. *The Contours of America's Cold War*. Minneapolis: University of Minnesota Press, 2010.

Federal Aviation Administration (FAA). "Low Altitude Authorization and Notification Capability (LAANC) Concept of Operations." Version 1.1. May 12, 2017. https://www .faa.gov/uas/programs_partnerships/data_exchange/laanc_for_industry/media /laanc_concept_of_operations.pdf.

Ferrari, Marco, Elisa Pasqual, and Andrea Bagnato. *A Moving Border: Alpine Cartographies of Climate Change*. New York: Columbia University Press, 2018.

Fishel, Stefanie R. *The Microbial State: Global Thriving and the Body Politic*. Minneapolis: University of Minnesota Press, 2017.

Foucault, Michel. *Of Other Spaces, Heterotopias*. Translated from *Architecture, Mouvement, Continuité* 5 (1984): 46–49. Foucault.info website, March 1, 1967. https:// foucault.info/documents/heterotopia/foucault.heteroTopia.en.

Frampton, Adam, Jonathan D. Solomon, and Clara Wong. *Cities without Ground: A Hong Kong Guidebook*. San Rafael, CA: Oro Editions, 2012.

French, Howard W. "What's behind Beijing's Drive to Control the South China Sea?" *Guardian*, July 28, 2015.

Füzfa, André. "How Current Loops and Solenoids Curve Spacetime." *Physical Review D* 93, no. 2 (2016). https://doi.org/10.1103/PhysRevD.93.024014.

Gabrys, Jennifer. *Program Earth: Environmental Sensing Technology and the Making of a Computational Planet*. Minneapolis: University of Minnesota Press, 2016.

Gagné, Karine. "Cultivating Ice over Time: On the Idea of Timeless Knowledge and Places in the Himalayas." *Anthropologica* 58, no. 2 (2016): 193–210.

Gandy, Matthew. *The Fabric of Space: Water, Modernity, and the Urban Imagination*. Cambridge, MA: MIT Press, 2014.

Garcia, Michael John. "Barriers along the US Borders: Key Authorities and Requirements." Congressional Research Service (CRS) report, April 8, 2015. https://fas.org
  /sgp/crs/homesec/R43975.pdf.
Garelli, Glenda, Charles Heller, Lorenzo Pezzani, and Martina Tazzioli. "Shifting Bordering and Rescue Practices in the Central Mediterranean Sea, October 2013–October 2015." *Antipode* 50, no. 3 (2018): 813–21.
Garrett, Bradley L. *Explore Everything: Place-Hacking the City.* London: Verso, 2013.
Garrett, Bradley L. "Who Owns the Space under Cities? The Attempt to Map the Earth
  beneath Us." *Guardian*, July 10, 2018. https://www.theguardian.com/cities/2018/jul/10
  /who-owns-the-space-under-cities-the-attempt-to-map-the-ground-beneath-our-feet.
Gauhar, Feryal Ali. "Siachen: The Place of Wild Roses." *Dawn*, November 2, 2014.
  http://www.dawn.com/news/1141375.
Ghosh, Sahana. "Relative Intimacies: Belonging and Difference in Transnational
  Families." *Economic and Political Weekly* 52, no. 15 (2017): 45–52.
Goh, Brenda, and Prak Chan Thul. "In Cambodia, Stalled Chinese Casino Embodies
  Secrecy, Risks." *Reuters World News*, June 5, 2018. https://www.reuters.com/article
  /us-china-silkroad-cambodia-insight/in-cambodia-stalled-chinese-casino-resort
  -embodies-silk-road-secrecy-risks-idUSKCN1J20HA.
Goldstein, Miriam C., Marci Rosenberg, and Lanna Cheng. "Increased Oceanic
  Microplastic Debris Enhances Oviposition in an Endemic Pelagic Insect." *Biology
  Letters* 8, no. 5 (2012): 817–20.
González, Roberto J. González, Hugh Gusterson, and Gustaaf Houtman. *Militariza-
  tion: A Reader.* Durham, NC: Duke University Press, 2019.
Goodman, Steve. *Sonic Warfare: Sound, Affect, and the Ecology of Fear.* Cambridge, MA:
  MIT Press, 2010.
Gordillo, Gastón. "Terrain as Insurgent Weapon: An Affective Geometry of Warfare
  in the Mountains of Afghanistan." *Political Geography* 64 (2018): 53–62.
Graham, Stephen. "Vertical Geopolitics: Baghdad and After." *Antipode* 36, no. 1 (2004):
  12–23.
Graham, Stephen. *Vertical: The City from Satellites to Bunkers.* London: Verso, 2016.
Green, Sarah. "Crosslocations: Rethinking Relative Location in the Mediterranean."
  University of Helsinki website. Accessed October 14, 2019. https://www.helsinki.fi
  /en/researchgroups/crosslocations.
Green, Sarah. "Lines, Traces and Tidemarks: Reflections on Forms of Borderli-ness."
  COST Action IS0803, working paper no. 1 (2009): 1–18. http://www.eastbordnet.org
  /wiki/Documents/Lines_Traces_Tidemarks_Nicosia_2009_090416.pdf.
Green, Sarah. *Notes from the Balkans: Locating Marginality and Ambiguity on the Greek-
  Albanian Border.* Princeton, NJ: Princeton University Press, 2005.
Green, Sarah. "Performing Border in the Aegean." *Journal of Cultural Economy* 3, no. 2
  (2010): 261–78.
Green, Sarah. "A Sense of Border." In *A Companion to Border Studies,* edited by Thomas M.
  Wilson and Hastings Donnan, 573–92. Chichester: Wiley-Blackwell, 2012.
Gregory, Derek. "From a View to a Kill: Drones and Late Modern War." *Theory, Culture
  and Society* 28, no. 7–8 (2011): 188–215.

Griffin, Dale W., Christina A. Kellogg, Virginia H. Garrison, and Eugene A. Shinn. "The Global Transport of Dust: An Intercontinental River of Dust, Microorganisms and Toxic Chemicals Flows through the Earth's Atmosphere." *American Scientist* 90, no. 3 (May–June 2002): 228–35.

Griffiths, Melanie B. E. "Out of Time: The Temporal Uncertainties of Refused Asylum Seekers and Immigration Detainees." *Journal of Ethnic and Migration Studies* 40, no. 12 (2014): 1991–2009.

Grinker, Roy Richard. *Korea and Its Futures: Unification and the Unfinished War*. New York: St. Martin's Press, 2000.

Hagood, Mack. *Hush: Media and Sonic Self-Control*. Durham, NC: Duke University Press, 2019.

Hall, G. E. "Space Debris—An Insurance Perspective." *Proceedings of the Institution of Mechanical Engineers* 221, part G:J, Aerospace Engineering (2007): 915–24.

Hameiri, Shahar, and Lee Jones. *Governing Borderless Threats: Non-Traditional Security and the Politics of State Transformation*. Cambridge: Cambridge University Press, 2015.

Haner, Josh, Edward Wong, Derek Watkins, and Jeremy White. "Living in China's Expanding Deserts." *New York Times*, October 24, 2016.

Hannigan, John. *The Geopolitics of Deep Oceans*. Cambridge: Polity, 2016.

Hansen, Peter. *The Summits of Modern Man: Mountaineering after the Enlightenment*. Cambridge, MA: Harvard University Press, 2013.

Haraway, Donna. "Situated Knowledges: The Science Question in Feminism and the Privilege of Partial Perspective." *Feminist Studies* 14 (1988): 575–99.

Haraway, Donna. *When Species Meet*. Minneapolis: Minnesota University Press, 2008.

Harms, Jan. "Terrestrial Gravity Fluctuations." *Living Reviews in Relativity* 18 (2015): 3–150. https://doi.org/10.1007/lrr-2015-3.

Harris, Andrew. "Vertical Urbanisms: Opening up Geographies of the Three-Dimensional City." *Progress in Human Geography* 39 (2015): 601–20.

Heller, Charles. "Traces Liquides." May 26, 2015. Vimeo video, 17:59. https://vimeo.com/128919244.

Helmreich, Stefan. *Alien Ocean: Anthropological Voyages in Microbial Seas*. Berkeley: University of California Press, 2009.

Herzfeld, Michael. *Cultural Intimacy: Social Poetics in the Nation-State*. London: Routledge, 1997.

Herzfeld, Michael. *Ours Once More: Folklore, Ideology, and the Making of Modern Greece*. New York: Pella, 1986.

Hevesi, Dennis, "James F. Calvert, 88, Sub Captain Who Surfaced at North Pole, Dies." *New York Times*, June 16, 2009.

Heyman, Josiah M. "Putting Power in the Anthropology of Bureaucracy: The Immigration and Naturalization Service at the Mexico-United States Border." *Current Anthropology* 36, no. 2 (1995): 261–87.

Hidden Plymouth. "Plymouth's Tunnel Myths." *Hidden Plymouth* (blog), August 6, 2012. http://hiddenplymouth.blogspot.com/2012/08/plymouths-tunnel-myths.html.

Hoffman, Danny. *The War Machines: Young Men and Violence in Sierra Leone and Liberia*. Durham, NC: Duke University Press, 2011.

Holbraad, Martin, and Morten Axel Pedersen. "Planet M: The Intense Abstraction of Marilyn Strathern." *Anthropological Theory* (2010). https://doi.org/10.1177/1463499609360117.

Hoy-Colon, Rebecca. "Rippling Borders in Latina Literature." In *The Image of the River in Latin/o American Literature: Written in the Water*, edited by Jeanie Murphy and Elizabeth G. Rivero, 95–116. Lexington, KY: Lexington Books, 2017.

Hu, Tung-Hui. *A Prehistory of the Cloud*. Cambridge, MA: MIT Press, 2015.

Hughes, John A., David Randall, and Dan Shapiro. "Faltering from Ethnography to Design." *Proceedings of the 1992 ACM Conference on Computer-Supported Cooperative Work* (1992): 115–22.

Humphrey, Caroline. "Odessa: Pogroms in a Cosmopolitan City." *Ab Imperio* 4 (2010): 1–53.

Hunt, Elle. "British Antarctic Research Station to Be Moved Due to Deep Crack in the Ice." *Guardian*, December 7, 2016. https://www.theguardian.com/world/2016/dec/07/british-antarctic-research-station-crack-ice.

Immerwahr, Daniel. *How to Hide an Empire: A History of the Greater United States*. New York: Farrar, Straus and Giroux, 2019.

Ingold, Timothy. "Footprints through the Weather-World: Walking, Breathing, Knowing." *Journal of the Royal Anthropological Institute* 16, no. S1 (2010): S121–39.

Ingold, Tim. "The Temporality of the Landscape." *World Archaeology* 25, no. 2 (1993): 152–74.

International Seabed Authority. "Continental Shelf." Official website of International Seabed Authority. https://www.isa.org.jm/continental-shelf. Accessed January 17, 2019.

Irwin, Aisling. "The Dark Side of Light: How Artificial Lighting Is Harming the Natural World." *Nature*, January 16, 2018. https://www.nature.com/articles/d41586-018-00665-7.

Iqbal, Iftekhar. *The Bengal Delta: Ecology, State and Social Change, 1840–1943*. London: Palgrave Macmillan, 2010.

James, William. *Essays in Radical Empiricism*. Whithorn: Anodos Books, (1912) 2017.

Jańczak, Jarosław. "Baarle-Hertog and Baarle-Nassau: Functional Interdependence of the Nested Territorial and Political Structures." In *European Exclaves in the Process of De-Bordering and Re-Bordering*, edited by Jarosław Jańczak and Przemysław Osiewicz, 57–70. Berlin: Logos Verlag, 2012.

Janssen, Marijn, and Anneke Zuiderwijk. "Infomediary Business Models for Connecting Open Data Providers and Users." *Social Science Computer Review* 32 (2014): 694–711. https://doi.org/10.1177/0894439314525902.

Jenner, Bob. "Mount Wise Plymouth Maratime HQ." Subterranea Britannica, December 13, 2004. https://www.subbrit.org.uk/sites/mount-wise-plymouth-maratime-hq/.

Jensen, Casper Bruun. "Introduction: Contexts for a Comparative Relativism." *Common Knowledge* 17, no. 1 (2011): 1–12.

Ji, Dagyum. "K-Pop, Handbags and Democracy: South Korean Payback for North's Nuclear Test." *Reuters*, January 8, 2016. https://www.reuters.com/article/north-korea-nuclear-speakers-idUSKBN0UM0UZ20160108.

Johansen, Herbert. "US Army Builds a Fantastic City under the Ice." *Popular Science*, February 1960.

Johnson, Chalmers. *Blowback: The Costs and Consequences of American Empire*. American Empire Project. New York: Holt Paperbacks, 2004.

Johnson, Corey, Reece Jones, Anssi Paasi, Louise Amoore, Alison Mountz, Mark Salter, and Chris Rumford. "Interventions on Rethinking 'the Border' in Border Studies." *Political Geography* 30 (2011): 61–69.

Jones, Clive G., John H. Lawton, and Moshe Shachak. "Organisms as Ecosystem Engineers." *Oikos* 69 (1994): 373–86.

Jones, Reece. *Border Walls: Security and the War on Terror in the United States, India, and Israel*. New York: Zed Books, 2011.

Jones, Reece. *Violent Borders: Refugees and the Right to Move*. London: Verso, 2016.

Joniak-Lüthi, Agnieszka. "Orbital." Volumetric Sovereignty forum. *Society and Space*, April 10, 2019. http://societyandspace.org/2019/04/09/orbital.

Jorgensen, Timothy J. *Strange Glow: The Story of Radiation*. Princeton, NJ: Princeton University Press, 2016.

Junod, Tom. "The Falling Man: An Unforgettable Story." *Esquire*, September 4, 2016.

Kaplan, Caren. *Aerial Aftermaths: Wartime from Above*. Durham, NC: Duke University Press, 2018.

Kaplan, Caren. "The Balloon Prospect: Aerostatic Observation and the Emergence of Militarised Aeromobility." In *From Above: War, Violence and Verticality*, edited by Peter Adey, Mark Whitehead, and Alison J. Williams, 119–40. Oxford: Oxford University Press, 2013.

Kaplan, Caren. "Drone-O-Rama: Troubling the Temporal and Spatial Logics of Distance Warfare." In *Life in the Age of Drone Warfare*, edited by Lisa Parks and Caren Kaplan, 161–77. Durham, NC: Duke University Press, 2017.

Kaushik. "The Camouflaged Military Bunkers of Switzerland." *Amusing Planet* (blog), July 13, 2015. https://www.amusingplanet.com/2015/07/the-camouflaged-military-bunkers-of.html.

Khan, Anisur. "Excavation of Eighty-Three Canals a Must." *Independent BD*, May 8, 2017. http://www.theindependentbd.com/printversion/details/93677.

Khan, Naveeda. "River and the Corruption of Memory." *Contributions to Indian Sociology* 49, no. 3 (2015): 389–409.

Kim, Eleana. "Invasive Others and Significant Others: Strange Kinship and Interspecies Ethics near the Korean Demilitarized Zone." *Social Research: An International Quarterly* 84, no. 1 (2017): 203–20.

Kim, Eleana J. "Flyways." Theorizing the Contemporary. *Cultural Anthropology*, June 27, 2018. https://culanth.org/fieldsights/flyways.

Kindynis, Theo. "The Subterranean-(In)Security Nexus?" Paper presented at Volumetric Urbanism: Charting New Urban Divisions—An International Workshop, University of Sheffield, UK, May 24–26, 2017.

King, Charles. *Odessa: Genius and Death in a City of Dreams*. New York: Norton, 2011.

King, Geoffrey, Derek Sturdy, and John Whitney. "The Landscape Geometry and Active Tectonics of Northwest Greece." *Geological Society of America Bulletin* 105 (1993): 137–61.

Klingan, Katrin, Ashkan Sepahvand, Christoph Rosol, and Bernd M. Scherer. *Textures of the Anthropocene: Grain, Vapor, Ray*. Cambridge, MA: MIT Press, 2015.

Klinke, Ian. *Cryptic Concrete: A Subterranean Journey into Cold War Germany.* Chichester: Wiley-Blackwell, 2018.

Knouf, N. Adriana. *How Noise Matters to Finance.* Forerunners: Ideas First. Minneapolis: University of Minnesota Press, 2016.

Knox, Hannah, and Dawn Nafus. "Introduction: Ethnography for a Data-Saturated World." In *Ethnography for a Data Saturated World,* edited by Hannah Knox and Dawn Nafus, 1–29. Manchester: Manchester University Press, 2018.

Kohel, James M., Robert J. Thompson, James R. Kellogg, David C. Aveline, and Nan Yu. "Development of a Transportable Quantum Gravity Gradiometer for Gravity Field Mapping." Paper presented at NASA Earth Science Technology Conference, University of Maryland, Maryland, June 24–26, 2008.

Konopinski, Natalie. "Borderline Temporalities and Security Anticipations: Standing Guard in Tel Aviv." *Etnofoor* 26, no. 1 (2014): 59–80.

Kopardekar, Parimal, Joseph Rios, Thomas Prevot, Marcus Johnson, Jaewoo Jung, and John E. Robinson III. "Unmanned Aircraft System Traffic Management (UTM) Concept of Operations." Paper presented at the American Institute of Aeronautics and Astronautics Aviation Technology, Integration, and Operations Conference, Washington, DC, June 13–17, 2016.

Korea Tourism Organization. "Cheorwon Peace Observatory (철원평화전망대)." Visit Korea website. Accessed June 1, 2018. http://english.visitkorea.or.kr/enu/ATR/SI_EN_3_1_1_1.jsp?cid=1733136.

Krishna, Sankaran. "Cartographic Anxiety: Mapping the Body Politic in India." *Alternatives: Global, Local, Political* 19, no. 4 (1994): 507–21.

Krishna, Sankaran. "Cartographic Anxiety: Mapping the Body Politic in India." In *Challenging Boundaries: Global Flows, Territorial Identities,* edited by Michael Shapiro and Hayward Alker, 193–214. Minneapolis: University of Minnesota Press, 1996.

Kucherenko, Olga. "Reluctant Traitors: The Politics of Survival in Romanian-Occupied Odessa." *European Review of History* 15, no. 2 (2008): 143–55.

Kvezereli-Kopadze, N. I. "The Problem of Year-Round Traffic through the Pass of the Cross on the Georgian Military Highway." *Soviet Geography* 15, no. 3 (1974): 163–74. https://doi.org/10.1080/00385417.1974.10770662.

LaFlamme, Marcel. "A Sky Full of Signal: Aviation Media in the Age of the Drone." *Media, Culture and Society* 40 (2018): 689–706. https://doi.org/10.1177/0163443717737609.

Lajeunesse, Adam. *Lock, Stock, and Icebergs: A History of Canada's Arctic Maritime Sovereignty.* Vancouver: University of British Columbia Press, 2016.

Lammes, Sybille, Kate McLean, and Chris Perkins. "Mapping the Quixotic Volatility of Smellscapes: A Trialogue." In *Time for Mapping: Cartographic Temporalities,* edited by Sybille Lammes, Chris Perkins, Alex Gekker, Sam Hind, Clancy Wilmott, and Daniel Evans, 50–90. Manchester: Manchester University Press, 2018.

Lammes, Sybille, and Clancy Wilmott. "The Map as Playground: Location-Based Games as Cartographical Practices." *Convergence* (2016). https://doi.org/10.1177/1354856516679596.

Langway, Chester. *The History of Early Polar Ice Cores*. US Army Corp of Engineers, Cold Regions Research and Engineering Laboratory, January 2008.

Larkin, Brian. "The Politics and Poetics of Infrastructure." *Annual Review of Anthropology* 42 (2013): 327–43.

Lash, Scott. "Deforming the Figure: Topology and the Social Imaginary." *Theory, Culture and Society* 29, nos. 4–5 (2012): 261–87.

Lasky, Jesse, Walter Jetz, and Timothy Keitt. "Conservation Biogeography of the US–Mexico Border: A Transcontinental Risk Assessment of Barriers to Animal Dispersal." *Diversity and Distributions* 17 (2011): 673–87.

Lata, Iulian Barba, and Claudio Minca. "The Surface and the Abyss/Rethinking Topology." *Environment and Planning D: Society and Space* 34, no. 3 (2016): 438–55.

Latour, Bruno. *Facing Gaia: Eight Lectures on the New Climatic Regime*. London: Polity, 2017.

Lattimore, Owen. *Inner Asian Frontiers of China*. Hong Kong: Oxford University Press, 1940.

Law, John. "After ANT: Complexity, Naming and Topology." *Sociological Review* 47, no. S1 (1999): 1–14.

Leary, William. *Under Ice: Waldo Lyon and the Development of the Arctic Submarine*. College Station: Texas A&M University Press, 1999.

Lebedev, Valentin. *Diary of a Cosmonaut: 211 Days in Space*. New York: Bantam Books, 1990.

Lefebvre, Henri. *The Production of Space*. Chichester: John Wiley, 1991.

Light, Ben, Jean Burgess, and Stefanie Duguay. "The Walkthrough Method: An Approach to the Study of Apps." *New Media and Society* 20 (2018): 881–900. https://doi.org/10.1177/1461444816675438.

Lin, Weiqiang. "AIR | Spacing the Atmosphere: The Politics of Territorializing Air." In *Territory beyond Terra*, edited by Kimberly Peters, Philip Steinberg, and Elaine Stratford, 35–49. London: Rowman and Littlefield, 2018.

Linnell, John D. C., Arie Trouwborst, Luigi Boitani, Petra Kaczensky, Djuro Huber, Slaven Reljic, Josip Kusak, et al. "Border Security Fencing and Wildlife: The End of the Transboundary Paradigm in Eurasia?" *PLOS Biology* 14, no. 6 (2016). http://journals.plos.org/plosbiology/article/metrics?id=10.1371/journal.pbio.1002483.

Lord, Austin. "Turbulence." Volumetric Sovereignty forum. *Society and Space*, March 17, 2019. http://societyandspace.org/2019/03/17/turbulence.

Lowe, Celia. "Viral Clouds: Becoming H5N1 in Indonesia." *Cultural Anthropology* 25, no. 4 (2010): 625–49.

Lower Colorado River Multi-Species Conservation Program (LCR MSCP). "Western Yellow Bat." LCR MSCP website, last updated December 21, 2018. https://www.lcrmscp.gov/species/western_yellow.html.

Ludden, David. "Maps in the Mind and the Mobility of Asia." *Journal of Asian Studies* 62, no. 4 (November 2003): 1057–78.

Luttrell, Markus. *Lone Survivor*. New York: Black Bay Books, 2007.

Lyon, Waldo K. "Sonar, the Submarine and the Arctic Ocean." *Journal of the Acoustical Society of America* 32 (1960): 1513.

Lysen, Flora, and Patricia Pisters. "The Smooth and the Striated." *Deleuze Studies* 6, no. 1 (2012): 1–5.

MacDonald, Kevin, dir. *Touching the Void*. FilmFour, 2003.

Malkin, Irad. *A Small Greek World: Networks in the Ancient Mediterranean*. Oxford: Oxford University Press, 2011.

Malkki, Liisa. "National Geographic: The Rooting of Peoples and the Territorialization of National Identity among Scholars and Refugees." *Cultural Anthropology* 7, no. 1 (1992): 24–44.

Malkki, Liisa. *Purity and Exile: Violence, Memory, and National Cosmology among Hutu Refugees in Tanzania*. Chicago: Chicago University Press, 1995.

Marshall, Shawn J. *The Cryosphere*. Princeton, NJ: Princeton University Press, 2012.

Martin, Lauren, and Anna J. Secor. "Towards a Post-Mathematical Topology." *Progress in Human Geography* 38, no. 3 (2014): 420–38.

Masco, Joseph. *The Theater of Operations: National Security Affect from the Cold War to the War on Terror*. Durham, NC: Duke University Press, 2014.

Massey, Doreen B. *For Space*. London: Sage, 2005.

Massey, Doreen. "Imagining Globalisation: Power-Geometries of Time-Space." In *Global Futures: Migration, Environment and Globalization*, edited by Avtar Brah, Mary J. Hickman and Máirtin Mac an Ghaill, 27–44. Basingstoke: Macmillan, 1999.

Mattern, Shannon. "All Eyes on the Border." *Places Journal* (September 2018). https://doi.org/10.22269/180925.

Maudlin, Tim. *The Philosophy of Physics: Space and Time*. Princeton, NJ: Princeton University Press, 2012.

Maxwell, Neville. *India's China War*. New York: Pantheon, 1970.

McCormack, Derek P. *Atmospheric Things: On the Allure of Elemental Envelopment*. Durham, NC: Duke University Press, 2018.

McCurry, Justin. "Sonic Attack: Why South Korea Bombards the North with News, K-Pop and Good Times." *Guardian*, December 3, 2017. https://www.theguardian.com/world/shortcuts/2017/dec/03/sonic-attack-why-south-korea-bombards-the-north-with-news-k-pop-and-good-times.

McGlynn, Evangeline. "Quake." Volumetric Sovereignty forum. *Society and Space*, March 12, 2019. http://societyandspace.org/2019/03/12/quake.

McLean, Stuart. "Black Goo: Forceful Encounters with Matter in Europe's Muddy Margins," *Cultural Anthropology* 26, no. 4 (2011): 586–619.

McNeill, Donald. "Airports and Territorial Restructuring: The Case of Hong Kong." *Urban Studies* 51 (2014): 2996–3010.

Megoran, Nick. *Nationalism in Central Asia*. Pittsburgh: University of Pittsburgh Press, 2017.

Meillassoux, Quentin. *After Finitude: An Essay on the Necessity of Contingency*. New York: Continuum, 2008.

Melo Zurita, Marilu. "Sinkhole." Volumetric Sovereignty forum. *Society and Space*, March 17, 2019. http://societyandspace.org/2019/03/17/sinkhole.

Merleau-Ponty, Maurice. *Phenomenology of Perception*. New York: Routledge, (1945) 1985.

Messeri, Lisa. *Placing Outer Space: An Earthly Ethnography of Other Worlds*. Durham, NC: Duke University Press, 2016.

Mezzadra, Sandro, and Brett Neilson. *Border as Method, Or, the Multiplication of Labor*. Durham, NC: Duke University Press, 2013.

Miéville, China. *The City and the City*. London: Pan Books, 2009.

Mikhailova, Ekaterina. "Broadcast." Volumetric Sovereignty forum. *Society and Space*, March 3, 2019. http://societyandspace.org/2019/03/03/broadcast.

Min, Lisa Sang Mi. "Marching through Suffering: Loss and Survival in North Korea by Sandra Fahy (Review)." *Anthropological Quarterly* 89, no. 3 (2016): 987–92.

Minh-ha, Trinh T. "Scent, Sound, and Cinema with Mary Zournazi." In *Cinema Interval*, 247–66. New York: Routledge, 1999.

Moodie, Megan. "'Why Can't You Say You Are from Bangladesh': Demographic Anxiety and Hindu Nationalist Common Sense in the Aftermaths of the 2008 Jaipur Bombings." *Identities* 17, no. 5 (2010): 531–59.

Morris, Jeremy Wade, and Sarah Murray. "Introduction." In *Appified: Culture in the Age of Apps*, edited by Jeremy Wade Morris and Sarah Murray, 1–19. Ann Arbor: University of Michigan Press, 2018.

Morton, Timothy. *Hyperobjects: Philosophy and Ecology after the End of the World*. Minneapolis: University of Minnesota Press, 2013.

Moshe, Ron. "The Restricted Abyss: Nine Problems in the Theory of Mise-en-Abyme." *Poetics Today* 8, no. 2 (1987): 417–38.

Murphy, Alexander B. "Territory's Continuing Allure." *Annals of the Association of American Geographers* 103, no. 5 (2013): 1212–26. https://doi.org/10.1080/00045608.2012.696232.

Mustafar, Shabbir H. "—SEA STATE, Some Measurements." In SEA STATE, by Charles Lim Yi Yong, 10–18. NTU CCA Singapore, April 30–July 10, 2016. Exhibition catalog.

Nares, George. *Narrative of a Voyage to the Polar Sea During 1875–6 in HM Ships Alert and Discovery*. London: Sampson Low, Marston, Searle, and Rivington, 1878.

NASA's Jet Propulsion Laboratory. "A Transportable Gravity Gradiometer Based on Atom Interferometry." *NASA News Briefs*, May 2010. https://ntrs.nasa.gov/archive/nasa/casi.ntrs.nasa.gov/20100019615.pdf.

Navaro, Yael. *The Make-Believe Space: Affective Geography in a Postwar Polity*. Durham, NC: Duke University Press, 2012.

Negarestani, Reza. *Cyclonopedia: Complicity with Anonymous Materials*. Melbourne: re.press, 2008.

Neiva, Rui. *Institutional Reform of Air Navigation Service Providers: A Historical and Economic Perspective*. Northampton, MA: Edward Elgar, 2015.

Netz, Reviel. *Barbed Wire: An Ecology of Modernity*. Middletown, CT: Wesleyan University Press, 2004.

New Indian Express. "Centre to Set up 42 ITBP Border Outposts." June 3, 2015. http://www.newindianexpress.com/nation/Centre-to-Set-Up-42-ITBP-Border-Outposts/2015/06/03/article2847427.ece.

New York Times. "China Won't Yield Inch on Sea, Says President." June 28, 2018.

Newton, Isaac. *The Principia: Mathematical Principles of Natural Philosophy*. New York: Snowball Publishing, (1687) 2010.

Ng, Jun Sen. "Masterplan of Singapore's Underground Spaces Ready by 2019." *Straits Time*, February 5, 2018. https://www.straitstimes.com/politics/masterplan-of-spores-underground-spaces-ready-by-next-year.

Ng, Mee Kam. "The State of Planning Rights in Hong Kong: A Case Study of 'Wall-Like Buildings.'" *Town Planning Review* 85 (2014): 489–511.

Nilsen, Thomas. "NATO Subs Kick off North Pole Exercise." *Independent Barents Observer*, March 8, 2018. https://thebarentsobserver.com/en/security/2018/03/nato-subs-kicks-north-pole-exercise#.WqZ7EBGI38c.twitter.

Nielsen, Kristian H., Henry Nielsen, and Janet Martin-Nielsen. "City under the Ice: The Closed World of Camp Century in Cold War Culture." *Science as Culture* 23 (2014): 443–64.

Nissim, Roger. *Land Administration and Practice in Hong Kong*. Hong Kong: Hong Kong University Press, 2011.

NovAtel. "Understanding the Difference Between Anti-Spoofing and Anti-Jamming." *Velocity Magazine*, 2013. Accessed November 16, 2018. https://www.novatel.com/tech-talk/velocity/velocity-2013/understanding-the-difference-between-anti-spoofing-and-anti-jamming/.

Nye, Joseph S. *Soft Power: The Means to Success in Global Politics*. New edition. New York: PublicAffairs, 2005.

Nyíri, Pál, and Danielle Tan. *Chinese Encounters in Southeast Asia*. Seattle: University of Washington Press, 2017.

Odenwald, Sten. *Patterns in the Void*. New York: Basic Books, 2002.

Oduntan, Gbenga. *Sovereignty and Jurisdiction in the Airspace and Outer Space: Legal Criteria for Spatial Delimitation*. London: Routledge, 2012.

Office of the Chairman of the Joint Chiefs of Staff. *DOD Dictionary of Military and Associated Terms*. Washington, DC: Joint Staff, 2018. http://www.jcs.mil/Portals/36/Documents/Doctrine/pubs/dictionary.pdf?ver=2018-05-02-174746-340.

Ogden, Laura A. *Swamplife: People, Gators, and Mangroves Entangled in the Everglades*. Minneapolis: Minnesota University Press, 2011.

Olson, Valerie. *Into the Extreme: U.S. Environmental Systems and Politics beyond Earth*. Minneapolis: University of Minnesota Press, 2018.

Olson, Valerie, and Lisa Messeri. "Beyond the Anthropocene: Un-Earthing an Epoch." *Environment and Society: Advances in Research* 6, no. 1 (2015): 28–47.

Ong, Aihwa. "The Chinese Maritime Silk Road: Re-Territorializing Politics in Southeast Asia." Keynote address, International Conventional of Asian Studies, Chiangmai University, July 20, 2017.

Ong, Aihwa. *Flexible Citizenship: The Cultural Logics of Transnationality*. Durham, NC: Duke University Press, 1999.

Ong, Aihwa. "Island-Nations." In *Patterned Ground*, edited by Stephan Harrison, Steve Pile and Nigel Thrift, 270–72. London: Reaktion Books, 2004.

Ong, Aihwa. *Neoliberalism as Exception: Mutations in Citizenship and Sovereignty*. Durham, NC: Duke University Press, 2006.

Ong, Aihwa. "What Marco Polo Forgot: Asian Art Negotiates the Global." *Current Anthropology* 53, no. 4 (2012): 471–94.

Ong, Aihwa. "Zoning Technologies in East Asia." In *Neoliberalism as Exception*, 97–118. Durham, NC: Duke University Press, 2007.

Ortner, Sherry. *Life and Death on Mount Everest: Sherpas and Himalayan Mountaineering*. New York: Columbia University Press, 1999.

Osawa, Jun. "China's ADIZ over the East China Sea: A 'Great Wall in the Sky'?" *Brookings*, December 17, 2013. https://www.brookings.edu/opinions/chinas-adiz-over-the-east-china-sea-a-great-wall-in-the-sky.

Ossman, Susan. *Moving Matters: Paths of Serial Migration*. Stanford, CA: Stanford University Press, 2013.

Packer, Jeremy, and Joshua Reeves. "Taking People Out: Drones, Media/Weapons, and the Coming Humanectomy." In *Life in the Age of Drone Warfare*, edited by Lisa Parks and Caren Kaplan, 261–81. Durham, NC: Duke University Press, 2017.

Pallasmaa, Juhani. *The Eyes of the Skin: Architecture and the Senses*. Chichester: Wiley Academy, 2005.

Pandolfo, Stefania. *Knot of the Soul*. Chicago: University of Chicago Press, 2018.

Paprocki, Kasia. "All That Is Solid Melts into the Bay: Anticipatory Ruination on Bangladesh's Climate Frontier." In *Frontier Assemblages: The Emergent Politics of Resource Frontiers in Asia*, edited by Jason Cons and Michael Eilenberg, 25–39. London: Wiley, 2019.

Paprocki, Kasia, and Jason Cons. "Life in a Shrimp Zone: Aqua- and Other Cultures of Bangladesh's Coastal Landscape." *Journal of Peasant Studies* 41, no. 6 (2014): 1109–30.

Parks, Lisa, and Caren Kaplan. *Life in the Age of Drone Warfare*. Durham, NC: Duke University Press, 2017.

Parks, Lisa, and Nicole Starosielski. "Introduction." In *Signal Traffic: Critical Studies of Media Infrastructures*, edited by Lisa Parks and Nicole Starosielski, 1–27. Urbana: University of Illinois Press, 2015

Parks, Lisa, and Nicole Starosielski. *Signal Traffic: Critical Studies of Media Infrastructures*. Urbana: University of Illinois Press, 2015.

Paterson, Simeon. "Korean Loudspeakers: What Are the North and South Shouting About." *BBC News*, January 12, 2016. https://www.bbc.com/news/world-asia-35278451.

Pelkmans, Mathijs. *Defending the Border: Identity, Religion, and Modernity in the Republic of Georgia*. Ithaca, NY: Cornell University Press, 2006.

Pérez, María Alejandra. "Exploring the Vertical: Science and Sociality in the Field Among Cavers in Venezuela." *Social and Cultural Geography* 16, no. 2 (2015): 226–47.

Peters, Kimberley and Philip Steinberg, "The Ocean in Excess: Towards a More-than-Wet Ontology." *Dialogues in Human Geography* 9 (2019): 293–307.

Peters, Kimberley, Philip Steinberg, and Elaine Stratford. *Territory beyond Terra*. London: Rowman and Littlefield, 2018.

Phillips, Jon. "WATER | Order and the Offshore: The Territories of Deep-Water Oil Production." In *Territory beyond Terra*, edited by Kimberly Peters, Philip Steinberg, and Elaine Stratford, 51–67. London: Rowman and Littlefield, 2018.

Pickles, John. *A History of Spaces: Cartographic Reason, Mapping, and the Geo-Coded World*. London: Routledge, 2004.

Pike, David Lawrence, *Subterranean Cities: The World Beneath Paris and London, 1800–1945*. Ithaca, NY: Cornell University Press, 2005.

Pinkerton, Alasdair, and Klaus Dodds. "Radio Geopolitics: Broadcasting, Listening and the Struggle for Acoustic Spaces." *Progress in Human Geography* 33, no. 1 (2009): 10–27.

Plantin, Jean-Christophe, Carl Lagoze, Paul N. Edwards, and Christian Sandvig. "Infrastructure Studies Meet Platform Studies in the Age of Google and Facebook." *New Media and Society* 20 (2018): 293–310. https://doi.org/10.1177/1461444816661553.

Protevi, John. *Political Affect: Connecting the Social and the Somatic*. Minneapolis: University of Minnesota Press, 2009.

Rabinow, Paul. "Artificiality and Enlightenment: From Sociobiology to Biosociality." In *Incorporations*, edited by Jonathan Crary and Sanford Kwinter, 234–52. New York: Zone Books, 1992.

Raknić, Damjan. "UZNEMIRUJUĆE FOTOGRAFIJE Na granicama Hrvatske s Mađarskom i Slovenijom zbog žice životinje ugibaju u strašnim mukama." *JutarnjiVijesti*, December 12, 2015. https://www.jutarnji.hr/vijesti/hrvatska/uznemirujuce-fotografije-na-granicama-hrvatske-s-madarskom-i-slovenijom-zbog-zice-zivotinje-ugibaju-u-strasnim-mukama/196525/.

Raleigh, C. B., J. H. Healy, and J. D. Bredehoeft. "An Experiment in Earthquake Control at Rangely, Colorado." *Science* 191 (1976): 1230–36.

Ramaswamy, Sumathi. "Visualising India's Geo-Body: Globes, Maps, Bodyscapes." *Contributions to Indian Sociology* 36, nos. 1 and 2 (2002): 151–89.

Rankin, William. *After the Map: Cartography, Navigation, and the Transformation of Territory in the Twentieth Century*. Chicago: University of Chicago Press, 2016.

Rayfield, Donald. *Edge of Empires*. London: Reaktion Books, 2012.

Reeves, Madeleine. *Border Work: Spatial Lives of the State in Rural Central Asia*. Ithaca, NY: Cornell University Press, 2014.

Reichert, Dagmar. "Weisen der Welterzeugung: Zur Möglichkeit einer Geographie aus der Welt." *Geographica Helvetica* 3 (1998): 112–18.

Richemond-Barak, Daphné. *Underground Warfare*. Oxford: Oxford University Press, 2018.

Richeson, David S. *Euler's Gem: The Polyhedron Formula and the Birth of Topology*. Princeton, NJ: Princeton University Press, 2008.

Rogers, Capt. Marshall M. "An Investigation into the Feasibility of Using a Modern Gravity Gradient Instrument for Passive Aircraft Navigation and Terrain Avoidance." Thesis, Air Force Institute of Technology, 2009.

Rogers, Douglas. *The Depths of Russia: Oil, Power, and Culture after Socialism*. Ithaca, NY: Cornell University Press, 2015.

Roorda, Eric Paul. *The Ocean Reader: History, Culture, Politics*. Durham, NC: Duke University Press, 2020.

Rozakou, Katerina. "Nonrecording the 'European Refugee Crisis' in Greece: Navigating through Irregular Bureaucracy." *Focaal: Journal of Global and Historical Anthropology* 77 (2017): 36–49.

Sailor, Craig. "He Reached the Top of Mount Rainier. On the Way Down, Skier Fell 150 Feet into Crevasse." *News Tribune*, July 17, 2017. http://www.thenewstribune.com/news/local/article161873348.html#storylink=cpy.

Sammler, Katherine Genevieve. "The Deep Pacific: Island Governance and Seabed Mineral Development." In *Island Geographies: Essays and Conversations*, edited by Elaine Stratford, 10–35. London: Routledge, 2016.

Sammler, Katherine Genevieve. "The Rising Politics of Sea Level: Demarcating Territory in a Vertically Relative World," *Territory, Politics, Governance* (2019). https://doi.org/10.1080/21622671.2019.1632219.

Santos, Fernanda. "No Environmental Impact Study? No Border Wall, Lawsuit Says." *New York Times*, April 13, 2017. https://www.nytimes.com/2017/04/13/us/no-environmental-impact-study-no-border-wall-lawsuit-says.html.

Sassen, Saskia. *Territory, Authority, Rights: From Medieval to Global Assemblages*. Updated edition. Princeton, NJ: Princeton University Press, 2008.

Schmitt, Carl. *Nomos of the Earth in the International Law of Jus Publicum Europaeum*. New York: Telos, (1950) 2003.

Schwenk, Theodor. *Sensitive Chaos: The Creation of Flowing Forms in Water and Air*. Translated by Oliver Whicher and Johanna Wrigle. New York: Schocken Books, 1976.

Scott, James C. *The Art of Not Being Governed: An Anarchist History of Upland Southeast Asia*. New Haven, CT: Yale University Press, 2009.

Scott, James C. *Seeing Like a State: How Certain Schemes to Improve the Human Condition Have Failed*. New Haven, CT: Yale University Press, 2002.

Scott, Jared, dir. *The Age of Consequences: How Climate Impacts Resource Scarcity, Migration and Conflict through the Lens of US National Security and Global Stability*. PF Pictures, 2016.

Scranton, Roy. "When the Next Hurricane Hits Texas." *New York Times*, October 7, 2016. https://www.nytimes.com/2016/10/09/opinion/sunday/when-the-hurricane-hits-texas.html?mcubz=0.

Secor, Anna. "Between Longing and Despair: State, Space and Subjectivity in Turkey." *Environment and Planning D: Society and Space* 24 (2007): 33–52.

Seepage," *Oxford English Dictionary*. https://www.oed.com/view/Entry/174831?redirectedFrom=seepage#eid.

Seo, Alex Y. I. "Borders, Borderlands, and Frontiers." PhD dissertation, Cambridge University, 2017.

Sepp, Lt. Col Eric M. "Deeply Buried Facilities: Implications for Military Operations." Occasional paper, Air War College, 2000.

Shainin, Jonathan. "Rods from God." *New York Times*, December 10, 2006. https://www.nytimes.com/2006/12/10/magazine/10section3a.t-9.html.

Shaw, Ian G. R. *Predator Empire: Drone Warfare and Full Spectrum Dominance*. Minneapolis: University of Minnesota Press, 2016.

Shelton, Barrie, Justyna Karakiewicz, and Thomas Kvan. *The Making of Hong Kong: From Vertical to Volumetric*. London: Routledge, 2010.

Shields, Rob. "Cultural Topology: The Seven Bridges of Königsburg, 1736." *Theory, Culture and Society* 29, no. 4–5 (2012): 43–57.

Simpson, Joe. *Touching the Void*. New York: HarperCollins, 1994.

Sloterdijk, Peter. *In the World Interior of Capital: Towards a Philosophical Theory of Globalization*. Translated by Wieland Hoban. Cambridge: Polity Press, 2013.

Smith, Susan J. "Beyond Geography's Visible Worlds: A Cultural Politics of Music." *Progress in Human Geography* 21, no. 4 (1997): 502–29.

Smith, Susan J. "Soundscape." *Area* 26, no. 3 (1994): 232–40.

Solis, Julia, *New York Underground: The Anatomy of a City*. New York: Routledge, 2005.

Some, Kamalika. "Say Hi to CIMON, the First AI-Powered Robot to Fly in Space." *Analytics Insight*, July 3, 2018. https://www.analyticsinsight.net/say-hi-to-cimon-the -first-ai-powered-robot-to-fly-in-space.

Sontag, Sherry, and Christopher Drew. *Blind Man's Bluff: The Untold Story of Cold War Submarine Espionage*. London: Arrow Books, 1998.

Sörlin, Sverker. "The Arctic Ocean." In *Oceanic Histories*, edited by David Armitage, Alison Bashford, and Sujit Sivasundaram, 269–95. Cambridge: Cambridge University Press, 2018.

Spagat, Elliot. "Border Wall Tests Find Heights Should Keep Out Crossers." *AP News*, January 20, 2018. https://www.apnews.com/a7c524fcd45e4c99959970d337dbdc3c.

Spivak, Gayatri. *Death of a Discipline*. New York: Columbia University Press, 2003.

Squire, Rachael. "'Do You Dive?': Methodological Considerations for Engaging with 'Volume.'" *Geography Compass* 11, no. 7 (2017): 1–11.

Squire, Rachael, "Immersive Terrain: The US Navy, Sealab, and Cold War Undersea Geopolitics." *Area* 48, no. 3 (2016):332–38.

Squire, Rachael. "Rock, Water, Air and Fire: Foregrounding the Elements in the Gibraltar-Spain Dispute." *Environment and Planning D: Society and Space* 34, no. 3 (2016): 545–63.

Stallybrass, Peter, and Allon White. *The Politics and Poetics of Transgression*. Ithaca, NY: Cornell University Press, 1986.

Starosielski, Nicole. *The Undersea Network*. Durham, NC: Duke University Press, 2015.

Steinberg, Philip. "Navigating to Multiple Horizons: Toward a Geography of Ocean-Space." *Professional Geographer* 51, no. 3 (1999): 366–75.

Steinberg, Philip E. "Of Other Seas: Metaphors and Materialities in Maritime Regions." *Atlantic Studies: Global Currents* 10, no. 2 (2013): 156–69.

Steinberg, Philip E. *The Social Construction of the Ocean*. Cambridge. Cambridge University Press, 2001.

Steinberg, Philip, and Kimberley Peters. "Wet Ontologies, Fluid Spaces: Giving Depth to Volume through Oceanic Thinking." *Environment and Planning D* 33, no. 2 (2015): 247–64.

Steinberg, Philip E., Jeremy Tasch, and Hannes Gerhardt. *Contesting the Arctic: Politics and Imaginaries in the Circumpolar North*. London: IB Tauris, 2015.

Steinbuch, Yarun. "This Is What's Left after the 'Mother of all Bombs' Hit Afghanistan." *New York Post*, April 24, 2017. https://nypost.com/2017/04/24/this-is-whats -left-after-the-mother-of-all-bombs-hit-afghanistan/.

Stewart, Kathleen. "Atmospheric Attunements." *Environment and Planning D: Society and Space* 29, no. 3 (2011): 445–53.

Stewart, Kathleen. *Ordinary Affects*. Durham, NC: Duke University Press, 2007.

Stolarczyk, Larry G. *Detection and Imaging of Underground Structures by Exploiting ELF/VLF Radiowaves*. Hanscom AFB: Air Force Research Laboratory, 2000.

Strathern, Marilyn. *After Nature: English Kinship in the Late Twentieth Century*. Cambridge: Cambridge University Press, 1992.

Strathern, Marilyn. "Cutting the Network." *Journal of the Royal Anthropological Institute* 2, no. 3 (1996): 517–35.

Strathern, Marilyn. *Partial Connections*. Walnut Creek, CA: AltaMira Press, (1991) 2004.

Straughan, Elizabeth, and Harriet Hawkins. "Conclusion: Reimagining Geoaesthetics." In *Geographical Aesthetics: Imagining Space, Staging Encounters*, 283–98. London: Routledge, 2015.

Streland, Lt. Col. Arnold H. "Going Deep: A System Concept for Detecting Deeply Buried Facilities from Space." Research report, Air War College, 2003.

Stuart, Jill. "Unbundling Sovereignty, Territory and the State in Outer Space." In *Securing Outer Space*, edited by Natalie Bormann and Michael Sheehan, 8–23. London: Routledge, 2009.

Sturgeon, Janet. *Border Landscapes: The Politics of Akha Land Use in China and Thailand*. Seattle: University of Washington Press, 2007.

Sullivan, Robert E. "Introduction." In *Underneath New York*, by Harry Granick, xi–xxviii. New York: Fordham University Press, 1991.

Sunberg, Juanita. "Diabolic *Caminos* in the Desert and Cat Fights on the Rio: A Posthumanist Political Ecology of Boundary Enforcement in the US-Mexico Borderlands." *Annals of the Association of American Geographers* 101 (2001): 318–36.

Sur, Malini. "Divided Bodies: Crossing the India-Bangladesh Border." *Economic and Political Weekly* 49, no. 13 (2014): 31–35.

Survey and Mapping Office (Lands Department). *Explanatory Notes on Geodetic Datums in Hong Kong*. Hong Kong: Hong Kong Government, 1995.

Sutherland, John. *Bestsellers: Popular Fiction of the 1970s*. London: Routledge, 2010.

Tarkovsky, Andrei, dir. *Stalker*. Mosfilm, 1979.

Tawil-Souri, Helga. "Checkpoint Time." *Qui Parle* 26, no. 2 (2017): 383–422.

Tawil-Souri, Helga. "Digital Occupation: Gaza's High-Tech Enclosure." *Journal of Palestine Studies* 41, no. 2 (Winter 2012): 27–43.

Telesca, Jennifer E. *Red Gold: The Managed Extinction of the Giant Bluefin Tuna*. Minneapolis: University of Minnesota Press, 2020.

Te Punga Somerville, Alice. "The Great Pacific Garbage Patch as Metaphor: The (American) Pacific You Can't See." In *Archipelagic American Studies*, edited by Brian Russell Roberts and Michelle Ann Stephens, 320–38. Durham, NC: Duke University Press, 2017.

Toal, Gerard. *Critical Geopolitics*. Minneapolis: University of Minnesota Press, 1996.

Torpey, John C. *The Invention of the Passport: Surveillance, Citizenship and the State*. Cambridge: Cambridge University Press, 2000.

Tran, Marc. "Georgia Admits Dropping Cluster Bombs, Says Rights Group." *Guardian*, September 1, 2008. https://www.theguardian.com/world/2008/sep/01/georgia.russia

Trouwborst, Arie, Floor Fleurke, and Jennifer Dubrulle. "Border Fences and Their Impacts on Large Carnivores, Large Herbivores and Biodiversity: An International Wildlife Law Perspective." *Review of European, Comparative and International Environmental Law* 25, no. 3 (2016). https://papers.ssrn.com/sol3/papers.cfm?abstract_id=2848898.

Tsing, Anna Lowenhaupt. *The Mushroom at the End of the World: On the Possibility of Life in Capitalist Ruins*. Princeton, NJ: Princeton University Press, 2015.

United Nations. *Agreement for the Implementation of the Provisions of the 1982 United Nations Convention on the Law of the Sea Relating to the Conservation and Management of Straddling Fish Stocks and Highly Migratory Fish Stocks*, A/CONF.164/ 22/Rev. 1 (New York: United Nations, 1995)

Uras, Alessandro. "The South China Sea and the Building of a National Maritime Culture: A New Chinese Province in the Making." *Asian Survey* 57, no. 6 (2017): 1008–31.

Valentine, David. "Atmosphere: Context, Detachment, and the View from Above Earth." *American Ethnologist* 43, no. 3 (2016): 511–24.

Valentine, David. "Gravity Fixes: Habituating to the Human on Mars and Island Three." *HAU: Journal of Ethnographic Theory* 7, no. 3 (2017): 185–209.

Valentine, David, Valerie A. Olson, and Debbora Battaglia. "Extreme: Limits and Horizons in the Once and Future Cosmos: Introduction." *Anthropological Quarterly* 85, no. 4 (2012): 1007–26.

Vallet, Elizabeth. "Introduction." In *Borders, Fences and Walls: State of Insecurity?*, edited by Elizabeth Vallet, 1–8. Burlington: Ashgate Publishing, 2014.

van Houtum, Henk, Olivier Kramsch, and Wolfgang Zierhofer, eds. *B/Ordering Space*. Aldershot: Ashgate, 2005.

van Schendel, Willem. *The Bengal Borderland: Beyond State and Nation in South Asia*. London: Anthem Press, 2005.

van Schendel, Willem. "Geographies of Knowing, Geographies of Ignorance: Jumping Scale in Southeast Asia." *Environment and Planning D: Society and Space* 20 (2002): 647–68.

Vaughan-Williams, Nick. *Europe's Border Crisis: Biopolitical Security and Beyond*. New York: Oxford University Press, 2015.

Verma, Virendra. *Chewang Richen: A Legend in His Own Time*. Dehradun: Young India Publications, 1998.

Vinokurov, Evgeny. *A Theory of Enclaves*. Lanham, MD: Lexington Books, 2007.

Wadhams, Peter. *After the Ice*. Oxford: Oxford University Press, 2016.

Wagner, Roy. "Figure-Ground Reversal among the Barok." *HAU: Journal of Ethnographic Theory* 2, no. 1 (2012): 535–42.

Wagner, Roy. "The Fractal Person." In *Big Men and Great Men: Personifications of Power in Melanesia*, edited by Marilyn Strathern and Maurice Godelier, 159–73. Cambridge: Cambridge University Press, 1991.

Walker, Andrew. *The Legend of the Golden Boat: Regulation, Trade and Traders in the Borderlands of Laos, Thailand, China, and Burma*. Honolulu: University of Hawaii Press, 1999.

Wall Street Journal. "Australia Strengthens Darwin's Defenses." May 25, 2018.

Wall Street Journal. "China Takes Territorial Dispute to New Depths." December 2, 2013.

Wallerstein, Immanuel. *Modern World-System I: Capitalist Agriculture and the Origins of the European World-Economy in the 16th Century*. Berkeley: University of California Press, 2011.

Washington Post. "A 'Great Wall of Sand' in the South China Sea." April 8, 2015.

Weindling, Paul. *Epidemics and Genocide in Eastern Europe, 1890–1945.* Oxford: Oxford University Press, 2000.

Weizman, Eyal. *Hollow Land: Israel's Architecture of Occupation.* London: Verso, 2007.

Whitington, Jerome. "Modernist Infrastructure and the Vital Systems Security of Water: Singapore's Pluripotent Climate Futures." *Public Culture* 28, no. 2 (2016): 415–41.

Whitt, Clayton. "Fluid Terrain: Climate Contestations in the Mudflats of the Bolivian Highlands," in *Territory Beyond Terra,* ed. Kimberley Peters, Philip Steinberg, and Elaine Stratford (London: Rowman and Littlefield, 2018), 91–106.

Whyte, Brendan R. "'En Territoire Belge et à Quarante Centimètres de la Frontière': An Historical and Documentary Study of the Belgian and Dutch Enclaves of Baarle-Hertog and Baarle-Nassau." Research paper 19, University of Melbourne, School of Anthropology, Geography and Environmental Studies, 2004.

Wikipedia. S.v., "United Nations Convention on the Law of the Sea." Last modified October 5, 2019, 02:10. https://en.wikipedia.org/wiki/United_Nations_Convention _on_the_Law_of_the_Sea.

Williams, Alison J. "A Crisis in Aerial Sovereignty? Considering the Implications of Recent Military Violations of National Airspace." *Area* 42, no. 1 (2010): 51–59.

Williams, Rosalind. *Notes on the Underground: An Essay on Technology, Society, and the Imagination.* Cambridge, MA: MIT Press, 2008.

Wilmott, Clancy. "Surface." Theorizing the Contemporary. *Cultural Anthropology,* October 24, 2017. https://culanth.org/fieldsights/surface?token=540.

Wilson, Thomas W., and Hastings Donnan, eds. *Border Identities: Nation and State at International Frontiers.* Cambridge: Cambridge University Press, 1998.

Winichakul, Thongchai. *Siam Mapped: A History of the Geo-Body of a Nation.* Honolulu: University of Hawaii Press, 1994.

Woodman, Richard, and Dan Conley. *Cold War Command.* Barnsley: Seaforth Publishing, 2014.

Wylie, John. "Landscape, Absence, and the Geographies of Love." *Transactions of the Institute of British Geographers* 34 (2009): 275–89.

Yu, Nan, James M. Kohel, Larry Romans, and Lute Maleki. "Quantum Gravity Gradiometer Sensor for Earth Science Applications." Paper presented at NASA Earth Science Technology Conference, Pasadena, CA, June 11 and 13, 2002.

Yurchak, Alexei. *Everything Was Forever, Until It Was No More: The Last Soviet Generation.* Princeton, NJ: Princeton University Press, 2006.

Yuval-Davis, Nira, Georgie Wemyss, and Kathryn Cassidy. *Bordering.* Cambridge: Polity, 2019.

Zak, Anatoly. "A Rare Look at the Russian Side of the Space Station." *Air and Space Magazine,* 2015. https://www.airspacemag.com/space/rare-look-russian-side-space -station-180956244/#dfGdcbof80WVQ7sv.99.

Zapruder, Matthew. "Poem for Japan" (2012). American Academy of Poets website. Accessed June 28, 2018. https://www.poets.org/poetsorg/poem/poem-japan.

Zee, Jerry. "Groundwork: Symbiotic Governance in a Chinese Dust-Shed." In *Frontier Assemblages: On the Emergent Politics of Resource Frontiers in Asia,* edited by Jason Cons and Michael Eilbenberg, 59–73. London: Wiley, 2019.

Zee, Jerry. "Holding Patterns: Sand and Political Time at China's Desert Shores."
    Cultural Anthropology 32, no. 2 (May 2017): 215–41.
Ziering, Joshua. "Abstraction as a Service Comes to Drones." *Kittyhawk* (blog), January 3, 2018. https://kittyhawk.io/blog/abstraction-as-a-service-comes-to-drones.
Ziering, Joshua. "LAANC Fact Check: Can You Hear Me Now?" LinkedIn post, October 23, 2017. https://www.linkedin.com/pulse/laanc-fact-check-can-you-hear-me
    -now-joshua-ziering.

CONTRIBUTORS

Debbora Battaglia received her PhD in social anthropology from the University of Cambridge. Focusing ethnographically on insular environments, she has presented and published extensively on identities and differences and on questions concerning world making, most recently at intersections of technoscience and conceptual art. She has been awarded fellowships from the John Simon Guggenheim Foundation, the National Endowment for the Humanities, the ACE/SLOAN Foundation, and the Smithsonian Institution. She was awarded a Five College Fortieth Anniversary Professorship in 2010.

Franck Billé is a cultural anthropologist/geographer based at the University of California, Berkeley, where he is program director for the Tang Center for Silk Road Studies. He is currently finalizing two books, *Somatic States: On Cartography, Geobodies, Bodily Integrity* (Duke University Press), and *On the Russia-China Border*, coauthored with Caroline Humphrey. More information about his current research is available on his website: www.franckbille.com.

Wayne Chambliss is a writer currently based in Southern California.

Jason Cons is associate professor of anthropology at the University of Texas at Austin. He is the author of *Sensitive Space: Anxious Territory at the India-Bangladesh Border* (2016) and the coeditor, with Michael Eilenberg, of *Frontier Assemblages: The Emergent Politics of Resource Frontiers in Asia* (2019). His work explores climate, territory, development, and the politics and ecology of the India-Bangladesh border and the Bengal Delta.

Hilary Cunningham (Scharper) is associate professor of anthropology at the University of Toronto, where she teaches courses on animals, posthumanism, and multispecies ethnography. She is currently conducting research on what she terms *gated ecologies*, with a focus on animal sanctuaries. She is also a Canadian novelist who publishes eco-Gothic fiction and is writing a series of (mysteriously) waterly stories, each unfolding on one of the five Great Lakes.

Klaus Dodds is a professor of geopolitics at Royal Holloway, University of London, and a fellow of the Academy of Social Sciences. His latest books are *Ice: Nature and Culture* (2018) and a coauthored volume with Mark Nuttall called *The Arctic: What Everyone Needs to Know* (2019). Between 2017 and 2020, he held a Major Research Fellowship funded by the Leverhulme Trust.

Elizabeth Cullen Dunn is a professor of geography at Indiana University, Bloomington. Her work focuses on displaced people and the aftermath of violent conflict. She is the author of *No Path Home: Humanitarian Camps and the Grief of Displacement* (2018) and *Privatizing Poland: Baby Food, Big Business and the Remaking of Labor* (2004). She is also the author of numerous articles about forced migration, labor, and postsocialist Eastern Europe in *Science, American Ethnologist, Cultural Anthropology, Slavic Review,* and other journals.

Gastón Gordillo is a professor in the Department of Anthropology at the University of British Columbia. A Guggenheim Scholar, his most recent book is *Rubble: The Afterlife of Destruction* (Duke University Press, 2014; honorable mention, Victor Turner Prize for Ethnographic Writing). He is also the author of *Landscapes of Devils: Tensions of Place and Memory in the Argentinean Chaco* (Duke University Press, 2004; winner of the Sharon Stephens Book Prize by the American Ethnological Society) and *En el Gran Chaco: Antropologías e historias* (2006), among other books.

Sarah Green is an anthropologist of place, borders, and location, with an interest in Balkan, Greek, Mediterranean, and British regions. She focuses on changes in what it means to be somewhere in particular, and the diverse techniques and logics through which the value and significance of location are established. She is currently working on the crisscrossing coexistence of such diverse "locating regimes" in the Mediterranean region. She is professor of social and cultural anthropology at the University of Helsinki.

Tina Harris is an assistant professor of anthropology and Codirector of the Moving Matters research group at the University of Amsterdam. Her book, *Geographical Diversions: Tibetan Trade, Global Transactions* (2013), investigates how state power is both articulated and circumvented by crossborder traders in the Himalayas. She is coeditor of the *Asian Borderlands* book series (Amsterdam University Press) and is an editor of ROADSIDES. Her current work focuses on how aviation personnel deal with increasing air traffic in the skies and on the ground.

Caroline Humphrey is an anthropologist who has worked across Asia and countries of the former Soviet Union. She is currently based at the Mongolia and Inner Asia Studies Unit at Cambridge, which she cofounded, and she is a director of research at the Department of Social Anthropology. She has been a Fellow of King's College since 1978.

Marcel LaFlamme is a postdoctoral researcher at the Ludwig Boltzmann Gesellschaft (LBG) Open Innovation in Science Center in Vienna, Austria. He is, with Alex

Blanchette, coeditor of "An Anthropological Almanac of Rural Americas," published as a special issue of the *Journal for the Anthropology of North America* in 2019. His current work concerns data reuse and the design of ecosystems for open, collaborative, and public scholarship

Lisa Sang-Mi Min is a PhD candidate in anthropology at the University of California, Berkeley. Her work explores the problem of the communist cult, borders and the imagination, and the trouble of seeing North Korea.

Aihwa Ong is a professor and Robert H. Lowie Distinguished Chair in Anthropology and Chair of the Center of Southeast Asian Studies at the University of California, Berkeley. She serves on the Academic Committee of International and Area Studies, Tsinghua University, Beijing. Professor Ong conducts research on science, technology, and society (STS), governance, citizenship, neoliberalism, cities, and contemporary art. Her approach examines novel interactions among these disparate phenomena, and the emergence of global contexts that span Southeast Asia, East Asia, and the United States. Her concepts *flexible citizenship*, *graduated sovereignty*, and *global assemblages* are recognized in the social sciences. Her most recent book is *Fungible Life: Experiment in the Asian City of Life* (Duke University Press, 2016).

Clancy Wilmott is assistant professor in critical cartography, geo-visualisation and design with the Berkeley Center for New Media and the Department of Geography at the University of California, Berkeley. She previously held positions at RMIT University, Manchester, and Warwick. Her research bridges geography and media studies, focusing on the intersections between cartographies, digitalities, and spatial practices, with an emphasis on the politics of knowledge and representation. She is the author of *Mobile Mapping: Space, Cartography and the Digital* (2020).

Jerry Zee is an assistant professor in the Department of Anthropology and the Princeton Environmental Institute at Princeton University. His forthcoming book, *Continent in Dust*, explores experiments in politics and environment through phase shifts in sand, wind, and dust along a hemispheric airstream moving from China's desertifying interior across the Pacific.

INDEX

borders: aesthetics of, 232; biodiversity on, 131–42; checkpoints at, 81, 141; ecology and, 131; evasion of, 222; demarcation of, 82, 212, 221, 230, 235; fences at, 131, 133–36, 139, 142–43, 206–7, 212; floodlights at, 16, 134, 139, 145n24, 212; fuzzy, 80; infrastructure of, 85, 235, 238, 242n38; landscape, 21, 80–81, 124–25, 134, 136, 140, 146–51, 156–57, 177, 181–83, 206–7, 215n21, 231–38; life on, 132; lines, 7, 11, 16, 20, 79–87, 107, 133–36, 175–78, 180, 184, 217–27, 230, 232, 238; maritime, 39–45, 196; militarization of, 135; moving, 11; outpost (BOP), 80–87; posts at, 235; seasonality of, 78–87; security and, 52, 59, 84–85, 133, 144n15, 205; as skin, 176; and sound, 230–39; technology and, 11, 135–36, 232; urban, 74; walls, 3–4, 6, 8, 16, 20, 25n22, 125, 132–43, 176, 192, 206, 214

borders, specific: Greece-Albania, 175–87; India-Bangladesh, 205, 207, 212, 215n17; India-China, 11, 79, 87; India-Pakistan, 78–79; US-Mexico, 6, 16, 61, 80, 120, 131–45

British Antarctic Survey, 106

buffer zone, 60, 230–39

Camp Century, 107–10

cartography: anxieties about, 5, 12, 82, 86; fictions of, 16, 207; practice of, 81, 146, 148; and representation, 4, 11, 14, 20, 23, 81, 87, 134, 146, 231

catacombs, 8, 27n44, 41, 43, 45–50

Caucasus, 9, 52–60

Chechnya, 54, 58, 61

China, 4, 6, 15, 19–20, 27n40, 79, 82–87, 99–100, 115, 119–29, 193–201; dust in, 119–29; East China Sea, 199; South China Sea, 1, 5, 7, 11, 198

Chinese People's Liberation Army (PLA), 84

chokepoints, 9, 28n49, 53, 55, 61, 62n2

Civilian Control Zone (CCZ), 230–31, 241n19

Clean Air Act, 120, 128

climate, 204, 207, 211–12, 214–15; catastrophe, 206; change, 204, 207–8, 211, 213–14, 215n17; security, 207. See also global warming

Cold War, 13, 60, 107–15, 192, 199, 202n17, 230–33, 237

commons: cosmic, 243; global, 200; high seas, 7–8, 28n57

communism, 19; in Albania, 181; Communist Bloc, 191; and modernity, 232

continental shelf, 2, 24n9, 30n76

crime: cartels, 192; criminals, 49; drugs, 4, 44, 53, 192

Crimea, 44–45

cryosphere, 115

data: open civic, 94

Defense Advanced Research Projects Agency (DARPA), 67, 69, 73

Deleuze, Gilles, 177, 243; and Félix Guattari, 9, 28, 47, 56–57, 162

demarcation: line, 13, 82, 134, 197, 212, 235; territorial, 212, 216n26, 221, 230

demilitarized zones (DMZs), 21, 144n15, 230–39, 241n18; ecology and, 144n15, 230, 239n2

desert, 15, 18, 64, 74, 81, 108, 114, 121–24, 131–35; desertification, 120, 128

deterritorialization, 6, 19–20, 23, 79, 196, 200, 243–50; reterritorialization, 196

digital: devices, 91–104; enclosure, 13; imaging, 2; mobile devices, 147; technologies, 176–77. See also mobile applications

downstream: air, 34, 120–29; gray water, 226–27; water, 205, 208, 210, 212

drones, 5, 12, 53, 64, 69, 83, 87, 91–100, 131, 141, 162, 167

drought, 123

dust, 13, 15, 30n87, 119–29

earthquakes, 73, 77, 164, 181

echolocation, 230–39; echocardiograms, 141. See also sonar

ecology: border, 131–45; ecological change, 205–14; ecological destruction, 16; ecological haven, 230, 239; forestry, 124; interface, 132; manipulation, 195–98; transition zone, 132
edge effects, 132–41
Einstein, Albert, 161–63
Elden, Stuart, 4–5, 53–56, 66, 78, 134, 137, 160–61, 185, 189n14, 235
embodiment, 13, 17–18, 135–36, 154, 164–65, 168–69, 176
enclaves, 10, 23, 44, 80, 217–29
Epirus, 175–87
erosion, 60; land, 131, 195, 210–12
European: airports, 7; allies, 52; geography, 165, 176, 192; infrastructure, 7, 19; integration, 227; philosophy, 240; space agency, 70; Union, 218, 223
exclusive economic zones (EEZs), 2, 7–8, 24n9
extrastatecraft, 3, 92, 94, 99
extraterritoriality, 34n135, 44, 194, 200–201

Federal Aviation Administration (FAA), 93–94, 96–97, 99
Fimbulisen Ice Shelf, 106
flooding, 204–6, 208, 210–11, 213–14
forests, 55, 82–83, 123–29, 159, 205, 208
Foucault, Michel, 244, 246
fracking, 9, 21

Ganges river, 207–8
geometry, 147, 160, 164–65, 175–87; affective, 160; Cartesian, 149, 163, 169, 183; Euclidian, 17, 160, 163, 183, 188n14; fractal, 177, 181, 183–86, 188n14, 221–23, 245; Newtonian, 160–65; non-Euclidian, 163; political, 121–22; post-Euclidian, 178; urban, 149, 155–57
geophilosophy, 162
geophysics, 62n2, 64–75, 181
geopolitics, 72, 249; icy, 114; vertical, 56
Georgia, Republic of, 33n117, 52–61

global warming, 205–7
GPS, 13, 72
gradiometer, 68–70
Graham, Stephen, 18, 55, 65
gravimetry, 68–75
gravity, 62, 64–75, 159–70, 236; measuring, 9, 68–69; microgravity, 248; signature, 9, 67; variations in, 72; weaponization of, 167–68
Gravity Recovery and Climate Experiment (GRACE), 70
Gravity Recovery and Interior Laboratory (GRAIL), 70
Great Pacific garbage patch, 14–15, 30n81
Great Wall: Great Firewall, 20; of sand, 20, 199; in the sky, 20, 199
Greece, 175–87
Greenland, 107–14
ground: higher, 159, 168; troops, 168. See also land

habitat, 40–42, 131–32, 136, 138
heterotopia, 244, 248
high seas, 7–8, 24n9, 28n57, 44
Himalayas, 78–87, 165
Hollywood, representations, 113–15
Hurricane Harvey, 204

ice, 105, 165–67; cap, 109; fissure, 105–16; floes, 1, 14, 133; glacial erratics, 66; island, 14; melt, 13, 109, 204; pack, 108, 111–15; polynyas, 111, 114; research on, 108; sea, 107–15, 110–15; sheet, 5, 105, 108–9; shelf, 106
Ice Worm, Project, 13, 107–9
impactor, 119–21
India, 4, 20, 78, 81–85, 196, 198, 205, 207–8, 212–13, 215–16, 218; army, 80, 84–85
infrastructuralization, 99
infrastructure, 19–20, 23, 29n61, 39, 61, 79, 86–87, 92, 99, 108, 115, 124–25, 131, 136–39, 191, 197–200, 202n13, 225–26;

www.ingramcontent.com/pod-product-compliance
Lightning Source LLC
Chambersburg PA
CBHW050337270326
41926CB00016B/3502